POVERTY IN COMMON

POVERTY IN COMMON

THE POLITICS OF COMMUNITY ACTION
DURING THE AMERICAN CENTURY

Alyosha Goldstein

Duke University Press | Durham and London | 2012

© 2012 Duke University Press
All rights reserved
Printed in the United States of America on acid-free paper ∞
Designed by Heather Hensley
Typeset in Garamond Premier Pro by Keystone Typesetting, Inc.
Library of Congress Cataloging-in-Publication Data appear
on the last printed page of this book.

For Rebecca and Alia

CONTENTS

ACKNOWLEDGMENTS

This book began as a dissertation in the American Studies Program at New York University. I am grateful to my dissertation chair, George Yúdice, for his intellectual verve, unwavering support, and all around geniality. I had the benefit of working with a truly outstanding dissertation committee: Robin D. G. Kelley, Andrew Ross, Danny Walkowitz, and Marilyn Young were each insightful readers and inspiring mentors. I am also thankful to Andrew Ross, Lisa Duggan, Arlene Dávila, and Phil Harper for making the NYU program such a vital and exciting place to pursue engaged critical scholarship.

The American Studies Department at the University of New Mexico has been an exemplary context within which to begin my academic career and to complete the research and writing for this book. It has been my great fortune to have had an extraordinary group of past and present colleagues: Beth Bailey, Amy Brandzel, Amanda Cobb, David Correia, Jennifer Denetdale (a fabulous all-around co-conspirator), Laura Gómez, Jake Kosek, Gabriel Meléndez, Vera Norwood, Michael Trujillo, and Gerald Vizenor. I am especially indebted to Alex Lubin. Thanks also to the tireless effort of our department administrator, Sandy Rodrigue. Beyond my department, I very much appreciate the friendship and intellectual generosity of Sam Truett, Carmen Nocentelli, Jason Smith, Ronda Brulotte, Les Field, Judy Bieber, Brian Herrera, Liz Hutchison, Adrian Johnston, Jeremy Lehnen, Leila Lehnen, Walter Putnam, Mary Quinn, Beverly Singer, Bill Stanley, Mary Tsiongas, Claudia Valdes, Kathryn Wichelns, and Rich Wood. Many thanks to Clare Daniel, for her diligent research assistance, and to all the incredible graduate students with whom I have had the pleasure of working at UNM.

This book has greatly benefited from the support and encouragement of many friends and colleagues, including Nikhil Singh, Audra Simpson, Enrique Aguilar, Michael Alexander, Joanne Barker, Sophie Bell, Natalie Bimel, Eileen Boris, Neil Brenner, Laura Briggs, Jayna Brown, Kevin Bruyneel, William Fowler Collins, Rosemary Cosegrove, Carlos Decena, Roxanne Dunbar-Ortiz, Joseph Entin, Tanya Erzen, Grant Farred, Julian Go, Mishuana Goeman, Cathy Gudis, Lisa Kahaleole Hall, Christina Hanhardt, Laura Harris, Adria Imada, J. Kēhaulani Kauanui, Richard Kim, Dave Kinkela, Kitty Krupat, Alex Ku, Stephanie Lipkowitz, Stuart Lipkowitz, Andrea McArdle, Pat McCreery, Mireille Miller-Young, Scott Morgensen, Derek Musgrove, Alondra Nelson, Marcelo Montes Penha, Jerry Philogene, Sujani Reddy, Mark Rifkin, Jim Roeber, Emily Rosenberg, Josie Saldaña, Malini Johar Schueller, Micol Seigel, David Serlin, Andy Smith, Julie Sze, Thuy Linh Tu, Penny Von Eschen, Jane Yeomans, and Cynthia Young. The opportunity to present portions of this project at conferences of the American Studies Association, Organization of American Historians, the Harvard Graduate Conference on International History, and International Studies Association provided indispensable feedback. Discerning commentary from Kandice Chuh, Julie Greene, Michael Latham, Craig Murphy, Emily Rosenberg, and Nikhil Singh helped shape this project early on. For the formative inspiration they provided, I will forever be grateful to Rosalyn Deutsche, Douglas Crimp, Hans Haacke, Ron Clark, Peter Hitchcock, and Stanley Aronowitz.

Research funding was generously provided by a number of institutions and organizations. A dissertation fellowship at NYU's International Center for Advanced Studies (ICAS) was invaluable, and it was especially rewarding thanks to the accompanying seminar discussions with Marilyn Young, Koray Çalişkan, Tina Chen, Kim Gilmore, Greg Grandin, Allen Hunter, Rob Kroes, Anna McCarthy, Molly Nolan, Corey Robin, and Robert Vitalis. In addition to ICAS, financial support for this project was provided by a Moody Grant from the Lyndon Baines Johnson Foundation, a Horace Samuel and Marion Galbraith Merrill Travel Grant in 20th-Century American Political History from the Organization of American Historians, an NYU Graduate School of Arts and Sciences Dean's Dissertation Fellowship, the Research Allocations Committee at the University of New Mexico, and a Dean's Summer Research Fellowship from College of Arts and Science at UNM. It was an honor to have been the recipient of the American Studies Association's Ralph Henry Gabriel Dissertation Prize, and I thank the award committee of Kevin Gaines, Priscilla Wald, and Susan Curtis.

This book would not have been possible without the knowledge and gracious assistance of a number of dedicated archivists and librarians. Special thanks go to Joellen Elbashir, Moorland-Spingarn Research Center, Howard University; Allen Fisher, Lyndon B. Johnson Library and Archives; Claire-Lise Benaud, Terry Gugliotta, Ann Massmann, and Beth Silbergleit of the Center for Southwest Research, University of New Mexico; Carolyn Hanneman, Carl Albert Congressional Archives, University of Oklahoma; Mario Ramírez and Pedro Juan Hernández at the Centro de Estudios Puertorriqueños, Hunter College; Margaret Jessup, Sophia Smith Collection, Smith College; Nik Kendziorski, Center of Southwest Studies, Fort Lewis College; David Klaassen, Social Welfare History Archives, University of Minnesota; Cynthia Lewis, King Library and Archives, The Martin Luther King Jr. Center for Nonviolent Social Change; Susan McElrath and Daisy Njoku of the National Anthropological Archives, Smithsonian Institution; Harry Miller, Wisconsin State Historical Society; Kristen Nyitray, Special Collections, Stony Brook University; Becky Schulte, Wilcox Collection of Contemporary Political Movements, Spencer Research Library, University of Kansas; Mary Beth Sigado and Wendy Chmielewski of the Swarthmore College Peace Collection; and Stephanie Smith, Ralph Rinzler Folklife Archives and Collections, Smithsonian Institution. I am also grateful to the remarkable photographers Dick Bancroft, Frank Espada, and Stephen Shames for allowing me to include their important work in this book, and particularly to Robert Houston, for permission to use his magnificent photograph of Resurrection City for the cover of the book.

Parts of chapter 1 were included in "The Attributes of Sovereignty: The Cold War, Colonialism, and Community Education in Puerto Rico," in *Imagining Our Americas: Toward a Transnational Frame*, edited by Sandhya Shukla and Heidi Tinsman (Duke University Press, 2007). I received helpful feedback on this portion of my chapter from Sandhya and Heidi, as well as the anonymous reviewers for the collection. An earlier version of chapter 2 was published as "On the Internal Border: Colonial Difference, the Cold War, and the Locations of 'Underdevelopment,'" in *Comparative Studies in Society and History* 50.1 (January 2008); and I am grateful to Andrew Shryock, David Engerman, and the anonymous readers for their thoughtful criticism, and to Cambridge University Press for permission to include the revised chapter.

At Duke University Press, I wish to acknowledge the steadfast enthusiasm and time devoted to this book by Valerie Millholland, Gisela Fosado, Miriam Angress, Rebecca Fowler, Jeanne Ferris, and Heather Hensley. The close reading and recommendations for revision provided by the anonymous readers for the press improved this book immeasurably.

I wish to thank my family members, including Malcolm Goldstein and Carol Marcy; Marin Goldstein and Pilar Goldstein-Dea; Carol and Sandy Schreiber; and Maddy Schreiber and Blaine Keese.

Most of all, I would like to thank Rebecca Schreiber and Alia Schreiber-Goldstein. My love and appreciation goes to my daughter Alia, who helps me keep in perspective what is most important in life, and is such a kind and wonderful person. Words are inadequate to express my gratitude for everything that Rebecca has contributed to this book and for the joy that she brings to my life.

"NOW, WE'RE OUR OWN GOVERNMENT"

"We are not truly a democratic country now, for the wealthy and politicians make all the decisions for us (the poor)," proclaimed Dorothy Perez in a statement at the Cleveland Community People's Conference in February 1965. She had traveled to the conference from Chicago with two other members of JOIN (Jobs or Income Now), one of the first "community unions" organized under the auspices of the Students for a Democratic Society's Economic Research and Action Project (ERAP). Perez declared: "From community, to city, to state, to federal government[,] poverty can and must be abolished . . . We must act for ourselves, for the wealthy and the politicians have failed to [act]."[1] At that time, grass-roots activists were not the only people to advocate the development of antipoverty initiatives within local communities, with the active participation of poor people. Legislators, social scientists, international development specialists, and community organizers alike concluded that the poor should be involved in the design and implementation of such projects. Yet there was no general agreement on exactly what including the poor meant in practice, or what the specific consequences of this were supposed to be.

During the same month as the Cleveland conference, the city of Chicago opened its first Urban Progress Center, with funding from the federally sponsored War on Poverty. Mayor Richard J. Daley's contention that the new centers would "create programs for self-help"

and "enlist adults and youth from impoverished families 'as progress repre-
sentatives'" did little to convince JOIN that this was anything more than a
scheme to use antipoverty funds to bolster his administration's power.[2]
JOIN picketed the opening ceremony and handed out pamphlets charging:
"Nobody in Uptown [the neighborhood where both the new center and
JOIN were located] was informed about plans to open this 'Urban Progress
Center' until yesterday. No poor person in Chicago has been consulted
about the City's War on Poverty plans. These facts not only reveal a contempt for the poor and their participation in democratic decision making;
they also spell disaster for the success of Chicago's plans to fight poverty."
The pamphlets further asserted: "The Economic Opportunity Act of 1964
recognizes [the importance of poor people organizing on their own behalf]
. . . and therefore emphasizes 'community action projects.' But the City of
Chicago has chosen to ignore the spirit of this Act and . . . has adopted a
democratic rhetoric without any attempt to allow a single decision to be
made by the poor whom the program affects." From the perspective of the
protesters, not only did federal legislation support their position, but "social
scientists believe, and poor people in JOIN know, that successful poverty
programs must be democratic, they must mobilize movements of poor
people who will act on their own behalf."[3] Invoking the authority of the
federal government and academic expertise was a way for JOIN to challenge
the Daley administration and rally the disenfranchised, even if ultimately
the activists' vision of participatory democracy demanded more substantial
change than anything espoused by President Lyndon B. Johnson or the War
on Poverty legislation.

JOIN's initial surge of activity faltered as a result of the organization's
internal conflicts. In 1968, Peggy Terry described the growing feelings of
resentment toward ERAP organizers on the part of poor people like herself
involved with JOIN: "As tensions deepened between the organizers and the
organized, charges of elitism (some of which were true) against the 'students'
began to be voiced by community people." The consequences of this antagonism included the spring 1967 disbanding of JOIN's welfare committee,
which reformed and expanded independently under the leadership of Dovie
Coleman as Welfare Recipients Demand Action (WRDA). Terry writes that
"the remaining core of community people," dissatisfied with the control
exerted over JOIN by ERAP leaders and encouraged by the WRDA example,
reconstituted and redefined JOIN based "on the perspective of poor and

working people organizing their own people and community," eventually voting to no longer include "organizers with student backgrounds" and strengthening their alliance with WRDA. According to Terry, "it was up to us to build an organization that will speak to, for, and about our people in a language and with actions that they can understand and relate to."[4] But this assertion—even with the split that Terry describes in JOIN—was not altogether dissimilar from the positions advocated by either ERAP organizers or the federal government. How this apparent convergence worked and did not work is a principal concern of this book.

Indeed, in the United States during the mid-twentieth century, policy-makers, social scientists, and grass-roots activists championed the idea of community as an indispensable means of alleviating poverty. This book explores why and how this relationship between community and poverty took the forms that it did. I examine the ways in which the prescription for community action as an antidote for poverty was linked to the exercise of self-governance, the integrative purpose of citizen participation, and the negotiated tension between demands for self-determination and self-help. I argue that the early Cold War doctrines of international development and modernization—with their abiding faith in the transformative power of economic growth and political democratization, as well as their anxieties about anticolonial insurrections and socialist revolutions—were intimately and increasingly associated with US policy on domestic poverty during the thirty years following the Second World War. Throughout this study, I consider how people collectively used federal legislation, community development initiatives, and the 1960s antipoverty program for their own purposes, and why people participated in programs that supplied so little in the way of financial benefits. Rather than write a history from "above" or "below," this book examines the way divergent conceptions of the politics of poverty and community shaped each other.

Building on precedents that I discuss below, Great Society liberalism expanded the prospects and procedures of governance.[5] Its social programs —in particular, the community-based programs of the War on Poverty— worked to generate decentralized local initiatives that kept direct state intervention or mediation at a distance.[6] This was not an abdication of the liberal state's authority, but rather indicated a belief that social order, individual liberty, and other commitments of liberal democracy were best served by a capacious yet exacting distribution of governance. The state alone could not perform the task of governance. At the same time, liberal policy honed the capacity of state agencies for enforcement and coercion in an effort to advance normative governmental and economic purpose. A reservoir of force secured the exercise of freedom. According to the sociologist Mitchell Dean, "the liberal reliance on authoritarian techniques is a consequence of understanding government as a limited sphere that must operate through forms of regulation that exist outside itself."[7] The limited purview of the state thus concentrates the means of compulsion in defense of liberal freedoms and makes order a prerequisite to liberty. Liberalism in this sense is not a totalizing system, but a framework that requires and deploys coercive measures in the name of security and stability.

Poverty posed an especially significant and constant dilemma for governance. From the liberal perspective, destitution appeared to be external to— rather than a consequence of—market forces, a result of exclusion from the opportunities of the market and not the outcome of the imperative for unequal economic interdependency. Crucial for liberal policy was the production of "the poor" as a discrete and singular category, and the enlistment and participation of poor people—sometimes strategically compliant, sometimes openly defiant—in the planning and implementation of antipoverty policy. Liberal antipoverty initiatives were comparable to the high modernist projects of socialist countries, but what made their organizing logic distinctly liberal—rather than simply modernist—was the concerted dispersal of governance and the ultimate focus on individuals. During the mid-twentieth century, the conventions of liberal citizenship were oriented toward the rights and responsibilities of individuals as members of the nation-state. Local and national horizons of belonging were crucial, but only to the extent that they reinforced the efficacy of possessive individualism in the final instance. Self-government, self-improvement, and community development were at this historical moment to be the means toward decentralization and incorporation, even as the relative autonomy and collective action of poor people often proved more unruly and antagonistic than envisioned by liberal policymakers.

Whether defined by a shared "culture of poverty" or perceived as inhabiting a world apart, the poor were collectively cast by mainstream journalism and social science as isolated, unfamiliar, and alien. Thus, in 1962 Michael Harrington declared that "the United States contains an underdeveloped nation, a culture of poverty. Its inhabitants . . . are beyond history, beyond progress, sunk in a paralyzing, maiming routine." If elements of Harrington's democratic socialist perspective resonated with liberal policymakers, it was because he so unequivocally advocated the inclusion of those for whom the benefits and promise of America remained elusive. Rather than a thorough overhaul of the systemic conditions that produced poverty, Harrington's aim was "the political, economic, and social integration of the poor with the rest of society. The second nation in our midst, the other America, must be brought into the Union."[8] Not only was the disaffection of this "other America" ethically deplorable, but it also threatened to undermine the security of liberal democracy. Notably, on the eve of the civil rights triumphs of 1964 and 1965, the integration that Harrington outlined seemed to be both about and not about race. Just as the United States provided economic development and international aid to win the hearts and minds of the third world abroad—underdeveloped and perhaps perilously nonaligned—it needed a reinvigorated politics of belonging to incorporate and make less volatile the world of the domestic poor, to secure their attachment to the free world of liberal democracy and capitalist markets.

In the mid-twentieth century, US liberal policymakers endeavored to secure the allegiance of Americans who were materially least well served by the prevailing social, economic, and political relations of society. There could be no mere going through the motions, no perfunctory or languid consent. Liberal policies had to offer real and substantive incentives to attract the enthusiasm and participation of those who were effectively dispossessed. The integration of this other world into US society also required ethnographic authority grounded in the everyday lives of poor people, a credible interlocution between worlds. The operation of liberal governance, in this sense, resembles Fredric Jameson's theorization of ideology as a strategy of containment that must manifest and perhaps even accentuate the conditions that it seeks to subsume and redispose. For Jameson, ideology invents "imaginary or formal 'solutions' to unresolvable social contradictions," calling attention to those contradictions as the source of its vitality and emotive force so as to establish credibility for their fictive resolution. Ideology, in other words, "brings into being that very situation to which it is also, at one and the same time, a reaction."[9] The liberal conjunction of poverty and community during the mid-twentieth century performed a similar and always vulnerable maneuver.

What makes this strategy of containment so compelling and so much

more than the simple machinations of the elite is precisely how it functioned as both a reactionary means of inclusive political management and a
dynamic condition of possibility. The form of liberal democracy practiced
in the mid-twentieth-century United States generated procedures for incorporating dissent and governing conduct—the political entwining of expressive desire and normative constraint—with a new intensity and zeal. The
cultivation of self-governance, individual liberty, and the simultaneously
affective and contractual relations of civil society all advanced liberal hegemony. Within this context, the specifics of race, gender, sexual orientation,
and class—manifested through innumerable everyday relations of inequity,
indignity, violence, intimacy, and collective identification—were mediated
through claims of national purpose and common interest. In order to be
plausible, the grandiosity of the liberal enterprise had to perpetually define
itself in terms of, and grapple with, the antagonisms and material inequalities that it sought ultimately to disclaim. A focus throughout this study is
thus how particular groups of poor people seized on this liberal staging of
incorporation as a way to disrupt or transform these containment strategies'
normative terms of political closure and imagined resolution.

Worlds Within

The tenuous character of governmental endeavors to at once attract and
contain the people most dispossessed by the prevailing order is especially
evident in the arena of Cold War geopolitics. Here the tensions and reciprocities between foreign and domestic were especially pronounced. On
October 6, 1965, for instance, the Washington headquarters of the United
States Information Agency (USIA) sent a telegram to the agency's international bureaus describing the significance of the Johnson administration's
Great Society. The telegram urged USIA officials "to make the Great Society
meaningful to foreign audience groups because an understanding of the
Great Society is fundamental to an understanding of the U.S. of today and
of the future." In order to help officials appropriately frame US policy, the
telegram explained: "We want to demonstrate that, even while deeply committed to the defense of free nations and free institutions in many parts of
the world, the U.S. is equally committed to the preservation and the development of the basic American institutions which provide this nation
with the strength and vigor required to meet its foreign commitments."
Thus, "we want the Great Society to illustrate what 'government of the

people, by the people, and for the people' means—how progress towards national goals engages efforts of many individuals acting through a wide variety of voluntary nongovernmental and civic groups, and how the system of free choice encourages and responds to the concern and initiative of these concerns." In order to convey the relevance of this grand mission for people throughout the world, the USIA encouraged its staff not only to respect the particularities of their host countries, but to demonstrate US enthusiasm for drawing on lessons from abroad: "Recognizing that every people has its own ideals of excellence, we want to suggest American readiness to learn from the experience of other peoples in progressing toward peaceful goals, and to share the evolving American experience of the Great Society where it is applicable."[10] Presenting the United States as a world leader prepared to put its foreign-policy doctrines into domestic practice expressed a keen awareness of the bad publicity that US civil rights abuses had generated over the past decade. But this last quoted comment also acknowledged the important advantages of the participatory strategies championed in the field of community development, an approach that was in vogue around the world during this period. Eschewing the technocratic unilateralism often associated with Cold War international development discourse, the USIA directive emphasized the value of democratic technologies of incorporation. This book examines how precisely this "system of free choice" and imperative for local involvement deployed poverty as a dilemma that was both international and national, and as a target for measured intervention and remediation by the US government.

The new emphasis on poverty during the late 1950s and early 1960s, and its troubled legislative culmination in the Great Society's War on Poverty, is a standard narrative theme in histories of the United States after the Second World War. Scholarly accounts are fond of citing John Kenneth Galbraith's *The Affluent Society* (1958), Michael Harrington's *The Other America* (1962), and Dwight MacDonald's 1963 *New Yorker* article "Our Invisible Poor" as decisive in bringing poverty to popular and political attention, leading to legislative action.[11] With the intellectual genesis of antipoverty legislation attributed to Galbraith, scholarship on the War on Poverty and the Community Action Program's call for "maximum feasible participation"—the unexpectedly notorious phrase used in the 1964 Economic Opportunity Act—has rarely considered precedents prior to the early 1960s Ford Foundation Gray Areas program and the President's Committee on Juvenile

Delinquency. Yet the USIA telegram above reveals the inadequacy of this peculiar omission. This study explains why this narrowed historical perspective and geopolitical frame are inadequate, and how they impoverish our understanding of both past and present conditions of US liberal democracy.

There have been exceptions to the conventional limits of scholarly inquiry. In 1969, the sociologist Lillian Rubin argued that a "history of the idea [of maximum feasible participation] suggests that its roots lie in community development programs for underdeveloped nations. The civil rights movement, coupled with a growing disquietude with existing welfare policy, gave the impetus for translating community development notions to the domestic scene."[12] Likewise, Daniel Patrick Moynihan, in a brief 1966 article and in his widely read 1969 book *Maximum Feasible Misunderstanding*, asserted that the Community Action Program was partially modeled on the Peace Corps's community development programs abroad.[13] And in 1971, the social scientist Anatole Shaffer suggested that the Cincinnati Social Unit Organization of the early twentieth century was a noteworthy precursor to War on Poverty community action.[14] Nevertheless, these preliminary observations and their implications have yet to be elaborated in any detail. More significant still, even studies that do acknowledge a broader historical and geopolitical context do little to address how the people who were the focus of such programs contributed to making poverty a prominent issue for federal policy.

A number of questions thus guide my inquiry. How significant were the continuities between constructions of the problem of poverty in US domestic and foreign policy during the thirty years after the Second World War? How were conditions of international underdevelopment both conflated with and differentiated from poverty in the United States? Did the focus on poverty integrate or obscure demands for social, economic, and racial equality galvanized by the mobilization against fascism, the accelerated collapse of the colonial system, and the black freedom movement? Why were policymakers and social scientists preoccupied during this period with the promotion of local initiatives and community participation as means of fighting poverty? What were the consequences of this emphasis? What can we learn from the extended history of community development as a field for government intervention? How did poor people respond to, negotiate, and reorient the practices of this intervention?

The principal message of the October 1965 USIA telegram was that the

Great Society embodied a democratic ethos that unified citizens in the local and national project of progress, an ethos that confirmed the US claim to enlightened world leadership through its irrepressible pursuit of improvement and political inclusion. This endeavor would further substantiate the coming "American Century" that the publisher Henry Luce famously advocated in *Life* on February 17, 1941. As the war in Europe proliferated, Luce had urged the United States to abandon its isolationist stance and accept its historical role as the champion of liberal democracy globally: "our vision of America as a world power" must begin with "a devotion to great American ideals," including those things that are "infinitely precious and especially American—a love of freedom, a feeling for the equality of opportunity, a tradition of self-reliance and independence and also cooperation." After the Second World War, with the effects of the Great Depression still felt by many and the fault lines of the Cold War remapping the globe, how to define and decrease world poverty were constitutive questions in the making of US postwar global hegemony. Moreover, these questions were accentuated by the decline of European colonial rule, with former colonies forcefully linking the issue of self-determination to the problem of poverty. India, with its national program for community development, provided US policymakers with an attractive model contrasting with the revolutionary trajectory of China. In the foreword to an influential edited collection on community development, Sarvepalli Radhakrishnan, then vice president of India, recommended that "the best way of securing the stability of a state from subversion within or attack from without is by promoting welfare and solidarity among the people themselves." He concluded: "Whatever differences there may be between the industrially developed countries of the West and the underdeveloped countries of the East, the Community scheme attempts to raise the welfare of the common people without imperiling the dignity and the liberty of the individual. If it succeeds . . . then it will be a great victory for democracy."[15]

At the intersection of questions of sovereignty and poverty, US policymakers and social scientists seized on the value of local community and participation.[16] The political scientist Uday Singh Mehta's analysis of the imperial formation of liberal thought in the British context suggests how this can be understood as a constitutive feature of modern liberalism. Mehta argues: "The will to power that liberals do express for the empire is always as a beneficent compensation for someone else's powerlessness relative to a more elevated order."[17] Although US policymakers and legislators were slow to recognize the advantages of embracing this perspective domestically, by the 1960s a focus on democratically inclusive, community-based solutions to poverty had become a central—if nonetheless embattled—premise of the War on Poverty. Although an emphasis on local initiatives and community participation to combat poverty was not without important precedents, the particular exigencies of US Cold War policy served both to focus legislative and public attention on poverty and to make community action a democratic imperative.

Particular forms of knowledge production and interpretations of poverty underwrote this enterprise. The historian Alice O'Connor provides a superb account of the role that liberal social science research played in establishing poverty as a category for Cold War policymaking. She argues that over the course of the twentieth century, although not in any uniform or unchallenged trajectory, "poverty knowledge has been perhaps most effective as a form of cultural affirmation: a powerful reassurance that poverty occurs outside or in spite of core American values and practices, whether those are defined in terms of capitalist markets, political democracy, self-reliance, and/or a two-parent, white, middle-class, family ideal." Since poverty was understood as an aberration or anomaly rather than as requisite for capitalism, mainstream research on poverty held that mitigating or even eliminating poverty was possible within the framework of capitalism. Poverty was not considered to be an aspect of racial or gender inequality but an alternative discourse. O'Connor suggests that, functioning in this way, poverty "offers a substitute language, of deviance and deprivation, for the language of inequality." Poverty knowledge, then, was a way for an "educated elite to categorize, stigmatize, but above all to neutralize the poor and disadvantaged through analysis that obscures the political nature of social and economic inequality."[18] Prior to the 1960s, the study of poverty on behalf of the state was dispersed across the distinct classifications and constituencies of the social policy bureaucracy (indigent mothers with children, the elderly, the unemployed, the disabled). Only with the advent of the War on Poverty did research on poverty become an official component of investigation for the state, institutionalized and unified under a single administrative category and aligned with an overarching policy mandate.[19]

This domestic policy frame functioned in tandem with the forms of knowledge and techniques of power that projected development on a global scale. Recounting the formulation of the international development paradigm during the years immediately following the Second World War, the anthropologist Arturo Escobar has analyzed the discursive and institutional production of the category of the Third World. He argues that, through the creation and administration of particular knowledges and "client categories," development was a method of governance that "proceeded by creating abnormalities (such as the 'illiterate,' the 'undernourished,' 'small farmers,' or 'landless peasants'), which it would later treat and reform." In an effort to detach poverty from its incriminating political contexts and universalize it as an object of reform by experts, social scientists set about formulating empirical abstractions that helped make development an approach to social and economic management. According to Escobar, within this paradigm not only was "the essential trait of the Third World . . . its poverty," but economic growth and development were the self-evident, necessary, and universal solutions to this immanent attribute.[20] These solutions, however, were never simply orchestrated from above, as many accounts of international development suggest. Instead, working through models such as community development, they required the involvement and enthusiasm of the people that they targeted. Thus, despite the solutions' purported universality, their implementation was always contingent on the particularities of local context, even if such particularities may have at times been lost on US policymakers and development administrators.

The Government of Poverty

The Economic Opportunity Act (EOA) of 1964 was a concerted rejection of income maintenance and job creation as mandates for federal policy. Instead of dealing with poverty as a condition tied directly to economic inequalities, it advanced the notion of equal opportunity as an expression of democratic participation. It was thus a logical complement to the 1964 Civil Rights Act and the 1965 Voting Rights Act, each of which addressed de jure practices of discrimination rather than de facto inequality. The EOA established the Office of Economic Opportunity as the coordinating agency for the programs it created, including the Neighborhood Youth Corps, Volunteers in Service to America (VISTA), the Job Corps, Upward Bound, and the Community Action Program (CAP), as well as, later, the preschool Head Start and Legal Services programs. President Johnson initially promoted the CAP as the hallmark of the EOA, although ensuing controversies led him to shift emphasis to the successes of programs such as Head Start. Nevertheless, the CAP—with its extensive complex of community action agencies, each overseeing a diverse array of neighborhood community organizations and projects—was considered by most policymakers and scholars to be the embodiment of the War on Poverty.[21]

When the Johnson administration launched its War on Poverty with the EOA, it deployed poverty as a category predicated on specific political calculations. The legislation was both a reaction to sustained pressure from an increasingly forceful civil rights movement and a preemptive strike intended to contain the growing insurgency of the economically and politically disaffected. Incorporating a variety of historical precedents, the EOA was a sweeping attempt to rally liberals, social conservatives, and politically marginalized people of color under a single platform for reform sponsored by the Democratic Party. Its mandate for economic opportunity cautiously avoided direct reference to racial politics, while also jettisoning the language of class conflict and gender inequality. It was an attempt to secure the electoral allegiance of African Americans, who had proven to be a pivotal constituency in John F. Kennedy's 1960 presidential victory, while simultaneously disclaiming the explicit language of race in order to retain the support of Southern Democrats.[22] Despite its colorblind rhetoric, the EOA was initially a strategy to circumvent state and municipal control of funding that might otherwise have obstructed African American access to programs—particularly in the South—and to establish precedents for direct allocations to local constituencies. The EOA thus dramatically recast the relationship between the federal government and localities through the framework of antipoverty community action. In doing so, it made local entities and resident interlocutors into representatives of communities, but it also required the consent and participation of local constituencies to substantiate the political viability of community. Through this process the EOA sought to incorporate and contain these constituencies within the established protocols of electoral politics. In practice, however, this meant that the implementation of federal antipoverty policy was contingent on an ongoing negotiation between local exigencies and national politics. Ultimately this relationship proved to be much more volatile than the Kennedy or Johnson administrations anticipated.

The so-called rediscovery of poverty after the Second World War was one particular moment within the extended configuration of liberal modernity. Two principal historical formations broached the problem of poverty within the making of Euro-American modernity.[23] The liberal democratic revolutions of the late eighteenth century and the early nineteenth signaled the demise of absolutist monarchies and hereditary social status, establishing a premise of formal equality and the rights-bearing subject, and precipitating a concern with the causes and management of social inequality.[24] The process of industrialization contributed to the ascendance of the bourgeoisie and the emergence of the proletarian classes, but it also produced a new form of mass poverty constituted within rapidly expanding capitalist relations of production. As Henry George observed in 1879, "The 'tramp' comes with the locomotive, and almshouses and prisons are as surely the marks of 'material progress' as are costly dwellings, rich warehouses, and magnificent churches."[25] Together, industrialization and the dilemmas of modern democracy contributed to a distinctly modern form of poverty.

The sociologist Giovanna Procacci provides an important analytical framework for linking the conditions produced by the liberal democratic revolutions and industrialization to a theorization of twentieth-century conceptions of poverty.[26] She describes how, during the course of the nineteenth century, poverty was constituted as a "social question," a concern for society as a whole, and an essential term for the political rationale of modern societies. The connection between labor and poverty was crucial in this regard. According to Procacci, the political utility of poverty for liberalism was a result of denying any direct correlation between poverty and the relations of production. Liberal approaches to the alleviation of poverty thus asserted a categorical distinction between social policy and the regulation of labor and market relations.[27]

Procacci argues that in the modern context, a moralistic interpretation of poverty acquired a reinvigorated double utility in constituting the social character of poverty. First, she suggests that "if poverty was still regarded as in part the 'fault of the poor,' it began to seem possible to moralize society as a whole by means of the techniques inspired by the treatment of poverty."[28] Poverty thus became a heuristic device. The historian Daniel Rodgers has similarly noted how the moral opprobrium of idleness was contrasted to the virtue of work in the United States in the mid- to late nineteenth century.[29] Second, Procacci concludes that by prompting inquiries into the causes of individuals' pauperism, moral explanations included terms of difference that qualified but did not undermine the rule of formal equality: "Together, these outcomes led to an analysis of the social question which was the effect of depoliticizing problems of inequality in a society of equals: that analysis described inequality as a difference in sociability or in the level of socialization."[30] Moreover, the task of governing poverty did not seek to end poverty —which after all was essential to capitalist relations of production—but to channel the aspirations of the poor so that they might imagine the satisfactions of their desires through the "means permitted them by the social regime."[31] In other words, the target for intervention was pauperism, not poverty.

In the United States, the distinction between deserving and undeserving poor people was intimately connected to the boundaries distinguishing free and unfree labor. With the expansion of the franchise to white male wage earners during the Jacksonian era, citizenship was tied to economic independence rather than property ownership. Economic independence for the white male working class was nonetheless further underwritten by westward expansion and the legalized dispossession of American Indians and Mexicans promoted by such state-sponsored transfers of property as the 1862 Homestead Act. During the second half of the nineteenth century, industrial capitalism moved from a tacit connection with the slave economy to a combination of rapid expansion with the abolition of slavery and increased suffrage. Even as the Emancipation Proclamation ostensibly universalized free labor, racial and gender categories segmented labor, relegating people of color and white women to jobs that were the least desirable, the worst paying, and subject to the most intensive forms of coercion. Vagrancy laws enforcing the obligation to work were applied more intensively after the Civil War than before. The historian Evelyn Nakano Glenn has noted: "These laws became a central component of white efforts to regain control of black labor in the South and of conservative efforts in all regions to achieve what Eric Foner called a 'compulsory system of free labor.'"[32] Moreover, a distinction between virtuous economic independence and reprobate economic dependence associated the most coercive and exploitative labor relations with the putative dependency of people of color and was only partially qualified by the ideological inscription of white women's properly dependent status.

During the Progressive Era, reformers sought to neutralize what they perceived as the social crisis and potential class warfare fomented by laissez-faire capitalism and accelerated industrialization. Beginning in the late nineteenth century, the settlement house movement emerged as an effort to promote interclass contact and social harmony as a remedy for this crisis. Foreshadowing the community development approach after the Second World War, settlement workers—primarily young women from professional families—took up residence in the impoverished neighborhoods that were the target of their reforms and worked among their urban working-class constituencies to ease the difficulties of tenement life. Despite claims to work with, rather than for neighborhood residents and an emphasis on democratic participation, even those most committed to social justice worked in predominantly top-down endeavors for uplift and social accord.[33] According to the social work educator Robert Fisher, "it was ultimately corporate leaders and national political figures, the most conservative elements in the reform movement, who set the tone and parameters of reform activity in the years 1900 to 1920. And it was within the limits of the emerging political economy of corporate liberalism that urban communitarian reformers formalized the first neighborhood organization movement in American history."[34] Nevertheless, during the 1910s a movement toward professionalizing community work was accompanied by initiatives to actively involve neighborhood residents in social reform.[35]

Whereas the settlement house movement established important precedents for community-based antipoverty work, the social programs generated by New Deal legislation were crucial for extending the interventionist purview of the state. Before 1935, there were no national social programs in the United States. The New Deal policies that emerged during the profound worldwide economic crisis transformed the capacities of the state but reinforced the uneven distribution of resources and social citizenship. The New Deal established a bifurcated welfare state, with programs that were either punitive, means-tested relief policies or universal social insurance. Provisions for income security in case of unemployment or injury, and in old age, were created for white industrial working-class families. But while the 1935 Social Security Act institutionalized selected benefits as entitlements, the Democratic Party's coalition of northern workers and Southern voters vigorously preserved racial inequality in New Deal policy. Concerned with the possible effect of relief policies for African American sharecroppers and domestic servants, Southern Democrats in Congress—with the support of Franklin Roosevelt's administration—opposed any form of direct cash transfers to black laborers. Thus, farm workers and domestics were excluded from both old-age and unemployment insurance. Furthermore, New Deal subsidies promoted agricultural automation that resulted in the dramatic contraction of sharecropping as a livelihood and the eviction of massive numbers of sharecroppers.[36]

Poverty, apart from the general crisis of the Great Depression, was not directly the concern of the Roosevelt administration. The administration shifted through the rubble of economic collapse in an effort to restore and secure the status quo of capitalist accumulation. In an often-quoted passage from his 1935 State of the Union address, Roosevelt declared: "The lessons of history . . . show conclusively that continued dependence upon relief induces a spiritual and moral disintegration fundamentally destructive to the national fibre. To dole out relief in this way is to administer a narcotic, a subtle destroyer of the human spirit. It is inimical to the dictates of sound policy. It is in violation of the traditions of America."[37] The administration conspicuously aimed its newly endowed powers for intervention at the crisis in the capitalist economic order, not at economic inequality and exploitation.

During the early 1960s, the emergence of what one economist called "poverty as a public issue"[38]—which might more accurately be understood as the deployment of poverty as a field for political action—was closely tied to the preoccupation with economic growth on the part of policymakers and social scientists. Brought to prominence with the 1936 publication of John Maynard Keynes's *General Theory of Employment, Interest, and Money*, but without significant influence on US policy until the appointment of Leon Keyserling to the Council of Economic Advisers in 1949, the necessity of economic growth rapidly became an article of faith.[39] Among the principal features of growth theory was the notion of increasing economic activity as a means of producing full employment. Beginning with the Korean War, however, state-sponsored growth also served as a justification for the economic feasibility of the military-industrial complex and for a fixation with fortifying the US national security state. Government-affiliated economists promoted a neoclassical faith in the allegedly incontrovertible laws of supply and demand and the inherent efficiency of competitive market forces. During the 1950s and early 1960s, much of this so-called neoclassical revival in economics focused on the theory of human capital, which defined individuals as rational, self-interested, profit-maximizing agents who operated along the same principles as capital itself.[40] Thus, as with capital markets, it was possible to make investments—in the individual through such means as education and training—that would increase future returns, including enhanced individual economic mobility and improved aggregate productivity. Oddly enough, although human capital theory was conceived in response to macroeconomic conditions, it provided a way to individualize the causes of poverty by reducing people to quantifiable attributes and behaviors ideally in accord with the logic of economic competition. In this way, the notion of a culture of poverty was compatible with the way that the problem of poverty was defined from the perspective of human capital theory.

The gospel of growth was the core principle of US development and modernization initiatives, both abroad and at home. In countries diagnosed as underdeveloped, economic growth ostensibly required industrialization fostered by (not altogether altruistic) direct foreign investment and the development of the labor force through investments in human capital. Notions of the modern economy as a self-evident totality underwrote a new conception of the nation-state through such concepts as the gross national product. According to the political theorist Timothy Mitchell, "the development of the economy as a discursive object between the 1930s and 1950s provided a new, everyday political language in which the nation-state could speak of itself and imagine its existence as something natural, spatially bounded, and subject to political management." Moreover, this rendering of economic logic derived its significance not only from the imperial foundations of classical economics as a way of theorizing a colonial world system, but also with respect to the dilemmas posed by the subsequent collapse of European empires and the consolidation of US hegemony. It provided a geospatial representation of the economy "in which the world was pictured in the form of separate nation-states, with each state marking the boundary of a distinct economy." Mitchell argues that "once economic discourse took as its object the fixed space of the national economy . . . and began to picture this object as a dynamic mechanism, it became both possible and necessary to imagine economic growth in new terms: not as material and spatial extension but as the internal intensification of the totality of relations defining the economy as an object."[41] Situated within national economic units, poor people were quantified and classified as an operative category— composed of groups defined by such factors as per capita income—within the calculations of growth. In the United States, this statistical disposition resulted in the Office of Economic Opportunity's 1965 decision to adopt as its official poverty level the threshold designed by Mollie Orshansky, an analyst at the Social Security Commission. Despite the fact that Orshansky herself was critical of the nationwide application of her statistical calculations to define the poor, this demographic profile institutionalized the poor as a discrete social category.[42]

The abundant 1960s literature on the persistence of poverty in the midst of US postwar affluence did not so much question the imperative of growth as sound a clarion call for state intervention to accelerate and focus its effects.[43] Policymakers shifted their attention to the limits of economic growth and to devising and managing the question of scarcity.[44] Indeed, it was the exigencies of scarcity that authorized intervention and management. In the 1964 report that set out many of the key terms adopted by the Economic Opportunity Act, the Council of Economic Advisers highlighted the declining rate of poverty reduction and emphasized that the economic gains of the postwar period had not affected the remarkably unequal distribution of income in the United States. The council concluded that "even if poverty should hereafter decline at the relatively more rapid rate of the 1947–1956 period, there would still be 10 percent of the Nation's families in poverty in 1980 . . . We cannot leave the further wearing away of poverty solely to the general progress of the economy."[45] On the one hand, the council's conclusion aimed to mandate certain forms of state action and regulation. On the other hand, perhaps more significantly, this verdict worked in tandem with the rhetoric of opportunity, insisting that the institutionally enforced isolation and nonparticipation of the poor was intolerable. The state would therefore act through the self-actualization of individuals— providing not jobs, but training; not direct access to income, but political incentives. Thus, as the cultural critic Andrew Ross has observed, "the assumption of scarcity is not simply an invention of modern affluent societies; it is the necessary premise for all social institutions and value systems that promote competitive individualism."[46] The normative effect of the War on Poverty was precisely its efforts to increase the capacity for possessive individualism within the poor, directing a desire for social change inward.

Self-Help or Self-Determination

The governmental constitution of poverty as a field for political action during the mid-twentieth century was a precarious project. If it was an injunction to possessive individualism, nonetheless individuals were to be awakened through the political process of democratic community. Initiatives to induce the participation of the poor, catalyzed by the Cold War and the dilemmas of decolonization, were sustained by a protracted tension between the conceptions of self-help and self-determination. The elasticity and contingent meaning of these terms, with frequent rhetorical slippage between the two, served as the means for attracting the interest and commitment of those marginalized people identified as candidates for inclusion.

Examining the War on Poverty, the political scientist Barbara Cruikshank contends that reform doctrines of self-improvement and the liberal democratic constitution of citizens saw "self-help as a mode of government that works through the maximization of citizenship . . . [and provides] an example of how individual citizenship is linked to 'society as a whole.'" She argues that an idea of the poor as powerless was used by radicals, reformers, and social scientists "to act on others by getting them to act in their own interests." Within this process, she contends that the construction of the poor "is founded not on the abnegation of their real interests but on the production of their interest in helping themselves." Rendering the poor as a group with a shared set of problems and interests entailed a normative mode of governance that sought to incorporate refractory social elements through particular modes of citizenship. Like Procacci, Cruikshank argues that "the novelty of social techniques of government was that they made it possible to target individuals and society as a whole in a single aim."[47]

But, contrary to Cruikshank's analysis, the incitement to self-activity, mobilization of interests, and quantification of needs perpetually cut against the grain of incorporation, more often than not increasing the suppressed tension between self-help and self-determination. In 1966, Ida Mae Lawrence, chair of the Mississippi Freedom Labor Union Local, proclaimed in a press conference: "You know, we ain't dumb, even if we are poor. We need jobs. We need food. We need houses. But even with the poverty program we ain't got nothin' but needs." This was after she and a group of over seventy poor African Americans had occupied the barracks of the Greenville Air Force Base to protest the conditions of poor blacks in Mississippi. At the same press conference, Isaac Foster, a plantation worker from Tribbett, Mississippi, declared: "The people are going to set up a tent city out at Tribbett and work on getting poor people to come and build a new city. Because of the fact that we was refused by the Federal Government and evicted, it's important that we start planning our own government." Lawrence added: "Now, we're our own government: government by poor people. Where do we go from here? To brighter days on our own."[48] During the mid-twentieth century, the federal government was persistently forced to confront both the affinities and contradictions of self-help and self-determination.

Self-help appears more complicit than self-determination with the ideology of American social mobility. Self-help evokes notions of individualism, voluntarism, free will, and independence.[49] But, without diminishing this prevailing connotation, the specific historical uses of self-help discourse reveal more complexity. Early and mid-twentieth century ideologies of African American racial uplift are a prime example. As the historian Kevin Gaines has argued, uplift ideology "represented the struggle for black identity in a deeply racist society, turning the pejorative designation of race into a source of dignity and self-affirmation through an ideology of class differentiation, self-help, and interdependence." At the same time, "its orientation towards self-help implicitly faulted African Americans for their lowly status, echoing judgmental dominant characterizations of 'the Negro problem.' "[50] In this sense, self-help simultaneously internalized and rejected the discriminatory premises of white society. The capacity for self-help offered a potential rebuttal to the racist ascription of incompetence and inferiority to African Americans.

Both self-help and self-determination were related to the dominant frameworks of dependency and autonomy. The social theorist Nancy Fraser and the historian Linda Gordon provide an invaluable genealogy of dependency. They note that after the liberal democratic revolutions of the eighteenth century, dependency was transformed from an ordinary condition to a stigma, with the new articulation of citizenship and independence as its antithesis. With the onset of industrialization, capital-labor relations were exempted from the discursive purview of dependency, white workingmen were semantically constituted as economically independent, and dependency was "redefined to refer exclusively to those noneconomic relations of subordination deemed suitable only for people of color and white women." Moreover, "there emerged a drift from an older sense of dependency as a relation of subjection imposed by an imperial power on an indigenous population to a newer sense of dependency as an inherent property or character trait of the people so subjected." In the United States in the early twentieth century, dependency assumed an increasingly "moral / psychological meaning," with feminized and racialized connotations.[51] Likewise, the dominant ideology rendered the capacity for independence as both an individual competence and a prerequisite for social and political agency. During the 1960s, Latin American dependency theorists sought to reestablish dependency as a relation of subjection within the capitalist world system controlled by Europe and North America. The theorists tried to demonstrate that so-called underdevelopment was the direct consequence of international economic development. But their strategies for delinking national economic development from this world system, or pursuing so-called dependent development, often replicated the mystifications of self-help by suggesting that national economic autonomy and development were possible without changing the structural conditions of the capitalist world system.[52]

Since its inception, US social welfare policy has served the purpose of selective regulation, based on ideologies of race and gender frequently attached to conceptions of dependency and autonomy. The benefits of mothers' pensions in the Progressive Era, for instance, which were designed to enable single mothers to raise their children respectably by staying at home, were unevenly distributed according to racialized criteria. African American mothers were regularly considered to be capable of finding employment, which disqualified them for the pensions. Similarly, during the New Deal, the Federal Emergency Relief Administration's "employable mother" rule forced black and Latina mothers to accept agricultural work and domestic service by denying their eligibility for aid. The social work educator Mimi Abramovitz contends that social welfare policy is predicated on both a work ethic, aimed at men and women and functioning to maintain the low-wage labor market by setting welfare payments below bottom-tier wages, and a heteronormative, racially inflected "family ethic," directed exclusively toward women and intended to perpetuate women's unpaid domestic labor. She argues: "Targeted to and largely reflecting the experience of white, middle-class women who marry and stay at home, the family ethic denied poor and immigrant women and women of color the 'rights of womanhood' and the opportunity to embrace the dominant definition of 'good wife' and mother because they did not confine their labor to the home."[53] In this sense, dependency was not an altogether pejorative category, but it was qualified by the operations of racist ideologies that rendered certain forms of dependency proper and certain forms of independence unacceptable.

Like ideas of self-help, the notion of self-determination embodied conflicting trajectories and multiple variations. It served not only as the antithesis of dependency but also as an acknowledgment of the broader field of relations of power. Yet it also presumed an already constituted sovereign subject, predicated on Enlightenment principles of reason and progress. Moreover, during the thirty years following the Second World War, the concept of national self-determination served as a potent referent for the more general notion of self-determination. Although President Woodrow Wilson championed national self-determination as a principle for US foreign policy in 1918, it was not inscribed as a tenet of positive international law until the Soviet Union insisted on its inclusion in the 1945 San Francisco Conference on the United Nations.[54] During the early stages of the Cold War, the rising tide of decolonization and the logic of development directed US grand strategy toward demands for national self-determination.[55] As the sociologist Ramón Grosfoguel has pointed out, "the modern idea that treated each individual as a free centered subject with rational control over his or her destiny was extended to the nation-state level. Each nation-state was considered to be sovereign and free to rationally control its progressive development."[56] Self-determination was therefore premised on the normative consolidation of a social collectivity, cast in the form of the autonomous and self-possessed individual. Nevertheless, in the context of the Cold War and US hegemonic expansion, decolonization and the national self-determination of former colonies had the potential to destabilize world hierarchies and the terms of global governance.

Political, economic, and military concerns shaped US foreign policy toward decolonization.[57] Although US policy aimed at restoring and expanding the capitalist world system focused first on postwar economic reconstruction in Europe and Japan, initiatives to integrate the so-called periphery rapidly assumed considerable significance. This was partly because of the specific historical context of struggles for national liberation, staged as revolts not only against colonial rule and repression, but also against Western cultural hegemony and foreign control more broadly. Indeed, these insurgencies often articulated explicitly anticapitalist platforms. Postcolonial nonalignment was of little reassurance for a US policy elite who were obsessed with the advance of communism and who perceived the world in the dichotomous terms of the Truman Doctrine. As US officials promoted foreign policy in the putative cause of the free world, the hypocrisy glaringly evident in the domestic realities of democracy and justice undermined their credibility. Recent scholarship has drawn attention to how US policymakers were, in this context, forced to confront doctrines of white supremacy and institutional racism domestically.[58] Policymakers' attempts to confine these concerns to the legal sphere of African American citizenship rights acknowledged the changing significance of such rights in light of national liberation struggles attempting to cast off the yoke of white European rule.

Self-determination also had significantly different implications depending on whether it was asserted by groups addressing the juridical and political formations of colonial conquest—such as Puerto Rican nationalists or American Indian nations—or claimed by social movements in response to the more diffuse context of what the Peruvian sociologist Anibal Quijano has called the "coloniality of power."[59] In the first case, demands ranged from institutional self-governance to full-scale national sovereignty and political and economic decolonization. In the latter case, collective self-determination was not so much a literal affirmation of a nation-state as it was a means of claiming autonomy and authority while foregrounding the historical dynamics of subjection, expropriation, and dominion. During the late 1960s and early 1970s, in the US context, demands for self-determination often translated into campaigns for community control. Although the phrase "community control" has often been associated with struggles over public educational institutions (the 1968 clash in Ocean Hill–Brownsville, Brooklyn, being perhaps most emblematic of this struggle), campaigns for community control included efforts for local control over the administration and accountability of such diverse institutions as the police, social services, and commerce. The trajectory of self-determination was often ambivalent and evident across competing political imaginaries. With American Indian tribes, there was constant pressure from US legislators to reduce tribal status from the original international terms of treaty obligations to an administrative and fiscal autonomy akin to domestic municipal control. Rather than asserting self-determination based on treaty obligations to Indian tribes, US policymakers during the 1960s and 1970s defined tribal nations as what the scholars Vine Deloria Jr. and Clifford Lytle describe as "eligible recipients and sponsoring agencies for the administration of federal programs." According to Deloria and Lytle, "the progress of the sixties and seventies was purchased at an enormous price. In order to attach themselves to national social welfare legislation, Indians had to pose as another American domestic racial minority."[60]

Nationalist declarations of black power during the 1960s encompassed the socialist James Boggs's revolutionary anticapitalism and the black Republican Nathan Wright's call for black capitalism. In 1968, Julius Lester, a staff member of the Student Nonviolent Coordinating Committee, could argue that black power was but one manifestation of the worldwide movement for anticolonial liberation, while Richard Nixon, then a candidate for president, could endorse the slogan, claiming—with the support of the Congress of Racial Equality leaders Floyd McKissick and Roy Innis—that "what most of the militants are asking [for] is not separation, but to be included in—not as supplicants, but as owners, as entrepreneurs—to have a share of the wealth and a piece of the action."[61] Rather than attenuating the rhetorical allure of self-determination, these ambiguities invigorated the debates about it.

The work of the philosopher Denise Ferreira da Silva is especially useful for critically reexamining the common association of self-determination with freedom. Silva argues that the opposition between the self-actualized, self-conscious subject and those who are subjected to the conditions of others' power is constitutive for the conditions of self-determination and engendered by a global logic of race. She challenges prevailing claims—made by both liberal reformers and critical race theorists—that "racial emancipation comes about when the (juridical and economic) inclusion of the racial others and their voices (historical and cultural representations) finally realizes universality." Rather than insisting on the inclusion of those who have been categorically excluded from universality, Silva argues that the racialized subaltern is at once produced by, indispensable to, and extinguished by conceptions of the self-conscious sovereign subject as "the only existing thing whose essence lies in its ability to determine, to decide upon, its own essence and existence."[62] The sovereign subject is a fantasy of wholeness and unconditional will that generates potential for some by foreclosing such prospective mastery for others. In the United States, the historical condition of possibility for the liberal national subject, when confronted with the disappearance of the spatial distance that supposedly marks the racial other as foreign and inferior, has been to reconstitute this spatial dissociation through racial tropes such as the "vanishing Indian" and resignifying blackness as a morally suspect quality of Southern difference. Silva argues: "At the turn of the twentieth century, globality deployed *racial difference* to write the U.S. (Anglo-Saxon) American subject against virtually any other inhabitant of the U.S. American space."[63] Silva's far-reaching critique of conventional understandings of racial subjection provides a means of interrogating the accepted correlation between self-determination or self-help and freedom. With her analysis in mind, the chapters that follow examine the consequences of this presumed correspondence and the possibility of imagining it otherwise.

In this book, I argue that the deployment of poverty as a field for political action and the constitution of community as the horizon of political transformation were contingent on tensions within the paradigms of self-help and self-determination. I examine the antinomies and shifting inflections of self-help and self-determination in order to clarify the significance of poverty as a category for governance and contestation within and against mid-twentieth-century US liberalism. I am thus interested in the sense in which, according to the political theorist Graham Burchell, both "old" and "new" forms of liberalism "set out a schema of the relationship between government and the governed in which individuals are identified as, on the one hand, the *object* and target of governmental action and, on the other hand, as in some sense the necessary (voluntary) *partner* or accomplice of government."[64] I argue that, within the reciprocal endeavors of the mid-twentieth-century US consolidation of the nation-state and empire, liberalism was a political logic animated by the varying notions of self-help and self-determination, premised on the pluralist extension of formal political power as a strategy of containment, and required as a hegemonic project for the management of social inequality.

This book foregrounds the concurrently local, national, and global terms through which poverty was constituted as a rationale for community action by policymakers, social scientists, and grass-roots organizers. Chapter 1 analyzes historical continuities and disparities in the specific meaning and purpose attributed to "community" during the early and mid-twentieth century, as well as differentiating between the former moment's elite-administered, cooperative reform and the latter moment's efforts to cultivate the leadership and civic initiative of poor communities themselves. I argue that the First World War served as the impetus for the US government to establish formal links to neighborhood-based social programs and closely examine the People's Institute in New York City and the Social Unit Organization in Cincinnati, in order to study their emphasis on so-called efficient democracy, community organization, cultural pluralism, and cross-class social cooperation as the foundation for national unity. Despite the fact that many of the central elements and dynamics of community action aligned with government programs were established during the 1910s, it was only after the Second World War that there emerged a more sustained interest in their implementation and their methodological refinement. As a way to study the Cold War ascendance of the community development model, I focus on the local outreach initiatives of Puerto Rico's División de Educación de la Comunidad (Division of Community Education) during the 1950s, which defined its mission as teaching the tenets of self-governance and inspiring self-reliance in impoverished local communities. US Cold War strategists promoted Puerto Rico as a model for newly independent nations to emulate, following its transition to commonwealth status in 1952. This chapter thus focuses on the specificity of Cold War community-based antipoverty programs by studying their resemblance to and difference from early-twentieth-century reform.

Chapter 2 examines the ways in which the emerging discourse on underdevelopment articulated ideas about poverty and foreignness, and how this association was appropriated for other purposes. Each of the examples analyzed in this chapter demonstrates how articulations of poverty and place contributed to defining poverty and show how different groups sought to use these definitions in distinct ways. The National Congress of American Indians (NCAI) sought to oppose federal termination of US treaty responsibilities and to claim resources made available through President Harry Truman's Point Four foreign technical assistance program by highlighting parallels between territories on the margins of the US nation-state and impoverished nations abroad. I compare the NCAI campaign with Peace Corps field training initiatives during the 1960s intended to acclimatize volunteers to the conditions of poverty in "underdeveloped" countries and to immerse them in "foreign" cultures by sending them to places within the United States that were ostensibly similar to where they would later be stationed. I focus on community development field training that placed recruits in Hispano[65] villages in northern New Mexico in preparation for assignments overseas. The chapter emphasizes struggles over the conceptual divide between foreign and domestic in order to rethink the significance of the then newly ascendant term "underdevelopment," and to argue that this term provides one indication of the historical specificity of conceptions of poverty in the United States at this time—that poverty was in some sense another country.

The third chapter studies competing interpretations of poor people's participation in the design and implementation of programs on their behalf during the 1960s. The chapter examines the rhetorical and legislative slippage that often conflated the problem of political participation—which threatened to exceed the apparently more policy-neutral "maximum feasible participation" of the poor—and riots. I compare how grass-roots activists and policymakers debated the terms of political participation and urban disorder. The chapter begins with an exploration of the links and disjunctures between theories of delinquency, the Mobilization for Youth, the Office of Economic Opportunity's Community Action Program, and the welfare rights movement. I then address legislative efforts to curtail the Community Action Program's mandates for resident participation and to reassert municipal authority and control by the social welfare establishment over local antipoverty programs. Finally, I examine how the framework of participation and the question of violence were evident in the 1968 Poor People's Campaign and the government responses to it. This chapter demonstrates that the institutionalization of participation predicated the rights of citizenship on compliance with dominant political edicts. At the same time, it shows how the practice of participation—especially as it was extended to those traditionally excluded from the formal workings of democratic politics—perpetually threatened to disrupt and defy established protocols. This chapter highlights the tension between the participation of the poor and the coercive force of the state, or between the dispersal of governance and the targeted deployment of punitive state power.

Chapter 4 considers how specific intersections of place, poverty, and politics were imagined within competing claims to represent "community" in response to the implementation of the Community Action Program. This chapter analyzes conflicts over the creation and control of federally sponsored community action projects in central Appalachia, the Puerto Rican Community Development Project in New York City, and the Office of Navajo Economic Opportunity's Local Community Development Program in the Navajo Nation for the manner in which they broached new potential political capacities, as well as enabling political incorporation and containment. This chapter examines the frictions between policy and politics that resulted from seeing community as a principal remedy for poverty. Such dissonance was amplified by the encounter between official presuppositions of what and who constituted community and the associational formations already in existence. The Office of Economic Opportunity provided recognition for newly organized collective interests through the rubric of liberal pluralism, while also working to secure recognition of and attachment to the state.

Chapter 5 extends the discussion of the preceding chapter to consider how groups such as the Black Panthers and the Young Lords Party critically reframed the issues of belonging, self-determination, and community action. The chapter begins with an analysis of what the War on Poverty's treatment of street gangs revealed about the tolerable threshold of liberal reform. I then consider the state's careful policing of permissible community representatives with regard to the gang reform and community survival programs of the Black Panthers and the Young Lords. Both groups established a decisive link between community self-determination and anti-imperialism that incorporated certain tenets of community action but also violated politically normative strategies of containment. At the same time, militant anti-imperialist organizations—including the Panthers, the Young Lords, and indigenous coalitions such as the International Indian Treaty Council—each petitioned the United Nations in an effort to hold the United States accountable for violations of international law. The end of the chapter focuses on the ways in which radicals negotiated the parameters of liberalism internationally.

Finally, the book's conclusion briefly situates the historical themes addressed in previous chapters with regard to the current political situation. It also considers the underlying presumptions and consequences of the turn by neoliberal policymakers toward championing particular forms of grassroots development and community participation.

Together, these chapters explore how the interplay of global, national, and local conditions shaped approaches to governance and inequality in the United States during the thirty years following the Second World War. As will likely be evident by now, my title, *Poverty in Common*, is intended to evoke a prevailing logic of mid-twentieth-century politics and its operative tensions, rather than to suggest a stable or universal sense of poverty as an identical attribute. The title also refers to the philosopher Jean-Luc Nancy's reformulation of the idea of community, and his insistence that community is not a form of shared identity, "common being," or mutual understanding. He argues instead that community is a "being-in-common"—with "being" itself constituted in and as a relation. Nancy's conceptualization is thus critically opposed to the normative construction of community as a primordial attachment, lost authentic collective life, or social contract.[66] This book examines the ways in which modern liberal conceptions of poverty were deployed, appropriated, reworked, and challenged across the geopolitical dynamics of governance and inequality, and within particular social movements and political calculations. The chapters that follow demonstrate how the negotiation of boundaries—between foreign and domestic, empire and nation, violence and order, dependency and autonomy—were a vital part of struggles over the privileges and politics of belonging in the mid-twentieth-century United States.

CHAPTER ONE

FREEDOM BETWEEN
Inequality and the Democracy of "Felt Needs"

Community development programs after the Second World War were concerned with identifying and cultivating local democratic initiative and neighborhood-level leadership. But tangible evidence of such activity and disposition—especially of the conciliatory type that the programs hoped to encourage—proved to be elusive. Policymakers and social scientists described the concern with this type of activity as an imperative to begin from the "felt needs" of a local community— claiming that community development "must come *from within* through the greatest possible participation of the people in accordance with needs determined by their values."[1] Although reformers in the Progressive Era conceived of the local community as the principal site for their social initiatives, not until the late 1940s did reformers consider the full participation and self-determined transformation of those who were to be reformed as integral to the success of such initiatives. A brief example from a booklet in the Libros Para el Pueblo (Books for the People) series of the División de Educación de la Comunidad (Division of Community Education; DIVEDCO) in Puerto Rico during the 1950s shows how popular will and introspection were cast during the postwar era as a dilemma for government-aligned social action.

The story in the booklet, "La Voluntad que Ignacio no Tuvo" (Ignacio's lack of will), is simple, but skillfully enough written so as not to seem insincere or formulaic. Ignacio stares listlessly down the road and across a parched, weed-covered field, while behind him a small crowd of neighbors gathers before the beginning of a town meeting. He overhears Nico, a "nobody" like himself, complaining to the others that local farmers have no land to cultivate. "The government should bring industry to the countryside," says Nico. But Ignacio is lost in his own thoughts and pays little attention to the conversation. He is thinking of his young son, who cried inconsolably at night before his death. He remembers his child's awful fevers and the tears of his wife, Gabriela. He recalls that other children had been ill, too. A mangy dog drinking from the nearby town well catches his eye. A wall should be built to keep the animals away from the community's only source of potable water, reflects Ignacio, "But who is going to take care of that?" He shrugs and tries to think of something else. The town meeting begins with Isidro—a prominent citizen and an associate of Teyo, a land-owner who is also present—addressing those gathered. The well-spoken Isidro recounts his efforts to obtain government support for a new park for the town. It was difficult, but he had secured funds for the park's con-struction on land to be generously donated by Teyo. It occurs to Ignacio that providing many other basic necessities would better serve the town than creating a park: "He suddenly feels the impulse to stand up and to begin to speak. He would say that the park was a good idea, but as a future project. There were more urgent problems in the community . . . for exam-ple, dogs drinking from the public well and the fevers and the children dying." But fear silences Ignacio. What right did he have to challenge Isi-dro? Only later, after the park has been finished and Ignacio hears Isidro telling a neighbor that a public health official informed him that the town's well was contaminated, does Ignacio profoundly regret his inaction. Re-turning home, he encounters Gabriela, now pregnant, who cradles a bundle of kindling. "In that moment a sudden decision awakened his sleeping will. 'The same thing is not going to happen to this child that happened to the other. I swear it!,' he said out loud." But when Ignacio finally speaks there is no one there to hear him. The story ends without catharsis or confronta-tion, but with the possibility of inner transformation and the deferred promise of social action.[2]

"La Voluntad que Ignacio no Tuvo" was paired with a second short story in the 1953 booklet *Los Casos de Ignacio y Santiago*. The other narrative is about Santiago, who, unlike Ignacio, saves his child's life because he was able to overcome his passivity and help solve the problem of tainted communal water. As was DIVEDCO's practice, the agency not only produced and distributed the booklet, but it also conducted a study of the booklet's reception in the communities where it was read. Contrary to the agency's expectations, its survey found that the vast majority of readers favored and identified with the "pessimistic" story of Ignacio's "failure of will" rather than the supposedly inspirational tale of Santiago.[3] Only traces of Santiago remained three years later when DIVEDCO produced the thirty-four-minute film *Ignacio* for community screenings. Responding to the readers' comments, the filmmakers cut the second narrative, emphasizing instead the oppressive paternalism of local elites, the apparently passive hope for rescue by government projects, and, above all, Ignacio's inner struggle to overcome his sense of resignation and powerlessness. A new ending, however, nudges Ignacio's inchoate social consciousness toward civic action. The scene shows a community meeting with amateur actors and people from the rural town in which the film was shot. This time Ignacio stands and addresses his neighbors. His voice is still tentative, but he has gathered his courage to speak publicly: "I don't know how it's to be done, but I do know the community should consult with someone who knows [how to make sure that we have clean water]. Something has to be done about this water problem that has made everyone suffer so much." A concluding voice-over informs the audience that "little by little, everyone began to talk. The problem had been hidden in everyone's mind. But now, Ignacio, the illiterate one, had made it clear and urgent with his words."[4] Ignacio thus personifies the aims of community development in practice, first recognizing his feeling of inadequacy and then overcoming it to initiate, with others like him, community transformation.

Ignacio was indicative of emerging government concerns about local community development during the 1950s. In 1951, the US delegation to the UN Social Commission presented a paper outlining a plan for community development centers. The paper maintained that the governmental agent "should not establish and run the center; he should help members of the community to learn to run it themselves as their own facility, to help them carry on the process of community self-development." The authors warned against "the creation of formal, collective institutions," instead recommending the development of "a cooperative individualism, functioning through *informal* neighborhood and community organizations." This would enable a "decentralized democratic development" shaped by the recognition that "*freedom is in the interstices'* between formal organizations."[5] For many policymakers, Puerto Rico's DIVEDCO became the embodiment of this strategy. Describing the Puerto Rican program, Ellery Foster, a US international aid consultant, observed: "Unlike specialized programs designed by experts to help people meet particular, predetermined felt needs, this approach recruits and trains village-level workers, not as purveyors of technical knowledge, but as catalytic or leavening agents to stimulate democratic processes of discussion, planning, and cooperation, in order to identify local problems and to develop local solutions to them." He stressed that "the 40 field workers in the Puerto Rico Community Education Program *are not extension agents* taking new technical knowledge to the people. Their function is to nurture the root-growth of democracy itself."[6] Although notions of expertise and guidance persisted, as the consultant's comments indicate, emphasis had moved toward facilitating the self-awareness and collective action of poor communities themselves in order to more intimately connect local and national purpose. A crucial difference between the programs after the Second World War and earlier locally focused ventures was the degree to which policymakers and social scientists identified the informalities and interstices of political life, and especially the collective initiative of poor people on their own behalf, as essential for this connection.

This chapter focuses on the specificity of mid-twentieth-century community-based antipoverty initiatives, examining their continuity with and divergence from reforms of the Progressive Era. The initiatives did not emerge as part of a trajectory toward self-determination by people living in poverty, in which the concern for addressing the local circumstances of poor people that we first glimpse in late-nineteenth-century social settlements evolves into full-fledged agency in the community-based programs of the 1960s. Nor was the conception and deployment of community a stable historical object from the 1890s onward, or ultimately only a disingenuous instrument for social control. Rather, I argue that at the beginning of the twentieth century and during the three decades following the Second World War, ideas and initiatives that centered around the idiom of community became especially significant for debates about social and economic inequality.

By starting the chapter with early-twentieth-century examples from the People's Institute in New York City and the Social Unit Organization in

Cincinnati, and then returning to the work of DIVEDCO during the 1950s and 1960s, I aim to show how these moments were analogous yet distinct, how multiple tensions and uneven negotiations played out in the arena of what was called first "community organization" and later "community development," and how and why the notion of community served competing claims and disparate purposes. I endeavor to convey how the particularities of the postwar context, which are the focus of this book more broadly, were not the result of a chronological development but a distinct episode of reconstruction and conflict among various factions of government, radicals, reformers, and poor people over the politics of belonging, autonomy, and inequality. I suggest why it was not until after the Second World War that, to varying degrees, poor people were themselves involved in the design, organization, and oversight of such programs, although many of the key features of the model for governmentally aligned community action were developed during the 1910s.

Reaching the People

During the late nineteenth century, proponents of what was then called the new liberalism began to challenge the preeminence of laissez-faire doctrine. New liberalism shifted emphasis from the classical liberal concern with protecting individuals from the encroachments of government—defending negative liberties—to advocating government as a means of increasing the scope and capacity of individual freedoms—expanding positive liberties.[7] Thus, when the American Economic Association was established by Richard T. Ely in 1885, its founding platform declared: "We regard the state as an educational and ethical agency whose positive aid is an indispensable condition of human progress."[8] Citing the association's proclamation, the historian Brian Balogh points out that "new liberals embraced a wide range of options regarding the relationship between the state and society in the late nineteenth century," including both clearly "national statist solutions" and the delegation of "national authority to private and voluntary groups so that they, rather than the national government directly, could compel individuals to comply with policies that best served the greater good of the country."[9] An increasing concern with the everyday lives and local social status of the non-elite was one consequence of such delegation.

Community-based social initiatives in both the early and mid-twentieth century promoted their work as endeavors on behalf of "democracy," although the exact meaning of that word shifted substantially from one invocation to the next. In his 1916 study *Poverty and Social Progress*, Maurice Parmelee announced that "the coming of the democratic society will mean the abolition of poverty. For it is inconceivable that such a society would tolerate this condition for any of its members."[10] For Parmelee, democracy remained an aspiration that had not yet been achieved, but its realization promised the equivalence of political and material equality. The Progressive Era theorist Mary Parker Follett argued that politics "must satisfy the needs of the people," but she also contended that "the needs of the people are not now articulate: they loom out of the darkness, vague, big, portentously big, but dumb because of the separation of men." American democracy accordingly required the recognition of difference and interdependence across classes and races. Follett maintained that "we can never reform American politics from above, by reform associations, by charters and schemes of government . . . Political progress must be by local communities."[11] Reformers often simplified this distinction by construing "local community" as an organic whole equal to the common "below," rather than as a site that in turn was unevenly divided by race, class, and gender. Writing in the 1920s, the sociologist Jesse Steiner observed: "One of the striking aspects of the recent interest [since 1900] in social reconstruction has been the increasing emphasis on the community as a social unit of real significance."[12] Careful to respect the professional domain of social workers and other local authorities, he proposed that emphasizing "community organization means simply a greater concentration of attention on the problem of striking a proper balance between specialized agencies and the interests of the people as a whole."[13] Democracy would thus embody the "whole" community, establishing consensus and cooperation across classes on behalf of an ostensibly objective and impartial common good.

It was in this sense that reformers during the 1910s emphasized "neighborhood" as a means of nation building.[14] Although class war may have considerably preoccupied and motivated Progressive reformers, it was the First World War that made "community" an arena for state intervention and decisively aligned liberal projects with government initiatives. Following several decades of protracted labor conflict with intermittent mass strikes, violent standoffs, economic instability, and the steady advance of socialism that produced nearly a million votes for Eugene V. Debs in the 1912 presidential election, the First World War marked a significant turning point.

Not only did the war provide a justification for suspending hard-won labor regulations and suppressing radicals, it allowed legislators the opportunity to experiment with new forms of governance in the name of national unity and democratic revitalization. The administration of President Woodrow Wilson enlisted the support of community reformers such as John Collier in connecting local initiatives to national mobilization in what was called the war for democracy. Reformers cast poverty as a condition that made poor people inefficient citizens by artificially obstructing their participation in the larger society. In the context of war, this inefficiency presumably jeopardized national preparedness and productive capacity, as well as fundamentally undermining a collective sense of nation.

Wartime mobilization prompted the Wilson administration's interest in local community organizing and focused government efforts on the effective and efficient use of local initiatives combined with the social and administrative expertise of reformers.[15] The Council of National Defense launched state and local community councils in early 1918 under the slogan "every community a little democracy." Accordingly, Henry E. Jackson, the US Bureau of Education's special agent for community organization and a key administrator of the community councils, pronounced: "A man without a community is a man without a country. His membership in the nation depends on his membership in the local community."[16] This was not primarily a concern with poverty and public welfare, but an interest in how the government might better activate and use local communities in realizing the goals of public policy. However, because the federal government sought the advice and contribution of leaders of the social service profession and because targeting the whole community required addressing issues of social and economic inequality, wartime community organizing confronted— even if not as a principal consideration—the question of poverty and participated in the broader transition from charity to public welfare.

Community councils provided a localized scale of everyday life through which to affirm the vitality of democracy and wartime resolve, as well as potentially to demonstrate the enduring purpose and efficacy of such endeavors. The *New York Times* extolled community councils as "neighborhood democracy made efficient by organization, not an autocratic bureaucracy of the type against which this war is waged." The councils established "a direct means of communication between the Government and the people in their respective localities."[17] An editorial in the *Atlanta Constitution* promoted the idea of permanent community councils, reasoning that "time, duplicated effort, unnecessary expense and detail work can be avoided in every community where the permanent organization exists, with its clearing house membership plan. Within a very short time such an organization can call together its membership, and put in action everybody in the community for any phase of public welfare."[18] Other proposals for the postwar role of the community councils suggested that, in addition to helping reintegrate returning soldiers and disabled veterans into civilian life, the councils would coordinate "Americanization work . . . by providing education in English and in American institutions and ideals [and] by seeing that all foreign-born citizens are taken into the community activity and life in such a way as not to violate customs and ideals."[19] Writing in 1918, with what was probably the most hopeful assessment one could make of the underlying causes of trench warfare, Follett contended that "the lure of war is neither the instinct of hate nor the love of fighting; it is the joining of one with another in common purpose . . . If the essential characteristic of war is doing things together, let us begin to do things together in peace."[20]

There was substantial disagreement among reformers as to whether or not cooperating in the wartime mobilization advanced their goals for social progress. As numerous scholars have argued, reformers in the Progressive Era did not comprise an ideologically unified movement, and the First World War amplified their differences. Many of those who joined the domestic war effort did so in the belief that such initiatives would establish the precedents and infrastructure for postwar reform—that by aiding the federal government during the war, they would pave the way for postwar government support for social reconstruction. Whereas "new nationalist" liberals such as Walter Lippmann and Herbert Croly were strident champions of wartime mobilization in the name of democracy, numerous progressive reformers like Jane Addams and Paul Kellogg resolutely opposed US participation in the war. Randolph Bourne warned that "the 'liberals' who claim a realistic and pragmatic attitude in politics have disappointed us in setting up and then clinging wistfully to the belief that our war could get justified for an idealistic flavor." Chiding John Dewey and "the other prophets of instrumentalism" who endorsed the war effort, Bourne wrote that for them "democracy remains an unanalyzed term, useful as a call to battle, but not an intellectual tool."[21] Unmoved by such criticism, John Collier perceived in the war effort an opportunity for expanding the influence of his reform efforts and emerged as an eager propagandist for the community councils.[22] He was well positioned to pursue such an undertaking as the civic secretary and periodic interim director of the People's Institute in New York City, a prominent reform organization established in 1897 by Charles Sprague Smith.

The People's Institute, like the social settlements, was devoted to helping new immigrants adapt to the United States, alleviating class conflict, and improving the efficiency of municipal government. As Smith described it, the institute was "founded upon the confidence of the people, non-partisanship, freedom from class control, and faith in democracy." The institute would provide a "council of our most representative citizens, one that commanded the respect and support of all sections of the community . . . watching on the one side the conduct of public officials . . . and, on the other side, counseling and assisting whenever occasion demanded united civic action."[23] The focal point of the institute's activities was the People's Forum at Cooper Union, on Manhattan's Lower East Side, which sponsored free public lectures three times a week from October to May that regularly attracted audiences of more than 1,500 people, most of whom were new immigrants of the working class. According to Collier, "The People's Forum was meant to give knowledge, leadership, and public voice to the wage-earning masses . . . A wide range of lectures and debates was provided, the unchangeable rule being that half of each meeting should be devoted to questions and discussion from the floor. The audience was free to pass resolutions, organize committees and in any way translate its majority views into action."[24] By the early 1910s, the institute's programs also included the nondenominational People's Church, the People's Music League, the Department of Play Streets, and a Committee on Community Relations of the Foreign-Born. Its programs rejected the assimilationist paradigm and were conceived instead as pedagogy to promote pluralist citizenship that celebrated the new immigrants' cultural heritage. From the perspective of the institute, these diverse pasts, cultural traditions, and social cohesion could help produce new citizens. By giving ordinary people—especially new, working-class immigrants—the opportunity to express themselves in public debate, the institute sought to teach them liberal democratic norms.

Nevertheless, forum lecturers were regularly overwhelmed by questions or heckling from the audience.[25] At times audience sentiments were in accord with the disposition of the People's Institute—such as when a forum resolution contributed to blocking the Rapid Transit Commission's permission for the privately owned Metropolitan Street Railway Company to take over the subway system in perpetuity.[26] Likewise, in January 1900, during a debate on the US military occupation of the Philippines, audience members cheered at the mention of the independence leader Emilio Aguinaldo and voted 850 to 250 against US policy.[27] But just as often the audience either failed to comply with the prescribed rules of behavior or strained against the terms of liberal reform. When, in February 1917, the *New York Times* reported that "several thousand men and women at the People's Institute at Cooper Union ... passed a resolution calling on Congress to take all necessary time and make every possible effort to avoid entering the European war,"[28] the institute's director, Edward Sanderson, felt compelled to respond. He explained that "owing to the wide publicity given the vote ... it should be made perfectly clear that the vote must in no way be construed as expressing the opinion of the People's Institute."[29] However, even while distancing the institute from the pacifist vote, Sanderson stressed the overarching good that the forum served by giving "voice" to the people in the name of teaching lessons in "progressive democracy."[30] Indeed, Collier took pride in the fact that "the temper of the people as they gathered at Cooper Union was radical from the beginning, and continues [to be] radical," but forum participants had not collectively advocated any "doctrinaire program."[31]

The lectures remained contentious even when audience opinion complemented the institute's position. During a discussion of the subway franchise, "Patrick Donahue ... [was] dragged bodily over a half dozen seats by a policeman and literally thrown out of the hall because he would not sit down when Chairman Smith ordered him to do so."[32] Such official acts nevertheless were ambivalent: "Five minutes later he was almost as forcibly dragged back to the hall by the same policeman, for Mr. Smith had not wanted the man thrown out and the audience, demanding 'fair play,' repeatedly called for his return."[33] In an exchange after a lecture on "the need for individuality," a woman from the audience stood and said: "There was a woman who was in a factory making boxes. She found that she could not make so many boxes if she talked. She stopped talking. She had a sick husband and five children to support. She found that she could not make so many boxes if she thought. She stopped thinking. Will the speaker tell me how such people can retain their individuality?"[34] Following a lecture on "equality," one audience member questioned the premise of the talk, stating: "Jack London says that man in the stone age was better off than the workingman in this day. What do you think about that?"[35] From the institute's perspective, such debate enhanced its tutelary role.

The public lectures were an expression of the institute's general interest in providing "wholesome leisure-time" activities for the "wage-earning masses" as constructive alternatives to the saloon, the dance hall, and the street. This concern was also evident in the central role Smith and his colleagues played in establishing in 1909 a committee for the "voluntary censorship" of films with the participation of the film industry.[36] These measures, according to Collier, would regulate "motion pictures in a scientific way" against both "thoughtless prejudice and powerful special interests."[37] In this regard the institute-run censorship board conceived of itself very much like the People's Forum, as an ostensibly objective arbiter of ethical propriety, a pedagogical force for social progress, and a rational intermediary above government corruption and political extremes. Moviegoing was a vital activity because it could foster the most positive elements and pleasures of communal interaction. Collier emphasized the manner in which the "democratic art" of film spoke "directly to the sentiments, the prejudices and passions, the romantic and social interests of more than a million American middle-class and laboring families."[38] Prefiguring interest in community-based uses of film by Puerto Rico's DIVEDCO and similar initiatives after the Second World War, Collier and the institute were enthusiastic advocates for transforming "the motion picture theater into an educational agency."[39]

The institute also experimented with workingmen's clubs and recreation centers as a means of promoting what it deemed to be socially constructive leisure activities. From the institute's perspective, the problem with the recreation centers had to do with the fact that, although activities were well attended, neighborhood residents were not actively involved in the centers' administrative decision making or operations. Like many other reformers of the time, the institute began exploring the use of public schools as community centers after school hours—capitalizing on the already established role and familiar place of public schools in local neighborhoods.[40]

Based on what it perceived to be a successful experiment of this sort at New York's Public School 63, the institute decided to launch a comprehensive neighborhood development initiative in the city's Gramercy district.

Collier and his colleagues opened a Training School for Community Workers that would combine course work and hands-on experience with other institute projects in the district. The institute created a Committee on Self-Supporting Community Clinics under the direction of Haven Emerson to evaluate health conditions in the district and provide limited medical services. The most extensive undertaking was the Wingate Experimental Community Center at Public School 40, which hosted public lectures, a "cooperative buying club," a drama troupe, Boy Scout and Girl Scout groups, a summer camp, soccer and basketball games, a weekly social dance, an Evening School for Foreigners, and membership activities of Local 25 of the International Ladies' Garment Workers' Union. Although theoretically self-governing and self-sustaining, the Gramercy projects received substantial administrative and financial support from the institute.[41]

In April 1916, the Training School for Community Workers sponsored the first National Conference on Community Centers, at which Collier was appointed president of the National Community Center Organization, a new association dedicated to promoting the community center model. The definition and composition of this model, however, remained a significant point of contention among conference attendees for the meeting's duration. One account reported that "there was a violent clash between the prevailing conventional standpoint, according to which public school work is administered by experts from central headquarters, and the new impulse[,] according to which the wider education of the whole public takes the form of local self-expression, with a strong tendency toward local home-rule and toward the development of small administrative units." Interestingly enough, critics of the "conventional standpoint" characterized it as "archaic and socialistic," while opponents of the "new impulse" called it "syndicalism" and an "I.W.W. [Industrial Workers of the World] philosophy," thus tarring it with the same brush. An observer noted that "equally heated debates grew out of the proposition . . . that community center work should be partially and increasingly self-supporting." A report submitted by the conference's committee on the financial support of community centers advocated the self-supporting model, arguing: "The spiritual essence of the community center is spontaneous, self-acting, free but co-operative assemblage of the people to secure the advantages which they want or can be led to want. Such responsible self-government can be developed only under conditions of fiscal responsibility, and of control over the local fiscal policy."[42] The formation of the National

Community Center Organization did not resolve these disagreements, but it did significantly advance the professionalization of community work.

During the 1920s an emphasis on professionalization would largely eclipse the pursuit of community control, but at first the two orientations uneasily coexisted. In response to the demands of the war effort on community work, Collier promoted his school for community workers by insisting that "it became evident that . . . the whole [community] movement was being retarded and in some places menaced through a lack of specially trained leaders."[43] The institute produced grandiose publicity materials for the training school, including a pamphlet titled "Community Work—The Local Community Will Save the Nation by Saving Itself" that advertised "well-paying positions and a career for young men and women with social vision and personality."[44] But the training school's college-educated tuition-paying students expressed considerable dissatisfaction with the curriculum, complaining: "We cannot secure for a small group the needed expert advise [sic] and instruction," "the practise [sic] work does not give the practical training needed in various subjects," "we have initiated things and then dropped them," and "we are without adequate means or personel [sic] for supervision."[45] According to these students, neither the professional instruction nor the practical training conducted in conjunction with neighborhood residents in the institute's Gramercy area projects was sufficient.

Although wartime mobilization established a direct link between government and community-based reform, the effect of this connection was not so much to invigorate local self-governance as to disseminate federal propaganda. In a presentation on the "crisis of democracy," Collier argued that the exigencies of war seemingly compelled "democratic nations . . . to emulate their adversary . . . [and] adopt schemes of organization which are like the schemes . . . that made Germany efficient." The community center was the answer to this crisis, as a "way to enlist a passionate and continuous personal response from the individual," while bringing "the mass of people into day-by-day working relations with the constructive operations of the government."[46] Such "working relations" had far-reaching consequences for the institute's Gramercy area projects and the training school. The governing board of the Wingate Experimental Community Center, for instance—which had previously been comprised primarily of neighborhood residents, with representatives of the institute and the city's Board of Education—lost all semblance of autonomy. Once Wingate was designated a Community

Council War Headquarters and a community council center under the Council of National Defense, the board was reorganized as a committee that included members from twenty-eight other agencies, including the Red Cross, the Liberty Loan Committee, Bellevue Social Service, and the Mayor's Committee of Women. Although this expanded board certainly provided Wingate with new resources, it turned the center into an instrument for programs planned outside the neighborhood—especially those designed for "patriotic" purposes—rather than a means of supporting locally initiated projects. Likewise, instead of working with a broad range of Gramercy area activities, training school students were enlisted to conduct classes and present lectures that would further the cause of "Americanizing" foreign-born residents. Although the institute did not sponsor programs focusing on immigrant culture to the degree that it had before the United States entered the First World War, it nonetheless resisted mounting pressure to adopt assimilationist imperatives.[47]

In October 1919, Collier spoke at the National Social Unit Conference on the community organization project then under way in Cincinnati, Ohio. Pronouncing the social unit plan "one of the two or three momentous experiments in democracy" in America, he contended that "significantly conservative . . . community work" would "bring about a gradual modernization of industry and government without violent fractures, without civil wars, without combines of hate." Collier used such elevated language partially in response to accusations made the previous year in Cincinnati that the social unit was a Bolshevik conspiracy, but his terms of praise also concisely explained why the social unit idea appealed to a broad spectrum of progressive liberals. The social unit was, according to him, "the kind of community organization that will make possible the carrying over into the Twentieth Century the moral and human liberalism of our Anglo-Saxon past."[48] This racially inflected notion of reform scarcely seemed to consider the white hatred on display during the bloody 1919 race riots in Washington; Chicago; Omaha, Nebraska; and Elaine, Arkansas. But it fully informed the social unit's approach to galvanizing the civic sentiments of a typical American urban neighborhood. Indeed, the social unit plan encouraged social conformity and envisioned the community as a cooperative and amicable whole. More than any other social welfare undertaking of its time in the United States, the social unit plan involved local residents as planners and participants in its operations—although, notably, these residents were largely white and not themselves impoverished. During its brief and widely publicized existence, the Cincinnati experiment anticipated many of the tactics of mid-twentieth-century community development, and—regardless of its emphasis on cooperation—the circumstances of its demise foreshadowed the outcome of numerous 1960s community action initiatives.

The Boundaries of Consensus

Allegations that the neighborhood work in Cincinnati was in some way socialist—although certainly exaggerated and opportunistic—were harder to refute than Collier might have expected. The social unit approach was largely derived from Wilbur Phillips's work with the New York Milk Committee and the Milwaukee Child Welfare Commission. The charity-oriented New York Association for Improving Conditions of the Poor established the Milk Committee as part of a campaign against endemic infant mortality among the poor and the working class. Phillips served as the first secretary of the new committee from 1907 to 1911, setting up neighborhood facilities to educate mothers about child hygiene and to provide fresh milk for babies. When Milwaukee became the first large city in the United States to be governed by socialists, electing Emil Seidel as mayor and sending Victor Berger to the House of Representatives, this seemed to Phillips an opportunity to implement a more substantive public health project. He and his wife and collaborator, Elsie Phillips, were members of the Socialist Party. Elsie was active in the trade union movement, working for the National League of Women Workers and the Manhattan Trade School for Girls. Wilbur had become a Socialist Party member "because I knew at that time no other way of registering my opinion that poverty could and should be abolished—and that it could not be abolished through charity."[49] He approached Seidel about the possibility of organizing a comprehensive pediatric health program and, with support from the municipal government, established the Milwaukee Child Welfare Commission in 1911. The commission's work began in the neighborhood of St. Cyril's Parish with an infant healthcare center and an extensive local network of participating doctors, nurses, social workers, midwives, and nonspecialist residents, but it ended prematurely when Seidel lost his bid for reelection in 1912.

The social unit plan that the Phillipses drafted two years later represented a moderate reformist version of socialism, focusing on what the authors described as "genuine and efficient democracy" and no longer directly associated with the Socialist Party. Consequently, they felt compelled to explain that "to many people the statement that one is a Socialist implies that he believes in violence, hate, and sudden change. This . . . is not true of us."[50] When asked about what distinguished the social unit idea from British Guild Socialism or Soviet cooperatives, they emphasized the social unit's lack of any predetermined political program and its focus on social unity across classes, while also affirming their belief that "the means of producing and maintaining what is essential to life, liberty, and the pursuit of happiness should, in theory, be owned and controlled democratically."[51] The Phillipses, however, "left the Socialist Party because we came to believe . . . [that] no sound immediate program by which to work toward an ideal social state had ever been developed . . . [and we] desired to serve the entire community rather than any part of it."[52] This perspective was common among progressive liberals who were significantly influenced by socialism, but convinced that it was possible and preferable to achieve class reconciliation and inclusive social consensus. The Phillipses' intention was to develop a practical program that did not focus exclusively on the condition of the working class, but that would cooperatively promote the interests of a whole neighborhood—"the basic unit of national life"—and, eventually, of the city and the entire United States.

Between 1912 and 1916, the Phillipses set about elaborating their ideas for the social unit plan and developing an organizational structure that could raise enough funds to sponsor a trial project. In New York, they founded the National Social Unit Organization (NSUO), with Gifford Pinchot as president and an advisory council of prominent reformers, including Herbert Croly, the editor of the *New Republic*; S. S. Goldwater, a former New York City health commissioner; Lillian Wald, a public health nursing advocate and a founder of the Henry Street Settlement; and John Lovejoy Elliott, the head of the Hudson Guild settlement house. Pinchot later described the organization as "interested not so much in doing things for people as in helping them to do things for themselves. The one is charity, the other is democracy."[53] The *New York Times* reported the inaugural meeting of the NSUO, explaining that the new organization would "finance, organize, and advise in some typical city . . . the 'development of a model program for community organization, with the counsel and advice of national social experts'" to address locally identified issues and needs in a three-year experiment.[54] The Phillipses argued, as did many reformers in the

Progressive Era, that scientific methods would allow social planning to rise above self-interested factionalism and impetuous social antagonisms. Wilbur Phillips later wrote: "Gradually it came home to us that experimental processes, worked out on a laboratory basis under the control of a body representative of every economic class, would be the soundest and sanest method and the one fairest to all concerned."[55] When the NSUO announced its intent to launch a trial of the social unit plan, sixteen cities competed to serve as the designated "municipal laboratory," and Cincinnati won.

Cincinnati appealed to the NSUO as a typical American city, with an active and well-coordinated alliance of social agencies willing to support the experiment. The city's bid to host the social unit was led by Courtenay Dinwiddie, superintendent of the Cincinnati Tuberculosis League, and John Landis, the city's health officer—both of whom were working at the time to develop neighborhood health centers to provide early diagnosis and treatment of tuberculosis. The city's professional and business elite and its Republican mayor, George Puchta, also enthusiastically endorsed the initiative, committing municipal funds to match the NSUO's contribution of $15,000 annually for the three-year demonstration project.[56] Once Cincinnati was chosen by the NSUO, the Phillipses worked closely with Dinwiddie, Landis, and the municipal government to establish two citywide committees—a council made up of influential private citizens and businessmen, and a professional council comprised of doctors, lawyers, social workers, and other prominent specialists—to oversee the implementation of the neighborhood-based project. The city's Chamber of Commerce, Council of Social Agencies, and Academy of Medicine backed the experiment. In an effort to make the social unit concept appeal to the city's elite and to prevent future jurisdictional conflicts, the councils appointed Mayor Puchta as honorary executive and invited members of the city council and municipal administration to nominate representatives to the occupational council. An extensive local newspaper campaign followed to solicit interested neighborhoods to participate in, among other ventures, "the development of a 'model child welfare program' . . . [and] a 'general preventative health program."[57] Five districts, each roughly comparable in socioeconomic makeup, competed for the project. Mohawk-Brighton was chosen, due to its residents' considerable expression of interest. A majority of the five hundred people attending the public meeting to select the district were from Mohawk-Brighton, with many of them presenting prepared speeches on why their neighborhood should be chosen. Mary Hicks, a public librarian, and Ruth Gottlieb, a schoolteacher, assembled a committee of 145 Mohawk-Brighton residents and coordinated a massive letter-writing campaign and a petition drive that collected 2,900 signatures, as well as recruiting local business and school support for the project. The Mohawk-Brighton Social Unit Organization (MBSUO) began operations in December 1917.[58]

The choice of this district exemplified the essentially conventional orientation of the social unit plan. This was a subsection of the city's West End and one of a number of predominantly middle-income areas situated between the wealthier hilltop suburbs and the "slums" of the semi-industrial area surrounding the central business district. Mohawk-Brighton, according to Courtenay Dinwiddie, was "the most typical section that could be selected in the city. It includes a good many tenements with some blocks in which bad housing conditions exist, but the majority of the residents are an independent, fine type of American citizens."[59] Eighty-three percent of the neighborhood's inhabitants were native-born, with a small number of new immigrants from Hungary, Romania, and Germany. And, although the NSUO considered this population ratio favorable for "Americanization," the social unit experiment deliberately avoided addressing racial inequality. For instance, its extensive self-studies and program reports never mention that, in comparison to other northern cities, Cincinnati had a considerable African American population, or that, at the time of the unit demonstration project, a large percentage of African Americans lived in the West End near Mohawk-Brighton. That the city's black population grew by two and a half times between 1910 and 1930 seems to have been extraneous to the concerns of the social unit planners, who strove undaunted for the innocuously "typical" neighborhood.[60] For the NSUO, what seems to have mattered most was that a majority of the residents appeared to be ordinary people—second- or third-generation Americans; white members of the lower middle class— awaiting civic inspiration and tutelage.[61] Yet, despite the district's proportion of "working families," one journalist reported that "most of the large, flat area of Brighton is on the decline, anciently elegant residencies housing from five to twenty families."[62] The close proximity of the city's "slums" may have alerted the neighborhood's residents to their own fragile economic security and made the prospect of neighborhood improvement and citizen self-government especially appealing.[63] Whereas the People's Institute sought to transform the foreign-born into active and ultimately loyal citizens, the social unit aimed to rouse the civic passions of everyday citizens and make them into agents of reform and Americanization for those still on the margins of social conformity.

Starting from this majoritarian predilection, the social unit was designed to establish a broadly participatory and democratic structure that, mirroring the citywide committees organized at the outset of the project, brought together neighborhood residents and professional specialists. Mohawk-Brighton was comprised of thirty-one blocks, with a total population of about fifteen thousand. Under the social unit plan, every resident over the age of eighteen could participate in the activities of an organized block council and vote for a block worker as his or her representative on the citizens' council that was responsible for promoting the needs of the entire district. Block workers were local women, paid a weekly salary by the NSUO, whose duty was to be in ongoing contact with their neighbors and to serve as liaisons between residents and the citizens' council. The block elections were to serve as a training ground for democratic participation. Indeed, the average 71 percent turnout of adult residents to vote for block workers, although not evenly distributed across all participating blocks, was considerably higher than the turnout for other local elections and implied substantial neighborhood interest.[64] The citizens' council was complemented by an occupational council that consisted of representatives of local professional groups—doctors representing a physicians' council, nurses a nurses' council, social workers a welfare council, and so on. The citizens' and occupational councils met regularly together as a general council that was responsible for policymaking and budgetary oversight of the project.[65] The unit plan intended the residents to organize and plan on behalf of themselves and their neighbors, and work in conjunction with the cooperative association of trained experts to provide public services and technical support. A reporter approvingly described this as "placing control for all policies completely in the hands of the people and at the same time giving their executives the maximum of administrative scope and freedom."[66]

Partially resembling the subsequent "maximum feasible participation" premise of the 1960s War on Poverty, the social unit model aspired to what one observer called "the evolution of a new form of political control"—"a plan of government designed to make popular control and technical skill function together."[67] However, Dinwiddie, elected as the executive of the occupational council, noted that local residents routinely "attended joint meetings of all the block councils, and special meetings in each block, with a fair degree of interest. But, insofar as assuming responsibility for carrying out agreed-upon policies or for directing the activities of the block workers is concerned, they failed completely." He speculated that because block workers were paid to serve as representatives, neighborhood residents may have expected that further ideas and implementation was the job of the block worker rather than a sustained collective endeavor.[68]

Block workers were therefore the hub of unit operations. Embodying what Mary Hicks and Roe Eastman call "the possibilities of neighborliness," block worker visits served to "link up the thought and the personnel of the individual family with that of the whole community." Their roles conveyed the presumptions of heteronormativity, but within the limited professional opportunities available to most women at the time, the position of block worker also provided access to public life and authority. Their predominantly lower-middle-class or working-class status and local identity distinguished them from the more privileged settlement house workers. Hicks and Eastman argue that "there were hundreds of women whose lives were limited by the four walls of their homes . . . [and with] the creation of the block worker, these women found a means at hand which enabled them to brush aside these limitations and become part of the life and the thought of all the women of the community."[69] One woman recalled: "I was so busy I didn't want to be a block worker at first, but I decided when I heard about the baby work it was something I couldn't be left out of."[70] Informally called "block mothers," these women were encouraged to build on and surpass the ostensibly innate motivations that led them to promote the health and happiness of their own family, and use this impulse toward the improvement of the community as a whole.

Defining the job of the block worker required making certain distinctions. Hicks and Eastman explain: "The block worker is not a gossip. The news she brings is not scandal or worthless chatter; she is concerned with the babies' health, the general welfare of the family, the big issues that are before the people of the nation." Therefore, "her visits are usually welcome because she can interpret the events and the plans which are of interest to the neighborhood." Moreover, block workers were invaluable interlocutors for the occupational council: "Without the elected block workers to make policies and execute plans, the organization of occupational groups for expert planning, consultation and service would not have the same funda-

"'Self-governed neighborhoods—One plan for Americanization': A Block Worker and District Nurse Making Rounds," Mohawk-Brighton Social Unit Organization, Cincinnati, Ohio, circa 1918. PHOTOGRAPH BY C. H. LONGLEY, COURTESY OF THE WILBUR C. AND ELSIE C. PHILLIPS PAPERS, SOCIAL WELFARE HISTORY ARCHIVES, UNIVERSITY OF MINNESOTA.

mental relationship to the neighborhood."[71] And although the local coordination of professionals into specialized committees working closely with neighborhood laypersons was a unique contribution to community organization practice, the block worker arrangement was even more significant for the involvement and direct self-governance of local residents. Nonetheless, the irony in the fact that female block workers served as the foundation of "local democracy" in a country that did not grant women the right to vote until three months before the end of the Cincinnati experiment remained unstated.[72]

An initial block worker undertaking, on which much of the subsequent work of the MBSUO relied, was a districtwide census. One of the women conducting the survey noted: "I soon saw, like most of the other block workers, that if the district was to get the full benefit of the Unit we had to learn more about our people. Blocks are different; each one has a body and a mind of its own you might say." Collectively, the block workers decided that this information would be crucial to their efforts on behalf of the neighborhood: "Before we could really help the doctors and nurses we had to know all about the families that made ours different. So we settled on a plan to take a general census."[73] The block workers requested that the occupational council devise the census questions. What emerged from the social unit census taking was less a regime of classification than the transfer of specialized competence to the block workers. Their initiative and actions served as a tutelary exercise—"learning by doing," as Wilbur Phillips called it[74]—that simultaneously qualified and reinstated the authority of experts.

Phillips's account of this episode is interesting. Describing the meeting where the block workers first requested to conduct the census, he writes: "Elsie shot a joyous glance at me. We'd got one of the thrills of our lives. A census! Asked for! Because they'd learned by doing! How we ourselves had yearned to suggest starting with a census!" But, of course, they had resisted the urge to suggest it. The objective of the experiment was self-direction by "the people," but this was nevertheless most gratifying when it mirrored the tacit desires of the reformers. Phillips thus celebrated the initiative of the block workers and, by association, his project: "So our theory had worked again—and worked in a way which . . . had a very important lesson to teach in government." Even more exciting was the fact that after receiving the census questionnaire drafted by the occupational council, the block workers insisted that the questions on income and place of employment be removed, so as not to offend or undermine the trust of those being surveyed. Phillips was elated: "Here a community of plain ordinary people had, through their representatives, not only asked a group of experts to work out a plan, but when that plan had been formulated and submitted to them, had checked it up and modified it to actual conditions and human psychology before giving approval."[75] The combination of neighborhood-level initiative and citizen-expert cooperation was, for Phillips, the utmost affirmation of the social unit idea.

Moreover, this apparent triumph of popular will lent itself to other forms of self-surveillance and normative ends. Although downplayed in accounts of the social unit, the census system of categorization and classification—minutely calculating statistical means, policing boundaries, and identifying abnormalities—nevertheless remained significant for the practical knowledge and majority aspirations of Mohawk-Brighton. One aspect of this regimen was a further sorting out and identification of those who might require additional neighborhood intervention and remediation. The census data were thus used by block workers to "find every foreigner who did not speak English and persuade him to go to night school."[76] This persuasion, however, was still ostensibly intended to respect cultural differences and in no way advance coercive assimilation. Thus, one social unit pamphlet suggested: "Why not let the foreign born Americanize themselves?" It was in this sense that "the foreign-born American is given an opportunity to tackle the problems at his own doorstep before he is pushed out into the complex social and political life of his municipality."[77] The empirically directed but immanently tolerant and welcoming neighborhood would presumably serve as the secure democratic incubator of citizenship.

Although the social unit model was not intended to focus exclusively on health and infant care, this primary orientation allowed the project to offer tangible benefits to the neighborhood and make direct use of the Phillipses' prior experience as a starting point.[78] The MBSUO was widely acclaimed as an innovative demonstration of the efficacy of community-based public health centers, especially with its success in gathering pediatric statistics in conjunction with the national Children's Year Campaign and in responding to the 1918 influenza epidemic. In 1918, the chairman of the Medical Division of the Council of National Defense, Franklin P. Martin, commended the unit plan, declaring: "If the Social Unit can build up, as I believe it is doing, a model system of medical administration, we shall be ready, when the war is over, to take it, adjust it to various environments, and apply it generally."[79] Although this general application never materialized, the medical historian George Rosen retrospectively described the social unit as "one of the most seminal experiments in social organization for health undertaken in the United States," noting that even by the late 1950s, many of the organizing principles introduced by the social unit were only beginning to be substantively explored.[80] In addition to staving off influenza, the MBSUO provided prenatal and postnatal care for mothers; infant and preschool health services; general nursing services, including home care for the sick and infirm; and treatments for tuberculosis patients.[81]

These public health endeavors demanded ongoing partnerships and negotiations with the city's physician and nursing associations. Phillips had secured the short-term endorsement of the Cincinnati Academy of Medicine by arguing that the social unit's preventative health measures would diminish the case for health insurance—the bête noire of the academy—and that its free diagnostic care would expand the patient base for profit-driven private medical practice. Phillips also sought to appeal to both physicians and nurses by suggesting that the social unit services would contribute to ending midwifery. Conflict between the social unit and the West End Medical Society was likewise provisionally overcome, but underlying tensions regarding professional jurisdiction persisted. The fact that the operations of the MBSUO neighborhood health clinic were as efficient and successful as Phillips had promised only accentuated the potential threat it posed to the status quo of the city's medical establishment. Plans to make the experiment citywide, beginning with medical inspections in public schools and annual health examinations for all adults, further increased these anxieties.[82] The Visiting Nurses Association remained antagonistic to the social unit, with the support for the MBSUO of the National Organization for Public Health Nursing and the city's Graduate Nurses Association in no way serving to reduce its animosity. Despite the Phillipses' insistence that "the people and the doctors will decide how far the process is to go," the question was eventually put to them: "Would not such a plan amount to the socialization of medicine ... [and] alter radically the economic organization of medical service?"[83] Professional hostility and political opportunism, rather than the limits of ordinary citizens' participation, led to the social unit's undoing.

The first allegations of socialism emerged soon after the MBSUO was created. During the summer of 1918, James O. White, superintendent of the city's Department of Public Welfare, triggered a minor uproar when he proclaimed that the social unit had moved away from its stated purpose of providing social services and was becoming a "national party with socialistic tendencies." White was among the municipal advocates initially responsible for bringing the experiment to Cincinnati, but he quit the unit's citywide occupational council soon after leveling these charges.[84] Landis, the city's health officer who was originally an outspoken advocate of the social unit plan, expressed his concern to Phillips that "there is real cumulative evidence justifying the impression . . . that the real object of the Social Unit Organization is political." Landis claimed: "Your assistant, Mr. Hart, met with a group of radicals in Pittsburgh and made the statement, 'In Cincinnati we have socialism with its feet on the ground,'" and worse still, "the meeting was attended by a group of extreme radicals and . . . anarchists and members of the I.W.W. were present."[85] These accusations may well have been hyperbolic, but the social unit premise of representing the thought of the whole community—as well as the assumption that this unified thought was manifested in impartial consensus—left it especially vulnerable to criticism that highlighted discord or dissent.

White's departure was followed by the resignation of a city councilman and the secretary of the city's Chamber of Commerce from the council, and it prompted the social unit to initiate a series of defensive measures that included inviting a local social research foundation to investigate White's accusations. The foundation published a report in February clearing the unit of all charges,[86] but the following month, the newly elected mayor, John Galvin, joined in the opportunistic spirit of the nationwide "red scare" to denounce the social unit as a "dangerous institution in our city and but one step away from bolshevism."[87] The Sands Business Men's Club and the West End Medical Society enthusiastically supported the mayor's condemnation, adding that the social unit's "motive was to establish a Soviet in Cincinnati." Others were quick to join the chorus of denunciation. A dean of a local university remarked that "the movement only wore the garb of democracy," and a local minister declared that "luckily someone discovered the snake in the grass before it bit."[88] The city government and the Council of Social Agencies withdrew their financial contributions to the MBSUO. Hicks wrote the mayor, asking: "Are you aware that intensive community organization has been urged by the United States Government, both during the war and since, as one way of solving the many problems confronting our life[?] . . . Do you consider this action of the United States Government and the Community Council Bolshevistic?"[89] Wilbur Phillips protested: "The mere fact that the experiment was launched and accepted as an 'experiment in democracy' implied the existence of unsatisfied social needs and the necessity of devising new and sounder and more fundamental satisfactions for them—implied, in a word, that 'changes' were imperative." He remarked that "only those who are opposed to democracy in practice (while, perhaps, giving lip-service to democracy in theory) have anything to fear from the unit plan."[90] But "democracy in practice" as imagined by Phillips remained an idealized political form that categorically excluded antagonism and incommensurability. Phillips contended that at the community level, "the things which divide us most readily fall away and our common interests as human beings are most clearly seen as paramount."[91] In the final instance, the hypothesis that the social unit success depended on the "mutuality," "goodwill," and full commitment of the "whole community" could not withstand the conflict and controversy evident in the accusations—inflated or not—brought against it.

In an attempt to discredit the mayor and provide public verification of neighborhood support for continuing the social unit experiment, the MBSUO held a districtwide referendum. The vote, with close to a 70 percent turnout, was nearly unanimous in its favor.[92] In a letter to the referendum committee, one neighborhood resident observed: "I cannot but wonder whether the present opposition to the Social Unit may not be due in part to the very fact that it makes the people so independent that they cannot be controlled by any small group or individual." But, in a local newspaper article republished in the *Social Unit Bulletin*, another resident commented: "I understand that Socialism means equality . . . This is what the block workers of the Social Unit preach." What apparently bothered this person was that "they say we are all one family and that we should not consider ourselves better than the Hungarians or Rumanians who live around here . . . that we ought to make friends of the foreigners. I told [them] . . . that I was able to select my own friends." By republishing the article, the social unit presumably aimed to demonstrate its own impartial presentation of differing opinions, as well as to provide an example of the intolerant views of those who opposed it. Another letter included in the same bulletin testified: "You will never hear [the Social Unit] say one word in regard to religion or politics."[93]

A special committee appointed by the Council of Social Agencies to investigate the MBSUO officially exonerated it of all charges. The committee's final report went so far as to assert that "the whole experiment is avowedly an attempt to proceed by methods of orderly democracy and . . . has aimed consistently to enable the people of the district to discover for themselves, without any aggressive tutoring by outsiders, just what their own needs are and how those needs should be met."[94] Despite these findings, the council refused to reinstate funding for the experiment. As a journalist for *Harper's* observed in her account of the episode, "social changes cannot be made without political changes. The balance of power would shift."[95] Phillips seemed unwilling to concede this point and instead maintained an obstinate belief in democracy as a form of collective life entirely without political conflict. In his memoirs, he recollects that after Milwaukee, he and Elsie had decided they "were through with politics! Hereafter, we told ourselves, we're for non-partisan democracy."[96] Whether or not this was a rhetorical maneuver intended principally to open possibilities for mainstream coalition remains unclear. Nevertheless, the social unit aspiration to build a broad alliance uniting Socialists, industrial workers, new immigrants, owners of small businesses, and members of the professional classes in certain respects anticipated the forms of Popular Front Americanism during the 1930s and 1940s that comprised what Michael Denning describes as the "Age of the CIO [Congress of Industrial Organizations]."[97] In the interim, however, the Phillipses were unable to sustain the coalition they had assembled in Cincinnati.

The social unit project retreated back to the not-so-typical city of New York, where the Phillipses and the NSOU pursued the idea of merging with the New York Community Council (NYCC) established by the Council of National Defense. Unfortunately for all involved, the postwar years featured not only heightened anticommunist hysteria and race riots, but also a dwindling commitment to the community-based initiatives so exuberantly championed during the First World War. Neither the NSUO nor the NYCC remained solvent for long, and—following a jointly sponsored Neighbor's Day event in 1920 and deteriorating relations between the two groups—the decline of philanthropic support and government interest quickly led to the dissolution of both organizations.

The catalyst of the First World War produced interim experiments in government involvement with community organization but did not lead to a sustained interest in the decentralized prospects of mobilizing local initiatives in alignment with governance and social welfare. Moreover, even in projects such as the Social Unit Organization, where attention was focused on cultivating citizens' participation in the definition of program goals and carrying out operations, poverty was only one issue among many. The red scare, the unbridled collective violence of whites against African Americans and other people of color, and rising anti-immigrant sentiment contributed to making a context in which those government-endorsed community-based initiatives that did exist sought to be unequivocally inoffensive. Although community center initiatives did not disappear in the 1920s, they were increasingly associated with top-down projects such as adult education, case-work-oriented social work, and expert-driven social engineering.

In contrast, the Cold War provided the sustained sense of emergency and social anxiety, combined with the expansion of US global economic and political preponderance, necessary for a more enduring turn to community development. Many of the social preoccupations and methods associated with the Cold War built on, intensified, and extended political dynamics already evident during the First World War, including the threat of communism and the democratic promise of community.[98] Nowhere were the conditions and consequences of the combination of expanded geopolitical economy and anxiety after the Second World War more clearly evident than in Puerto Rico and its community education program, where the terms of being "foreign to the United States in a domestic sense"—as the US Supreme Court had designated the island and other territories acquired as a result of the Spanish-American War in its efforts to sidestep the taint of colonialism—enhanced strategic possibilities.[99]

Insular Democracy

Although faith in expertise and social engineering remained robust after the Second World War, alternative approaches to development gained institutional ground. In 1953, the community development advocate William Biddle argued that the problem with the "expert" is that usually this person "comes from somewhere else." For Biddle, this was part of "a tendency among Americans to 'pass the buck' of responsibility to professionals." In order to remedy this problem, he called for cultivating "participant-leaders," based on the "belief that leadership can emerge when ordinary people take responsibility for solving their own problems" and on "faith in the potentialities and the ultimate decency of ordinary people." According to him, this sort of leader "is no longer remote and removed from followers. He is part of and growing with the group of which he is a part. The leader and the led are closer and more readily interchangeable, for both have become stronger together. Decision is democratized, less concentrated in a few."[100] This perspective was evident in the widely acclaimed Community Development Program of India established in 1952, which drew on Indian precursors such as the Institute of Rural Reconstruction, founded in West Bengal by the poet Rabindranath Tagore in 1921, and the efforts of Mahatma Gandhi beginning in 1931 to make villages self-sufficient units using local "constructive workers" as catalysts for cooperative community self-help.[101] But this viewpoint was also apparent in the British colonial strategies of indirect rule and, during the 1920s, British colonial educational policy whose aim was "to promote the advance of the community as a whole."[102] England's focus on education directed by local people was further advanced in the Colonial Development and Welfare Acts of 1940 and 1945. As the British Empire began to lose hold over its territories, it increasingly turned to inclusionary strategies in an effort to maintain at least the vestiges of colonial rule.

During the late 1940s, US foreign policy strategists and social scientists found community participation both relevant and useful in development plans. The State Department promoted programs for economic development and modernization in the noncommunist and nonaligned world as the beneficent counterpart to US military and covert security measures.[103] Policymakers viewed poverty as a problem for modernization because it was a threat to political stability and an impediment to the socialization of the largely agricultural rural peasantry of the "underdeveloped" world. From a normative policy standpoint, poverty was associated with backward subsistence economies and the worldviews of those not yet fully incorporated into the wage labor regimes of industrial production and the modern nation-state. In the bipolar worldview of the Truman Doctrine, poverty posed a problem for winning the hearts and minds of Third World populations susceptible to the revolutionary promise of communism. US foreign policy experts reframed poverty as an implicitly depoliticizing discourse that detached inequity and discontent from the volatile domain of class struggle, legacies of colonial exploitation, and the structural necessities of capital accumulation. In addition to discouraging the revolutionary impulse and lure of the communist bloc, this separation continued to place blame for the conditions of poverty on the poor themselves. But expert intervention would supposedly provide the means with which to break their chains of backwardness and passivity, channeling social action into established modes of democratic citizenship, possessive individualism, and the teleology of growth. At the same time, for much of the formerly colonized world, the development paradigm was not simply the latest form of imperialist expropriation, but it also promised to improve national health standards and social welfare. In addition, the specter of communist incursion provided leverage for winning political and financial support from the United States.

During the early Cold War, as global conflict was displaced to the nominal periphery, Puerto Rico assumed an increasingly strategic role in US policy toward Latin America and the so-called developing world. In a 1955 memo to all US diplomatic missions in Latin America, John Foster Dulles, a noted cold warrior who was then secretary of state, warned that "criticism of the proportional amount of United States aid to Latin America, as compared with economic assistance in other areas, especially Europe and the Far East, is so persistent as to constitute a serious factor in our good relations with other governments of this hemisphere."[104] US policymakers promoted Puerto Rico as a hemispheric object lesson in noncommunist political and economic transformation produced in association with private capital from the United States rather than by US aid. In a 1956 speech delivered at the Annual Convention of the Associated Harvard Clubs, Puerto Rican Governor Luis Muñoz Marín proclaimed: "We have insisted in making Puerto Rico a training center for technical assistance, a laboratory for visitors from the New World and even Africa and Asia, so that they may see for themselves our unrelenting and peaceful war on colonialism, poverty, disease, ignorance, and hopelessness—carried out in terms of a deep sense of friendship, of brotherhood with the U.S."[105] Muñoz's Partido Popular Democrático (Popular Democratic Party; PPD) capitalized on the island's strategic significance for US policy in such a way as to consolidate the party's political authority, change the political status of Puerto Rico, and attract US investment capital to promote industrialization.

The PPD also cultivated a dedicated following among the island's peasants and working class during the late 1940s and 1950s. Legislation such as the PPD-sponsored 1941 Land Act, which provided *agregado* (landless) families with small parcels of land arranged in planned rural communities and established an institutional infrastructure for breaking up the system of rural labor peonage controlled by the *hacendados* (large landowners), secured the rural poor's enduring loyalty to the PPD.[106] The party undercut sugar plantation interests, promoted land redistribution, and enfranchised the rural poor in exchange for their electoral support. The Puerto Rican example proved all the more compelling for elites within the context of Latin America's conservative retrenchment in the late 1940s. As the histo-

"Land Authority Program at the drawing lots for *parcelas*, small plots of land upon which landless farmer workers can erect their homes," near Toa Baja, Puerto Rico, July 1946.

rian Ian Roxborough has observed, the Lombardista alliance between workers and domestic entrepreneurs that supported industrialization with substantial income redistribution was overcome by a distinctly conservative version of import-substitution industrialization "in which foreign capital played a leading role and a central concern was the control of labor." Nevertheless, Roxborough points out: "Despite their victory in the struggles of the 1940s, Latin American elites failed to develop a widespread legitimation for the new model of capital accumulation."[107] It was precisely such popular legitimation that Muñoz managed to achieve. As the economists John Kenneth Galbraith and Carolyn Shaw Solo recognized, "the Muñoz Marín administration, in the process of coming to power in 1940, did a singularly effective job both of defining the issues facing the Puerto Rican people and in developing a popular understanding and identification of the people with solutions and goals."[108] Such popular identification with government purpose was a primary ambition of liberal community-based approaches to poverty and governance during the postwar era.

In 1952, an islandwide plebiscite authorized by the US Congress officially transformed Puerto Rico into the newly conceived political category of *estado libre asociado* (free associated state, or commonwealth). According to Muñoz, the new commonwealth status provided "a dramatic refutation of the communist claim that the United States position is narrow, colonialistic, and reactionary." Moreover, "the social and economic surge in Puerto Rico clearly demonstrates that a people of different historical background can find a way out of their former anguish and despair, in close association with the United States."[109] Public Law 600 similarly disavowed the colonial preconditions of "free association" and affirmed the resolutely democratic character of the new political status, stating that "fully recognizing the principle of government by consent, this Act is now adopted in the nature of a compact so that the people of Puerto Rico may organize a government pursuant to a Constitution of their own adoption."[110] The power of the Puerto Rican people to establish their own constitution made the formal terms of consent the means through which the substance of democracy trumped colonial inequality. In January 1953, five months after Puerto Rico's new constitution was ratified, the United States successfully petitioned the United Nations to remove the island from its list of non-self-governing territories.[111] Clearly, the terms of the new constitution and the maneuvers of the Muñoz administration were strategic, just as the character and consequences of this strategy were directly linked to the Cold War context, the US relationship to decolonization, and ascendant doctrines of economic modernization.

The PPD and the US State Department collaborated in publicizing Puerto Rico as a "showcase of democratic development." This was done in part by promoting the apparent political innovations of Puerto Rico's "free associated state" status and its new constitution.[112] These were heralded variously as a "middle road to freedom," "America's answer to communism," and, later, a crucial antithesis to Castro's Cuba.[113] These political novelties were undergirded by the Muñoz administration's export-oriented economic development program, called Operation Bootstrap (Operación Manos a la Obra), a plan combining capital importation and export processing that was

"Artists from the Division of Cinema and Graphics of the Parks and Recreation Commission [precursor to the Division of Community Education] making sketches of agricultural workers, who live on a Land Authority Settlement area, building a community road for themselves" near Fajardo, Puerto Rico, May 1947. PHOTOGRAPH BY LOUISE ROSSKAM, COURTESY OF THE ARCHIVES OF THE PUERTO RICAN DIASPORA, CENTRO DE ESTUDIOS PUERTORRIQUEÑOS, HUNTER COLLEGE, CITY UNIVERSITY OF NEW YORK.

launched by the Puerto Rico Development Company (known as the Economic Development Administration after 1950) that vigorously courted US private capital and industry with the help of tax-abatement arrangements and the promise of a no-strike, no-union pledge for factories. As with the changing ideological and policy alignment of the PPD, the initial state-run companies created under the auspices of Operation Bootstrap were rapidly privatized to avoid the perception that Puerto Rico was anything less than a beacon of free-market entrepreneurialism.[114]

The División de Educación de la Comunidad—begun as a pilot program for civic education in 1947 and established as an agency within the island's

Department of Education in 1949—was indispensable to Puerto Rico's "showcase" status.[115] Whereas Operation Bootstrap was characteristic of the elite-driven centralized approach typically associated with the modernization agenda, DIVEDCO translated the demands of liberal capitalism into everyday democratic practices that were initiated locally and crucial to anticommunist discourse. As one education scholar summed up more broadly, "the Free World . . . is developing a new approach to community education, which depends on the understanding and acceptance of the desirability of change by the people who will be affected, so that their conscious and enthusiastic participation in making the change is assured."[116] Not only did modernization require a labor force supportive of and adapted to the new industrial regime, but it could substantially benefit from a political order that conscientiously affirmed the requisites of popular consent.

In order to appeal to the island's rural poor, many of whom were illiterate, DIVEDCO produced motion pictures and graphic pamphlets, books, and posters. Pamphlets were distributed and films screened in rural communities by field organizers, who used the material as a catalyst for group discussion and getting residents interested in local civic endeavors. Legislation defined DIVEDCO's mission as teaching the tenets of self-governance and inspiring in local communities "the wish, the tendency, and the way of making use of their own aptitudes for the solution of many of their own problems of health, education, cooperation, [and] social life through the action of the community itself."[117] Local meetings served to identify collective concerns and mobilize community participation to address them through government-supported small-scale education, social service, and infrastructure projects.

Popular identification with the island's government was grounded in a sense that the state was the people's advocate, even when localized antagonisms suggested disagreements between municipal authorities and islandwide programs. Interviews conducted by the anthropologist Ismael García-Colón provide examples of the localized activities through which the rural poor came to identify with the state. Describing the process of neighborhood meetings and film screenings, Práxedes Collazo Ramos, a DIVEDCO group organizer during the 1950s in the town of Cidra, told García-Colón that "this program motivated neighbors to discuss their problems. In this way, many community projects emerged through the [DIVEDCO] movies." His colleague Francisco Zayas recollected: "As neighbors became more knowledgeable, began holding meetings, and discuss[ed] their problems . . . we began to help them and inform them on how to seek assistance from the government." According to one resident, Concepción Rivera Santiago, this led to the creation of formal committees to petition the city government for assistance: "We would discuss our needs and then we would head to the Mayor's Office. There, they would tell us whether or not they could help us. If they couldn't help us, they would give us some help for the moment and tell us to continue forward doing the rest on our own." Another resident, Monserrate Reyes Ramos, recounted that when no action was taken on demands for access to potable water and for improved roads, neighbors went to protest at the Municipal Hall.[118] Even when such conflicts challenged local authority, they had the effect of reinforcing a broader identification with the PPD-directed state, under whose auspices the community had mobilized to begin with.

DIVEDCO was thus a cornerstone of the PPD hegemonic project because of its capacity to officially associate the daily life of the rural poor with state policy, while championing the economic independence and self-initiated enterprise of the people. Furthermore, this capacity for independence was a partial surrogate for Puerto Rico's ever-deferred political sovereignty. Of course, small-scale local cooperation and mutual aid existed long before the introduction of state-sponsored programs such as DIVEDCO. Despite intermittent claims to the contrary, the rural poor did not have to be taught such forms of collective support and reciprocity. Thus, DIVEDCO field organizers were instructed to be "aware of the history of the 'juntas' " and to locate existing "centers where community activity is already underway."[119] What was significant about PPD programs—and DIVEDCO in particular— was that they established a formal link to the state through such activities and institutionalized these localized mechanisms for survival within the state itself. Thus, although not new, local cooperation and mutual aid assumed an unprecedented significance. The political and administrative recognition of these activities gave them value as expressions of the state. Because they were associated with the tangible gains of redistribution and employment, the incorporation of such activities confirmed the PPD's embodiment of what Muñoz frequently called the "nacionalismo pueblo" (people's state).

Targeting the local poor, DIVEDCO sought to reform what it diagnosed as their subservient and fatalistic tendencies. Kalevro Oberg—an anthropologist affiliated with the US International Cooperation Administration mission in Brazil who would later introduce the notion of "culture shock" into social science and policy discourse, as discussed in the next chapter—alleged that when poor rural people in Puerto Rico resist the liberating overtures of community education, "this resistance is rooted in the traditional paternalistic type of rural society in which the community does little or nothing for itself but expects everything from the government through the intercession of its formal leaders, such as political bosses, large landowners, priests, and even school teachers." According to Oberg, the persistence of such locally entrenched paternalism was the failure of enlightened self-interest on the part of the peasants themselves. He contended that DIVEDCO could bring these recalcitrant peasants into the fold of the nation, better harmonizing their aspirations with those of the larger polity: "The rural folk are intellectually isolated, they are in the nation but not really part of it . . . With a properly oriented community education program the people will be brought to a cultural level in which the national objectives are their objective, in which action and self-help will originate among the rural masses."[120] Only once they were properly reconstructed as energetic citizens could the "rural masses" assume their rightful place as the democratic source of national purpose.

División de Educación de la Comunidad planners intended each component of the division's operations to serve as a heuristic device, informed by community concerns and conducive to making local people into active, self-sufficient citizens. The Production Unit made films and illustrated booklets about problems identified during community discussions arranged by DIVEDCO group organizers. Films were produced on location, often with amateur actors recruited from the surrounding community. The process of producing films and graphic publications also served as a training ground for local technicians and artists, many of whom subsequently assumed leadership roles in DIVEDCO projects. The Field and Training Unit enlisted local residents to serve as group organizers, who in turn coordinated community discussions and planning sessions. Writers in the Editorial Unit not only drafted DIVEDCO's pamphlets but were responsible for providing screenplays for the Production Unit; for each project, they lived in the communities they were writing about for several days or weeks.[121] The Analysis Unit gauged the efficacy of DIVEDCO materials by surveying community reaction and measuring changes in attitude toward the subjects addressed.

Altogether, the division's pedagogical enterprise simultaneously accentuated local issues and made local communities an embodiment of the Puerto Rican free associated state.

DIVEDCO's compulsion for localization was paralleled by its drive to improve the conduct and consciousness of individuals. The division substituted a focus on producing the democratic citizen as a normative political subject for a concern with establishing conduits for collective mobilization and inclusionary policymaking. In its programs, an understanding of democracy as a form of state power was essentially replaced by concerns for internal psychological transformation. This focus on individual mental and emotional adjustment as a political end in and of itself was indicative of the ubiquity of psychological concepts after the Second World War. It also fit well with the psychological diagnostics of Oscar Lewis's "culture of poverty" thesis, which—although not given that name until 1959—provided a convenient phrase for social scientists' already widespread belief in the family as the agent responsible for social inequality and intergenerational poverty.

DIVEDCO emphasized process over outcome, as was the case with the community development model more generally. This focus on process, with its notably therapeutic overtones, privileged the normative ambitions of community development. Prominent community development theorists William and Loureide Biddle define the value of community development as a "social process by which human beings can become more competent to live with and gain some control over local aspects of a frustrating and changing world . . . The essence of process does not consist in any fixed succession of events . . . but in the growth that occurs within individuals, within groups, and within the communities they serve."[122] The sociologists Stephen B. Withey and Charles F. Cannell reiterate a theme evident throughout published accounts of DIVEDCO when they write that "the Division centers its work on the community—its perception of itself and its own potential . . . The problems are the community's own; the motivations and processes by which the community grows as it solves these problems are the concerns of the Division."[123] Fred Wale, director of DIVEDCO, further stipulated the terms of this process, stating that "material facilities must be accompanied by internal growth for community well-being and . . . this cannot be accomplished without the use of democratic methods in all matters effecting [sic] the related lives of those within the community."[124] Introspection is facilitated through group discussion and culminates in an emerging democratic consciousness, but ultimately it serves the transformation of individuals.

In typical descriptions of DIVEDCO fieldwork, problems are similarly detached from the broader social context and individualized. Social, economic, and political dilemmas were construed as issues of community self-esteem and confidence. Individuals needed to overcome their internalized sense of resignation and inferiority in order to begin to work collectively. Moreover, most DIVEDCO narratives omitted any significant discussion of the outcome of collective efforts except to note that a milk station (a dispensary with information on pediatric care and fresh milk for infants), bridge, or road was built. For instance, the field organizer Zacarías Rodríguez reports: "For more than a year the people of Cuyón talked and worked together, individually and in groups, seeking a solution to a problem common to all." He recounts triumphantly that "through many disappointments but with even greater accomplishments, through sickness and poverty, often delayed by rain and mud, the community finally reached the place where today . . . the community is building its own milk station."[125] Reports such as this accentuated the protracted duration of the process, as well as persistent poverty and struggle. Of course, these forms of collective discussion were not inherently therapeutic narratives of personal psychological catharsis, and they could also lead to more extensive and overtly political mobilizations. However, the administrative organization of DIVEDCO discouraged this by maintaining the program's closely circumscribed and assertively local character.

Whereas activities within communities themselves continually threatened to exceed the procedures of introspection, the selection and training of field organizers demonstrates the therapeutic imperative to an even greater degree. In describing the training design, Wale and Carmen Isales, the director of field programs, reflect: "We believed that democracy began with the stimulus given each individual to search into his innermost resources."[126] Group organizers were selected on the basis of criteria that included the following: "Was he a man of the people?" "Could he work in his own community?" "Was he a happy man at home?" "What were his attitudes towards authoritarian behavior?" "Was he a secure person?" "Was he a static personality or did he possess the capacity for growth?"[127] Here a candidate's psychological profile was translated into a quantifiable political value. Democracy was an internal capacity, a propensity for a distinct set of moral values based on a stable emotional foundation. Consequently, democracy in practice became focused on liberating oneself from neurotic disorders and internalized constraints.

Both training and supervision also appear as a process of confronting and overcoming inherited attitudes. Wale and Isales insist: "To assure the fulfillment of the aims of the program, attention must be given to the field man as a personality. His whole life is a subject that comes often into discussion during supervisory conferences."[128] Although this approach certainly replicated social work training and supervision, it also projected the distinctly social and economic struggle of local communities into purely psychological dimensions. The connection between training and the frame of community action is clearly articulated in the reflections of Higinio Rivera, a field organizer:

> I could not have been more surprised. There were no lectures on how to build roads or latrines, or how to rotate crops. We were told government technical people would help when they [the local community] needed such aid. Instead the instructor threw open to discussion such problems as can a poor, uneducated jíbaro without any land do much to affect the welfare of his community? We spent three months discussing such questions. I had to dig deep into my own attitudes to find the answers . . . What it did was to prepare me to go into a community that lacked even the minimum facilities and to recognize that the tragedy was not that the people lacked latrines or paved roads or even pure water, but rather the spiritual isolation in which they lived.[129]

The material conditions of poverty and deprivation were thus reduced to symptoms of "spiritual isolation." Organizers for DIVEDCO were taught to bypass the apparent complexities of such symptoms in order to concentrate on the more profound process of spiritual transformation.

The inspiration for community involvement undoubtedly followed from budgetary restraints as much as from rhetorical claims. Part of the appeal of community development for Muñoz and the PPD was its low cost to the island's government. With financial resources historically depleted by the dispossessions of colonialism and further constrained by Operation Bootstrap's tax-abatement tariff-free strategies to attract private investment, the means for backing such projects were limited. Self-help ideology offered the possibility of working in such conditions of scarcity. The political scientist Henry Wells has noted that DIVEDCO's budget was too small for the agency to have any significant impact on the island's underlying troubles. The early decision to shift the bureaucratic mechanisms for small-scale self-help community projects to the Social Programs Administration of the Department of Agriculture and Commerce further diminished DIVEDCO's ability to support community-generated endeavors.[130] However, it was precisely this limited funding and disinterest in structural change that propelled the community development model to begin with. Rather than merely embodying grand and unrealized aspirations, community development—and DIVEDCO specifically—approached the ethical substance of democracy in the details of everyday life, with little attention to systemic change.

This narrow scope also affected the thematic repertoire of DIVEDCO's literature, graphic publications, and films. The new forms of labor, new relations of production, and social consequences of the accelerated programs for industrialization and modernization initiated under Operation Bootstrap were peculiarly absent from DIVEDCO's depictions of peasant life. Although local communities were indeed prompted to organize and to work collectively, and were even assisted in their efforts to challenge entrenched local leadership based on landed and mercantile power—as evident in the booklet *Los Casos de Ignacio y Santiago* and the film *Ignacio* discussed at the beginning of this chapter—the agency's work remained localized and very rarely addressed the profound effects of the collapse of agriculture and the new realities of industrial production and urbanization on the island.[131] Indeed, similar comments could be made about community development programs generally. Even as community development forced local contingencies and specificities into the universalized abstractions of modernization theory, the salience and utility of local community was precisely its clear limit as local.

DIVEDCO's stubborn myopia did little to address in either image or narrative how Puerto Rico's broader socioeconomic circumstances changed over time. Apart from single projects on the issues of women's rights and migration—which reflected little concern for the complexity of Puerto Rican feminist discourse on sterilization or the realities of economic opportunity on the US mainland—the narratives of DIVEDCO films and pamphlets, as well as the division's objectives for fieldworker organizing, remained static.[132] However, especially as industrialization and urbanization threatened to overwhelm familiar ways of life, DIVEDCO's truncated framing was more than merely sentimental. The division's recourse to images of traditional Puerto Rican life and its avoidance of the realities of massive social dislocation and modernization worked in conjunction with the multiple currents of cultural nationalism on the island at the time.

Indeed, the broad resonance of Muñoz's cultural agenda allowed him to weather the various contradictions of his political and economic platforms. As the anthropologist Jorge Duany has argued, over the course of the 1940s, Muñoz gradually disavowed political nationalism in favor of an assertive and advantageous cultural nationalism. That DIVEDCO's legacy has been almost entirely its role in Puerto Rican cultural history, and not in the expansion of local political and economic power, reaffirms this turn to cultural nationalism. For the island's elite, cultural nationalism promised an autonomous national identity still conducive to a strategic compromise with US colonial rule. It partially displaced the political implications of insisting on a distinct national identity and thus also appealed to advocates for statehood.[133]

The PPD's precipitous decline made DIVEDCO's function increasingly uncertain. Efforts to depersonalize and institutionalize the PPD after Muñoz stepped down in 1964 foundered on internecine party politics, petty rivalries, and ineffectual leadership. During the decade following Muñoz's retirement, social, economic, and political factors converged to fragment and destabilize both DIVEDCO's role as a legitimating force for the PPD and the PPD's as a persuasive interlocutor of colonial power. PPD-sponsored industrialization and migration to the US mainland, as well as largely unpopular urban resettlement programs during the early to mid-1960s, contributed to the erosion of the party's traditional support and made the rural orientation of its populism appear antiquated. Moreover, rural electoral support for the PPD notably declined in the 1968 election. Even before the global economic recession of the early 1970s, competition for the low-wage, labor-intensive production that was the hallmark of Operation Bootstrap had spread to other Caribbean, Latin American, and Southeast Asian sites.[134] During the 1970s, DIVEDCO was increasingly underwritten by US federal funds, which by the end of the decade made up more than 60 percent of the agency's budget.[135] This dramatic decrease in fiscal sponsorship by the island's government only further weakened DIVEDCO's position as the everyday instantiation of the PPD.

The global economic crisis of the early 1970s thus heralded less a renunciation of US colonial rule than growing disillusionment with PPD populism, which by then seemed incidental to rather than essential for the negotiation of US colonial policy. Rather than evidence of acquiescence to colonial rule, continued popular support for "association" with the United States expressed a particular class politics. During the 1970s, the advantages of that association seemed more apparent to the poor and working class. Direct US government transfers to the Puerto Rican poor increased from $517 million in 1973 to $2.5 billion in 1980. Sixty percent of Puerto Rican families qualified for food stamps, compared to only 11 percent of families on the mainland. Thus, during the 1960s and 1970s, a common saying among Puerto Ricans was: "Better to be a colony than to be independent like Haiti or the Dominican Republic." Indeed, more often than not, the corollary of decolonization appeared to be neocolonial exploitation. As the sociologist Ramón Grosfoguel has argued, "given the drastic differences between the situation of working classes in modern colonies and neo-colonial nation-states" of the Caribbean, it is not surprising that the Puerto Rican working class and poor favor the material incentives of colonial rule. Grosfoguel contends that the economic burden of independence would fall disproportionately on the most materially vulnerable. Why, therefore, would people want to relinquish the social entitlements and economic assistance accorded by "association," especially when political independence includes the likely prospect of neocolonial domination without accompanying compensation?[136] This was a question beyond the purview of community education.

Felt Needs and Anxious Government

"It is always worth remembering," advised the prominent community development specialist T. R. Batten in 1957, "that the community is primarily a social group, and based on the *feeling* that people have for one another ... In essence, it is the feeling of belonging to, and sharing responsibility for, the welfare of the group." He argued that "there are two main kinds of development agency: the one which tries to introduce specific changes and is mainly interested in material development; and the other which is primarily interested in people." The aim of the first type was "to get things done," whereas the second approach sought to "develop the people's own abilities for leadership, wise judgment, and co-operative action." According to Batten, the decisive weakness of the first approach was that it obstructs "the growth of the basic feeling of 'belonging' in the groups and institutions it creates." The second, however, enabled more substantial and lasting change because it aims "to leave the people free, to consider their feelings and their needs, and to try to serve their *wants*."[137] Although much community development discourse existed primarily at the level of rhetoric—speaking in terms not corroborated in practice or subscribed to by the people it named as its agents—the substantial frictions, incongruities, and aspirations it articulated remain significant for understanding liberals' thinking about inequality and the conditions of possibility for social action. At the same time, the community development model was potentially appealing to the people toward whom such programs were directed precisely because it encouraged those who were often the most disenfranchised to perceive themselves as possessing the capacity to influence and change both themselves and the world around them.

Elements of the second approach described by Batten are evident in both early- and mid-twentieth-century community-based reform initiatives, but the intensity with which this method was deployed and the scope of its application changed during the decades following the Second World War. Certainly, during both periods reformers often claimed to act on behalf of the "felt needs" of the people themselves. One significant difference between the two eras, however, was the shift in focus from advocating neighborhood democracy to encouraging community action with the alleviation of poverty as its specific object—a move away from the typical toward the poor. After the Second World War, community development attention to nurturing democracy as a psychosocial capacity became a corollary to the idea of community development as a strategy of localization. Whereas reformers in the Progressive Era argued for neighborhood cooperation as key to nation building, community development programs strove to channel broader social aspirations toward local transformation. Community development still promoted local initiatives as a means of nation building, but—especially as such nation building emerged internationally in the context of decolonization and Cold War bipolarity—it was subsumed within the containment objectives of US grand strategy.[138]

The relationship between early-twentieth-century community-based social welfare and postwar programs was often not explicit. Reference to the Social Unit Organization appeared cursorily in histories of community organization and public health, but by midcentury there was little substantive discussion of the Cincinnati project by policymakers or social scientists. In contrast, the Collier-era philosophy of the People's Institute did have considerable, though indirect, national consequences. In his subsequent career as the US commissioner of Indian Affairs, John Collier's contribution to the Indian Reorganization Act of 1934 encompassed a set of contradictions similar to the People's Institute's cultural pluralism. His efforts to administratively formalize tribal self-government and recognize traditional cultural practices both provided considerable opportunities for autonomy and authority for indigenous peoples who were amenable to the types of reform Collier proposed, and made these opportunities vehicles for federal control and incorporation into broader US society. It was in this arena that his plans for community-based democracy were most fully articulated, albeit as paradoxically as were his People's Institute endeavors.

It is perhaps not surprising that reformers' preoccupations in the early twentieth century with community—especially local community as the way to foster national identity—coincided with an anxious, ambivalent, yet insistent concern with foreign-born immigrants. Indeed, this seems indicative of the ways in which the political theorist Bonnie Honig has analyzed "foreignness as a site at which certain anxieties of *democratic* self-rule are managed." Honig notes: "In the various versions of the myth of immigrant America, it is . . . the immigrant's *foreignness* that positions him to reinvigorate the national democracy," and yet this foreignness remains "itself a problem for the regimes that seek to benefit from its supplement,"[139] a problem where the foreign remains always already within and provisional. This was and is still the case with regard to the innumerable ways in which foreignness is deployed as a trope that justifies inequality and hierarchy as somehow provisional forms of internal exclusion—fully entwined, as it were, with the stratified ascription of racial and colonial differences. The cultural theorist Rey Chow contends that the idea and category of the "ethnic" is shaped in relation to "ever-intensifying processes of collective commodification." Chow argues that "the ethnic as such stands in modernity as the site of foreignness that is produced from within privileged societies and is at once defined by and constitutive of that society's hierarchical divisions of labor."[140] The premise of social unity and cooperation as a managerial strategy during the early twentieth century simultaneously disavowed and depended on this relation. The expanded geopolitical exigencies of the Cold War further amplified the significance of this concurrently internal and external foreignness—resonating across civil rights confrontations, the specter of the communist threat, and the disavowal of US imperialism.

For community development after the Second World War, the local leader or democratic catalyst was likewise an uncanny subject. On the one hand, Cold War bipolarity institutionalized the presumption of rational choice as an interpretive lens for understanding social action, while on the other hand such abstractions were never fully persuasive on the ground. Once identified as a necessary constituent for development, the bona fide member and plausible representative of community sentiment in some sense continued to appear foreign—his or her position as interlocutor always potentially suspect from the perspective of governance. "Felt needs" remained elusive—always entangled in representational practices that threatened to destabilize the claims to credibility of such collective sentiments. In the first section of this chapter, the US international aid consultant Ellery Foster was quoted as referring disparagingly to "predetermined felt needs." For Foster, this was an oxymoron that haunted community development. In this sense, DIVEDCO's dramatization of Ignacio's story sought to provide an object lesson, complete with the requisite procedures of introspection, in genuine felt needs. Partially qualified by audience response, but in fact no less "predetermined," DIVEDCO conjured the inner life of the *jíbaro* (Puerto Rican peasant) in an effort to substantiate its mission.

In Puerto Rico, the "tutelary colonialism" that the sociologist Julian Go argues served as the overarching justification for US rule in the early twentieth century gathered momentum as it was refracted through the gradual advance of populist educational policies, self-help programs, and the tenets of free association.[141] The work of DIVEDCO reveals the reciprocal relations between often elaborately localized relations of power and the wider horizon of US preponderance. In turn, these relations demonstrate how community development was a liberal strategy for governing the poor and circumscribing dissent. Community as envisioned by the PPD and developed by DIVEDCO fieldwork was a crucible for liberal democracy inasmuch as it respected certain political limitations while encouraging people to feel unencumbered by the conditions of colonialism. That Puerto Rico continued to appear "foreign in a domestic sense" was also symptomatic of how poverty was viewed by many US policymakers and social scientists at the time.[142] In the next chapter, I turn to the ostensibly foreign quality of poverty and the supposedly universal value of liberal rehabilitation.

CHAPTER TWO

ON THE INTERNAL BORDER
Colonial Difference and the Locations of Underdevelopment

I n 1962, the recently established Peace Corps announced plans for
an intensive field training initiative that would acclimatize the agency's growing number of volunteers to the conditions of poverty in so-
called underdeveloped countries and to seemingly foreign cultures.
The initiative was to take place in parts of the United States that were
considered similar to the volunteers' future stations abroad. This
training was designed to be "as realistic as possible, to give volunteers a
'feel' of the situation they will face." With this purpose in mind, the
Second Annual Report of the Peace Corps explained: "Trainees bound
for social work in Colombian city slums were given on-the-job training in New York City's Spanish Harlem . . . New Mexican Indian
reservations and Spanish-speaking villages make realistic workshops
for community development trainees. Puerto Rico provides experience in living in a Latin American environment. The Island of Hawaii, with its multiracial population, remote valleys and varied rural
economy, performs a similar function for volunteers headed for
Southeast Asia."[1] Communities throughout the United States were
chosen for their apparent similarities to locations abroad, to serve as a
staging ground for President John F. Kennedy's vaunted Cold War
diplomatic venture.

In this chapter I argue that US policymakers' conceptions of the
foreign shaped economic underdevelopment as an emergent category

of poverty during the early Cold War. Whereas the previous chapter examined how "community" was variously defined and deployed at two distinct historical periods, this chapter considers the ways in which "poverty" was seen as a site for intervention and remediation during the mid-twentieth century. In this chapter I analyze the strategic associations of poverty as at once foreign and provisional, arguing that these associations remained significant for a broader understanding of "community action" to alleviate poverty. The Peace Corps is one important example of how the foreign served not simply as a boundary, counterpoint, or disruption to domestic norms, but as integral to the dynamics of liberal reform. The discursive link between foreignness and underdevelopment, however, also served political and economic strategies not limited to the prescriptive agendas of reform.

I begin with a brief discussion of underdevelopment and its association with the foreign in postwar United States policymaking and social science. In order to demonstrate the rapid appropriation of this logic for other purposes, I then examine a series of legislative proposals by the National Congress of American Indians (NCAI) during the 1950s that explicitly sought to draw on the confluence of US policy constructions of the foreign and underdevelopment. These proposals were modeled on the US Point Four foreign technical assistance program.[2] However, rather than promoting industrialization and market expansion that US policymakers might readily define as foreign, the NCAI proposals aimed to safeguard tribal treaty rights while also securing economic assistance from the US government. The NCAI proposals and lobbying efforts demonstrate both the inadvertent promise of Point Four rhetoric and the decisive barriers to leveraging this rhetoric beyond certain limits.

The chapter then turns to Peace Corps community development field training as a way to explore the proliferation of investment in the discursive junction of foreignness and underdevelopment, following its official transposition to the margins of the domestic scene. First conceived in 1957 as a Point Four Youth Corps, the Peace Corps became the preeminent international agency of US liberal reform during its heyday in the 1960s. I compare Peace Corps field training to the NCAI campaign in order to study the ways in which such government initiatives existed in tension with the competing policy objectives, political claims, and economic demands that strategically combined underdevelopment and foreignness. My examination of Peace

Corps field training aims to parse the multiple agents that competed for symbolic and material resources through the foreign-underdevelopment rubric. I also focus on the training program in New Mexico, as well as a pretraining initiative for American Indians called Project Peace Pipe, in order to consider how state-sanctioned conceptions of underdevelopment, cultural difference, and foreignness ran up against the limit of colonial difference during the 1960s. "Colonial difference," as Walter Mignolo uses the term, refers to the disavowal and subalternization of peoples and knowledges—through colonial regimes of racialization, labor exploitation, forced assimilation, and territorial dispossession—upon which Euro-American world power has been historically predicated.[3] I use the notion of colonial difference to underscore specifically how this disavowal and subalternization has remained essential to formations of liberal democracy in the United States. I examine the Peace Corps' plans for its training program, the circumstances of its implementation in New Mexico, and the oppositional uses of the foreign at the local level that the program could not accommodate (especially the Alianza Federal de Mercedes). Project Peace Pipe provides an additional vantage point from which to interrogate the permissible variations and forbidden referents of foreignness as a provisional catalyst.

US policymakers seized on the alignment of the foreign with underdevelopment when it could be cast as a transitional moment in the process of incorporation and assimilation, but when the conjunction threatened to seem a consequence of market or colonial relations, they considered it not only inassimilable but impermissible. Such groups as the Alianza quite deliberately mobilized in opposition to colonial dispossession, while other New Mexicans, aiming to take advantage of Peace Corps training models for their own purposes, adopted strategies similar to those of the NCAI and sought to capitalize on the tension between provisionality and colonial difference. The discursive combination of underdevelopment and foreignness during the early Cold War provided ways for specific groups—including American Indians, Puerto Ricans, and southwestern Hispanos[4]—to negotiate political and economic concessions from the federal government. The outcome of such negotiations depended in part on each group's respective status with regard to the historical conditions of US colonialism and the shifting dynamics of the Cold War. At the same time, the past and present of US colonialism were categorically excluded from the mid-twentieth-century liberal discourse of the foreign, and in fact marked the limit of its capacity to assimilate difference as a provisional form that would be replaced under the guidance of the United States as leader of the free world.

Locating Underdevelopment

Conventional accounts of US history often compartmentalize the politics of poverty. According to this view, throughout the 1950s poverty was an international problem framed by the problem of underdevelopment, and during the 1960s it was a domestic issue defined in terms of opportunity. In his 1949 inaugural address, President Harry S. Truman outlined a plan to extend US foreign assistance through technical aid for "the improvement and growth of underdeveloped areas." World poverty, according to Truman, was of particular concern because "the economic life [of the poor] is primitive and stagnant . . . Their poverty is a handicap and a threat both to them and to more prosperous areas."[5] Significantly, whether underdeveloped or prosperous, "area" in this sense was synonymous with "nation-state." Only with the 1957–58 economic recession did this concern for the political and economic repercussions of poverty begin to officially translate to the US territory. The 1964 Economic Opportunity Act consummated a domestic policy concern with poverty as distinct from and a menace to the norms of US liberal democracy. That same year, in its report to the president, the Council of Economic Advisers warned that "poverty is costly not only to the poor but to the whole society . . . It is a social and a national problem." The council worried—in language echoing Michael Harrington's *The Other America* and subsequently recast in explicitly racial terms by the 1968 Kerner Commission—that "the poor inhabit a world scarcely recognizable, and rarely recognized, by the majority of their fellow Americans. It is a world apart, whose inhabitants are isolated from the mainstream of American life and alienated from its values."[6]

The idea that poverty was in some fundamental way a question of culture had particular salience in this shift. The Cold War established the terms through which the poor were constituted as a distinct and singular social group, with a discernible culture and psychology to be studied. Poverty was not a consequence of capitalist market relations, but rather a lack of attachment to the capitalist economy. The postwar ascendancy of the behavioral sciences focused attention on the family as the crucible of culture and personality, and isolated psychological dynamics from social and economic conditions. During the Cold War, social scientists set about enumerating the psychological traits that they argued personified a distinctive national character. The American character—as a singular, homogeneous disposition—was supposedly oriented toward achievement, acquisition, individualism, and deferred gratification in the service of long-term objectives. This psychological and cultural explanation for affluence and American exceptionalism positioned poor people in the United States as foreign to white middle-class familial heteronormativity and as lacking the national character.[7]

Underdevelopment, moreover, was not conceptually incidental to the Cold War. US policymakers promoted a specific social, cultural, and political worldview in their efforts to stabilize and expand capitalist markets. The Marshall Plan aimed to reestablish political and economic stability in Western Europe and Japan and to provide a bulwark against communist encroachment. The Point Four program expanded on this precedent, promoting the supposedly disinterested reason of technical assistance as a means for the comprehensive reeducation of strategically selected countries with limited industrial and market infrastructures. The development paradigm was a product of eighteenth-century Enlightenment thought, but the economic logic broached at Bretton Woods in 1944 and advanced by Point Four in 1949 defined the specific conditions through which development and underdevelopment became organizing principles for the Cold War. As noted in the introduction, the political theorist Timothy Mitchell argues that between the 1930s and 1950s there emerged a new conception of "the economy" as a coherent, territorially aligned object amenable to political calculation and administration. The "fixed space of the national economy" as a self-evident totality was likewise understood to correspond with the nation-state as the exclusive political form sanctioned and recognized by the international system. Thus, from this new perspective, the world was divided into discrete territorial nation-states, each with its own internal economy and distinct national history.[8] The former UN Development Program administrator Majid Rahnema contends that with this epochal shift "entire nations ... [came] to be considered (and consider themselves) as poor."[9]

For many US policymakers after the Second World War, underdevelopment was increasingly defined as an identifiable collection of cultural deficiencies, shaped in isolation from the capitalist marketplace. From this vantage point, underdevelopment could be remedied through the disciplining procedures of capitalism, measures that were not simply economic but also cultural. Modernization theorists enthusiastically adapted Weber's cultural analysis of capitalist development through the lens of Talcott Parsons, who conveniently discarded Weber's unfavorable assessment of modernity itself in order to prescribe normative cultural change.[10] The "culture of poverty" thesis of the anthropologist Oscar Lewis subsequently delineated an inherited assemblage of personality traits used by many social scientists and policymakers during the 1960s to justify market-oriented remediation. Lewis's "culture of poverty," like George Orwell's "Cold War" and Alfred Sauvy's "Third World," was initially a critical description of prevailing power relations. Mainstream discourse transformed and depolemicized the meaning of each of these terms. Although Lewis intended his term to highlight the generational survival strategies of poor people, most social scientists and policymakers using the notion of a culture of poverty focused on cataloging behaviors that defined as passive, apathetic, impulsive, and reprehensibly deviant specific—often racialized—groups of poor people.[11] Building on this inverted account, US policymakers and social scientists extricated the culture of poverty from the circumstances of capitalist exploitation and reframed the problem of poverty as poor people's lack of integration into normative capitalist society. Defined as a discrete culture, poverty could be understood as inherently foreign to liberal American values. Indeed, here underdevelopment served as a teleological mandate for the benevolent exporting of US liberal capitalism.

In order to strategically claim underdevelopment, groups occupying the incriminating grounds of US territorial conquest had to contend with a number of political and legal precedents. In 1831, for instance, Chief Justice John Marshall's ruling on *Cherokee Nation v. Georgia* invented for American Indian tribes the new legal category "domestic dependent nations" in an effort to undermine their sovereignty and rationalize the economic and political needs of US expansionism. In the southwest, the 1848 Treaty of Guadalupe Hidalgo finalized the vast seizure of Mexican territory in the settlement of the US-Mexican War and conferred on annexed Mexican nationals the rights of US citizens—provided that they relinquish their Mexican character (which by implication was racial as well as national and cultural). At the beginning of the twentieth century, a series of constitutional decisions produced the *Insular Cases* in response to the national controversy over the status of the territories acquired through the 1898 defeat of Spain. The doctrine of unincorporation was adopted in an effort to resolve the messy business of US colonialism. This doctrine was a means of establishing the essential difference of the peoples of those unincorporated territories, while still proclaiming US jurisdiction and control over them.[12]

Reframing Accountability

With policymakers historically intent on denying the existence of US colonialism and with Cold War geopolitics decisively shifting to the so-called periphery, Truman's Point Four program deliberately projected the conditions of underdevelopment abroad. However, the emphatically universal promise of the development paradigm left open other then-unforeseen possibilities.

In 1951, D'Arcy McNickle, chairman of the Indian Tribal Relations Committee of the National Congress of American Indians (NCAI), proposed a ten-point plan targeting Indian poverty that was modeled on Truman's foreign aid program but directed toward "our underdeveloped areas." Although "Congress has been giving warnings for the past several years that appropriations for Indians must come to an end," McNickle's plan entailed technical support and planning, a revolving credit fund, vocational training, and increased federal funding for Indian tribes. His proposal emphasized poverty as the pervasive problem facing Indian Country, contending that "unless some fundamental attack is made on the problem of poverty— and it is the problem which underlies all else—we will stand here 10 and 25 years from now, and will have come no closer to solutions for the problems of our Indian people." It was nevertheless for the particular conditions of American Indians that McNickle defined and reoriented the idea of underdevelopment. Even while framing his proposal as "a domestic Point 4 Program," he asserted in his ten points the fundamental question of land and self-determination for Indian peoples. He recommended "an adequate land-purchase fund," "the immediate transfer to tribal ownership of submarginal lands acquired with emergency relief funds for tribal use," legislation that limited "the taking of Indian lands for public purposes," and concentrated throughout on tribal authority and control. His proposal met with little success.[13]

Two years later, Congress adopted House Concurrent Resolution 108 to terminate federal trusteeship of Indian reservations. As McNickle noted, beginning in the mid-1940s, a concerted backlash against the Indian Reorganization Act of 1934 had attempted to undo the so-called retribalization promoted by Commissioner of Indian Affairs John Collier. Culminating in the 1953 legislation, federal termination policy sought rapid and total assimilation for Indians into the dominant white society. Termination also mandated an accelerated effort to seize valuable tribal land and natural resources for non-Indian private industry through the selling off of property that the federal government defined as surplus—land in excess of individual Indians' designated allotments. Termination advocates nevertheless framed their arguments in ways intended to resonate with Cold War rhetoric by associating collective tribal landownership with communism and tribal autonomy with segregation.[14] The National Congress of American Indians was founded in 1944 largely as a response to the growing threat of termination. As the only national intertribal organization at the time, the NCAI was in a unique position during the 1950s to campaign against termination policy.[15]

In 1953, McNickle reasserted the parallel between domestic and foreign underdevelopment. "Surely the United States," he insisted, "which would like to see undeveloped and under-developed areas of the World brought into more fruitful functioning, is capable of achieving the development of its own native population."[16] During its annual convention the following year in Omaha, Nebraska, the NCAI put forward another proposal largely based on McNickle's earlier plan.[17] The proposal was submitted to Congress as the Point IX Program (one of McNickle's ten points having been resolved), again deliberately invoking US technical assistance abroad as an alternative model to forced termination. The text of the proposal asserted Indian autonomy while also stipulating specific rights with regard to US society, originating from the historical conditions of colonization: "It is declared . . . that this program shall be offered to the American Indian communities without exacting termination of the federal protection of Indian property or of any other Indian rights as its price; that Indian culture and identity shall not be restricted or destroyed; that technical guidance and financial assistance shall be made available; that the request for assistance shall come from the Indians themselves after each Indian group has studied itself in terms of its own needs."[18] The terms of the proposal replicated the language supporting technical assistance to impoverished nations abroad, where US policymakers' focus on technical support and the expansion of industry and market relations was combined with an emphasis on national self-determination in order to attract the participation of newly decolonized states.

National Congress of American Indians research trip to Puerto Rico to study Operation Bootstrap, March 1958. COURTESY OF THE NATIONAL CONGRESS OF AMERICAN INDIANS COLLECTION, NATIONAL MUSEUM OF THE AMERICAN INDIAN, SMITHSONIAN INSTITUTION.

Opposed by a coalition of influential legislators and a small but vocal group of protermination Indians, the NCAI's Point IX Program was never implemented. The Association on American Indian Affairs, led by Oliver La Farge and LaVerne Madigan, pursued a parallel Point Four–based initiative that resulted in Senate Concurrent Resolution 3 in 1957, but this was likewise defeated.[19] Undaunted, the NCAI worked to generate publicity in support of its campaign against termination. With this objective, it organized a fourteen-member delegation to travel to Puerto Rico in March 1958 to learn about Operation Bootstrap, the island's highly touted program for industrialization. The administration of Puerto Rican Governor Luis Muñoz Marín had succeeded in rallying diplomatic and economic support in Washington for its new status as a "free associated state" and in generating international attention as a US State Department showcase. Muñoz's Partido Popular Democrático had used the Point Four program to push the legal logic of the *Insular Cases* to their limit by insisting on being "foreign in a domestic sense" so as to most benefit from this alliance while also securing the greatest possible political autonomy.[20] In February 1958, the NCAI announced to its membership that, in addition to continuing the organization's efforts to cultivate a Point Four approach to developing "human and natural resources in Indian communities," the trip would be valuable for understanding the ways in which "the Puerto Rican people in the last twenty years have learned much about public relations, about getting great men to champion their cause, about bringing about community development."[21]

The NCAI leaders believed that much could be gained from the trip. As with the visitors and diplomats who streamed into Puerto Rico from Africa, Asia, the Middle East, and Latin America, they thought something in the Puerto Rican model could be applicable to their own situation. American Indians, perhaps more than visitors from the formerly colonial world, could look to Puerto Rico for lessons in negotiating and transforming an ongoing colonial predicament. Their sojourn was thus equal parts publicity endeavor and informational tour. For a week they toured new production facilities, visited community development projects, and met with various officials.[22] When they returned home, the NCAI leaders sought to implement the lessons they had learned. They hired the public relations firm Sontheimer-Runkle, which also represented the Commonwealth of Puerto Rico in the United States.[23] More important, they proposed legislation titled "Operation Bootstrap for the American Indian" that succeeded in prompting congressional hearings in 1960.

During these hearings, non-Indian politicians demonstrated considerable support for programs geared toward tribal economic development. Representative Lawrence Brock, a Nebraska Democrat, emphasized the inefficiency of the current situation, testifying: "For the good of this Nation, with its present tensions and international problems, it seems a sacrilege not to utilize the now terrible waste of human resources on the Indian lands . . . Now is the time to do something material and constructive to put those many thousands of idle hands into a production program, one that will return material and lasting benefit to a nation that owes something to the American Indian."[24] Representative E. Y. Berry, a South Dakota Republican who cosponsored the bill, detailed economic incentives and tax abatements modeled on the Puerto Rican case to encourage private investment and industrial development in Indian reservations. Other testimony promoted reservation industrialization as an untapped business opportunity with the distinct benefit of operating outside of US regulatory standards and minimum wage laws, while still benefiting from federal oversight.

The NCAI delegates and other tribal representatives, however, were not solely concerned with attracting capital investment and industry from outside the reservations. Instead, they clearly articulated political and cultural concerns as inseparable from economic development. Allen Quentone, a member of the Kiowa tribe who had traveled to Puerto Rico in the NCAI delegation, affirmed that such a plan "must provide many alternatives for development, and that encouragement to find better solutions to Indian problems should begin in economic and social areas before there is any more headlong rushing into changing the political status of Indians."[25] Helen Peterson, the NCAI's executive director, highlighted the importance of Puerto Rican initiatives in community development that worked in conjunction with the industrialization program. She testified: "We hope that the Congress . . . will not only enact the bills under consideration with amendments, but will continue to do those other things that go along with industrial development that may make for the kind of progress among American Indians that has been possible and that we have seen achieved in Puerto Rico in 20 years."[26] American Indians forcefully asserted that their political and cultural self-determination were essential to any program for economic development. In direct opposition to termination legislation, witnesses testified in favor of preserving a US presence on the reservations that upheld past treaties and responsibilities while strengthening Indian independence.

Although the bill did not become law, the federal government abandoned its pursuit of a policy of termination in the face of escalating American Indian activism that underscored tribal sovereignty and federal liability. The founding of the National Indian Youth Council and the success of the Washington State fish-in protests in 1964 signaled American Indians' move toward more overtly assertive political strategies.[27] During the second half of the 1960s and the 1970s, a growing number of organizations built on and extended the NCAI's intertribal work for economic and political self-determination without relinquishing US government responsibilities, and some advanced a decidedly more radical and confrontational stance. The Nixon administration espoused the language of tribal "self-determination," and Congress made attempts to both accommodate and contain Indian pressure for change. In his proposal titled "A Plan for Navajo Economic Development," prepared as part of the 1969 congressional study *Toward Economic Development for Native American Communities*, the anthropologist David Aberle asserted: "The argument set forth here is that the Navajo country is an underdeveloped area, and that the cause of its underdevelopment is its historical and current relations with the larger polity, economy, and society." He prodded the federal government to commit economic resources and technological support to the Navajo Nation, while insisting that the Navajos independently plan and manage development projects.[28] During this period, many tribes and intertribal groups went beyond calls for economic development and demanded access to financial support and investment—to be controlled by the tribes—that respected their economic, cultural, and political autonomy.[29]

The Discomfort of Strangers

The mission of the Peace Corps appears at first to confirm US policymakers' view of underdevelopment as a problem for other countries. The agency's field training initiatives, however, insisted on a foreignness closer in proximity. Although this affirmed none of the causal relations that Aberle insisted on with regard to the Navajo situation, it did potentially authorize multiple claims in the name of underdevelopment.

In 1957, Representative Henry S. Reuss, a Wisconsin Democrat, returned from a trip to Cambodia worried about US credibility among formerly colonized nations. He recommended establishing a program to send young American volunteers to these countries as a demonstration of US goodwill. Such a program would provide technical staffing for US foreign aid projects, convey American ideals and aspirations to the peoples of other nations through direct contact with American youth, and provide a sense of purpose and inspiration for the volunteers themselves.[30] Reuss and Senator Richard Neuberger, a Democrat from Oregon, cosponsored a bill to create a Point Four Youth Corps. Although the project received limited congressional support, the idea of dedicated American youth engaged in the "shirt-sleeve diplomacy" of technical assistance abroad generated a good deal of favorable publicity.[31] Three years later, Hubert Humphrey made the idea, now called the Peace Corps, part of his brief presidential campaign, passing on the details of his plan to John F. Kennedy on withdrawing from the race. For Kennedy, the Peace Corps served as a tangible demonstration of how youth inspired by his call to service might help their country and the world simultaneously. The idea was thus aligned with Kennedy's belief in the strategic importance of the Third World for US policy, while it also embodied the youthful idealism and higher purpose with which his administration was eager to be associated.[32]

Soon after the Peace Corps was formally established, its administrators began to consider the question of training its volunteers as a first step in getting the initiative under way. A central concern expressed by administrators was how volunteers would adjust to cultural differences abroad, and they used the concept of "culture shock" to address this concern.[33] During the mid-1950s, as US power rapidly expanded abroad, managers, educators, and social scientists paid increasing attention to the problems they believed confronted businessmen, diplomats, and students working outside the United States. With funding from the Carnegie Corporation, Harlan Cleveland, then dean of the Maxwell School at Syracuse University and later assistant secretary of state, coauthored one influential book on the topic and coedited another.[34] The first—*The Overseas Americans*—highlighted culture shock and the importance of cultural empathy, and it became part of the core curriculum of Peace Corps training.

The conceptual framework of culture shock relied on liberal universalist constructions of the foreign. On one hand, culture shock was predicated on the assumption that the foreign precipitated a confrontation with absolute difference beyond recognition. On the other hand, it served as a means of assimilating and comprehending this difference. Cultural empathy provided a way to negotiate this disconcerting encounter and to raise "overseas Americans" to a universal vantage point above the fray of unfamiliarity.

The term "culture shock" had been coined during the mid-1950s by Kalervo Oberg, an anthropologist affiliated with the US International Cooperation Administration mission in Brazil. Oberg defined "culture shock" as a psychological condition "precipitated by the anxiety of losing all our familiar signs and symbols of social intercourse. These signs or cues include the thousand and one ways in which we orient ourselves to the situations of daily life." He provided a list of what he considered everyday examples: "when to shake hands and what we say when we meet people, when and how to give tips, how to give orders to servants, how to make purchases, when to accept and when to refuse invitations, when to take statements seriously and when not [to]."[35] The fact that such concerns applied both to the US diplomats who were the audience for Oberg's initial observations and to Peace Corps volunteers reveals the presumed class privilege of both. When stripped of familiar convention, these preoccupations with and anxieties about etiquette and class position apparently assumed traumatic proportions. The Peace Corps sought to develop distinct instructional methods to counteract culture shock and give its volunteers the means of maintaining a confident, if empathetic, posture abroad.[36] Descriptions of culture shock moved easily between cultural and economic registers in Peace Corps literature. In training materials, accounts of culture shock often described the trainee's shock at conditions of abject poverty as an encounter with cultural difference. Similarly, culture shock conflated culture and poverty, deeming Peace Corps volunteers, as ostensible models of ingenuity and fortitude, to be agents of change simply because of the cultural example they provided.

One initial purpose of field training was to provoke culture shock. Producing this trauma prior to sending volunteers overseas would both minimize its later effects and allow monitoring of trainees as they passed through Oberg's stages toward reestablishing psychological equilibrium.[37] Peace Corps planners assumed that culturally unfamiliar poor communities in the United States would be similar to impoverished countries abroad and looked for US contexts to simulate foreign conditions.

An early example of this approach to training was Columbia University's placement of volunteers in New York City social work offices in poor, Spanish-speaking neighborhoods.[38] Affirming the presumptions of the new training regime, one Columbia University trainee testified: "The most valuable part of my field work experience has been what one might call a cushion in preparation for a cultural shock. The experience has, to a large extent, been a shock and opened my eyes to the realities of city life that I had not known before. I am sure that I will encounter similar shock in Colombia but now I feel much better prepared to meet it."[39]

Numerous other locations facilitated this experience. The Waipio Valley in Hawaii, for instance, provided a "remote tropical" and "exotic" location where trainees bound for Indonesia, the Philippines, and other regions of the Far East learned to grow rice and taro and build thatched huts.[40] The training fit well with the overall posture of the Peace Corps as a noble experiment of motivated US youth "living poor" and voluntarily sharing the conditions of austerity and deprivation of the struggling peoples they went to serve abroad.[41] It also complemented what the historian Michael Latham has described as the Peace Corps' dual mission to make international role models of American youth and, in the context of Kennedy's New Frontier, to regenerate the volunteers themselves through a rediscovery of the Turnerian frontier's role as a crucible for the American character.[42]

Among the most extensive and enduring of these programs was the Peace Corps Training Center of the University of New Mexico (UNM), which had one of only four year-round Peace Corps training contracts. Writing UNM's proposal for training Peace Corps volunteers slated to serve in Latin America, Marshall Nason—a UNM professor and the future director of the training center—argued that New Mexico offered an exemplary context for training because it provided a "state-wide laboratory" and was "itself an underdeveloped area" with "people speaking Spanish and Indian languages as well as English." Nason continued: "The populations of many Latin American countries are also composed in large part of indigenous peoples. Many of these countries, therefore, have Indian problems much like those found in the Southwestern United States." Similarly, in his letter confirming arrangements with the Peace Corps, UNM President Tom Popejoy emphasized "the unique features of New Mexico—its combination of cultures, its islands of primitive peoples and underdeveloped communities, its first-hand experience with problems of cultural adaptation in the process of economic development."[43]

If notably facile, as well as patronizing toward New Mexico's impoverished Hispanos and indigenous peoples, Nason's and Popejoy's characterizations of New Mexico were nonetheless in keeping with contemporary social scientists' views of the state. The anthropologist Margaret Mead had recently published *Cultural Patterns and Technical Change*, sponsored by UNESCO, in which she included New Mexico's Spanish Americans alongside Burma, Greece, the Palau Islands, and the Tiv people of Nigeria as case studies for the cultural impact of technological modernization on underdeveloped societies.[44] In 1962, the sociologist Clark Knowlton observed: "In the past few years New Mexico has reached a position comparable to many underdeveloped countries in the world." He stressed that "rapid social and cultural changes are bringing with them rising rates of welfare and dependency, family breakdown, juvenile delinquency, the creation of chronically depressed areas, large scale population movements, and cultural breakdown among minority groups." Concluding that New Mexico's economy was "a colonial economy in every sense of the word," Knowlton speculated: "If these distressed areas had the good fortune to be located in Africa,

Asia, or Latin America, they would be the recipients of foreign aid, peace corps groups, and a concerted effort to resolve their problems."[45]

Indeed, in many respects the history of New Mexico presents a striking chronicle of conquest, resistance, and colonization. This history is remarkable even if we consider only the period since the US-Mexico War. Following the territory's seizure, congressional fears that its mixed-race population would erode Anglo-Saxon predominance in the country served to postpone the territory's admission into the Union. In 1850, New Mexico—which then included what is now the state of Arizona—was formally designated a US territory, ruled by Congress and without political representation. Despite repeated petitions for statehood, New Mexico was not admitted into the Union until 1912. With the complicated exception of Puerto Rico, this sixty-two-year interval between territorial status and statehood remains unsurpassed in US history. Between 1902 and 1912, Senator Albert Beveridge, a Republican from Indiana and chairman of the Senate Committee on Territories, became well known for his unflagging efforts to maintain the territory's unincorporated subordinate status. During subcommittee hearings on the matter, he harped incessantly on the racial composition of New Mexicans as well as on their persistent use of the Spanish language. Notably, racial categories themselves were in flux in New Mexico, where elite Hispano families sought to claim whiteness in contrast to the mixed-blood poor and Indians, and the demographic disadvantage of Anglos fostered widespread intermarriage and racial accommodation in the service of class consolidation.[46]

By the time of UNM's proposal to administer Peace Corps training, the Hispano villages and Indian pueblos of north-central New Mexico had already been subject to a long history of Anglo fascination and intrusion. In the mid-twentieth century, the descendants of Spain's sixteenth-century conquest and late-seventeenth-century reconquest of the region remained a relatively close-knit group of people living on properties collectively held through Spanish and Mexican land grants. An influx of anthropologists into the region during the 1920s and 1930s had been supplemented by Anglos who sought to recapture the supposed premodern authenticity of rural village life.[47] The 1930s craft revival celebrated both Spanish colonial and pueblo traditions and began to integrate artisanal labor into expanded market relations. However, indigenous forms of community organization were often either romanticized by Anglo settlers or, through the lens of postwar community development, incorporated only to the degree that indigenous methods and institutions were recognizable and amenable to such inclusion.[48] Moreover, for the purpose of Peace Corps training, "community" was decisively not urban and would not involve the substantial Hispano and Indian populations in Albuquerque.[49]

In order to win community participation, UNM launched a publicity campaign that included contacting city councils, local officials, civic organizations, and local professional groups. Historically entrenched divisions of power and resources not only characterized the places where the training took place, but often determined who in a given town or area initiated contact with UNM's Training Center.[50] For example, one account of an early planning meeting in the town of Chama notes: "The meeting hall was quickly filled before eight o'clock with about sixty of what might be termed 'middle-class'—businessmen, teachers, etc.—of Chama. Both the Spanish-American and the Anglo segments seemed to be equally represented. Conspicuously absent were the Negro of which Chama had a small but noticeable percentage." Another report describes an irrigation project that was started but eventually abandoned because it had been initiated by an Anglo rancher with a vested interest in it, but no support from the majority Hispano population of the town.[51] To a certain extent, the abstract universalism of Peace Corps training discourse could accommodate such conflicts. After all, it was exactly this sort of fractured civic engagement that volunteers were to mend abroad. However, the Peace Corps Training Center's solicitations, even as they purportedly sought out community involvement, remained focused on officially sanctioned institutional representatives.

Toward the end of the 1950s and throughout the 1960s, long-standing and often violent Hispano struggles to retain or reclaim land grants in north-central New Mexico intensified. Actions by the US government and judicial system had consistently denied the region's Spanish American families the territorial rights guaranteed in the Treaty of Guadalupe Hidalgo. During the late nineteenth century, government surveyors, local Anglo banks and ranchers, and real estate speculators such as Thomas B. Catron defrauded grantees out of thousands of acres of land. Furthermore, in violation of the treaty, the government refused to recognize the communal system of land tenure formalized in the land grants. During the late nineteenth century and the early twentieth, clandestine Hispano groups such as Las Gorras Blancas (The White Caps) and La Mano Negra (The Black

"Almost all 900 residents of the northern New Mexico town of Chama turned out for the mass meeting at which local and Peace Corps officials explained the objectives of the Peace Corps Project there," 1963. COURTESY OF THE UNIVERSITY OF NEW MEXICO PEACE CORPS COLLECTION (UNMA 150, BOX 4), CENTER FOR SOUTHWEST RESEARCH, UNIVERSITY LIBRARIES, UNIVERSITY OF NEW MEXICO, ALBUQUERQUE.

Hand) waged campaigns of sabotage to protest Anglo encroachment.[52] At midcentury, the Abiquiu Corporation sent out eviction notices to Anglo occupants of land grant territories, organized armed patrols of the Tierra Amarilla land grant perimeter, and initiated legal action in an attempt to reclaim stolen territory.[53] During the early 1960s, the US Forest Service, perceived by many Hispanos as an occupying army terrorizing their communities, stepped up efforts to drive farmers off disputed properties and rescind grazing rights on land the agency deemed to be in the public domain. To add insult to injury, just as the displacement of Hispano farmers accelerated, the Forest Service was busy transferring rights to use these same territories to private timber and agriculture businesses.

In 1963, the grass-roots organizing efforts of Reies López Tijerina, a controversial advocate of what he termed "Indo-Hispano rights," and local land grant heirs created the Alianza Federal de Mercedes (Federal Alliance of Land Grants). As with the campaign by the National Congress of American Indians, the Alianza framed its land claims in explicitly international terms that highlighted US colonization and imperialism on the mainland.

FREE PEOPLE BORN OCT. 19, 1514

U. S. A. IS TRESPASSING IN NEW MEXICO.

U. S. A. HAS NO TITLE FOR NEW MEXICO.

THE TREATY OF GUADALUPE HIDALGO IS A FRAUD and INVALID.

ESTADOS UNIDOS NO TIENEN JURISDICCION N. MEX.

ALL TRESPASSERS MUST GET OUT OF NEW MEXICO ¡NOW!

ALL PIRATES GO HOME.

All SPANISH and INDIAN PUEBLOS are FREE FOREVER.

All TRESPASSERS WILL BE PUNISHED BY LAW.

VIVAN LOS PUEBLOS REPUBLICAS LIBRES DE NUEVO MEX.

LAS INDIAS BORN APRIL 17, 1492

Document 129 of State Department Exposes the **U. S. A. Crime Against ALL Spanish and Indian Rights and Freedom**

Alianza Federal de Mercedes handbill asserting that the United States is a foreign country that is "trespassing" and "has no jurisdiction in New Mexico." COURTESY OF THE REIES TIJERINA PAPERS, CENTER FOR SOUTHWEST RESEARCH, UNIVERSITY LIBRARIES, UNIVERSITY OF NEW MEXICO, ALBUQUERQUE.

Alianza pamphlets brazenly announced that the "USA is trespassing in New Mexico." In 1964, Tijerina began planning a two-hundred-car caravan to Mexico City to publicize the Alianza's efforts and to request that Mexican President Adolfo López Mateos submit to the United Nations formal charges against the United States for violating the Treaty of Guadalupe Hidalgo.[54] While Tijerina was in Mexico making arrangements for the caravan, he was arrested by undercover Mexican police—probably working in conjunction with US agencies—and deported to the United States. During October 1966, members of the Alianza occupied the Echo Amphitheater area of the Kit Carson National Forest, a section of the territory included in the San Joaquín del Río Chama land grant. There they proclaimed the autonomous Republic of the Pueblo San Joaquín del Río Chama and hoisted a national flag of blue and gold. Although this episode—and others, like the 1967 storming of the Tierra Amarilla county courthouse by armed members of the Alianza to depose and arrest District Attorney Alfonso Sánchez for his ongoing harassment of land grant activists—proved unsuccessful in achieving the Alianza's quest for recognition of their autonomous land rights, it did establish the group's importance within the burgeoning movement for Chicano nationalism.[55] Throughout the Alianza's existence, the FBI and New Mexico state police subjected the group to surveillance, infiltration, defamation, and violent attacks.[56]

The inability of Peace Corps community development training to accommodate and address forms of community action that challenged the established organization of power and resources—not only regionally, but in terms of the federally orchestrated appropriation of local Hispano resources on behalf of corporate capital—is not surprising. Future Peace Corps agents of change were, after all, agents of the federal government. What this inability makes exceedingly clear, however, is the acutely selective manner in which the framework of locality was deployed in Peace Corps training. The understanding of what locality was supposed to accomplish varied considerably and somewhat predictably according to the administrative level of the Peace Corps bureaucracy. In fact, different administrative sectors of training embraced different methodological abstractions (of cultural difference, underdevelopment, and experience), while these abstractions in turn offered people outside the Peace Corps a variety of forms of strategic negotiation and engagement.

When UNM's Peace Corps Training Center opened in 1962, its programs consistently framed the trainees' field experience in local communities with extensive instruction on the theoretical principles of community development. Richard Poston, a well-known expert in the field and the author of such books as *Democracy Speaks Many Tongues*, was hired to coordinate community development instruction. Training included lessons on the "dynamics of the community development process," "community as a social structure," and "patterns of behavior of peasant societies." Lectures covered the theoretically distinct "phases" of community development, which were to progress successively from "investigation" to "organization" to "implementation." Techniques were introduced for "the development of a viable citizens' organization that will stimulate the local population toward responsible citizenship."[57] Once in the field, trainees were expected to keep thorough, daily logs of their activities and provide profiles of the families they met that described their "socio-economic characteristics," "migration history," "orientation and aspiration," and the family's "formal and informal relationships" to the larger community. At the conclusion of the field training, trainees would write a summary of their work and a formal evaluation of the community where they had been placed.[58]

Although trainees expressed mixed reactions to the classroom instruction, most of them viewed the field training as invaluable. A trainee placed in the northern town of Canjilon wrote: "The culture and way of life of these people was very different from anything I had previously encountered . . . I really got a taste of what it may be like to fit myself into a community in a foreign country." A trainee in Jemez Springs stated: "We were not in an extremely rural area, but even so, there was a degree of 'culture shock.' "[59] In contrast to the academic training they received, trainees considered the field experience to be real, a credible approximation of what they imagined their work in Latin America would be like. They rarely questioned the intended contrast between themselves and the New Mexican villages into which they were inserted.

Outside evaluations of UNM's Peace Corps Training Center reiterated this emphasis on field experience as an encounter with cultural difference. The author of one such appraisal commented: "The classroom cannot replace the field in terms of presenting the actual difficulties of putting a community development program into effect." Indeed, the evaluator was "surprised and pleased to see that the frustrating, monotonous aspect of community development—the feeling of inadequacy that often confronts a Volunteer—could be duplicated." This duplication was possible because a purportedly universal set of characteristics was readily discernible. These qualities were easily transposable in the same manner that for many social scientists a culture of poverty supposedly transcended the particular circumstances of specific societies. Thus, the evaluator concluded: "The correlation of problems encountered in the neighborhoods of Las Vegas [New Mexico] to those *veredas* of Colombia was high, e.g., fatalism, pessimism, lack of faith in government, lack of faith in their neighbors."[60] Although it was precisely this belief that it was possible to replicate in poor and culturally unfamiliar contexts in the United States the situations and experiences that volunteers would encounter abroad that underwrote the logic of Peace Corps field training, the necessity of enlisting the cooperation of actual people for such projects complicated the simple transposition of universals.

Training materials for new volunteers, written by Bill McKinstry, a community development consultant in Pecos Valley, New Mexico, explained that fieldwork was intended to accomplish two main goals: "(1) to give you a training ground to practice application of Community Development principles; (2) to provide a service to the community itself." Emphasizing the need to establish reciprocal benefits, he insisted: "Although the community is serving as a training ground and recognized as such by many people, we must do all we can to convince the people that we have something to offer them in return—a stimulus toward the development of a comprehensive community improvement program with a problem-solving mechanism (organization) which will perpetuate itself and reap benefits long after we are gone. In this sense, favors are being exchanged."[61]

McKinstry endorsed the imperatives of the Peace Corps training curriculum—that trainees learn to develop a "comprehensive community improvement program"—but conceded that this goal would be impossible unless the people with whom such a program was organized considered it suitable to their particular needs. As outlined in a trainee handout, in order to avoid making the community a "victim" of "a continual barrage of unrelated activities causing confusion and possible resentment," the activities of one cohort of trainees were to be coordinated with the work of those who had preceded them and those who would follow.[62]

Trainees' desires were often at odds with the realities of field training. Obviously annoyed, John Arango, the community development coordinator at UNM's Peace Corps Training Center following Poston's departure, reported:

> The trainees are constantly seeking something new in the experience, some accomplishment which no other group or trainee has before managed. In every group, one or more trainee reports begin: "I was glad to accept Ribera as my research site because (as opposed to many towns) it has been relatively untouched by previous trainees and I could do a realistic investigation." . . . One of the main problems facing the consultants is getting each trainee group to build on the work of previous groups. Because groups about to go into the field normally pay little attention to the reports from groups that have just returned, the consultants are now giving quizzes on the first day that the trainees are in the field.[63]

In this sense, trainees' expectations were what the upper levels of the Peace Corps administration envisioned. Both groups believed that field training should provide an encounter with the radically unfamiliar and thus make "training as realistic as possible, to give volunteers a 'feel' of the situation they will face."[64]

In contrast, Arango distinguished between two approaches to training that he saw in the Peace Corps' preparation of its volunteers. In the first approach, "acculturation training[,] . . . the goal is to place the trainee in a situation much different from those he is accustomed to, in order to test his ability to adapt to different cultures." The objective of the second more strictly vocational approach, "community development field training[,] . . . is to give the trainees practical experience in a community development program."[65] The tension and slippage between these two distinct paradigms is an indication of competing political imaginaries of place and the tactical maneuvering for material resources and political legitimacy by those communities involved in the training program.

Responding to criticism of UNM's field training program expressed in a memo from the director of the Peace Corps in Colombia, Arango detailed his perspective on why the UNM program was geared toward the community development field training approach. His rejoinder reveals differences that also existed between the official training rhetoric of UNM, which often promoted the ostensible realism of its cultural simulation instruction, and the outlook of training staff with ongoing relationships with the communities where training took place. Arango went so far as to contrast UNM training to other Peace Corps field training, asserting: "Most Volunteers readily adapt to strange living conditions, but have difficulty applying the community development method. The situations we choose for field training are selected not for their similarities with Latin America . . . , but because they present close parallels to the community development situation in Latin America." Instead of emphasizing the adjustment of trainees to "a new culture," Arango stressed the techniques of community development. After traveling to Ecuador, Peru, and Bolivia, he observed, "it is significant that groups which were trained in community development field situations, as opposed to acculturation situations, produced more Volunteers who were community organizers, or organization oriented community workers."[66] As the UNM Peace Corps Training Center's community development coordinator, Arango's perspective shaped the training curriculum. However, his agenda went directly against the grain of field training descriptions provided by Marshall Nason, the former director of the center, and UNM President Tom Popejoy, as well as the higher echelons of the Peace Corps administration responsible for training.

After a tour of South American Peace Corps projects in early 1965,

Arango reported his observations to Jules Pagano, acting director of Peace Corps university relations and training. Frustrated with the Peace Corps' training practice of treating host countries as culturally homogeneous places, Arango protested: "I personally believe that the training of Volunteers for a whole country at a time is wasteful, and that for community development training at least, the training should be structured around regional assignments."[67] He noted, for instance, how inappropriate it was to teach all volunteers assigned to Peru a single dialect of Quechua. He outlined significant differences in the dynamics of the communities he had visited in Huancayo, Cuzco, and Puno, and recommended how instruction might be variously tailored to local needs.

In *Education in the Peace Corps*, an official summation of Peace Corps training written by Jules Pagano several months after Arango's letter to him, the indiscriminate term "cultural immersion" remained at the forefront of the agency's training agenda. Pagano emphasized the benefits of cultural immersion and the transposability of the foreign: "Trainees must be prepared to operate in a culture which is not only *foreign*, but also *non-Western* —a great leap in thought and mores. And their subjects will speak a different language—both literally and figuratively . . . The fundamental principle of Peace Corps training . . . is the notion of total cultural immersion; the ultimate effect is a 'liberally educated' Volunteer."[68]

In his description of everyday field training activities, the predominance of "total cultural immersion" appears more ambiguous but is still apparent:

The State of New Mexico has been the scene of much of our rural community action field work . . . One group recently spent two weeks scattered in the outer reaches of New Mexico, going through a field exercise surveying communities. The trainees become deeply involved in the life of their respective towns, and they were enraptured by the experience. Their typically American composure was shaken. What they saw and the conditions they found gave them a somewhat different slant on the "great society." One trainee summed up his worry about his ability to be useful in Chile. "If I can transport my feelings of humility with me overseas, maybe I will have some degree of success."[69]

Vocational training was subsumed under an explicit imperative to engage the emotional and psychological dimensions of trainees. Despite running counter to the guidelines provided by McKinstry and the vocational em-

"Part of the training program conducted by the University of New Mexico consists of exposure to the elements of community development work. Here a Colombia trainee helps a farmer near Taos build another room on his house out of adobe brick," 1963. COURTESY OF THE UNIVERSITY OF NEW MEXICO PEACE CORPS COLLECTION (UNMA 150, BOX 4), CENTER FOR SOUTHWEST RESEARCH, UNIVERSITY LIBRARIES, UNIVERSITY OF NEW MEXICO, ALBUQUERQUE.

phasis of Arango, the overarching model of field training prioritized the inner transformation of individual trainees that was triggered by an unsettling encounter with the unfamiliar.

Local support for Peace Corps training in north-central New Mexico provides a sense of the calculated invocation of the foreign. Such support often simply reproduced the language and logic of the trainers. For instance, an editorial in Santa Fe's *New Mexican*, expressing concern that Peace Corps training activities in the Taos area were going to be closed down, used almost exactly the terms of the UNM Peace Corps training proposal. The author of the unsigned editorial asserted: "The nearest these students will ever come to their foreign assignments, without actually leaving the United States, is in the economically depressed rural areas of the Southwest where even the language is similar to that spoken in the areas in which they will later serve." The author observed that the Peace Corps training had provided invaluable services in northern New Mexico that facilitated ongoing development in the region. Trainees, the writer argued, "demonstrated the kind of outside help many in the rural villages want—not a person who tells the local folks what to do, but persons who roll up their sleeves and show them things can be done."[70]

Local criticism of the field training, in contrast, often asserted the indigenous forms of community organization already in operation. Residents argued that local forms of community organization were disrupted or undermined by the field training initiatives. For instance, a community organizer from the town of Llano complained to the Training Center's director: "It has always been my understanding that what the trainees are doing is learning how to organize communities[,] not to create new groups and frictions among them."[71]

In one newspaper, the Las Vegas *Daily Optic*, whose front page regularly featured republished international and national news wire items alongside coverage of high-school debate team activities and the minutiae of municipal budget meetings, Peace Corps field training appears as just another public works project. A typical story in the paper read: "The Peace Corps will visit homes, talk to people, investigate problems and seek solutions with existing organizations."[72] Ironically, it was not local controversy that precipitated the end of UNM's program. Rather, bureaucratic conflicts between the university and the Peace Corps office in Washington led to the cancellation of the training contract in 1967.[73] In all, UNM trained over 1,800 volunteers for service in eight Latin American countries.

By the time the UNM program ended, the Peace Corps' Washington office was trying to systemize its training efforts more clearly. In 1968, this process was entrusted to the Center for Research and Education in Estes Park, Colorado. Two years later, the center published a four-volume study and manual titled *Guidelines for Peace Corps Cross-Cultural Training*. The authors concluded: "One thing most if not all Peace Corps Volunteers have in common is that they have to enter, live, and work in a culture quite different from their own." Thus, of foremost concern was acculturation that allowed trainees to be empathetic toward the local people while maintaining their exemplary role as Americans: "Trainees need to develop an understanding and tolerance of differences between values, beliefs, assumptions, needs, attitudes, and behavior, particularly of individuals from different social and cultural backgrounds, and an awareness of the conflicts and problems that can arise from these differences. They need to learn to adapt their own values, needs, etc. to those of the culture within which they wish to work, without losing their identity as Americans."[74]

What the guidelines make exhaustively clear is how the emerging educational philosophy of experiential learning easily integrated vocational training into the acculturation model and was capable of dissolving the methodological distinction that Arango had underscored. In his comparison between "acculturation" and "community development field training" the distinction between the two often appeared tenuous, but his emphasis on the latter grounded training in explicit interaction with the people the trainees were working with.

At the Limit of Colonial Difference

If Peace Corps field training presumed a coherent and universal form of difference, it also imagined an equally generic Peace Corps volunteer. The calculated shock of difference supplied by field placement in local communities was conceivable only to the degree that such communities were perceived as different and unfamiliar. To be sure, the lens of universality engendered recognizable tropes, such as the simplicity and authenticity of pre-industrial life. That the cross-cultural experience could be rendered within an anticipated narrative, however, did not diminish the expectation that for the trainee, it was to be a dramatic encounter with the foreign and unknown.

The presumption of a single volunteer type posed difficulties for an assertively liberal agency rhetorically committed to inclusivity during the peak of the civil rights movement. Thus, throughout the 1960s, the Peace Corps sought to counter the image of its volunteers as all white and economically privileged. The agency widely promoted its efforts to recruit African Americans and native Spanish speakers, but it often found its liberal colorblind philosophy at odds with existing structural inequalities and unable to accommodate the realities of racial prejudice.[75] The total number of African American volunteers, estimated at a meager 5 percent between 1961 and 1965, dropped to less than two percent by 1969.[76] The agency's few explicitly class-based recruitment initiatives fared similarly. A blue-collar embassy of mechanics, machinists, and welders was organized by the agency and dispatched in 1965 to Chile, but no comparable endeavor followed.[77] For many Americans, two years of volunteer service without other guarantees of economic support was an impossible luxury. The Peace Corps' vow of poverty was an incongruous indulgence in terms of the daily lives of people struggling with racially overdetermined conditions of poverty.

In late 1966, representatives of the Oklahomans for Indian Opportunity

(OIO), a group funded by the Office of Economic Opportunity and led by the Comanche activist LaDonna Harris, approached the Peace Corps with the idea of developing a program to recruit and train American Indians to serve as Peace Corps volunteers in Latin America. The initial proposal promoted the project as "a way of interesting American Indian youngsters in the Peace Corps and many American Indian Peace Corps volunteers returning to be of service to the Indian community in this nation. Part of the purpose of [this project] . . . is to develop American Indian leadership. Peace Corps service is an excellent vehicle for reaching this end."[78] The OIO and the Peace Corps devised a five-week pretraining program called Project Peace Pipe and publicized the endeavor with funding from the Bureau of Indian Affairs.[79]

In an article on the project in the *Journal of American Indian Education*, Harris and Leon Ginsberg, a professor of social work at the University of Oklahoma, stressed that "reaching persons who are closely identified with their groups and who are also socio-economically deprived probably requires special recruitment efforts . . . Normal Peace Corps advertising and recruiting efforts, which focus on major college campuses, are not enough."[80] Moreover, in addition to recruitment, Harris and Ginsberg concluded that pretraining would facilitate volunteer retention. There was little doubt that young, middle-class whites would believe they have something to contribute to impoverished people abroad; Project Peace Pipe focused on dispelling the doubts of Indian trainees that they too could make a contribution. Concerned with redressing the psychological effects of internal colonization, the project emphasized the racialized and economic inequalities within the United States rather than impending culture shock abroad. Thus, Harris and Ginsberg argued: "While the rigors of overseas life could pose adjustment problems to middle and upper socio-economic class volunteers, they would be less frightening, it seemed, to reservation-reared or rural Indian young persons. It was the fellow trainee group that could cause the most serious difficulties—perhaps a failure in training—for the American Indian."[81] Causes of Indian trainees' failure were more likely to be related to disparities between relatively privileged white trainees and the recruits. Inverting the Peace Corps' cross-cultural training model, the OIO sought to use training as a way to address structures of dominance in the United States rather than to prepare volunteers for encountering those structures abroad.

If the Peace Corps was concerned with the recruitment of people of color

Project Peace Pipe recruits speaking with Senator Fred Harris during training in Puerto Rico, 1967. COURTESY OF THE NATIONAL ARCHIVES, WASHINGTON, D.C. (490-G-63-82068-C2-19).

largely for the sake of appearance, the OIO project seized on this anxiety as a concrete means of intervening in dominant institutional relations of power. This intervention was aimed both at transforming the local, individual consequences of internal colonialism and at appropriating the representational power of the Peace Corps' role in US diplomacy.

Scholars such as the historian Fritz Fischer have pointed to Project Peace Pipe as a failed Peace Corps endeavor, and an example of the ethnocentric and exceptionalist Peace Corps mission to "make them like us."[82] This interpretation misunderstands the genesis of the project. Initiated by La-Donna Harris and the OIO, Project Peace Pipe used the conventions and prestige of the Peace Corps idea as a counterforce to the social and institutional constructions of "domestic dependency."[83] That the Peace Corps retreated from the project after only three years and two cohorts of trainees was indeed evidence of the agency's racial and class-based presuppositions.[84] Only two Indian recruits completed training and overseas assignments: one went on to work for Americans for Indian Opportunity (an outgrowth of the OIO), and the other later became vice president of the Jicarilla Apache.[85] However, to focus only on this failure is to miss the significance of the fact that the project was initiated by American Indians. Fischer reads the project as yet another chauvinist gesture toward assimilation, but the attempt to place on the world stage American Indian youth working with communities in the so-called Third World provided an opportunity to unsettle relations of colonialism and to underscore the historical interdependencies of European and US colonialism. Such a possibility was important precisely because of the constructions of difference and universality that underwrote Peace Corps field training. Indeed, the colonial difference of the American Indian trainees, and the still-operative conditions of US colonialism underscored by their participation, proved to be fundamentally incompatible with US Cold War liberal universality and the versions of foreignness that it authorized. To recognize colonialism as constitutive of the United States would render the country perilously foreign to itself and destabilize the moral and cultural claims that sustained the "internal border" of US national unity. The radical conditionality of this unity, in the context of US Cold War grand strategy, embraced an ethic of liberal pluralism only inasmuch as the United States claimed to be an exceptional nation.[86]

Provisional Subjects and "Real Universality"

Perhaps most striking about the Peace Corps' field training initiatives is the manner in which they drew attention to the very conditions that the Peace Corps sought to disavow. How, after all, could the United States claim the expertise to solve the problems of poverty abroad if it was unable to do so within its own borders? The explicit parallel between impoverished, culturally distinct domestic areas and poor nations overseas revealed the existence of two competing versions of US globalism. First, the State Department promoted the United States as the fulfillment of human history, a paragon also devoted to assisting underdeveloped parts of the world in realizing their aspirations to reach this ideal. The US example seemingly transcended the particularities of culture and place, but it qualified universal inclusion with a hierarchically differentiated teleology emphasizing the developmental distance between itself and other nation-states. Second, US competence to intervene in matters of underdevelopment globally could be claimed through this ongoing practice of domestic intervention. Thus, the affluent society's knowledge of and experience with—in the words of UNM President Tom Popejoy, quoted above—the "problems of cultural adaptation in the process of economic development" were exactly the qualifications required for world leadership. Weighing against the conceits of both affirmative versions of US globalism was the fact that territories or peoples within the United States and the world at large shared a history of colonization and dispossession. This suggested lines of conflict decisively at odds with the interests of US Cold War policy.

Although Truman firmly placed underdevelopment outside the United States, the examples discussed in this chapter suggest ways in which the global logic of development proved less tidy and manageable than US policymakers had anticipated. Rather than simply stigmatizing entire nations and naturalizing an apparently irrepressible process of economic growth, underdevelopment also introduced a new space for strategic negotiations. Nevertheless, these negotiations ran aground whenever the conditions of US colonialism became too visible a point of reference.

The particularities evident in both the NCAI campaign and the local contexts of Peace Corps training challenged the abstraction of universality, specifying explicit histories of exclusion while still pursuing a strategic inclusivity. In each case, the global paradigms of poverty and cultural difference functioned as arenas for action rather than ways to impose seamless social meaning. In none of these instances is the significance of poverty and cultural difference exhaustively universalized; rather, they are always remade in their concretely manifest forms. The philosopher Étienne Balibar has described "real universality"—one of three salient forms of universality—as the historical moment when "humankind" is experienced as an actual condition of global interconnectivity rather than as an ideal or utopian future. Balibar insists, however, that "far from representing a situation of mutual recognition, it actually coincides with a generalized pattern of conflicts, hierarchies, and exclusions."[87] Under conditions of real universality, identity is increasingly strategic because of the inequities that globalized interdependency intensifies. In other words, inequities—often themselves the residue of historical dispossessions wrought by preceding globalizations such as colonialism—animate identity as strategy. It is in this sense that underdevelopment served as an arena for action and intermediation rather than as a dictated and fixed term of identity.

The observations of the political scientist Uday Singh Mehta on the imperial constitution of liberal thought are particularly useful here. Taking shape in the British colonial context, liberal universalism was less an unfulfilled ideal toward which its progenitors aspired than a particular logic of colonial administrative practices. Mehta focuses on the exclusionary strategies embedded in liberal universalism and, rather than suggesting that such strategies incite contradiction, points to the circumstances of colonial India within which liberal philosophers such as John Stuart Mill and James Mill conceived of the liberal project.[88]

Foregrounding this imperial context, Mehta poses an important question: "What was the response of liberal theorists as they cast their gaze on an unfamiliar world?" According to him, these theorists perceived unfamiliar forms of experience and life as provisional. Particularities foreign to their own understanding and worldview were merely circumstantial details that obscured the essential truth of their own perspective. Their response to such provisionality, Mehta argues, was to insist that they were obligated to intervene on behalf of that which was "incomplete, static, backward, or otherwise regnant, and guide it to a higher plateau of stability, freedom, and purposefulness." Indeed, their claim was that such intervention was not pursued in self-interest but rather for the greater good and essential truth that liberal imperialists had the rational capacity to recognize. At the core of liberal justification for empire, and of the liberal social mission more broadly, was the judgment that the provisionality of other peoples' experience required normative remediation. Liberals, in this sense, based their authority on the higher purpose they claimed to pursue in order to help others.[89] The historical negotiations examined in this chapter, I suggest, were necessarily animated by this still-dominant liberal enterprise.

Significant historical differences separate the Truman era from the Kennedy and Johnson administrations, especially with regard to how domestic policy was cast in relation to US Cold War grand strategy, but discursive continuities did persist. In 1964, President Johnson appointed Peace Corps Director Sargent Shriver as head of the new Office of Economic Opportunity (OEO), to lead the domestic War on Poverty. For two years, Shriver served as director of both the OEO and the Peace Corps. His efforts to subsume both agencies into a single mission are immensely telling. He went so far as to insist: "The best evidence I have that both of the agencies I'm running are successful [is when a] guy who agitated for the poor in Peru for two years took that [Peace Corps] training and used it, and is now working for OEO to get the poor to demand that they be allowed to participate in city council meetings."[90] Likewise, seeking to recruit the support of the American Society of Newspaper Editors for the War on Poverty in 1964, Shriver insisted that the programs were in tune with US free-market ideologies and joked: "The Communists have been calling me an agent of Wall Street imperialism ever since the Peace Corps got started. Not bad for a Democrat!! But for the first time they may be right." In this same address, Shriver noted: "Peace Corps Volunteers who have completed their service abroad were queried about the poverty program. Eighty-two percent of them said they were interested in joining. From this source alone we can anticipate 2,847 dedicated workers next autumn."[91] Because they suffered from the same ostensible cultural deficiencies as the underdeveloped hosts abroad, impoverished populations within the United States could benefit from the Peace Corps in the form of War on Poverty community action agents.

The construct of culture shock, however, also proved to be malleable. In 1970, the Navajo Nation, with the support of several prominent social scientists, challenged a negative evaluation of its OEO-funded Rough Rock Demonstration School by claiming that the OEO's evaluators had suffered from culture shock and thus were incapable of objectively appraising the project. The school's advisory board contended: "Our claim is that the Rough Rock evaluators, unknown to themselves, were overwhelmed by the impact of the new school culture and that their report was written under severe culture shock due to unfamiliarity with Navajo culture."[92] Among other points, the OEO report criticized the school for not fully implementing the War on Poverty mandate for community control. The board countered that the evaluators were in fact unable to recognize community control, blinded as they were by cultural preconceptions and disoriented by the unfamiliar context.

The strategic use of culture shock by the Navajo school board cut against the grain of liberal universality because it disallowed the assimilability of difference. The foreign, as I have discussed in this chapter, was vital to the mechanics of liberal reform because it served as a representation of the absolute other as essentially the same—that is, as a provisional subject awaiting transformation into its immanent sameness. By charging that OEO evaluators were debilitated by culture shock, Navajo leaders both insisted on the situated particularity of difference—that a group of white experts might not have the capacity to recognize what they observed—and called attention to this liberal presumption of sameness. The limit of liberal universality was the particularity of its own historical and material conditions of possibility. Liberal claims to universal truths were themselves symptomatic of the actual circumstances through which these claims were made. Examining the foundational role of the foreign for liberal reform, and its specific dynamics within the mid-twentieth-century discourse of underdevelopment, reveals the ways in which US colonialism served as both an impossible referent and a structuring absence in the US Cold War construction of the free world. The participation and civic integration of poor people in the United States, discussed in the next chapter, worked in tandem with poverty imagined as a foreign country that awaited remediation through development and modernization. From a normative standpoint, poor peoples' participation was an exercise in tutelary alignment that nevertheless perpetually threatened to unsettle the prescribed terms of incorporation.

CHAPTER THREE

THE CIVICS AND CIVILITIES OF POVERTY
Participation, Policing, and the Poor People's Campaign

In the months leading up to the passage of the Economic Opportunity Act (EOA) in August 1964, the first of the decade's violent urban uprisings convulsed the nation. On July 16, in the Yorkville neighborhood of New York City, an off-duty white police lieutenant shot and killed James Powell, a fifteen-year-old African American. Two days later, rioting erupted in Harlem, spreading to the Bedford-Stuyvesant neighborhood of Brooklyn and then beyond New York City—to Rochester, Chicago, Philadelphia, and, in New Jersey, Jersey City, Elizabeth, and Paterson. During the following month, as Congress debated the EOA, New York City Mayor Robert Wagner traveled to Washington. Reporting on his trip, the *New York Times* observed: "It would be highly surprising if Mr. Wagner—the Mayor of the city where the present epidemic of racial disturbances began—did not mean to remind members of the House of the intimate connection between the battle against poverty and the battle against riots . . . The antipoverty bill, in the new perspective given by the disturbances of this long, hot summer, is also an anti-riot bill."[1]

A number of factors made the association of antipoverty programs with domestic pacification increasingly salient during the mid-1960s. These included the rise of the Black Power movement and its challenge to federal integrationist policies, the white backlash against the social policies of Presidents Kennedy and Johnson, and popular reaction to the visibility of US military carnage in Vietnam. Responding to pressures such as the widespread appeal of the "law and order" rhetoric employed by Barry Goldwater's 1964 presidential campaign, the Johnson administration increasingly marketed its EOA legislative package to social conservatives as a strategy for civil peace. Massive violence and property damage in the Watts neighborhood of Los Angeles during the summer of 1965 stoked white fears of prolonged urban insurrection. Echoing legislation devoted exclusively to the problems of urban disorder, 1966 amendments to the EOA went so far as to explicitly include an antiriot clause to guard against any perception that employees of the Office of Economic Opportunity (OEO), the umbrella agency created to implement the programs of the EOA, might take part in future disorders.[2] This clause was a concession to conservatives, but it also expressed the liberal view that although the police powers of the state were insufficient to the task of governance, they were nevertheless indispensable. Conservative criticism of Johnson's antipoverty programs exerted political pressure to produce more overtly forceful means of maintaining order, but reliance on state coercion during this time was also consistent with liberalism's concern for enforcing norms of behavior and aspiration.

Addressing Congress on March 16, 1964, President Johnson proclaimed: "The war on poverty is not a struggle simply to support people, to make them dependent on the generosity of others . . . It is an effort to allow them to develop and use their capacities . . . so that they can share . . . in the promise of this Nation."[3] In extending this promise, the Johnson administration proved to be especially concerned with what it believed to be the incapacity of the dispossessed to exercise their citizenship responsibly, or to conform in their personal conduct to the obligations of liberal democracy. The EOA substantially recast the relationship between citizens and the state by linking neighborhood representatives directly to federal agencies and circumventing other political intermediaries. Title II-A of the EOA, the Community Action Program, required "the development and implementation of all programs and projects to serve the poor or low-income areas with the maximum feasible participation of the residents of the areas and members of the groups served." Ostensibly reversing a long tradition of social welfare paternalism, antipoverty efforts would be "carried out not *for* the community, but rather *by* the community."[4] The assumption was that, without disturbing the competitive spirit of capitalism, participation in social policy design and implementation would restore poor people's dignity as citizens and offset the demoralizing effects of poverty by giving them a voice in the government programs that most affected their lives.

Within this framework, Gayatri Spivak's provocative question "Can the subaltern speak?" provides a useful point of departure. Spivak notes the incongruity of calling for a subject to speak from the position of one who is silenced, whose very identity is purportedly constituted by a lack of agency. She specifies instead how an imperial project is always already present in the injunction that the oppressed must speak.[5] Rather than suggesting that there is a voice available for retrieval, she argues that Bhuvaneswari Bhaduri's suicide brings her "subalternity into crisis." It is this crisis as the undoing or destabilization of subalternity itself, and not the injunction to speak, that emerges as the crucial intervention.[6] Spivak's contention is not that representation ("speaking for") is impossible, but rather that representation is itself an action contingent on relations of power that are intimately and often violently structured by absence and incommensurability. In the context of the 1960s antipoverty programs, we can pose questions related to "Can the subaltern speak?": Of what significance is the compulsion that the poor and dispossessed participate in their own self-government, that they themselves become the primary agents of social reform and rehabilitation, and that they give voice to their needs and desires so as to enter the fold of governmental authority? Indeed, in what ways did participation make "the poor" a cohesive political category, a constituency expressive of common interests and wants? What were the circumstances, anxieties, and political stakes that animated this approach to governance? To what extent was this approach consonant with, or perhaps even constitutive of, liberalism more broadly at this time? Furthermore, how might the state's crisis of legitimation have amplified various ascriptions of disorder and violence as either a dangerous excess or troubling failure of poor people's participation?

This chapter considers the significance of "maximum feasible participation" by situating it within an expanded political and social frame. In order to examine the emergence of participation as a site of conflict, I begin by exploring the intersection between programs to combat juvenile delinquency, the Mobilization for Youth, and the welfare rights movement, and I trace their connection across the development and deployment of Richard

Cloward and Frances Fox Piven's "crisis strategy" for the political power of the poor.[7] The fact that juvenile delinquency programs were a model for federal antipoverty endeavors was especially significant for how those endeavors approached community as a conciliatory force and for the ways in which they associated poverty and criminal behavior. The disruptive tactics of the welfare rights movement were likewise construed by some critics as encouraging the association between criminal disorder and the poor. Next, I study the changing terms of participation within the Office of Economic Opportunity and the Community Action Program, looking specifically at how these reconfigurations of policy were shaped by governmental concerns over the urban disorders. Finally, I examine how the framework of participation and the question of violence played out in the 1968 Poor People's Campaign and the government's responses to it. However ill-fated the campaign, it successfully rallied a broad, national coalition of people with a significantly less predetermined, more heterogeneous notion of participation and more substantive commitment to economic justice than that envisioned by the Johnson administration. The campaign dispensed with the singular governmental category of "the poor," instead asserting a radical —though tenuous—solidarity that insisted on the specificity and distinct claims of each group involved and that challenged standard forms of political inclusion.

I consider each of these examples as a means of elaborating on the social resonance of participation—linked specifically to poverty—as a key term both for mobilizing political consent and for the recalcitrant social forces that could not be contained and curtailed by this manner of enclosure. Each instance also highlights the specific manner in which participation as a political idiom was articulated with or separated from violence, as well as suggesting the ambivalent sense in which participation framed participants as embodiments of the state. In discussing these examples, I do not intend to suggest a trajectory from a disingenuous, state-administered imperative to a liberatory grass-roots catalyst, but rather to specify the shifting and dynamic constellation of political tensions evident in each context. Likewise, I am not suggesting that state-authorized participation either wholly contained or preempted less-compliant participatory strategies. Instead, I consider official policy as a way to understand both the essentially normative impulse for participation and its unruly surplus.

Feasible Participation

During the 1960s, antipoverty policy mandates for participation were increasingly oriented toward the management of political instabilities. Within the liberal policy framework of the period, participation—long a key word in the lexicon of democratic governance—was an elastic term that moved expediently between the invocation of implicitly racially-specific constituencies, localized collective action by poor people, and representation of the formerly excluded.[8] The social welfare scholar Ralph Kramer argues that at its inception, OEO policy implied four distinct modes of participation: policymaking, program development, social action, and employment.[9] The requirement that low-income neighborhood residents make up at least one-third of a community action agency's governing board was the most definite example of the insistence on participation. Yet a legislative emphasis on participation also allowed the Johnson administration to suggest that social, economic, and political exclusion were matters of personal choice and to shift culpability for exclusion and dispossession to the supposedly willful negligence of individuals and groups. Moreover, the phrasing of the Economic Opportunity Act allowed only for "maximum *feasible* participation" (emphasis added). The qualifying language of feasibility insisted that the established order and relations of power were not to be disturbed, and existing limits were to be respected. According to accounts such as Daniel Patrick Moynihan's *Maximum Feasible Misunderstanding*, this stipulation unrealistically raised expectations, and the normative limit of "feasibility" was too easily trespassed.[10]

Participation as a policy directive presumably valorized and nurtured the political agency of those formerly excluded from the political establishment. Nevertheless, participation also transformed participants into political subjects whose actions were legible in the already operative terms of political institutions—to participate was to be remade in terms that conformed to recognizable expressions of agency.[11] More often than not, the institutionalization of participation demanded that multiple sociopolitical identifications and the capacity for opposition be relinquished as a precondition for political inclusion. In this sense, participation predicated the rights of citizenship on compliance with dominant political edicts and identifications. At the same time, the practice of participation—especially as it was extended to those traditionally excluded from the formal workings of democratic government—perpetually threatened to disrupt and defy established protocols. For conservatives such as the political scientist Samuel Huntington, this threat was inherent in the "excess of democracy" and was manifest in the widespread challenge to governmental authority during the 1960s. In his contribution to the notorious Trilateral Commission report *The Crisis of Democracy*, Huntington lamented that "the effective operation of a democratic political system usually requires some measure of apathy and noninvolvement on the part of some individuals or groups . . . Democracy is more a threat to itself in the United States than it is either in Europe or Japan where there still exist residual inheritances of traditional and aristocratic values."[12] Arguably the United States had a more oligarchic underpinning than Huntington acknowledged, but the form and function of democratic participation were indeed among the most volatile arenas of contention in the country during the 1960s and 1970s.

The language of the Johnson administration's programs presented the reciprocity between coercion and independence as an elemental feature of liberal governance—most overtly with the administration's declaration of "war" on poverty. The metaphor of war promised concerted federal action to address the political issue of poverty.[13] War was a supremely national enterprise that authorized a unified, nonpartisan effort, making support a moral obligation, embodying the nation-state in the intrepid actions of individual citizen soldiers, and rendering opposition equivalent to treason. Indeed, urging Congress to enact the Economic Opportunity Act, President Johnson declared: "On similar occasions in the past we have often been called upon to wage war against foreign enemies which threatened our freedom. Today we are asked to declare war on a domestic enemy which threatens the strength of our Nation and the welfare of our people."[14] But at issue was not only who waged the war and on whose behalf, but who was the enemy. In the beginning, the War on Poverty was championed as a moral crusade ignited by the beacon of world democracy, but it rapidly became more of a war—not so different in intent than the war in Vietnam—over the self-determination of subject peoples and the meaning of democracy itself. The war on poverty was rapidly literalized by the experience of internal conflict, racial polarization, and urban upheaval. Under conditions of escalating social unrest, the enemy targeted in such a war was more ambiguous than initially proposed. The historian Michael Sherry has suggested that, "given urban riots and black resentment, it became easy for some to see the enemy as poor and black people themselves."[15]

Numerous studies have treated the War on Poverty and the Vietnam War as competing endeavors, with domestic social policy quickly falling victim to military expenditures demanded by the domino theory of the spread of communism. However, the competition for resources between the domestic and foreign agendas should not lead us to overlook the manner in which liberal governance was crafted across this ostensible divide. The "strategic hamlet" program and the Mekong Delta dam project are two examples among many of how the United States deployed the "community development" paradigm as military strategy in Vietnam.[16] During this same period, the use of military technologies for urban policing dramatically reconfigured domestic law enforcement.[17] In the context of the burgeoning urban crisis, federally funded projects for community development and citizen participation operated in tandem with more conspicuously coercive counterinsurgency tactics, while simultaneously expanding poor people's access to previously unavailable economic and political resources.

From the outset of the War on Poverty, governmental imperatives for participation were entangled with efforts to claim legitimate force and ensure that domestic insurgencies were perceived as unreasonable—detached from any circumstances with which the state might be complicit—and as responsible for excesses that justified the most severe forms of state reaction. For the Johnson administration, the urban uprisings were a crisis that partially dissolved the effective distinction between agencies of the state's coercive apparatus: policymakers, law enforcement officials, and the military collaborated in strategies for domestic pacification. But although in 1965 and 1966 Johnson himself drew parallels between domestic law and order and the war in Vietnam to suggest the magnitude of the government's resolve, by 1967 this analogy too easily left the administration open to criticism on both fronts and was effectively abandoned.[18] In both the domestic and international arenas, however, officials strove to establish state violence as an indispensable civilizing and heuristic force.[19] To the degree that political challenges to the state could be rendered as violent and irresponsible—as juvenile and incorrigible, and as either apolitical or seditious—state repression could be made to appear equitable and reasonable. Likewise, although liberal reformers were quick to view collective urban violence as a response to conditions of poverty and racism, liberals found it inconceivable that poverty and racism were themselves forms of violence, symptoms of how social norms and capital accumulation actually worked. In its very ubiquity, the systemic violence of capitalism—a violence that the philosopher Slavoj Žižek points out in its most pervasive form "is no longer attributable to concrete individuals and their 'evil' intentions, but is purely 'objective,' systemic, and anonymous"[20]—remained imperceptible and therefore seemingly unimpeachable.

Delinquency and the Social Order of Opportunity

The use of programs and policies aimed at juvenile delinquency as prototypes for the 1960s antipoverty program remains significant far beyond the usual cursory inclusion of the programs in the origin stories of the War on Poverty. Indeed, juvenile delinquency initiatives reinforced the idea that poverty, crime, and race were correlated, as well as the prescriptive emphasis on community participation at the time.[21] According to most accounts, the President's Committee on Juvenile Delinquency and Youth Crime and the urban demonstration projects created by the subsequent 1961 Juvenile Delinquency and Youth Offenses Control Act directly contributed to the design of the OEO's Community Action Program. The 1961 legislation also marked the beginning of federal involvement in what had historically been the province of state and local policymakers, agencies, and law enforcement officials.[22] The sociologists Lloyd Ohlin and Richard Cloward proposed the concept of "differential opportunity structures,"[23] which provided the theoretical orientation for community-based demonstration projects funded through federal delinquency-prevention legislation such as Mobilization for Youth, Harlem Youth Opportunities Unlimited, and Bedford-Stuyvesant Youth-in-Action. These same projects were later transformed into flagship antipoverty organizations for the War on Poverty.

Yet there has been little consideration of precisely how opportunity and community action were prefigured by the juvenile delinquency programs in ways that were decidedly normative and oriented toward intensified self-policing. The most influential programs emphasized mobilizing local adult involvement and civic organizations to redirect the activities and aspirations of neighborhood youth prone to criminal behavior.[24] These were not programs for overhauling social, economic, or political norms, but—like mid-twentieth-century US liberalism more broadly—initiatives to facilitate access and dismantle impediments to living by these norms. Although Ohlin and Cloward's differential opportunity theory deliberately refrained from moralizing about young people's criminal conduct, the authors' objective was nonetheless to make "legitimate opportunity" the path taken, and they emphasized community as a means of shoring up social order.[25] Subsequently, the 1960s antipoverty programs advocated community as a stabilizing and, indeed, disciplinary force that militated against the criminal excesses of its most marginalized.

The federal experiments in juvenile delinquency prevention during the early 1960s inherited much of their approach to reform from earlier neighborhood-based delinquency programs such as the Chicago Area Project. Ohlin and Cloward's work differed on theoretical fine points, but it nevertheless owed a great deal of its applied community focus to the Area Project model. And Mobilization for Youth planners, for instance, traveled to Chicago to meet with Area Project staff and closely study its programs in action.[26] Clifford Shaw, a sociologist at the University of Chicago, established the Area Project in the early 1930s under the auspices of the Institute for Juvenile Research. It was the most comprehensive application of the so-called Chicago school approach to the causes and treatment of juvenile delinquency, which saw disorderly youth as symptomatic of what members of the school called the "social ecology" of particular inner-city environments.[27] Critical of a narrowly defined casework approach that pathologized and individualized youthful transgressions, Shaw focused on young people's misconduct situated within "delinquency areas"—urban neighborhoods, often inhabited by recent immigrants or migrants, with statistically high rates of juvenile crime.[28] The Area Project worked to organize and support neighborhood-based community committees, as well as to directly interact with local youth gangs within targeted areas, to remedy the problems associated with juvenile delinquency.

The Area Project relied on so-called detached or street workers, preferably recruited from the neighborhood, to identify and establish rapport with what Shaw called the natural leaders (both locally prominent adults and leaders of youth gangs) of a designated area. The cooperation of the pastor of St. Michael's Church, for instance, was essential to the formation of the Russell Square Community Committee, one of the most successful of the Area Project committees.[29] This was especially important when, as was the case in Russell Square, residents had had unsatisfactory encounters with University of Chicago sociologists in the past and were skeptical of the delinquency project's motives.[30] Concurrent with outreach to neighborhood adults, street workers strove to connect with young males affiliated with area gangs. Notably, Area Project efforts were selectively directed toward delinquent boys, who were considered the source of the most disruptive and dangerous behavior. After having gained the confidence of a particular gang, street workers engaged in informal "curbstone counseling,"[31] as well as actively mediating among local youth, neighborhood adults, and the juvenile justice system. Street workers did not directly express disapproval of gang activities but made extensive efforts to persuade youths to internalize social norms and forsake criminal pursuits.

The Area Project based its approach to neighborhood intervention and reform on research that Chicago school sociologists had initiated during the 1920s and 1930s. Concerned with metropolitan growth and the problems of residents in adapting to urban modernity, the researchers focused on recent immigrants from the Eastern and Southern European countryside, as well as African American migrants from the rural US South. Delinquency was perceived as a problem of cultural adaptation and a consequence of urbanization's weakening of traditional social bonds. Like those who approached underdevelopment as in some way foreign, as discussed in chapter 2, Chicago school analysts tended to construe delinquency and poverty as provisional attributes of foreignness that would be discarded as immigrants and migrants adjusted to their new urban circumstances. The new arrivals were foreign to American middle-class norms. At the same time, they were alienated by the unfamiliarity of US urban modernity. Following other Chicago school theorists such as William I. Thomas, Robert Park, and Ernest Burgess, Shaw did not advocate assimilation as a solution to the social problems of the newly arrived. Rather, he argued that adaptation demanded reinvigorating and revising traditional social bonds that had been left behind in the Old World or the plantation South as a means of regulating the behavior of neighborhood youth.

The Area Project initially targeted three "delinquency areas" and eventually included nearly eighty community committees by the end of the 1960s. The structure of the groups it organized sometimes included a coordinating board, as was the case with the Southside Community Committee, which was comprised of delegates elected from neighborhoods in Chicago's predominantly African American South Side. The Southside Community Committee served as an intermediary between the area's smaller committees and the Area Project, which supplied financial and technical assistance. According to committee rules, outside project support required local matching funds. This structure was intended to foster local autonomy and, in the committee's own words, to "elicit the maximum participation on the part of the greatest number of residents." The premise of delinquency areas was to reform youth by treating the social problems of the entire neighborhood. Programs were thus based on the belief that "delinquent conduct first gets established in a community because adults have compromised their own moral standards." In practice, this meant that social divisions internal to a given area were accentuated when adults sensitive to "the reputation of the community" were enlisted to police those who did not share their concerns. Campaigns were organized to boycott movie theaters and taverns that served as hangouts for truant youth, get rid of local houses of prostitution, and force out the men to whom young thieves sold stolen goods.[32]

Despite the Area Project's emphasis on the delegation of responsibility to local leadership, gang leaders and the delinquent youth targeted for reform were not included as members of community committees. Instead, the emphasis in the South Side, as in Area Project initiatives throughout Chicago, was to attract young people through recreational programs, chaperoned camping trips, and informal counseling and mediation by street workers. The Southside Community Committee believed: "The most important thing is to give the predelinquent or delinquent boy an opportunity to form an attachment to, or come under the influence of, a person or persons from whom he will receive recognition for conforming to the conventional standards of conduct ... This becomes the problem of substituting for the delinquent boy's leaders, law abiding men and women."[33] If, as suggested by Chicago school theorists, delinquent youth were caught between two worlds and lacked an adequate moral compass, the renewal of their community would bridge the generational divide among the new arrivals and provide adult guidance and legitimate role models for the youth.

Borrowing designs and methods from earlier neighborhood-based juvenile programs, the 1960s initiatives were conceived at a time of heightened concern with youth crime and street gangs. During the late 1940s and 1950s, juvenile delinquency once again became a national preoccupation. The subject of intermittent federal hearings, innumerable social science studies, and sensationalist mass media exposés, juvenile delinquency was depicted as a scandal of youth gone bad in the heyday of American affluence.

Fear of youth crime approached panic as the ethic of small-town America and traditional family networks seemed to give way to creeping urbanism and a depraved and incorrigible youth.[34] Sociological literature and popular journalism argued that the increasing disaffection in modern society led to a breakdown of individual responsibility, the collapse of moral authority, and impending social disorder. Media spectacles and social science analysis individualized social pathologies and targeted individual behavior for rehabilitation. What began in the late 1940s as a widespread panic about degenerate youth and the erosion of traditional methods of social regulation became by the late 1950s a white phobia about and fixation on youth of color and black and Latino gangs.[35] By the late 1960s, white racial fears of crime in general had largely replaced sensationalized concerns with juvenile delinquency and tended to conflate adult and youth offenses by people of color.

All the while, the political jargon of opportunity breathlessly evaded the structural inequalities that made the promise of opportunity appealing to begin with. At the most rudimentary level, poverty was simultaneously requisite to and potentially hazardous for capitalist accumulation. Opportunity supplied a heuristic structure for poor people, who like young people allegedly needed to learn how to defer short-term gratification in the service of long-term goals. The promise of deferred gratification held that deprivation and acceptance of the everyday tyrannies of wage labor—or even the hope of getting such work—held future rewards. If juvenile delinquency was in part seen as a threat to the reproduction of the heteronormative social order, opportunity was a measure of participating in and subscribing to the promise of order and bourgeois familial norms as a general social good. Opportunity thus provided another important discursive mechanism for displacing responsibility for the violence of poverty onto poor people themselves, while also allaying dominant fears and anxieties about the social and economic instabilities of liberal democracy in the mid-twentieth-century United States.

Disruption and the Subject of Participation

The early history of Mobilization for Youth (MFY) in New York City was indicative of the conditional and negotiated character of opportunity and participation as ideas for community action. The group was first conceived during a meeting at the Henry Street Settlement of the Lower East Side Neighborhood Association, an umbrella group for local social welfare agencies largely controlled by the settlement house establishment that emphasized increasing the capacity and scope of traditional, expert-driven social welfare intervention. A proposal to create MFY was submitted to the National Institute of Mental Health (NIMH) in 1957. The institute's technical review panel, chaired by Leonard Cottrell, rejected the proposal and insisted that a more substantive program for community involvement, as well as a research and evaluation component, be included. To meet those requirements, MFY was developed in partnership with the Columbia University School of Social Work Research Center, where Ohlin and Cloward were conducting research for *Delinquency and Opportunity*.[36] In 1959 NIMH awarded MFY a two-year planning grant, and in the summer of 1962 MFY opened its first neighborhood service centers with additional funding from the Ford Foundation, the President's Committee on Juvenile Delinquency and Youth Crime, the federal Department of Labor, and the city of New York.

During the planning phase, differing conceptions of what constituted community action figured prominently in the competition between the upper echelons of the Henry Street Settlement and the School of Social Work Research Center to control MFY's orientation.[37] Henry Street's director, Helen Hall, and board of directors chairman, Winslow Carlton, emphasized professional advocacy and consensus building with municipal leaders. MFY staff members, with the support of Ohlin and Cloward, focused on local residents' involvement. NIMH requirements for innovation helped ensure that the settlement house's top-down approach proved less influential in program development. However, during MFY's first year of activity, community participation primarily meant identifying already existing voluntary associations such as veterans' organizations, recreational clubs, Puerto Rican hometown clubs, and church groups.[38] Efforts were made to cultivate relations with these organizations and involve them in MFY projects, but little in the way of direct neighborhood organizing occurred. In this sense, jettisoning control by the social welfare establishment in favor of an emphasis on neighborhood-level authority did little to change the structural distribution of power. Participation in effect consolidated the power of neighborhood residents already aligned with institutions.

MFY's 1961 *Proposal for the Prevention and Control of Delinquency by Expanding Opportunities* underscored the importance of a communitywide organization that provided opportunities for adult residents to assume positions of community leadership. The authors wrote: "Participation by adults in decision-making about matters that affect their interests increases their sense of identification with the community and larger social order. People who identify with their neighborhood and share common values are more likely to try to control juvenile misbehavior. A well-integrated community can provide learning experiences for adults which enable them to serve as more adequate models and interpreters of community life for the young."[39] The goal was to bring local groups together and to cultivate the authority and investment of adult participants through a neighborhood-wide, coordinated effort. "Identification with the community" would in turn foster increased attachment to the "larger social order" for adults and youth alike.

In the summer of 1963, MFY's strategy shifted from a focus on recruiting local organizations to organizing unaffiliated poor people in the neighborhood. Many MFY staff members were frustrated by their limited success with institutional reform. Indicative of this frustration, one MFY memorandum noted: "The response from existing low-income groups was often misleading. Most of these were more interested in Mobilization's resources of money and staff than in programs for community change."[40] An MFY community organizer who had been attempting to work with a neighborhood ministers' council similarly mused: "I would say the effort was a failure . . . We weren't going anywhere with them. We didn't have anything to really fight for."[41] At the same time, many of those working with MFY became involved with the civil rights movement, participating in the 1963 March on Washington and local organizing with groups such as East New York Action and the Congress of Racial Equality (CORE).[42] Some staff members began to discard the conventional community development approach to local participation, which emphasized the transformative potential of collective process, instead advocating the use of conflict and grassroots protest to advance institutional change. Other staff members, more recently hired as community organizers, were—according to codirector George Brager—already considerably more militant than those who had been involved in drafting the program's initial proposal.[43] MFY directly supported and coordinated rent strikes (developing an informal relationship with Jesse Gray, a prominent Harlem housing activist), school boycotts, and voter registration drives, as well as backing attempts to establish a civilian review board for the Police Department. Ezra Birnbaum, an MFY social worker, explained his frustration with the lack of municipal accountability and his reasons for turning to disruptive action by stating: "The slum landlords aren't creeping in, they're marching in . . . The code enforcement down here is as unrealistic and deplorable as it is in any slum community."[44] In 1964, MFY staff members also helped organize the Welfare Recipients League, with whom MFY worked the following year in forming the City-Wide Coordinating Committee of Welfare Groups.[45] Moving from advocacy to organizing, the agency refined and expanded its activities, building coalitions of local residents around specific issues or campaigns.[46]

This shift in emphasis prompted a concerted and hostile reaction. During the summer and fall of 1964, Mobilization for Youth was the target of attacks by Lower East Side school principals, the mayor's office, the FBI, and Republican members of Congress. The assault began with a widely circulated telegram from twenty-six area principals to MFY, accusing the organization of turning its original plan of a "war against delinquency into a war against individual schools and their leaders." The principals charged that MFY staff members were "full-time paid agitators and organizers for extremist groups."[47] They said that "workers paid with public funds . . . have no right during their official working hours to misuse public funds by secretly proselytizing . . . their own private beliefs and affiliation [to] the innocents who do not realize they are being used to further someone's desire for a social revolution."[48] FBI monitoring of the organization had been under way since the previous year. The FBI deemed MFY's cooperation with CORE and participation in the March on Washington sufficiently treasonable to warrant planting two informers in the organization.[49] In February 1964, the New York Police Department's Bureau of Special Services entered the fray as well. Citing the bureau's findings, Mayor Robert Wagner contacted the MFY board director Winslow Carlton, claiming that the organization was "filled with Communists, from top to bottom," and naming 150 staff members who allegedly had "undesirable" political affiliations.[50]

A number of politicians, with the aid of the New York *Daily News*, seized on the controversy as ammunition for the upcoming elections. The *Daily News* alleged that MFY's mimeograph machines were used for anti–police brutality pamphlets distributed in Harlem and Bedford-Stuyvesant at the time of the riots. Daniel Patrick Moynihan, hoping to be elected president of New York's City Council, announced that "an ex-Trotskyite friend" had verified that MFY was "full of Communists."[51] Paul Screvane—the current City Council president who backed Moynihan as his successor and who was also head of the city's Anti-Poverty Operations Board and Wagner's chosen successor as mayor—reiterated allegations of leftist infiltration and added charges of financial impropriety. Screvane, with Wagner's approval, launched an investigation of MFY wrongdoing and suspended the city's contract with the organization for the duration of the investigation. Barry Goldwater's running mate, the Republican vice presidential candidate William Miller, jumped on the bandwagon as well, vowing to make the controversy a campaign issue. Even after an FBI loyalty check found that of 350 MFY employees, only two were members of the Communist Party and only three were affiliated with "other leftist organizations," efforts to discredit the agency continued.[52] The Republican New York City councilman Joseph Modugno railed: "If activities such as [the ones that] have been going on in Mobilization for Youth are duplicated in all major cities of the United States, we will then have a complete breakdown of law and order on a national scale."[53]

Mobilization for Youth rebounded from the attack. To begin with, it was in the Johnson administration's interest that one of its showcase organizations for the turn from delinquency prevention to antipoverty efforts be vindicated. Indeed, as Modugno's charge exemplified, many of the Republican condemnations of MFY sought to impugn Johnson's proposed War on Poverty, and to suggest that other antipoverty programs that the administration initiated would be as corrupt and subversive as MFY was alleged to be. In 1964, the Johnson administration still held sufficient sway over Congress and popular opinion to effectively counteract such criticism.[54] MFY defied new injunctions to purge supposed leftist agitators on its payroll, but continuing political pressure from City Hall—invigorated by the growing white backlash against Johnson's social programs—did succeed in November 1966 in forcing the agency to halt its local organizing activities.

Skeptical of the perfunctory forms of participation afforded by the War on Poverty, Richard Cloward and Frances Fox Piven, then an MFY research associate, concluded that the best prospect for increasing poor people's political power was their capacity to provoke political crises through institutional disruption. The scholars noted a peculiar confluence of liberal and leftist assumptions about political and social change based on the conviction that "the political system was open, accessible, permeable."[55] Thus, as African American protesters turned to increasingly confrontational tactics, the support for their cause of white liberal sympathizers waned. Cautioning that such tactics would alienate would-be reformers and allies, liberals emphasized the importance of working through established bureaucratic and political avenues. In contrast, leftists were galvanized by the rising tide of black political activism, but their goal was similarly to channel this unrest into stable, mass-based organizations. By joining such organizations, many leftists argued that poor people of color would increase their capacity to transform the existing political system. Liberals and leftists thus both focused on establishing formal organizations with the capacity to act through conventional political processes.

An emphasis on creating and sustaining a mass-based political organization of poor people, according to Piven and Cloward, was a strategy bound to fail. Poor people did not have the resources to effectively use and shape conventional legislative and judiciary institutions. Historically, the scholars argued, most mass-based political organizations gathered momentum in tandem with social protest and as protest abated, they either floundered or were co-opted by the establishment. The most effective political way to produce concessions was disruptive action. Whereas workers in the labor movement could withhold their participation as producers, the principal contribution that poor people made to dominant institutions was their acquiescence to institutional norms. Thus, Piven and Cloward argued that the poor's chief asset was their capacity to "defy the rules governing their behavior on which institutions depend."[56] Winning concessions for the poor required mobilizing around strategic sites of contestation.

The most common problem faced by Lower East Side residents who turned to MFY for help was the structure of public assistance. The ambiguities of eligibility, inadequate allowances, late checks, hostile caseworkers, and the byzantine inaccessibility of the municipal bureaucracy collectively ensured that the welfare system was a punitive and degrading ordeal. Piven and Cloward noted a significant and frequent discrepancy between the public assistance benefits to which people were entitled by law and the amount that they received. After further research, they discovered that perhaps as many as twice the number of people who were receiving welfare payments were actually eligible for them. The public welfare system actively suppressed the number of people receiving benefits by failing to inform recipients of their rights, fostering a climate of intimidation and shame that discouraged eligible people from applying for assistance, and using arcane policies to deny benefits to some of those who did apply.[57] Mobilizing poor people around economic assistance to which they were legally entitled would, in the short term, provide the immediate and tangible benefit of a welfare check. In the long term, with the proper strategic maneuvering, it would help make the case for a nationally mandated guaranteed income. If all those eligible for welfare asserted their right to welfare, they would overwhelm the welfare system and compel structural change.

Oddly enough, the public welfare system remained relatively untouched by War on Poverty legislation. For all the Johnson administration's rhetoric about poverty, the principal government institution established for direct economic assistance continued to operate with business-as-usual policies. This was partly because, as already mentioned, the War on Poverty was emphatically not a program for economic redistribution, but one for advancing the promise of opportunity. Independent from Piven and Cloward, welfare rights associations had already begun to appear across the country— Piven and Cloward put on paper what many welfare rights activists were in effect already doing. One of the first of such groups, the Alameda County Welfare Rights Organization, was established in California in 1962. Johnnie Tillmon organized the ANC (Aid to Needy Children) Mothers Anonymous in the Watts neighborhood of Los Angeles the following year. Tillmon was a shop steward in the local laundry workers union who, at age forty-five, had lost her job as a laundress after being hospitalized for acute tonsillitis. She later reflected: "We called ourselves ANC Mothers Anonymous—we got a dictionary and found *anonymous* meant 'nameless.' We understood that what people thought about welfare recipients and women on welfare was that they had no rights, they didn't exist, they was [sic] a statistic and not a human being."[58] The welfare rights movement thus emerged not as a result of new opportunities for participation, but as a response to the forms of exclusion already constitutive of the US semiwelfare state and reaffirmed by the doctrine of maximum feasible participation.[59]

In January 1966, at the Poor People's War Council on Poverty meeting in Syracuse, New York, Cloward and George Wiley discussed at length the proposal that Cloward and Piven had devised. Wiley had recently resigned from CORE over differences in political strategy and was enthusiastic about translating Piven and Cloward's plan into action. Wiley also met Beulah Sanders, a New York City welfare rights activist, at the conference in Syracuse. During the spring of 1966, Wiley moved to Washington, D.C., to work as the national coordinator of the Citizens' Crusade against Poverty, sponsored by the United Auto Workers. In April, he submitted a proposal to the organization for an "action center" that would coordinate grass-roots welfare rights initiatives: "The Center would be ideally equipped to coordinate the Cloward-Piven welfare crisis strategy, spearheading the drive for a guaranteed minimum income."[60] That same month, at the crusade's annual meeting, the board of directors rejected his proposal.

Although the crusade's leadership opted for a less contentious path, its members had lost patience with the platitudes of maximum feasible participation and the War on Poverty. When Office of Economic Opportunity Director Sargent Shriver, an honored guest speaker at the crusade's annual meeting, delivered a sanguine speech on his agency's many accomplishments, he was greeted with outright hostility. A large number of audience members from local antipoverty organizations interrupted his address and challenged him with questions and irate testimonials. Johnnie Tillmon was among those most vocal in their criticism. A stunned Shriver reportedly stormed out of the conference, after announcing: "I will not participate in a riot."[61]

Shriver's heat-of-the-moment word choice could not have been more revealing. Expecting a deferential and grateful audience, his bitter retort made the consequences of disloyalty explicit. To violate the protocols of participation, to disturb the polite and civil exchange between attendees at a conference who were all putatively committed to a common goal, was equivalent to violent insurrection. Poor people were expected to be thankful for the opportunity to voice their opinions, and their role was thus to assume the proper cadence of gratitude and to echo the policy priorities already articulated on their behalf. Outrage and indignation breached the confines of permissible expression and would not be sanctioned by the presence of the institution (embodied in this case by Shriver himself).

The welfare rights movement organized against such OEO-prescribed civility, embracing instead the crisis strategy described by Piven and Cloward.[62] The movement also placed greater emphasis than the scholars suggested on the specific predicament of poor African American women. Welfare rights activists demanded financial support as a basis for their social autonomy. In contrast to the largely middle-class orientation of the women's movement, these activists insisted that the decision to have a child was something quite different for poor women of color, for whom the capacity to do the work of mothering their own children had historically been secondary to the racialized norms and economic pressures that pushed them into the low-wage labor market. A guaranteed minimum income would provide poor women of color the financial independence that was prerequisite to decisions regarding familial norms and work.[63] Welfare rights activists thus challenged the combined lineage of the maternalist framework of economic assistance, which privileged whites, and the class hierarchies that expected deference and docility on the part of aid recipients.

On June 30, 1966, sixteen simultaneous welfare rights demonstrations across the country heralded the emergence of a national movement. These actions grew out of a plan by Edith Doering, of the Ohio Steering Committee for Adequate Welfare, for a march from Cleveland to Columbus to protest public assistance reductions. Wiley suggested making the protest a national cooperative effort and opened the Poverty/Rights Action Center in Washington, D.C., as a headquarters linking the demonstrations. The following year, Wiley officially established the National Welfare Rights Organization (NWRO), with Tillmon and Sanders as co-chairs, to connect and coordinate local grass-roots welfare rights groups. By 1968, the NWRO's network included more than two hundred groups in more than seventy cities and thirty-six states.[64] Its membership was 98 percent female and predominantly African American.[65] During its initial years, before its activities were impaired by internal struggles over leadership and organizational power, the NWRO succeeded in bringing significant pressure to bear on the welfare establishment to be responsive to the demands of welfare recipients, as well as making progress in promoting a guaranteed annual income as a policy objective. Although invectives like Daniel Patrick Moynihan's rant against the putative "tangle of pathology" birthed by black matriarchy or Senator Russell Long's infamous "brood mares" diatribe sought to further vilify and degrade single motherhood,[66] the NWRO promoted a guaranteed annual income as an explicit program for the economic and social autonomy of poor women. But rather than some unwitting confluence of Left and Right demolishing the rational—if perhaps misguided—compromise of the liberal center, as conventional histories often present the matter, the more salient juncture was that of liberal policy and the conservative quest for law and order. Even taking into consideration the relentless right-wing attacks against Great Society liberalism and its supposedly corrosive indulgence of militant radicals, liberal strategies to redistribute and reassert modes of control—to keep individual liberty free from direct state coercion—were not merely signs of acquiescence to partisan forces. Liberal conceptions of freedom insisted on a certain degree of dispassionate conduct and a guarantee of underlying social stability.

The Counterinsurgent Community

Nevertheless, for conservative and right-wing critics of the Office of Economic Opportunity, the urban riots appeared to be proof of the agency's subversive and incendiary character. The OEO's Community Action Program (CAP) was the most popular target of these criticisms. In 1966, Representative Gerald Ford, minority leader of the House, went so far as to call for President Johnson's resignation because of this purported connection. The Republican Party prepared to make what it termed "racial disorder" and the failures of community action central to its 1966 midterm election campaigns.[67] Accusations that CAP fueled the fires of urban disorder were perhaps most vociferously made by municipal leaders in Newark, New Jersey. Charges by Mayor Hugh Addonizio and members of the City Council that antipoverty workers were involved in the urban riots prompted the House Education and Labor Committee to reconvene its hearings on the Economic Opportunity Amendments of 1967. Newark officials testified that the city's community action program, the United Community Corporation, had been commandeered by radicals who operated as political agitators, made inflammatory public statements, undermined the authority of elected city leadership, and generally incited violence in the city's poor neighborhoods.[68]

The Newark accusations bolstered congressional critics of the EOA. Representative Edith Green of Oregon testified: "I would heartily disapprove of the expenditure of Federal funds to finance people who are outside of Government and who are working for the express purpose of changing the political structure and changing the democratic process and upsetting or overturning the decisions made by mayors or duly elected officials."[69] New York Congressman Paul Fino complained that with CAP, "troublemakers and malcontents have been bankrolled and pay-rolled in incredible numbers."[70] Representative James Gardner of North Carolina and Senators James Eastland of Mississippi and John McClellan of Arkansas led the attack in Washington. Gardner stressed that even if antipoverty workers were not directly involved in instigating the riots, "the important thing is that you people are agitating the poor sections of our cities, Newark for a prime example[,] . . . to go out and demonstrate against the authorized authority in that city, and what happens, it gets out of hand."[71] These criticisms, in addition to partisan grandstanding, were arguments for direct government control and authority—as opposed to the diminished overt role of state intervention promoted by Great Society policy in general and CAP in particular.

To make matters worse for the OEO, allegations that there was evidence of subversion, if not outright sedition, in OEO-funded community action programs were amplified by testimony before Senator Eastland's Judiciary Committee hearings in August 1967 on the Antiriot Bill and Senator Mc-Clellan's Permanent Subcommittee on Investigations hearings that began in September. In the case of the Permanent Subcommittee on Investigations, formerly chaired by Senator Joseph McCarthy, McClellan parlayed the urban riot investigation into a massive three-year affair that variously targeted OEO community action workers, student antiwar activities, and so-called domestic terrorists. McClellan worked closely with J. Edgar Hoover and the FBI to make the subcommittee hearings a deliberate counterpoint to the social focus of the Kerner Commission. Even prior to Senate authorization of the investigations, McClellan announced that the subcommittee would emphasize "law enforcement rather than the social issues underlying the disorders."[72]

Two widely publicized cases were especially damaging to OEO credibility.[73] Nashville Police Captain John Sorace charged that the OEO had funded a Student Nonviolent Coordinating Committee (SNCC) liberation school that supposedly taught black children to hate white people. SNCC had already been accused of playing a prominent role in the April riots in Nashville, and the link to OEO money was touted as proof that the agency was directly funding antiwhite revolutionaries. An incident in Houston compounded the appearance of OEO culpability in urban violence. In mid-August 1967, Houston Police Chief Herman Short announced to the press that the Harris County Community Action Committee was seeking to acquire telescopic rifle sights from a surplus depot at the Kelly Air Force Base. He reportedly mused: "I would hate to guess what they are for, but from what we have seen in the streets recently, I can imagine." Further aggravating the scandal, it was revealed that the Houston antipoverty agency had purchased a dozen walkie-talkies and four radios for monitoring police broadcasts, and had supposedly used this equipment during a civil rights demonstration. Although the charges in both the Nashville and Houston cases later proved to be exaggerated and inaccurate, they embroiled the OEO in public controversy that appeared to confirm critics' worst fears about how the agency was catering to extremist black militants and outright revolutionary conspiracy.[74]

In response to these allegations, the OEO mounted an extensive damage control campaign that included a major survey of OEO activities in sixty-four cities to underscore the conciliatory role of local antipoverty workers during the summer riots. The agency also went to great lengths to publicize its own stringent guidelines for hiring staff and employee activities, and to reassert and refine already existing agency policies. It highlighted the close cooperation between antipoverty workers and the police, noting cities in which joint ventures were orchestrated by the police department and CAP agencies, or where antipoverty workers served as conduits for information about possible future disturbances. The report was full of supportive testimonials by mayors, police chiefs, and local politicians. Rhode Island Congressman Robert Tiernan affirmed: "Rather than cause riots, economic opportunity programs are designed to prevent them by giving poor people a voice in their own destiny. In that sense, OEO has been the foremost deterrent to riots in our country's history."[75] The opposing views of the OEO as a pacifying or incendiary agent made clear that for either side of the debate, "participation" could be only a normative acquiescence to the already established political order.

Despite the extensive maneuvering to vindicate the OEO, in the mid-1960s a flurry of proposed amendments to the Economic Opportunity Act sought to rein in the parameters of participation. The first result of these actions was the OEO's capitulation to the demands by the US Conference of Mayors that the OEO prohibit CAP employees' involvement in voter registration and local political organizing, a potential challenge to the vested interests of municipal governments. In 1966, midterm elections had ousted many liberal Democratic Johnson supporters from the House of Representatives and added fifty-nine new Republicans. By the time it came to reauthorize the EOA in 1967, the Johnson administration was anxious to preempt congressional efforts to terminate the legislation. One proposed amendment by Democrats sought to formally bar members of SNCC—and possibly other allegedly militant organizations such as CORE and Students for a Democratic Society—from participating in the antipoverty program.[76]

Although these official exclusions never materialized, the administration did amend the EOA with provisions against the use of federal funds for "illegal picketing or demonstrations . . . participation by antipoverty employees in any form of direct action in violation of the law, or in partisan political activity." Efforts were to be made to prevent people with "violent antisocial behavior" from enlisting in the Job Corps, an OEO agency that provided employment for poor youth. With a nod to the fiscal scandal that had recently embroiled Harlem Youth Opportunities Unlimited, the amendments also required annual audits of all antipoverty programs.[77] At the close of 1967, the Green Amendment instituted municipal control over CAP funds, ending direct federal support for community autonomy from city supervision.[78] Cumulatively, the discretionary powers of local community action agencies were reduced and oversight by traditional government agencies increased. The fact that a majority of city governments throughout the country opted not to take over CAP operations only confirmed that community action was often already in tune with the interests of municipal authorities.

The OEO turned to its personnel policy as one way to work with the limited supervisory power written into its mandate for decentralized coordination. On July 20, 1967, OEO Director Sargent Shriver sent a memo to all regional directors stressing: "There will be absolute insistence that every OEO employee . . . scrupulously avoid and resist participation . . . in any activities which threaten public order in any community . . . I shall insist upon the withholding of OEO funds from any grantee or delegate agency which is shown to be encouraging or tolerating such behavior."[79] General Counsel for the OEO Donald Baker sent an administrative memo on August 19 about the "power to suspend and terminate personnel in OEO-assisted programs," in which he surveyed existing policy precedents. Baker noted that terminating or suspending entire programs in major cities posed definite problems unless the action had significant community support. However, there existed what he characterized as "considerable leverage" for firing any employee who "caused the grantee to violate applicable requirements." Among such requirements, he cited those included in the initial 1964 *Community Action Program Guide* that all contracted agencies "employ only capable and responsible personnel who are of good character and reputation, [who] are sympathetic with the objectives of the Economic Opportunity Act . . . and are not members of subversive organizations."[80] If at the outset CAP projects might have paid little attention to such guidelines and, with the intention of including dissenting opinions, actually aimed to attract participants inclined toward more militant political action, by 1967 this strategy threatened to be an irreparable liability.

These stipulations might not be surprising as guidelines for federal employment. However, the fact that they were vigorously reaffirmed and redistributed at this particular moment is significant. Not only were CAP employees being accused of inciting riots, but employees of flagship projects such as MFY were being labeled communist provocateurs. Almost all of these allegations were either dropped or proved to be false, but the OEO's efforts to exonerate itself from each ensuing scandal placed increasing constraints on the scope and character of the forms of participation sanctioned by the agency. Originally it had certainly intended nothing other than the most general stipulations for personnel, and because local circumstances varied widely, the agency was willing to forgo the rigid implementation of guidelines in order to maximize recruitment—an objective that the agency considered the most effective and durable means to neutralize radical insurrection. The OEO now sought to police these imperatives for responsibility with greater zeal and would no longer tolerate substantive political contestation in its name. The belief that the most advantageous counterinsurgent strategy was to provide outlets for expressions of dissent and political antagonism in order to redirect and domesticate those unruly impulses was replaced by a partisan pragmatism and concern for short-term appearances.

Outside of the agency, the OEO continued to advertise the virtues of its programs. Testifying before the National Advisory Commission on Civil Disorders in October 1967, Community Action Program Director Theodore Berry presented his agency as a model for others to emulate. He contended: "While we acknowledge we have no complete solution to offer for the problem of neighborhood riots, we are convinced that one approach is to increase the involvement of ghetto residents in the planning, policy making, and conduct of programs organized for their benefit." Citing an OEO survey of Watts after the riot there, he noted that most people from the neighborhood reported that conditions in Watts were simply not improving fast enough and felt that they had little influence on the institutions that governed their lives. According to the survey, respondents voiced support for the riots as a last recourse for affecting policy and obtaining much-needed economic resources for the neighborhood. Berry argued: "We must provide residents of the ghetto alternative means for effecting their destinies. The experience of [the] community action program suggests the alternative is resident involvement." Moreover, CAP-style community workers were invaluable for communication between local residents and government: "They interpret the ghetto to the agencies and the agencies to the ghetto. Because they live and work in the target areas and speak 'its' language they are better able to communicate with their neighbors." Berry concluded that "community action thus represents a model . . . of the way effective involvement can be implemented. If similar models were adopted by other institutions . . . it is our contention that much of the disaffection and alienation in our ghettos could be overcome."[81] According to Berry, community interlocutors translating between the state and the "ghetto," and facilitating "resident involvement" (participation) and open communication across racial and class divides, remained the most viable way toward civil peace.

The Poor People's Campaign and the Economy of Violence

Less than two weeks after Berry's deposition, Martin Luther King Jr. also testified before an executive session of the National Advisory Commission on Civil Disorders. He contended that the urban uprisings were "born of the greater crimes of white society," stating: "When we ask Negroes to abide by the law, let us also declare that the white man does not abide by the law in the ghettos." It was a lack of political will, not a lack of understanding, that stood in the way of resolving the current crisis.[82] Immediately following his testimony, King gave a press conference in which he announced: "The time has come if we can't get anything done otherwise to camp right here in Washington just as they did in the bonus march[,] just camp here and stay here by the thousands and thousands until the Congress of our nation and the federal government will do something to deal with the problem."[83] Mass civil disobedience had become the only recourse. King later elaborated: "We must fashion . . . new tactics which do not count on government good will, but instead serve to compel unwilling authorities to yield to the mandates of justice." Moreover, economic justice meant more than simply inclusion in the existing system. He insisted that "our economy must become more person-centered than property-centered and profit-centered . . . Let us not think of our movement as one that seeks to integrate the Negro into all existing values of American society," but as an endeavor to transform the essence of those values.[84]

Over the course of the following two months, King and the Southern Christian Leadership Conference (SCLC) developed plans for a nationwide Poor People's Campaign.[85] Highlighting the need for jobs and income, the campaign underscored connections between the Vietnam War, the War on Poverty, and the urban riots.[86] Calling attention to the trajectory of US state violence, King declared: "The bombs in Vietnam explode at home. The security we profess to seek in foreign adventures we will lose in our decaying cities."[87] An article in the newspaper of the SCLC's Trenton, New Jersey, branch recommended that Lyndon Johnson "assign our military personnel to constructive, rather than destructive tasks. . . . OUR troops will be on our soil, doing OUR work. Exterminating and killing rats and roaches is certainly less demoralizing, yet far more important to Americans, than killing other humans."[88] One draft of the campaign's statement of purpose noted that "millions of Americans lead lives scarred by the violence committed against the poor, the violence of the many indignities and inhumanities they suffer daily."[89] Another version of the statement proclaimed that the poor "are the captives, the colonized, of the colony, consigned to an island of abject poverty from the mainland of power and decisions."[90] The statement also directly referred to the urban riots. Like many involved in protesting white racism and economic injustice at the time, the authors of the statement insisted on the legitimacy of the insurgent impulse demonstrated in the urban riots, while simultaneously positioning nonviolent demands for economic and political power as alternatives to escalating violence.[91] The statement affirmed that the poor "are trapped in poverty because they are voiceless and powerless. The most militant poor have resorted to retaliatory violence in their demands for economic justice. They have burnt their Ghettos, out of the angry passion of their inflame[d] spirit, born in the dark hours of hopelessness. They have looted stores, as they likewise have been legally looted by the greed of the business world."[92] The vicious circle of violent dispossession, blurring distinctions between the legal and the criminal, materially linked imperialism abroad with the brutalities of exclusion at home. The violence of retaliation in this sense was neither voice nor power, but an unequivocal assertion of the systemic and unrelenting violence of poverty.

Throughout the winter and early spring, King tirelessly pursued his vow to direct the SCLC's nonviolent protest toward massive civil disobedience on behalf of the poor. The ambitious and daunting scope of the SCLC's organizing effort was complicated by resistance from within the organization as well as by outside forces. Many of the SCLC's leaders, including James Bevel and Jesse Jackson, were ambivalent in their support for the venture, unconvinced that the campaign was the most opportune direction for the SCLC to take. Marian Logan, an SCLS board member, and prominent black leaders such as Bayard Rustin publicly criticized King's intended "massive dislocation"[93] of the nation's capital, arguing that such disruptive tactics would alienate the movement's congressional allies rather than prompt positive legislative action. Fundraising faltered in the face of waning support from white liberals. Lack of funds undercut efforts to recruit local fieldworkers. In an attempt to galvanize grass-roots participation in the campaign, King embarked on what he called a people-to-people tour. At the first stop, in Michigan, he was confronted with a crowd of three hundred right-wing demonstrators who heckled him throughout his address, calling him a "commie" and a "traitor."[94]

Moreover, during this initial organizing phase and throughout the campaign, tensions between SCLC leaders and participating organizations constantly threatened to undo the campaign's coalition. For instance, the SCLC had in certain respects usurped the National Welfare Rights Organization's agenda, taking up the demand for a guaranteed income and belatedly opposing the injustices of the welfare system. In fact, NWRO Executive Director George Wiley had repeatedly tried to contact King and coordinate efforts between the two organizations but was flatly ignored until the SCLC began planning for the Poor People's Campaign. Even after planning was under way and the SCLC had requested a meeting in Chicago with NWRO leaders, King was not scheduled to attend. After Johnnie Tillmon and the other officers of the NWRO walked out, insisting that he be present, a subsequent meeting was arranged. When King finally met with the NWRO leaders, the meeting almost disintegrated again when he and other top SCLC leaders demonstrated their ignorance of welfare rights issues and the difficulties the welfare system posed for women in particular. Although King was able to save face and establish a partnership with the NWRO, the attitude of SCLC leaders was still evident in retrospective comments by Andrew Young, who had been the group's executive director at that time. He recalled: "They jumped on Martin like no one ever had before. I don't think he had ever been that insulted in a meeting. But I think he understood. In a way, they were testing him. Just to deal with those kinds of women took a hell of a lot of energy."[95] This underlying paternalism on the part of SCLC leaders exasperated the already difficult task of recruitment and called into question the presumed goals of a poor people's campaign, which necessarily required paying attention to gender discrimination in US society and social policy. In the end, the SCLC needed the support of organizations such as the NWRO, which provided the incentive for a certain amount of compromising to establish campaign objectives.

The SCLC sponsored a minority group conference in Chicago on March 23 in order to coordinate a collaborative nationwide effort.[96] George Wiley led efforts to involve the substantial membership of the NWRO in the SCLC's campaign. Rodolfo "Corky" Gonzales and Reies López Tijerina organized Hispanics in the Southwest to take part. Hank Adams, Tillie Walker, Mel Thom, and the National Indian Youth Council coordinated Native American participation. Gilberto Gerena Valentín and the Congreso de Pueblo organized a Puerto Rican contingent from New York City. Myles Horton and the Highlander Center orchestrated a delegation from Appalachia.[97] With such a broad coalition, conflicts over priorities and demands persisted, but not at the expense of the campaign itself.

On April 4, 1968, Martin Luther King Jr. was assassinated, and a groundswell of outrage and rebellion swept across America. But planning for the Poor People's Campaign continued. The Reverend Ralph Abernathy, successor to King as leader of the SCLC, fought to keep the momentum of the campaign going.

On April 22, the date King had intended to present the demands of the campaign to Congress, the NWRO held a vigil on Capitol Hill. At the vigil, Irene Gibbs, a member of NWRO, succinctly reiterated King's insistence on the relationship between US poverty and the cost of military violence in Southeast Asia, beseeching Congress: "Take the money from Vietnam and feed our children."[98] All participants in the vigil were arrested. When they were taken to court, the judge berated them for what he perceived as their commiseration with those who had rioted in Washington, D.C., after learning of King's murder. In response to the assertion that the vigil was in honor of King, the judge dismissively remarked: "That's what . . . [the rioters] said they were doing when they burned the town down." He interrogated defendants about their employment, asking questions such as "Is that an OEO organization?" and "Did the taxpayers pay your way out here?"[99] The vigil was accompanied by the NWRO's "Proposals for a Living Memorial" to King that demanded a national guaranteed minimum income, a federal job creation program, and the repeal of the punitive welfare sections of the 1967 Social Security Amendments. The NWRO framed its proposals as the first steps in establishing "the only fitting memorial to Dr. Martin Luther King— a society with liberty and justice for all."[100]

The following week, the SCLC assembled a Committee of 100, representing groups from across the country, for a preliminary round of meetings with federal officials. The SCLC identified five essential requirements for a bill of economic and social rights: (1) "a meaningful job at a living wage"; (2) "a secure and adequate income for all who cannot find jobs or for whom employment is inappropriate"; (3) "access to land as a means to income and livelihood"; (4) "access to capital as a means of full participation in the economic life of America"; and (5) "recognition by law of the right of people affected by government programs to play a truly significant role in determining how they are designed and carried out."[101] Emphasizing the reciprocal significance of political and economic participation for the poor—a materialist conception of participation distinct from the heuristic OEO model—these requirements were then expanded into specific demands addressed to various federal departments and agencies.

During three days of meetings, delegates from the Poor People's Campaign presented these demands to the Departments of Agriculture, Justice, Labor, Housing and Urban Development, State, Interior, and Health, Education, and Welfare, as well as to the Senate Subcommittee on Employment and the Office of Economic Opportunity. At the Department of the Interior, Mel Thom read a statement coauthored by the American Indian contingent declaring that this agency had failed them "because it was built upon and operates under a racist, immoral, paternalistic, and colonialistic system." He insisted that attention be paid to the specific conditions facing American Indians, explaining: "We are not white middle-class aspiring groups of people in need of direction." He was presenting neither demands for civil rights and integration, nor acquiescence to the termination of federal treaty obligations: "We make it unequivocally clear that Indian people have the right to separate and equal communities within the American system; our own communities that are institutionally and politically separate, and socially equal and secure within the American system."[102] Confronting Secretary of Labor Willard Wirtz on his department's failure to involve the poor "in decision-making about manpower training and other employment programs," the SCLC asserted: "Programs will continue to fail because of your problems with 'recruitment.' These recruitment difficulties simply reflect the failure to involve those who will participate in the programs in the planning process."[103]

Following an extended public meeting with Dean Rusk at the State Department, Abernathy announced to the press: "The leaders here for the first time heard the cries and groans of . . . poor people speaking in their own language . . . The poor are no longer divided . . . It's about poor power and we're going to use it."[104] Abernathy insisted that the subaltern spoke and were heard—that the subaltern spoke "their own language," a language of "cries and groans" that constituted "poor [people] power" as an effect of their abject powerlessness—and were comprehensible if legislators would only listen. If, from the perspective of the SCLC leadership, participation required a unified language that was both familiar and foreign, Abernathy's assertion that the campaign spoke in a manner intelligible and compelling to those who had been indifferent would appear increasingly untenable in the months to come.

During the preliminary meetings with government officials, representatives of the Poor People's Campaign reserved a special indignation for the Office of Economic Opportunity. Andrew Young and Victor Charlo, a representative of the National Indian Youth Council, met with the office's Acting Director Bertram Harding, at which time Charlo read the campaign's statement, which included an indictment of the OEO's failure to fulfill its mandate:

> OEO was the agency supposedly created especially to serve the poor—and to give them the power and the money to speak and to act for themselves. You have failed us. You were to be our spokesman within the federal government, but our needs have gone unspoken. You were to help us take our rightful places as dignified and independent citizens in our communities but our manhood and womanhood have been sold into bondage to local politicians and hostile governors . . . OEO became the middleman captured by the myriad of anti-poverty agencies that continued their traditional and abusive ways of dealing with poor people.[105]

Betrayed by the agency's bait-and-switch participation mandate, the campaign claimed to embody the form of direct democracy and self-determination called for in the Economic Opportunity Act.

At the beginning of May, Poor People's Campaign contingents gathered across the country to travel to Washington, D.C. Participants came on foot and by bus. The first of the campaign's Freedom Roads began after a mass rally at the Lorraine Motel in Memphis, Tennessee, where King had been slain. The Southern Caravan traveled with a mule train (with twenty-six mules and three wagons) to dramatize the plight of the rural poor, stopping at thirteen major cities on its journey through the deep South. This contingent included African Americans, Latinos, and poor white Southerners. The Eastern Caravan began in Brunswick, Maine, and accumulated eight hundred people, including two hundred Puerto Ricans from New York City, as it made stops in seven cities along the Eastern seaboard. The Appalachia Trail contingent consisted of poor whites and African Americans from largely rural areas in Tennessee, Kentucky, southwest Virginia, and West Virginia. The Western Caravan was composed of Chicanos from Los Angeles and Hispanos and American Indians from New Mexico, Colorado, and Oklahoma. The Indian Trail began in Seattle, Washington, and traveled east, stopping in Montana, North Dakota, and Minnesota.[106] Members of the Blackstone Rangers from Chicago, the Invaders from Memphis, and the Commandos from Milwaukee accompanied the marchers as safety marshals.[107] Surveillance by the FBI and the Justice Department's Interdivisional Intelligence Unit was in full force throughout the campaign. Undercover FBI and US military personnel infiltrated each branch of the march. The marchers proceeded so peacefully that undercover agents' reports complained the only violence they had to convey was local police harassment.[108] The multiple caravans' journey to the capital was marred only by scattered arrests during local rallies en route, a police riot in Detroit, and an incident in Wilmington, Delaware, where a white teenager attacked a youth in the campaign with a broken bottle.[109]

At first the Office of Economic Opportunity took measures to bar its employees from participating in the campaign. After significant protest, the agency relented, promising not to penalize employees for taking part as long as they did so as private citizens and no OEO money was spent on these activities.[110] The Department of the Interior initially sought to deny the campaign a permit to camp on federal property, but it finally conceded to campaign plans. Members of Congress introduced seventy-five separate bills during April and May to control the threat of what Southern legislators termed "mob rule."[111] By contrast, Representative Donald Fraser of Minnesota testified that "the best way for the citizens of Washington and the leaders of our government to counteract the efforts of militants is through a friendly welcome for the marchers."[112] For the duration of its activities, both direct repression and cursory gestures of appeasement continued to be characteristic of the federal response to the Poor People's Campaign.

Between the middle and end of May, the caravans arrived in Washington and assembled a vast shanty town called "Resurrection City, USA," adjacent to the Lincoln Memorial. At its peak, Resurrection City housed more than three thousand people, and demonstrations and solidarity visits drew many thousands more to the encampment during its six weeks of existence. Residents braved torrential rains and seemingly endless rivers of mud. Planning for the city was utopian, though inadequately implemented. City programs included a child-care center, health and social services, a Poor People's University with ongoing seminars and lectures, free meals for residents from Our Daily Bread, a daily newspaper called *True Unity News*, cultural activities in the Soul Center, a city council, a finance committee, and a public relations center. At the opening ceremony for the city, Abernathy pledged: "Here we will build a *Kiononia*, a community of love and brotherhood. American Indians, Puerto Ricans, Mexican-Americans, white poor Americans from the Appalachian area of our country and black Americans will all live together here in this city of hope. It may be that we will have some squabbles among ourselves. But I want to set the record straight for you now: that if we have squabbles, they are going to be all in the family and we are going to solve these squabbles among ourselves."[113] Resurrection City residents may have come to feel less celebratory than Abernathy's statement predicted, but solidarity did persist despite sometimes unfavorable conditions. First-person accounts, such as Charles Fager's highly critical *Uncertain Resurrection* and Walter E. Afield and Audrey B. Gibson's *Children of Resurrection City*, document the everyday frustrations created by the gap between rhetoric and reality in the city.[114] Nevertheless, the city presented precisely the heterogeneity and ambivalent alliances that refused a uniform and deferential representation of the poor. The utopian, disorderly, and ultimately thwarted symbolic metropolis that was Resurrection City was in this sense a perfect embodiment of the righteous discontent,

The day care center was among the many social, cultural, educational, political, and service programs organized in the Poor People's Campaign's Resurrection City in Washington, D.C., June 1968. PHOTOGRAPH BY THEODORE HETZEL, COURTESY OF THE THEODORE HETZEL PHOTOGRAPH COLLECTION, SWARTHMORE COLLEGE PEACE COLLECTION, SWARTHMORE, PA.

political challenge, fragile alignments, and destitute conditions on which the campaign had been built.

On May 12, the Poor People's Campaign launched the first of its demonstrations and direct actions with a Mother's Day march coordinated by the NWRO. Seven thousand protesters led by Coretta Scott King, the widow of Martin Luther King Jr., walked along streets decimated by the rioting following King's assassination, moving from the John F. Kennedy Playground to the Cardozo High School Stadium.[115] At the concluding rally, Coretta King spoke out against the violence of US state policy. "Suppressing a culture is violence . . . Ghetto housing is violence, the lack of will-power to help humanity is violence," she contended.[116] Her speech once again called attention to the brutality of liberal policy and capitalist accumulation that— though often shrouded in anonymity and abstraction—were palpable in the everyday lives of many of those to whom she spoke. As proposed by the NWRO, the march highlighted at the outset of the Washington encampment the coercive regulation of poor women and the injustices perpetrated by the welfare system.[117] The campaign's Women's Solidarity Committee worked for the duration of the campaign to underscore the specific manner in which poverty was gendered and targeted by punitive government policies.

Welfare rights march on Connecticut Avenue, with National Welfare Rights Organization signs demanding "¡Mas Dinero Ahora!" (more money now) as part of the Poor People's Campaign, Washington, D.C., June 1968. PHOTOGRAPH BY WARREN K. LEFFLER, COURTESY OF THE PRINTS AND PHOTOGRAPHS DIVISION, LIBRARY OF CONGRESS, WASHINGTON, D.C. (LC-U9-19271-33A).

Campaign participants presented a broad array of concerns and demands. As the demands made to federal departments and Congress made clear, a unified position did not require minimizing the diversity of the movement's interests. Rafael Duran, who had come from the Southwest, said: "My grandfather used to tell me how we were robbed of land by the U.S. government . . . I was always looking for a way to come to Washington to get it back." In a formal presentation before the Department of State, Duran also insisted on the "educational and cultural rights of Spanish-speaking children to a completely bilingual education."[118] Zola Petty from Mississippi reflected that "if this Campaign just united all the poor minorities against their oppressors that would be doing something." Melcenia Long from Pennsylvania put it succinctly: "Jobs and increased income for the poor is what it's all about." Mary Hyde of Chicago observed: "This country spends thousands of dollars apiece to kill people in Vietnam and about $50 on each poor person in this country . . . We got to straighten out these Congress people's values."[119] The diverse circumstances that motivated people to participate in the campaign produced multiple perspectives that demonstrated the inadequacy of the liberal governmental category of "the poor" and the need for sustained negotiation about differences and material inequality. Whereas liberal pluralism rendered inequality equivalent and commensurate, as will be discussed in the next chapter, the Poor People's Campaign made poverty a means of mobilizing the heterogeneity of its members.[120] The diverse claims and the particularity of the conditions faced by the petitioners were shaped by the overarching structure of dispossession, but that did not mean they were all identical. The form of the campaign itself—with its multiple contingents and numerous demands—underscored the irreducibility of its parts to a unified whole.

Throughout May and June, the campaign continued to lobby government officials and to stage demonstrations. Following up on the initial demands presented to cabinet officials, campaign representatives pressed for substantive action and reported back to Resurrection City's residents. The NWRO called for the repeal of the welfare sections of the 1967 Social Security Amendments, a "national guaranteed minimum income of $4,000 for every family," and "federal funds for [the] immediate creation of at least three million jobs for men."[121] Exasperated by the lack of response to their proposals from the Department of Health, Education, and Welfare, campaign representatives reported: "HEW did not respond to our demand for assurance that unless other needed services are provided, such as health care, additional social services, and effective training, mothers will not be forced to work; HEW also ignored our demand that mothers not be required to work at jobs that do not pay a minimum wage or provide for decent working conditions. These omissions imply that HEW is prepared to condone the certain exploitation of welfare recipients."[122] Likewise, a typical report on meetings with the State Department denounced Secretary of State Dean Rusk's lack of response to the campaign's grievances, which included demands to enforce the provisions of the Treaty of Guadalupe Hidalgo and withdraw US support for the governments of South Africa and Portugal. "The most crucial overriding issue with this agency is that of ending the war in Vietnam," an official PPC statement concluded. The war's "cost in lives, Vietnamese and American, its cost in domestic sacrifice which is paid largely by the poor, is intolerable and immoral."[123] The high point of the campaign was the Solidarity Day march on June 19, slated to commemorate the infamous day in 1865 when slaves in Texas learned of the Emancipation Proclamation—two and a half years after its passage. More than fifty thousand demonstrators arrived in Washington for the march.

Despite the explicitly nonviolent character of the Poor People's Campaign, law enforcement officials had anticipated violent confrontations.[124] Although fear of hostilities was magnified by the April riots in Washington following King's assassination, plans for covert surveillance and military action preceded these events.[125] An editorial in the *New York Times* argued: "Dr. King's plan to seek 'massive dislocation' of the national capital violates the principles of responsible protest."[126] After the April riots, Senator John McClellan's Permanent Subcommittee on Investigations convened a special conference with members of the US Army, the FBI, and Washington's Metropolitan Police Department to prepare for the worst.[127] High-level strategy sessions contemplated future ghetto revolts and concluded: "we must be prepared for guerilla-type warfare, incidents in the suburbs, use of children, Castro-trained commandos, and various other possibilities."[128] On a separate occasion, Senator McClellan called the campaign "a premeditated act of contempt for and rebellion against the sovereignty of government."[129] He announced that he had evidence that "anti-American" elements had infiltrated the Poor People's Campaign and were plotting to incite widespread rioting and disorder in the nation's capital.[130] Press coverage eagerly highlighted conflicts, disorder, and violence within Resurrection City during its six-week existence.

On June 24, 1968, Resurrection City was shut down by an immense show of paramilitary force, following two evenings of violent confrontation and escalated tension between residents and police. Police dogs had been set on protesters, and over one thousand tear gas grenades had saturated the encampment. An eyewitness SCLC report observed: "Most shocking of all was the deliberate brutality of the massive and unprovoked attack of tear gas against a whole city, including women and children. In all of the tear gassing and other military attacks we have experienced in the South, none was ever as vicious as this attack on Resurrection City."[131] Leaders of the campaign had petitioned Congress and met with legislators, but policymakers and President Johnson remained largely indifferent to their demands.[132] In the end, the conclusion of the Poor People's Campaign may have mirrored too closely the Veterans' Bonus March of 1932 invoked by King, which produced similarly disheartening legislative results and ended after eight weeks

Mel Thom, a Walker River Paiute activist and founding member of the National Indian Youth Council, arrested during a Poor People's Campaign march in Washington, D.C., June 1968.

PHOTOGRAPH BY DIANA DAVIES, COURTESY OF THE DIANA DAVIES PHOTOGRAPH COLLECTION, RALPH RINZLER FOLKLIFE ARCHIVES AND COLLECTIONS, SMITHSONIAN INSTITUTION, WASHINGTON, D.C. (FP-DAVI-BWNE-0469-33A).

of encampment in Washington in a deluge of fire and tear gas from US Army troops led by General Douglas MacArthur.[133]

Liberal Enforcements

The calculated orchestration of force was integral to Great Society liberalism. This was evident with the steady procession of presidential commissions on law and disorder. The President's Commission on Law Enforcement and the Administration of Justice (1965–67), the National Advisory Commission on Civil Disorders (1967–68), and the National Commission on the Causes and Prevention of Violence (1968–69) were more than the Johnson administration's frantic though frustrated search for political triage as Republicans seized the rhetorical high ground of "law and order." From the liberal perspective, social order—guaranteed in the final instance by coercion—was at once a corollary of and indispensable to individual liberty. In practice, the distribution of state violence in the name of order extended unevenly across racial and class lines.[134] Furthermore, critics such as Martin Luther King Jr. pointed out how the liberal quest for order in fact relied on violence, whether in the political economy of US militarism or the quotidian brutality of poverty and racism. Yet the cumulative direction of the presidential commissions was simultaneously to consolidate law enforcement activities (as with the Law Enforcement Assistance Administration) and to increasingly blur the boundaries of law enforcement and the community—bringing local communities into the governmental fold in a way that reinforced the perception that crime was external to both government and the social order of community life. That such endeavors were not largely successful—due in no small part to the resistance of law enforcement agencies—did not slow the proliferation of these community-based experiments during the late 1960s and early 1970s.

The US liberal state at this time combined its ever-expanding coercive branches with an accelerated reallocation of governance in and through civil society. The escalation of policing and military capacities in tandem with the diffusion of social and political regulation closely aligned governance with order maintenance as a prerequisite for freedom. On the one hand, liberal hegemony required that unreconstructed political opposition to the state appear irresponsible, violent, and criminal, so as to justify state coercion as a reasonable way of securing the social order apparently required by freedom. On the other hand, the dispersal of policing throughout civil society—the mobilization of community—reflected a manifestly liberal approach to governance that aimed to defuse the overt confrontation between law enforcement and unruly populations by making self-policing a form of citizen participation and community power. As in the Chicago Area Project juvenile delinquency programs, the idea was that revitalizing the community as a site of social management would achieve both neighborhood self-esteem and effective law enforcement.

During the mid-1960s, so-called police-community relations projects emerged as a growing trend in metropolitan law enforcement. Prompted by rising public expectations regarding due process and police accountability, the Supreme Court issued a series of historic decisions limiting police practices. In 1968, the National Advisory Commission on Civil Disorders identified the "deep hostility between police and ghetto communities as a primary cause of the disorders." It recommended that routine police operations be altered to "ensure proper individual conduct and to eliminate abrasive procedures," and that researchers conduct more studies of policing that emphasized the significance of police-community cooperation.[135] By the time of the commission, many police departments had added sensitivity and conflict management training, expanded their outreach programs for schoolchildren, established "ride along" programs to give residents a view of police work from the perspective of police officers, and decentralized police presence using neighborhood storefront outposts.[136] Although the majority of such initiatives were criticized as cosmetic policies that produced little substantive change, some appeared to have greater potential. Project PACE (Police and Community Enterprise) in San Francisco, for instance, was a relatively well-received program.[137]

The Office of Economic Opportunity was interested in this trend toward community involvement. In August 1968, the OEO announced that it would sponsor a Pilot Police Project, to be conducted by the Metropolitan Police Department, in Washington, D.C. The proposal focused on establishing an elected citizens' board to monitor police activities, making local communities responsible for certain non–law enforcement functions that had been performed by the police, and improving police services through in-service training. More broadly, the project was intended to improve the department's public image following the April 1968 riots, and to ease tensions between the police and residents in the city's third police district, made up mostly of African Americans.[138] Before Resurrection City had been demolished by the police, Abernathy had written OEO's Acting Director Bertrand Harding to protest the project. Abernathy noted that even if the project sprang from "noble motivations," it deliberately undermined the mandate for "the people of poverty in a community to participate in the determination of their own program needs and their own program priorities."[139] The original proposal had also included efforts to improve police intelligence sources in the target area, but this goal was dropped as a result of resident protest. Similar pressure succeeded in shifting the project's objectives from an emphasis on improved services to a focus on community control over the police and the project itself.

When local community members finally succeeded in establishing a broadly representative and influential board of directors for the project, the white officers in the Metropolitan Police Department largely abandoned it. Officers complained that it had become a platform for black militants and that the community refused to accommodate a law enforcement perspective on police work.[140] For them, police participation was predicated on the idea that the project would be an opportunity for the residents of the third district to empathize with the police and begin to police themselves according to the department's dictates. Marion Barry, then leader of a neighborhood organization called Pride Inc. and a future mayor of Washington, was among the most outspoken opponents to this interpretation of the project. He had moved to Washington in the summer of 1965 to launch SNCC's first experiment in urban organizing. Once there, he became convinced that SNCC had to change its organizing approach, noting: "We had to shift locally to be relevant. To be in Washington talking about voting in Mississippi was irrelevant when we weren't able to vote here."[141] Complementing his grass-roots Free D.C. Movement for home rule in the disenfranchised nation's capital, with its majority black population, Barry insisted that OEO funds should build community power, not police power.[142]

Participation as a normative prescript was not unique to the OEO during the 1960s. The political scientists Gabriel Almond and Sidney Verba devoted a chapter of their influential 1963 study, *The Civic Culture*, to "Competence, Participation, and Political Allegiance." They defined "competence" in terms of attitudes and behavior considered to be compatible with participation. Various degrees of civic competence corresponded to different forms of participation, and the one they lauded the most combined competence with a favorable orientation toward the existing political system. Conversely, they argued that negative attitudes toward the system were indications of a lack of, or inadequate, civic competence. Political allegiance was thus a prerequisite for participation. Such allegiance was linked to political stability on the one hand, and citizen satisfaction on the other hand.[143] This premise was deeply ingrained in the operative logic of federal initiatives such as the Community Action Program. Movements such as welfare rights and the Poor People's Campaign not only forced into relief and called into question the premise of allegiance but also suggested that participation might have to take the form of disruption and conflict.

My purpose in moving from a discussion of the Office of Economic Opportunity and the Community Action Program to an account of the Poor People's Campaign is not to suggest a progression from counterfeit to genuine participation of the poor. As commentators have shown in painful detail, the Poor People's Campaign suffered endless internecine battles and sharp divisions among a leadership composed entirely of men, who did not hesitate to speak in place of local community leaders, many of whom were women.[144] Moreover, as head of the SCLC, Abernathy often invoked the voice of the poor while maneuvering throughout the campaign to secure his own position as its spokesman. But the very heterogeneity of the campaign and the multivalence of the demands that petitioners presented meant that there could be no single spokesman or representative. What the Poor People's Campaign did was to unequivocally disaggregate "the poor" as a single governmental category and defy the state-sanctioned parameters of political participation.

Participation demonstrated extraordinary rhetorical elasticity, but it was nevertheless constrained by the everyday arena of political contestation. Maneuvers by the state to use participation as a mechanism to defuse and contain dissent were in turn shaped by social movements' attempts to use the state's legitimation strategy for increased leverage. The specter of collective violence was ever present. Over the course of the 1960s, increasing restrictions in OEO policy regarding the participation of the poor were repeatedly justified by allegations of violence and irresponsibility on the part of poor people. The Poor People's Campaign inverted these allegations, instead pointing to the violence perpetrated by the US state in both its actions and negligence toward the US poor and in its colonial war against peasant revolutionaries in Vietnam. In effect, the campaign affirmed a fundamental but tacit link between liberalism and militarism. It challenged what it believed to be the uneven and egregious deployment of the US state's monopoly on violence in the name of the liberal ideals of autonomy, sovereignty, and freedom. The state's demand that the poor and dispossessed speak was, therefore, inextricably linked to the interplay between freedom, order, and military force.

Martin Luther King Jr., in one of his last appearances on a university campus, associated the question of violence with the problem of participation and poverty in a potentially new way. Speaking at Ohio Northern University, King proclaimed: "In condemning violence it would be an act of irresponsibility not to be as strong in condemning the conditions of our society that cause people to feel so angry that they have no alternative but to engage in riots. What we must see is that a riot is the language of the unheard."[145] As King made clear in his condemnation of violence as a tool for political and social transformation, such a "language of the unheard" should not be read as an affirmative response to Spivak's question "Can the subaltern speak?" Instead it brings us back to her claim that an imperial project is always already present in the directive that the oppressed must speak. What is made evident by this injunction is the force through which signification and self-determination were foreclosed at the very moment when the subaltern subject was putatively recognized. The violence of this foreclosure occurred precisely in the manner in which subjection was extended through the subaltern as speaking subject, making the claim to be a forum for the subaltern voice essential for the legitimacy of liberal governance. The "language of the unheard" marked the brutality of silencing, while the call to speak effaced this same violence.

The 1960s urban riots approximated the illicit double of community participation. For some, these violent uprisings were evidence of the excesses of poor people's participation. For others, they were a symptom of the failure to institute substantive participation. The OEO articulated perhaps the most conciliatory version of this latter position. From this perspective, the demand that the dispossessed speak assumed a heuristic or tutelary tone and aimed at the production of responsible, competent, and compliant leaders formed in the image of those who called on the voice of the poor. For the Johnson administration to sustain its investment in the disciplinary capacity of participation, a threshold of acceptable trade-offs could not be breached.

Nevertheless, it would be a mistake to underestimate the significance of the OEO's mandate of maximum feasible participation. Although fraught with the exigencies of the historical moment, this turn of policy was remarkable for the possible confrontations and outcomes that it facilitated in excess of its normative logic. As Piven and Cloward acknowledged in outlining their crisis strategy, prospects for the politics of disruption were historically contingent and were predicated on the ambivalent rationalities articulated by the liberalism of a particular period.[146] The War on Poverty was intended to shore up the liberal dimension of democracy in the United States—guaranteeing the acquisitive disposition of poor people and positioning the democratic process as the political extension of market competition. The potential volatility of community action and the promise of democracy nevertheless continued to frustrate the enclosures of electoral formalism and the dictates of liberal order. OEO mandates for participation presumed a relatively unproblematic notion of local community, focusing instead on how to attach local belonging to national allegiance. But, as the next chapter explores at length, the substance and value of community remained mutable and contested in ways that both utilized and exceeded the conventions of liberal governance.

CHAPTER FOUR

THE SURPLUS OF INCLUSION
Poverty, Pluralism, and the Politics of Community

On January 7, 1964, the day before President Lyndon Johnson's auspicious declaration of an "unconditional war on poverty in America," twenty-nine mine workers from eastern Kentucky arrived in Washington, D.C. The delegation had arranged three days of meetings with members of Congress and other government officials to request emergency federal aid for the rapidly increasing number of miners left destitute by mechanization in the coal industry and dubious changes in union medical coverage.[1] George Reedy, one of Johnson's aides, assured them of the administration's concern for their difficulties and, according to one member of the delegation, "suggested that we go back home and organize so as to be in a better position to assist the Government's efforts in the War on Poverty."[2] Two weeks after returning to Kentucky, the miners formed the Appalachian Committee for Full Employment (ACFE) with this objective in mind. Confronted by the stranglehold of local political elites and coal operators, the ACFE defined as its mission to "organize the unemployed ... without regard to color or creed ... to bring union jobs with honest pay back into the area ... to see to it that the 'War on Poverty' gets to the people who need it ... [and] to obtain local government that works for us instead of against us."[3] Everette Tharp, the new organization's secretary, later recalled: "Our efforts to set up community action committees to help the President's fight against poverty were met with threats and coercion by local police"—and rather than support ACFE initiatives, the local press attacked the organization, charging that communists were invading Kentucky.[4] Following the Economic Opportunity Act's passage in August, ACFE community action funding proposals were rejected by the Office of Economic Opportunity (OEO), and no support for the group was forthcoming from Washington.

Perhaps the group's association with the so-called roving picket strikes and reprisals against coal-industry despotism made it suspect from the perspective of OEO administrators, but the official explanation—that the ACFE was not a legally incorporated organization and was therefore ineligible for community action funding—was also plausible.[5] What is clear is that "community" as defined for the purposes of government-sponsored community action was never simply a question of affiliation or self-identification but was a matter of certain institutional norms and social forms. Community in this context was at least partially an instrument of disciplinary remediation and normative recognition. The Johnson administration's peculiar elision of any direct means of addressing economic inequalities through the OEO must be understood with respect to the rhetorical centrality it accorded community as a means to self-sufficiency.[6]

This chapter focuses on the politics and political logic of community at work in the War on Poverty. Confrontations over the meaning of participation discussed in the previous chapter were also disagreements over the form and function of community. For the OEO, the prospective value of community prompted a number of speculations, including: Who exactly were the legitimate communities of community action? Who were a community's bona fide leaders, responsible interlocutors, and genuine members? For whom was opportunity a valued catalyst, and who were merely fraudulent opportunists? Who was included as part of the community and what substantiated their belonging was rarely the same from the perspective of policymakers, the people for whom policy was made, and others with political and economic stakes in the local implementation of an antipoverty program. Policy in practice sanctioned new political formations—within certain parameters—with new capacities for engaging with the existing political establishment. This chapter thus considers both who was and was not recognized by the OEO as community and what the mechanisms of incorporation in the name of community facilitated beyond the aims of the Johnson administration. In other words, for those defined as a community, what did recognition enable beyond the authorized and officially anticipated terms of political inclusion? Touting the alleviation of poverty and the integration of all citizens into the so-called affluent society, liberal policymakers nevertheless proved incapable of engaging the entwined inequalities and racial, gendered, and class conditions of mid-twentieth-century capitalism.

Recognizing Opportunity

The electoral significance of newly urban African Americans for the Democratic Party notwithstanding, the Johnson administration was careful to emphasize the absence of racial preference and the provisions for opportunity across racial groups in the design of the Economic Opportunity Act. "The war on poverty was in no sense a help-the-blacks program," Adam Yarmolinsky, a key figure in the development of the Johnson administration's antipoverty legislation, later insisted: "Color it . . . Appalachian if you are going to color it anything at all."[7] Considered suspect by Southern Democrats for his involvement in the Pentagon's efforts to desegregate Southern military bases, Yarmolinsky's defensive remark simultaneously suggests that the antipoverty program principally aided poor whites and that, because its beneficiaries were white, racial politics were not a primary consideration in the design of the War on Poverty.[8] President Johnson's April 1964 photo op with the Fletcher family on their front porch in the eastern Kentucky mountains similarly broadcast the iconic value of the region and was an important part of the publicity campaign to pass the antipoverty bill.[9] Appalachia remained peripheral, however, to the investigations of the President's Task Force in the War against Poverty and to the content of the Economic Opportunity Act, which included an all-purpose section called "Special Assistance to Rural Families" that was concerned with the plight of small-scale farmers and migrant agricultural laborers but largely inattentive to the dynamics of the coal industry that had decimated central Appalachia.[10] Actual economic assistance in the region was presumably the proper domain of the Area Redevelopment Administration and, later, the Appalachian Regional Commission.[11] Yet the notions that the EOA was conceived in response to a national dilemma called poverty that transcended racial difference and that its centerpiece program acted through a universal social field called community were crucial to the political configuration of the War on Poverty.

This chapter studies three examples as a means of understanding the

During his Appalachian "Poverty Tour" to gain support for the proposed War on Poverty, President Lyndon B. Johnson at the home of the Fletcher family in Inez, Kentucky, April 1964.

PHOTOGRAPH BY CECIL STOUGHTON, COURTESY OF THE LYNDON B. JOHNSON LIBRARY, AUSTIN, TEXAS.

politics of community within and beyond the War on Poverty: disputes over antipoverty organizing in central Appalachia, the Puerto Rican Community Development Project (PRCDP) in New York City, and the Office of Navajo Economic Opportunity (ONEO) in the Navajo Nation. These examples are especially important for the ways in which they underscore local and national struggles to define and operationalize the terms of inclusion and exclusion, autonomy and interdependence, and compliance and challenge. They reveal how notions of race, ethnicity, culture, and colonial difference were at once articulated with and disarticulated from poverty and community in relation to the antipoverty program. Looking first at Appalachia not only allows us to take seriously Yarmolinsky's suggestion that we "color" the War on Poverty Appalachian, but also to consider how the region's entrenched conflicts ultimately overwhelmed both OEO and New Left community action. In contrast, the PRCDP was exemplary in its use of the antipoverty program as a crucible for establishing a new political constituency—a political identity and municipal base for New York Puerto Ricans that was autonomous from island-centered authority—and consolidating the mechanisms of interest group pluralism through the terms of ethnicity. Like the PRCDP, the ONEO successfully used OEO's sponsorship as a way of obtaining political recognition and relative autonomy—in the Navajo context, to reassert government-to-government relations between the Navajo Nation and the United States, and Navajo independence from Bureau of Indian Affairs oversight. But unlike the PRCDP, the ONEO had to navigate the tension between asserting tribal sovereignty and maintaining the historical treaty obligations of the US federal government. In each of these examples, community meant something different, with distinct normative configurations, while also serving to authenticate claims to recognition and being partially remade through the protocols of the antipoverty program. In each example, I look specifically at how the idea that poverty could serve as the binding force and legitimating source of group interest variously contributed to the dynamics of community action in practice.

From the perspective of the OEO, community action embodied a form of belonging that was intended to be simultaneously local and national. The Economic Opportunity Act emphasized what it termed a "commonality of interest" as providing the social cohesion through which community action was to be mobilized.[12] The utility of poverty as a collective interest was derived from liberal pluralism, which during this period served as the predominant policy lens (and social science framework) through which community was politically legible.[13] Liberal pluralism insinuated an abstract formal equivalence between groups that afforded room to maneuver for some, while placing others beyond the pale of recognition. Liberal pluralism also provided the conceptual order through which community, poverty, and racialized difference were aligned with palliative forms of opportunity and interest. In liberal pluralist terms, the political system was a balance of power among social and economic groups, with each group constraining and constrained by other groups. Competing interest groups, in this perspective, shared a common system of beliefs and values, which allowed conflict to proceed within established limits and encouraged disagreements to be resolved through compromise. According to the liberal pluralist model, government provides diverse interest groups with a supposedly disinterested arena for debate, mediation, and reconciliation. The notion of interest is itself decisive here. Michel Foucault, for instance, contends that the formation of modern governmental reason pluralizes interest into "a complex interplay between individual and collective interests, between social utility and economic profit, between the equilibrium of the market and the regime of public authorities, between basic rights and the independence of the governed."[14] Government thus ostensibly serves as a mechanism for arbitrating formally comparable and always competing interests.

The Johnson administration supplied local communities with administrative forms intended to secure local participation in mainstream political norms. The economic resources that were forthcoming from War on Poverty programs were not channeled toward a politics of redistribution, but rather were aimed at shoring up official political procedures. Antipoverty funds provided limited resources for building institutions recognizable within the conventions of government and for promoting the recognition of state power. Although recognition appears initially to be an appeal for acknowledgment and consideration made by those subordinated or illegible in relation to the state, in effect recognition also—even primarily—serves as a means of affirming the authority of the state.[15] The antipoverty program thus sought to defuse the most egregious and politically embarrassing effects of racism and to co-opt political radicalism. For a select few, antipoverty programs were a means toward political mobility and professional advancement as representatives or intermediaries for the poor. Funding made possible the development of a new class of local political leaders and nonprofessional social workers habituated to the routines of the political process. Moreover, even as antipoverty programs enhanced the potential political capacity of the poor, in effect these programs depoliticized poverty and the broader field of social action by strictly limiting this political capacity to the status of a constituency within established electoral politics. Community was, in this sense, a means of acquiring the skills necessary to identify and pursue collective interests, and to participate in the prevailing political and economic system.

For the Office of Economic Opportunity, the quest for community initiated a relentless production and management of boundaries, the most literal of which were the various community corporation zones and economic opportunity council areas consolidated through board member elections. The legislation treated community as a homogeneous, intrinsic, and —for the most part—spatially delimited social group. Policymakers often assumed that territorially defined groups in the United States were in fact racially or ethnically defined groups—that, in effect, the segregated spatial logic of uneven development assembled groups of people with a common heritage and shared interests. A byproduct of this process, sometimes used by the OEO to its managerial advantage, was the ethnic or racial competition precipitated by such elections and community jurisdictions. Bertram Beck, the director of Mobilization for Youth, went so far as to argue that "the great sell out of the antipoverty program was the invention of these elections of community corporations," which he contended ended up "with groups of poor people fighting one another over an inadequate paltry sum of money that can do nothing."[16] Although these conflicts at times undermined the authority of the OEO, they were also integral to establishing a putative boundary between representative and fraudulent—and, by extension, authentic and inauthentic, responsible and irresponsible—community leadership. Confrontations in Appalachia over the control and orientation of community action programs, for instance, convey the relentless policing of belonging, the racial and class politics of place, and the failure of the OEO to address the structural reciprocities of economic and political inequality in the region.

Identifying Outside Agitators

Since the Second World War, coal industry automation and strip mining had resulted in ever-increasing mass unemployment and environmental devastation in central Appalachia.[17] These circumstances were compounded by the covert decision of the United Mine Workers of America (UMWA) to join forces with the Bituminous Coal Operators' Association against both rank-and-file miners and small-scale coal operators. The UMWA actively backed industrywide mechanization as the only way to keep coal competitive with other fuel sources. In eastern Kentucky, however, the partnership between the mine owners and the union neither forced independent operators out nor helped the union regain control over the region's labor market. Instead, these measures led to the proliferation of small, nonunion mining operations, with whom the Southern Coal Producers' Association sided during contract negotiations in 1958. These tensions led to a protracted and acrimonious general strike the following year, after which the UMWA bowed to intervention by the National Labor Relations Board and virtually abandoned the Kentucky miners.[18]

Central Appalachian mine workers increasingly had to fend for themselves. In 1960, the UMWA canceled its medical coverage for all miners who had been unemployed for more than a year or who were working in a nonunion mine, even if all their preceding employment had been with union operations. Two years later, the UMWA closed ten union hospitals in the region and withdrew hospital coverage for workers at companies that had not paid their royalty to the union of forty cents per ton of coal. Deprived of even the most rudimentary provision for their survival, mine workers throughout eastern Kentucky, joined by unemployed miners and their families, went on strike without union authorization. Strikers known as roving pickets moved from one mine to another, seeking to close down nonunion and royalty-delinquent operations. Violence between the picketers, coal operators' security forces, and the police intensified. *Time* did its best to frame the brutal conflict not as class war but as the struggle of "the desperate . . . against a permanent fact of life"—another unfortunate example of the mountaineers' backwardness.[19] Rather than portraying the unemployed miners as part of an indefatigable rank-and-file movement for labor rights or a people under economic siege, journalists depicted them as "yesterday's people," stubbornly mired in a culture of poverty.[20] Nonetheless, the roving picketers remained unwilling to concede their dispossession as an inevitable "fact of life" and sought to make the situation equally intolerable for those who saw them as expendable, a mere social surplus.

Local political fiefdoms and patronage networks were intimately aligned with coal industry preponderance in Appalachia. "Broad form" deeds—rights sold to underground mineral resources during the early twentieth century—were treated by local judges as giving coal companies carte blanche to devastate the land and water above designated coal deposits with no obligations to landowners and tenants. The callousness of the absentee coal owners and local courthouse duplicity were accompanied by the flagrant corruption of county politics, where control over federal revenue—especially money for education, welfare, and public works projects—was a primary means to power. School superintendents, for instance, not only controlled the hiring of teachers and staff, but they could easily hijack funds intended for school lunch programs, school bus transportation, and basic supplies. People given work by welfare programs, such as the unemployed fathers assembled into so-called Happy Pappy work crews to perform such menial tasks as roadside weeding or cleaning old cemeteries, were frequently used instead to provide services for the county elite. Even when not used for personal favors, the people in the program received only a dollar per hour (less than minimum wage), and the program did nothing to equip them with marketable skills.

Faced with hostile and intractable regional power brokers, the striking miners sought allies outside Appalachia. In February 1963, the labor organizers Stanley Aronowitz and Hamish Sinclair traveled to Hazard, Kentucky, to make a radio documentary on the roving pickets for WBAI, and the following summer they established the Committee for Miners (CFM) to provide financial and legal assistance to the picketers. The local politicians, coal operators, and police also sought help from outside, bringing in the FBI to help crush the picket movement. In June eight miners, including the picket leader Berman Gibson, were arrested and charged with conspiracy for allegedly planning to dynamite several bridges of the coal-transporting Louisville and Nashville Railroad Company. Roving picketers were subpoenaed to appear before the Perry County Grand Jury in October and were denounced in court as communists.[21] It was not until winter that the CFM could extend its efforts much beyond the immediate needs of the trial. Once the most serious charges failed to win convictions for the prosecution, Sinclair and Arthur Gorson arranged for speaking tours for Gibson, who met with college students and members of civil rights organizations and labor unions across the Northeast. As a result of these tours, a number of Students' Committees for Miners were established to help raise funds and generate publicity.[22] Neither the failed prosecution nor the initiatives in solidarity with the CFM diminished the ferocity of the confrontation between the miners and the coal industry and its allies. By the end of the year, with violence escalating and no resolution in sight, many roving picketers began to reassess their approach to the conflict and to consider ways to destabilize the political and economic compact underwriting the coal industry's intransigence. These were the miners who traveled to Washington and later formed the ACFE. As much as War on Poverty administrators may have wished otherwise, the political economy of poverty in Appalachia complicated their prescriptions for localized community self-help.[23]

The same month that Gibson and his compatriots were arrested on conspiracy charges, Students for a Democratic Society (SDS) sponsored a conference in Nyack, New York, on unemployment and social change that forecast the end of postwar economic growth and rising structural unemployment. Emphasizing the effects of automation, the conference working papers contended that "today unemployment is no longer confined to a few sick industries or underdeveloped areas."[24] Some SDS leaders wanted to redirect the organization's focus from campus to community and to develop a strategy analogous to the Student Nonviolent Coordinating Committee's local organizing in the South. By the fall, SDS had launched the Economic

Research and Action Project (ERAP) with funding from the United Auto Workers and had started several of its ten planned community-based initiatives.[25] Despite union financing, ERAP was premised on the notion that, in the context of increasing long-term joblessness, traditional shop-floor organizing had largely been supplanted by a need to appeal to the economically disenfranchised in the context of their everyday lives. In an influential series of articles in *Studies on the Left*, James O'Connor argued: "The focus of political activity [has shifted] from the work place to the neighborhood, the community, the region." At the same time, the political dispositions of community—the potential social orientation of poor "residential groups"—had also changed. According to O'Connor, "yesterday the residential group was 'intrinsically' conservative," but, under present conditions where working-class demands were community-based, "the residential group today is 'intrinsically' radical."[26] Community unions would bring together poor people in a neighborhood as an organized political force. Although they lacked certain strategic weapons available in the workplace (especially the threat of a labor strike), community organizers could use tactics such as picketing in front of welfare offices or outside the suburban homes of slumlords, rent strikes, and other forms of civil disobedience. Community unions became a defining feature of ERAP initiatives, the most successful of which were the Newark Community Union Project and Chicago's JOIN-Community Union.

The community union approach focused on poor people rather than the working class as primary historical agents in the opposition to capitalism. Todd Gitlin of the SDS argued that the poor "are less tied to the dominant values, . . . just as—and partly because—they are less central to the economy that creates, and expresses those values." In the most romanticized version of SDS discourse, the poor embodied by the very fact of their marginality a more authentic humanity uncorrupted by the modern forces of acquisitive individualism and compulsive consumerism. Gitlin urged "strengthen[ing] the poor as a source and reservoir of opposition to the final rationalization of the American system."[27] For SDS, the War on Poverty seemed an opportunity to use liberal policy for more radical ends. ERAP's director, Rennie Davis, suggested: "A 'strategy of insurgent response' begins by asking what is most worthwhile about Johnson's War on Poverty and in what ways we can encourage its better tendencies."[28] Tom Hayden and Carl Wittman explained: "We believe, of course, that nothing less than a wholly new organized political presence in the society is needed to break the problems of poverty and racism, but it must be a force which today explores for many of its allies within the liberal institutions."[29] Norm Fruchter and Robert Kramer of the Newark Community Union Project noted that "the project does not conceive of itself as a group within the pluralist network of city power," but is instead "committed to two kinds of change at once: the specific remedying of individual aggravating grievances, and basic structural changes which would replace the present systems of production, authority, and control with far more egalitarian and participatory institutions."[30] While SDS activists aspired to a fundamental political and social transformation of US society, they nonetheless—at least with ERAP—sought to achieve these ends by working within dominant institutions. From this perspective, much like that of the civil rights movement, desired change could be achieved by forcing these institutions to honor their self-proclaimed mandates and live up to the high-minded promise of American democratic equality.

ERAP's focus on community and poverty was also shaped by specific racial considerations that were distinct from liberal pluralist conceptions of race. Debates within the Student Nonviolent Coordinating Committee on the relationship between the civil rights movement and organizing poor whites contributed to the ways in which ERAP hoped to forge an "interracial movement of the poor."[31] Although many ERAP projects were organized in racially mixed areas, poor and unemployed miners in Appalachia seemed an ideal constituency for white organizers. In response to the ascendance of Barry Goldwater, George Wallace, and massive white resistance to civil rights more generally, the SDS organizer Richard Rothstein surmised that "ERAP's purpose grew out of concern that the objectives of the civil rights movement would be frustrated by working class white reaction. In part, therefore, our goal was to form organizations in white communities which could counter the backlash."[32] Carl Wittman, a principal organizer in ERAP's Chester, Pennsylvania, project, contended that "the shift of the movement away from an explicitly racial basis enhances the possibilities for the white student. The possibility of working in areas of high white unemployment makes the white student not secondary or supportive, but the catalyst of the movement."[33] Sinclair recollected that "Hazard was to be the Mississippi of the white unemployed because here there was already a movement, the militant 'roving pickets.' "[34] However, although the ACFE prioritized interracial organizing, it did not do this as a way to substantiate the existential needs of white student organizers.

For the ACFE, New Left organizers and student activists were not so much catalysts as a means of gaining national visibility and backing for their struggle. In March 1964, the ACFE, CFM, and SDS organized the Student-Miners Conference on Poverty and Unemployment. In its welcoming statement to the more than 150 conference attendees, the ACFE noted: "We do not believe that the conditions you see here today are the result of natural causes but stem from the desire of large corporate monopolies to preserve, for themselves, a one industry (coal) economy, to the destruction of all other natural resources." They warned that "such firms as the American Power Co., and the L&N Railroad Co., the absentee owners of large acreage of timber, coal, and other mineral resources, as well as the oil and gas corporations have a strong influence upon Congress . . . [and because of this], Congress is reluctant to enact a program that will satisfy President Johnson's declaration that he has launched a 'War on Poverty.' " In opposition to this pernicious influence, the ACFE asked for assistance in fulfilling the mandate of Johnson's declaration. As they defined it, prerequisites for a "true war on poverty" would be cheap electricity, federal legislation against strip mining, a program of reforestation and soil conservation, "the strict enforcement of our civil liberties," and reasserting "the right to organize and bargain collectively."[35] Based on the conference, SDS decided to commit ERAP resources and to work in conjunction with the ACFE and CFM in Hazard.[36] In spite of the enthusiastic reception at the conference, however, only a handful of students returned to Kentucky to work with the ACFE during the following summer. Local law enforcement was quick to express their enmity toward the students, arresting two on blatantly fabricated charges soon after their arrival. This harassment and intimidation was ongoing, while incidents such as rifle fire aimed at the ACFE office and the home of its vice president went uninvestigated.[37]

The ACFE's funding application to the OEO also encountered obstacles. The scope of the proposal was straightforward enough. It outlined the creation of five community centers in each county of eastern Kentucky, which would serve as community organizing and social service clearinghouses. Each center would include a medical clinic and offer short-term day care, remedial and adult education services, and recreation facilities. Each center would be staffed by a community organizer, secretary, program adviser, driver (to provide transportation for local residents to and from the center), pediatric nurse, field nurse, and custodial employees. The centers would publicize information on available federal and state assistance programs, as well as serve as a place for community meetings. Also proposed were long-range plans for jobs programs (with wages "the same as the scale for each trade under their union contract elsewhere in the nation") dedicated to building roads, waterworks and sewer construction, school construction, and local food and handicraft cooperatives. The ACFE explained that the primary objective was "to involve all the unemployed, the poverty stricken, the people in the hollows and creeks—through the community organizing centers—to develop the programs that they need." Included with the proposal was a petition signed by more than three hundred Perry County residents endorsing the project. Without commenting on the merits of the proposal, the OEO rejected it on the basis that the ACFE was not legally incorporated and recommended that the ACFE instead work with local officials.[38]

Based on this advice, the ACFE sought sponsorship of its OEO application from the Upper Kentucky River Area Development Council. In November 1964, members of the ACFE attended a council meeting on the antipoverty program to present their proposal and request the council's support. Tom Gish, a local newspaper editor, observed: "All the well known faces are there—the county agricultural agents, public welfare workers, health department workers, school board workers, a few ministers, a batch of poverty experts from the University of Kentucky extension center at Quicksand, state experts, etc.—and the vastly outnumbered handful of private citizens." Gish also described "a small group of 'outsiders' totally foreign to the usual group that attends such meetings. A group that one suspects may be the only true experts on poverty present." The council appeared unreceptive to the ACFE but allowed the group to present its proposal. After Everette Tharp had summarized its OEO application, an African American member of the ACFE spoke about the deplorable conditions of the Appalachian poor. Citing a personal example that countered charges of dependency and affirmed government responsibility, she declared: "It is just not right . . . for a mother to raise up her sons and see them taken away to war and then not be able even to see a doctor when she is going to have another child." According to Gish, there was an "almost visible tension between the two groups represented—one group in a sense representing the Eastern Kentucky power structure, the other representing the unemployed."[39] Although the council was ultimately willing to have the proposal submitted under its aegis, the application was once again rejected by the OEO, which remained unconvinced of the ACFE's feasibility as community organizers and local interlocutors.

However, it was not only the federal government that did not see the ACFE as representative of community in the anticipated sense. CFM and ERAP efforts were short-lived. Sinclair complained that the miners' failure was due in part to their misguided internalization of autocratic trade union organizing style. He later reflected: "I think the two years work was not a success, in terms of the aims we had—to develop a constituency for a left politics."[40] According to Sinclair, in the final analysis, the roving picket movement and the ACFE "had not yet developed an actual program and had only rudimentary political instincts."[41] Appalachia might have appeared to promise white activists a way out of their racial quandary with respect to the civil rights movement, but, as Sinclair put it, "when your own white people don't react to your organizing efforts, there is no escape to paternalistic [or] emotional reason, there is only politics and that is more subtle and more demanding."[42] Unable to make the miners conform to the political role that the CFM and ERAP had defined for them, the CFM disbanded and ERAP focused its efforts elsewhere.

The ACFE was, of course, one of many Appalachian groups hoping to solicit OEO support. The Appalachian Volunteers (AVs) are the most well known of these initiatives. In comparison with the ACFE, the AVs initially appeared markedly less threatening to business as usual in the region. One AV recruit, apparently concerned that locals might confuse the two organizations, contacted the AV main office for guidance on how best to deal with the "supposedly communistic" ACFE.[43] The Council of the Southern Mountains, an organization begun by missionaries in 1912, established the AVs in 1963. The group was subsequently funded as a demonstration project by the OEO and worked closely with the OEO's VISTA (Volunteers in Service to America) program. It won wide-spread accolades for its recruitment of college students to refurbish one-room schools during their summer vacation, but came under attack as its attention gradually shifted to the political and economic conditions of which the deteriorating schools were a symptom. In contrast, the Council of the Southern Mountains favored a partnership model of community work that made use of existing institutions and did not disturb the region's prevailing power dynamics.

Much as Mobilization for Youth came up against the conservative reformism of the Lower Eastside Neighborhood Association and the Henry Street settlement, disagreement between the AVs and the council led to their separation in May 1966. Changes in volunteer demographics compounded the effect of the AVs' split from the council. The number of volunteers grew from 150 in 1965—with a roughly equal number from the region and from outside—to more than 500 in 1966, the majority of whom were not from Appalachia. Perhaps to offset these changes, the AVs created positions for community interns and assembled advisory community councils to increase the number of poor people directly involved in their organization. The AVs' tactics also became increasingly confrontational. They began to focus on issues such as welfare rights, strip mining, black lung disease, and education, as well as developing craft cooperatives and community newspapers. In an effort to challenge control of community action by county elites and unresponsive administrators, the AVs organized people's committees of local poor people and staged electoral takeovers of community action programs. For instance, with the assistance of one people's committee, the AVs replaced the ineffective director of the Raleigh County Community Action Association with Gibbs Kinderman, a member of the AVs.[44] The OEO continued to fund the AVs following their split from the council, while also sponsoring many of the community action programs that had become targets for AV takeovers. Support from Harry Caudill, a member of the council's board and author of *Night Comes to the Cumberlands*, and admiring evaluations of the AVs by Robert Coles, a Harvard University psychiatrist and well-known author, helped secure continued OEO funding.[45]

The tactics of the AVs brought up once more the ever-present and highly contested question of who could rightfully claim to be agents of community action in the region, and toward what end. Writing to the national office, the director of the OEO in Kentucky explained: "Our chief aim ... is to unite the entire community—the rich[,] the just well-to-do[,] and the poor—*to work together against poverty*." He insisted that "any and all volunteers are, of course, needed and welcome in helping make our communities whole, and thus winning the War on Poverty. But they must do this under a unified command, or else they are a serious liability rather than a valuable resource." Not only were the AVs apparently indifferent to the imperative for united community action—making communities "whole"—but, the director complained, "to have some other group, funded by OEO and working in the community *against* OEO-CAP is simply unbelievable and most certainly unworkable."[46] Joe Mulloy, one of the AVs, later observed that, rather than help secure consensus and unitary purpose, "the Appalachian Volunteers and the VISTAs weren't beholden to anybody locally . . . [W]e were outsiders completely. And weren't part of the local power structure or part of the courthouse gangs . . . so [we] weren't cutting deals, and weren't back slapping." Yet Mulloy also pointed out: "I was a local person . . . [because] I was a native Kentuckian." This identity, however, was relative and easily shifted. According to Mulloy, "I was identified and promoted by the Council of Southern Mountains and the AVs as a local person. Once I got on the staff and stopped being a volunteer . . . I became something else."[47] And to be considered "something else" had potentially severe consequences.

Violence frequently awaited anyone who jeopardized the nepotistic status quo in the region. Sue Ella Easterling Kobak, an AV originally from Pike County, Kentucky, recalled later: "Every county in East Kentucky was controlled by a very small group. And when they started perceiving a challenge, their immediate reaction was to figure out ways to . . . threaten the people and push them back into kind of not questioning the power structure. And I think that we [AVs] were used [as an example] to . . . make people afraid to question the power structure." Kobak remembered sustained harassment by local police, as well as having her house shot at and destroyed by arson.[48] Roslea Johnson, an AV who went on to work for the multicounty Kentucky River Foothills Development Council, recounted similar incidents. She had gone to Powell County well aware of the widespread violence in the area, but she had believed that "they probably wouldn't harm a woman [at] least without some kind of warning." However, of the low-income people she persuaded to join the council's board of directors, Johnson noted: "all five of them were killed. Died under mysterious circumstances that were not investigated . . . I feel sure that . . . the reason for their deaths was because of their involvement in the War on Poverty programs. It was just too much of a threat to the power structure there."[49]

County elites utilized legal as well as illegal means for intimidation. Robert Holcomb, president of both the Pikeville Chamber of Commerce and the Independent Coal Operators Association, was among those who orchestrated the arrest of Joe Mulloy and three others on sedition charges in

1967. The indictment by the Pike County Grand Jury for conspiring in "a well organized and well financed effort" to promote "the violent and forceful overthrow" of the Pike County government was brought shortly after the high-profile confrontation between a local farmer, Jink Ray—allied with Mulloy and the Appalachian Group to Save the Land and People—and a Puritan Coal Company strip-mining bulldozer had involved Governor Edward Breathitt.[50] The incident prompted Breathitt to suspend and then revoke the company's mining permit and stop the demolition of Ray's land. Thomas Ratliff, an attorney; Holcomb; and others sought vengeance for the disruption of local business as usual and for bringing national scrutiny to the situation. They targeted Mulloy and others as communist-influenced outside agitators.[51] Although the charges were eventually ruled inadmissible, this approach proved a successful way to publicly undermine local support for the AVs. Moreover, the sedition trial provided the groundwork for establishing the Kentucky Un-American Activities Committee and staging the committee's 1968 show trials against the AVs, which contributed to the group's demise.[52]

Even as Appalachian county elites managed to stave off the incursions of those they deemed outsiders, chronic unemployment compelled increasing numbers of able-bodied local people to leave for cities such as Columbus, Cleveland, and Chicago. The steady procession of hearings and official findings on Appalachian poverty—including the President's National Advisory Commission on Rural Poverty 1967 report *The People Left Behind* and the Senate hearings chaired by Robert F. Kennedy on rural poverty and hunger in 1968—did little more than reiterate the region's dire conditions. OEO planners remained divided as to whether the rural poor should be encouraged to start their own self-help programs in the countryside or simply be incorporated into existing urban programs after relocating to more economically prosperous areas. Appalachian migrants to Chicago once again encountered SDS's ERAP in the form of JOIN-Community Union.[53] Many central Appalachians became involved in JOIN and, with other poor people in the Uptown neighborhood, as discussed briefly in the opening pages of the introduction, eventually took over the project and expelled the student organizers.

In central Appalachia, open class war did little to foster the modes of incorporation that liberal policy aimed to achieve. Highlighting the situation of poor whites as evidence of poverty's nonracial character—poverty as a social problem not linked to race in any specific way—may have been sufficient in Johnson's campaign to win support for the EOA. But when white poverty revealed the complexity of racialized capitalist social relations, it could no longer be used to conceal racism. The predicaments of poor whites in central Appalachia foregrounded the ways in which race was differentiated along axes of class, gender, place, heritage, education, employment, and other forms of social status and power. Rather than convey the colorblind character of the War on Poverty, the Appalachian poor threatened to call attention to the presumption of white privilege—in other words, how could it be that these people are poor, when as white people they should be able to access racial entitlement? Because they ultimately failed to fulfill white racial norms, they became especially undeserving in the eyes of policymakers and their prospects were inescapably bleak.[54]

Other analytic models for theorizing the whiteness of the Appalachian poor remained similarly entangled in the problem of how to address the context of racial difference. Critics who used the analogy to colonialism as a way to understand Appalachian poverty—an increasingly common formulation by the late 1960s—encountered a parallel problem.[55] What began as a description of the region's exploitation by absentee owners was analyzed in C. Vann Woodward's classic study of the South as a colonial economy and later elaborated on by some scholars to suggest that all aspects of Appalachian inequality could be traced to its status as an internal colony.[56]

The colonial analogy, however, was particularly incapable of conceptualizing race in the Appalachian context and tended to render all inequality as uniformly symptomatic of external domination. Indeed, whites in the region were themselves primarily the descendants of settler colonists who had moved westward and dispossessed indigenous inhabitants. In the case of Appalachians who relocated to the Midwest and Northeast in search of employment, whiteness had other precise local configurations. In metropolitan areas outside of Appalachia, migrants became, among other things, white "ethnics." But the ethnic specification of whiteness conveyed situation-specific social hierarchies of its own—hierarchies that might appear exclusively in class terms, but that in fact indicate the racial and ethnic nuance of economic relations. In New York City, negotiations between the making of a Puerto Rican ethnic identity and US colonialism, as well as the significance of poverty for community, assumed a decidedly different form.

Conforming Community

In November 1966, following a contentious meeting with prominent New York Puerto Ricans at Gracie Mansion, Mayor John Lindsay agreed to cancel a conference his administration was organizing with the Puerto Rican government on the social and economic problems of Puerto Ricans in the city. Since taking office at the beginning of the year, Lindsay had been severely criticized by civic and political leaders for not involving the city's Puerto Ricans in policy decisions. In January 1967, Lindsay announced plans for a new conference featuring local Puerto Rican leaders. When asked about the change of plans, the city's highest-ranking Puerto Rican elected official, Bronx Borough President Herman Badillo, said: "I suppose there was a time when most of the civic leadership for Puerto Ricans in New York had come from the island, but I am pleased to see that the Lindsay administration has come to realize that the local community has come of age and is quite prepared to handle its own affairs."[57]

Indeed, the War on Poverty was decisive in the shift toward New York–based Puerto Rican political power underscored by Badillo.[58] Nevertheless, it is important to note the ways in which Badillo's comments both paralleled and departed from the political connotation of community evident on the national scale. For the Johnson administration, the problem of local community was not an issue of any particular locality per se, but rather the institution and ordering of the national polity itself. Johnson's social policy was thus aimed at shoring up the authority of the federal government by establishing its presence in local communities. For Badillo, the political goal was Puerto Rican metropolitan power (and through that, his personal political career). The availability of federal antipoverty funds facilitated a move toward increased Puerto Rican political influence in New York City and worked in tandem with an emerging mainland Puerto Rican identity distinct from the previously dominant island-oriented identification.

In April 1967, the Lindsay administration sponsored a conference called Puerto Ricans Confront Problems of the Complex Urban Society. It was coordinated by Marte Valle, a Puerto Rican social worker recently appointed by Lindsay as assistant deputy director of community relations in the city's Human Resources Administration.[59] After the All-City Band had performed "The Star-Spangled Banner" and "La Borinqueña," the anthem of

Manuel Díaz Jr.—Puerto Rican Forum board member, former community outreach director for Mobilization for Youth and Puerto Rican Community Development Project executive director—at a project picnic, circa 1966. PHOTOGRAPH BY AND COURTESY OF FRANK ESPADA.

the Commonwealth of Puerto Rico, and Herman Badillo had given the keynote address, distinguished New York Puerto Rican leaders presented papers on topics including education, housing, community development, civil rights, economic development, and "Puerto Rico's Cultural Legacy to New York." Among those speaking was Manuel Díaz Jr., a Puerto Rican Forum board member (a discussion of the forum follows below) and former community outreach director for Mobilization for Youth. Díaz had chaired the forum committee that proposed and planned the Puerto Rican Community Development Project and had served for almost a year as the project's executive director. In 1966, he had become the first Northeast regional director of the Equal Employment Opportunity Commission.

Díaz cautioned against the self-evidence of "community." His comments emphasized community formation as a process of consolidation while foregrounding the centrality of conflict and disagreement: "To have seven hundred thousand Puerto Ricans in NYC, however, does not per se make a community. A community has to develop a self-awareness and a self-identification. It has to have a common heritage or interest. It needs the bond of language; but the real test of a complete community is the degree to which it can express its cultural strengths, define its problems, and confront relevant social and economic issues." Ethnicity did not therefore guarantee community. Díaz also warned: "We . . . need to learn that public officials, just because they are Puerto Ricans, do not necessarily serve the community well unless held to their responsibilities." He recognized that the antipoverty program served as the principal means through which to garner the federal support necessary for community organization, but he also envisioned an expanded influence for Puerto Rican institutions in the City: "Puerto Ricans and their institutions must be directed at issues and actions which will help decide the nature, design and implementation not just of welfare services, but of the nature and design of New York City as a commercial and industrial complex . . . It means, in short, that we have a role to play in the *total* life of the city—*not just on the ethnic issues.*"[60] The institutionalization of New York City Puerto Rican political power thus required moving beyond the localized focus of past Puerto Rican organizational and political efforts. It required the ethnic community to be a citywide force that both sustained and surpassed its particularities.

The conditions for changes in the municipal authority and mainland identity of Puerto Ricans began to take shape after the Jones Act conferred US citizenship on Puerto Ricans in 1917 and prompted large-scale migration from the island. Fleeing the impoverished conditions of colonial rule and the island's sugar oligarchy, a majority of migrants settled in New York City where there was a growing demand for semi-industrial labor. By the early 1920s, Puerto Ricans had established an enduring presence in East Harlem and South Brooklyn. Migrants arriving in the city could look to hometown associations, labor organizations, and political clubs for support and social networks.[61] In 1948, Puerto Rico's Department of Labor established its Migration Division as an integral counterpart to the island's industrialization program, Operation Bootstrap. The Migration Division served until the late 1950s as the main advocate for Puerto Ricans in New York City to non–Puerto Rican political and economic institutions.[62] Between 1948 and 1965, the industrial export-oriented economy rapidly expanded in Puerto Rico, while migration to the mainland contributed to decreasing both the size of the labor force and unemployment.[63] Net migration from Puerto Rico to the mainland reached its peak in 1953, when more than seventy thousand migrants arrived in the continental United States— just after the Popular Democratic Party had succeeded in changing the island's political status from an unincorporated territory to a free association state. Throughout the 1950s, the organization and authority of mainland Puerto Rican institutions advanced rapidly. Although these institutions did not eclipse island-based ones, or diminish the migrants' general sense of belonging to both the island and the mainland, many of these institutions did insist on the specificity of the Puerto Rican mainland urban predicament as well as diasporic Puerto Ricans' right to define and pursue their own agenda.

During the late 1950s and early 1960s, the role of the Migration Division as the official representative and arbiter for the Puerto Rican community came under increasing attack by an ascendant faction of young New York– based Puerto Rican professionals. The Puerto Rican Forum, one of the most influential of these new organizations, was established in 1954 with funding from private foundations. The forum initially concentrated on fostering a mainland Puerto Rican professional class and developing initiatives for small businesses and entrepreneurs. Aspira, an education-oriented leadership development program, was perhaps the forum's most prominent endeavor. By the early 1960s, this focus on leadership training segued into broader concerns over bilingual education and the dire economic conditions common among the approximately 750,000 Puerto Ricans living in New York City.[64]

On the island, the Popular Democratic Party, which had been the political force behind the island's rapid economic growth, unraveled between 1964 and the early 1970s. As noted in chapter 1, industrialization and migration to the US mainland, which the party had sponsored, as well as the unpopularity of urban resettlement programs in the early and mid-1960s, contributed to the erosion of the party's traditional base and made the rural orientation of its populism seem outdated. After Governor Luis Muñoz Marín left office in 1964, the party experienced debilitating internal conflicts, and suffered a momentous electoral defeat in 1968.

It was in the context of the party's decline that mainland organizations such as the Puerto Rican Forum were able to seize the political initiative. Josephine Nieves, a leader of the forum, recalled: "We began to see that the government of Puerto Rico . . . was not permitting new leadership. The Commonwealth . . . wanted to be the broker, the spokespeople, and the leaders [sic] . . . They were talking about how we were not really poor, and we were talking about how poor we really were."[65] For Nieves and other members of the forum, the "commonality of interest" made possible by programs for impoverished Puerto Ricans was a way to reject the commonwealth's paternalism and to promote local leadership. A former antipoverty program director from the predominantly Puerto Rican section of Williamsburg, Brooklyn, reflected: "The poverty program helped the Puerto Rican community organize itself. It was through politics that you got what you wanted. I saw it as a program to educate the community. I never thought the poverty program would stay forever. You had to use it right away before it would disappear . . . Most of us had to work all day and didn't have time to organize the community. The poverty program gave us that time."[66] This fleeting opportunity did indeed prove decisive in many ways, and it is therefore essential to understand the extent to which the notion of community was itself transformed by these processes of organization and education—in other words, how community was rendered as a "commonality of interest" by antipoverty initiatives.

The Puerto Rican Community Development Project (PRCDP) was the first federally sponsored citywide antipoverty program for New York Puerto Ricans.[67] Although other federally funded programs, such as the Real Great Society, were subsequently organized by Puerto Ricans in New York, none matched the scale or influence of the PRCDP. During the fall of 1963, the Puerto Rican Forum created a committee chaired by Manuel Díaz Jr. to investigate possibilities for establishing a youth project based on the Mobilization for Youth model—this was prior to MFY's mid-decade foray into the politics of disruption—and extending the activities of the forum's own community development unit. Antonia Pantoja—director of the forum's leadership education project, Aspira, and a member of the committee— argued that strengthening family cohesion and emphasizing cultural heritage must be central to any effort to alleviate poverty and mobilize mainland Puerto Ricans for collective social action.

In 1964, the Puerto Rican Forum submitted a proposal to the OEO to establish the PRCDP. The proposal focused on ethnic identification as a unifying force leading toward collective self-help and community formation. A section titled "Rationale for a Culturally Based Project" stressed:

"The way to motivate and prepare young Puerto Ricans to contribute services effectively and provide leadership for their own group is by affirming and strengthening their ethnic identification." Moreover, the proposal asserted that the difficulties Puerto Ricans regularly encountered with social services agencies "derive from cultural differences as reported by the agencies themselves." Puerto Ricans in New York were dispersed throughout the city's voting districts, in comparison with other ethnic or racial groups. As a result they lacked the capacity to elect local officials and had only limited access to political representation. The PRCDP would take the form of an umbrella organization, not only coordinating a number of distinct programs (including job training, family services, drug addiction prevention and rehabilitation, preschools, leadership development, and consumer education) but also coordinating the activities of neighborhood organizations in order to develop a citywide Puerto Rican cultural identity and political constituency.

The forum's proposal clearly showed that Puerto Ricans were not immigrants in the traditional sense, but it nonetheless argued that the historical formation of ethnic communities were a model to emulate. Thus, the proposal asked: "How can the social and emotional survival of persons with distinct cultural traits be assured within the democratic American tradition that recognizes the right of individuals and of groups to be different? How can their eventual integration into the larger society be assured? The traditional answer of all immigrant groups has been the immigrant community."[68] Careful to distinguish integration from assimilation, the forum promoted cultural pluralism as a way to achieve collective uplift, and to consolidate and promote group interest.

The middle-class professionalism of the forum quickly provoked hostility from grass-roots Puerto Rican community organizers. One of the first initiatives of the PRCDP was to conduct leadership workshops. These sessions were not well received. A typical response was: "Who the hell is the Forum to come into the community to give us training—to prepare us to deal with our problems?"[69] Puerto Ricans who had been engaged in organizing around local cultural and political concerns, often for many years but without the professional credentials recognized by forum leaders, were to be paternalistically brought under the wing of forum tutelage. Speaking critically of the forum's influence, Joseph Erazo, a PRCDP Board member, explained: "We don't want a minority of professional planners controlling the board ... The antipoverty act is concerned with how to strengthen so-called grassroots organizations ... We want the advice of professional planners but control will remain with the community leaders on the board."[70] Alfredo Lopez, a writer and activist, criticized the forum's antipoverty strategy, stating: "They are people whose aspirations never question the basis of this system but only the fact that Puerto Ricans aren't allowed a piece of the pie."[71] The forum was interested in poverty at least partly as a means to consolidate access to this "piece of the pie" and provide upward mobility for mainland Puerto Rican professionals.

The forum's professional-managerial class orientation, its efforts to control the PRCDP's Board of Directors, and its tendency to disregard PRCDP staff autonomy periodically erupted into vituperative stand-offs between the two groups and frequently hindered PRCDP operations. An important source for tracking these internecine battles was a 1967 evaluation conducted by New York City's Community Development Administration (CDA). The evaluation cataloged numerous problems with the PRCDP and its board and noted: "While the Board represents a geographical cross section of the Puerto Rican community, it does not include 1/3 representation of the poor as required by [the] OEO." This same lack of representation of the poor was evident in all PRCDP committees.[72]

The CDA evaluation was far from disinterested, given that the CDA was the city's conduit for federal antipoverty grants to local community action programs. The mayor's office and the Human Resources Administration, of which the CDA was a subsidiary, tended to insist on the "one-third representation of the poor" to gain leverage in the federal-to-community funding continuum. In this manner, municipal authority could intervene as a purportedly objective superintendent of local programs. At the same time, the OEO subjected the CDA to external audits and evaluations much as the CDA scrutinized the affairs of the local projects to which it distributed funds.[73] Local community served as an indispensable source of legitimation and authority, but this authority could be realized only through individuals claiming to be representative of local community and the poor. The forum-dominated PRCDP Board of Directors, PRCDP staff, and municipal politicians—and, it should be noted, the federal government—thus each claimed legitimacy by professing to speak in the interests of the poor, for which community became a synecdoche.

The PRCDP's Block Organization Program became the crux of claims that the project actually served poor Puerto Ricans. The block program demonstrated that the poor were something other than rhetorical figures for the PRCDP's claim on federal funding. The program provided neighborhood services by contracting with small, local Puerto Rican organizations throughout the city to provide access to job referrals, welfare, and housing advocacy services. Target areas were selected on the basis of having at least "50% housing dilapidation and deterioration and 30% or more Puerto Rican population."[74] Many of the contracted organizations were hometown clubs; others included church programs and neighborhood centers. During the first six months of its operation, the block program received more than two hundred applications for contracts, of which slightly less than half were approved. By September 1967, the program staff included a director, seven community coordinators, and ninety-nine block workers (also referred to as community workers). Statistics provided in PRCDP annual reports and program evaluations show increasing activity over the course of at least the first three years of the program's existence.[75]

Block workers were hired by the contract agencies with funds from the PRCDP. The workers were based in the neighborhood contract agencies' offices but were also supervised by community coordinators, who worked from the PRCDP's central office. Through the PRCDP the workers received training, including classes on community organization at the New School for Social Research. In the field, their duties included ongoing outreach to neighborhood residents; organizing collective meetings in response to needs identified by residents; facilitating access to public and private resources and services; and providing technical assistance, such as writing funding proposals, arranging for consultations with specialists, and managing project budgets and drafting reports.

The function of the block worker was in keeping with the tradition of community development after the Second World War.[76] A guidebook distributed to new block workers conveyed the centrality of their role, stating: "The primary organizing catalyst is the block worker." They were instructed that the block program "offers the poor and indigenous persons of an area an opportunity for mutual and individual self-help. Such an approach will demonstrate to neighborhood residents that by collective action involving neighbors within their own blocks, real, desired, and visible changes can be wrought in their everyday conditions." Although they were to serve as catalysts for neighborhood-level social change, the guidebook cautioned: "The program will emanate from the neighborhood, and develop in accordance with residents' needs, interests, aspirations, fears, successes and failures."[77]

In practice, the daily operation of the block program was hindered in several important ways. To begin with, as noted by the CDA evaluation, many of the contract agencies' offices had little visible presence in the neighborhood, and only a limited number of the agencies actively publicized their services. Second, the proficiency and orientation of the PRCDP's seven community coordinators varied substantially. The CDA evaluation observed: "As the link between the PRCDP and the contract agencies they fulfill a most crucial and pivotal role in the agency and structure."[78] But the inconsistent performance of coordinator duties often jeopardized this essential link. Among the coordinators there was a "range from those who take over the block workers and use them for their own community action activities to those who rarely visit their agencies."[79] According to the CDA, the block organization director "seems dedicated and has rapport with the contract agencies" but was unable to exert control over the coordinators because they were politically appointments of the PRCDP Board of Directors.[80] Thus, the legitimating connection to the local community remained central to the project as a whole, even if it was often inoperative in practice.

These conflicts revealed a split between neighborhood program implementation and PRCDP decision making. Local projects were supported by the PRCDP, but they had little effect on the direction of the PRCDP itself. Block workers were structurally positioned outside the organizational core of the PRCDP, and their subordinate position was reinforced by the arbitrary actions or inaction of coordinators. The Block Organization Program attracted neighborhood participation through the services it provided and the local organizing it facilitated. However, without reciprocal influence on the PRCDP as a whole, local activities were not so much atomized as they were rendered contingent on the priorities of the larger organization in the competition for municipal political power and resources. The primacy of the citywide organization reinforced the sense of a single community of interest united by ethnic identity.

This unified community of interest did not diminish the valorization and, in certain respects, accentuation of the neighborhood groups of which the overall community was comprised. While serving as the PRCDP's executive director, Manuel Díaz explained: "My basic commitment . . . is to strengthen this community and I feel I can do it better by supporting [neighborhood] organizations and helping them to develop and get resources and establish themselves on a par with community organizations of other ethnic groups."[81] In fact, Díaz's focus on coordinated localization was not unlike the methods of the Migration Division, which closely aligned itself with the voluntary work of hometown associations. The Migration Division may have encouraged an island-affiliated orientation, but—focused as it was on facilitating adjustment in the mainland—in practice it supported the organization of a close-knit, semi-autonomous Puerto Rican community in New York. The locus of authority may have remained in Puerto Rico, but its purview was tremendously dispersed. In this sense, individual groups in fact had more autonomy under the Migration Division than under the PRCDP. What distinguished the PRDCP, as Díaz noted, was the functional integration of neighborhood-based community organizations into a citywide form of ethnic community.

As a result of the federal antipoverty policy and funding during the decade after 1964, particularistic identifications, such as those embodied in hometown associations, gave way to a more comprehensive identification as mainland Puerto Ricans. Although the institutions established during this period facilitated some mainland Puerto Rican occupational upward mobility, the more significant outcome was a sense of Puerto Rican ethnicity. Thus, over the course of the 1960s, a collective ethnic identification emerged that promoted interethnic competition for available resources.[82] Such competition reinforced urban regime politics without fundamentally challenging the racial and ethnic terms of uneven development.

The antipoverty programs coincided with significant growth of the Puerto Rican, African American, and Afro-Caribbean immigrant populations in New York City. In the conventional logic of electoral politics, this numerical increase represented a potential gain in political clout. However, racially overdetermined uneven development, compounded by a declining manufacturing sector, left many blacks and Puerto Ricans without a secure source of income or in direct competition with each other for low-wage work. An emerging professional class among both blacks and Puerto Ricans sought to use increased population and the War on Poverty to gain political power in a manner that glossed over internal differences within each group, while accentuating divisions between blacks and Puerto Ricans. Thus, the Puerto Rican Forum's 1964 study emphasized through extensive empirical data, directly compared to statistics on black poverty, that Puerto Ricans were *the* poorest group in the city. The scholars William Sales and Rod Bush have argued: "Black and Latino competition . . . reinforces the status quo in which the largest segment of both populations is consigned to the margins of the social economy . . . [T]he logic of competition is driven by the narrow class needs of the middle class as a class 'for itself.' "[83] At the same time, the cross-racial alliances that did exist and were built by grass-roots activists were regularly disregarded by the press in favor of sensationalized narratives of competition.[84] During the 1960s, this logic of competition for political resources required articulating community in terms of poverty and localization as a requisite strategy of legitimation, as was evident in the case of the PRCDP.

What is important in this regard is not just that Puerto Rican ethnic identity was partially crafted from the political form of the War on Poverty and made possible a break with the authority of island-based governance. This severing and compartmentalization of political identity also served to obscure the possible role of US colonialism in the making of race and ethnicity. Likewise, it effaced the material conditions of what activist groups such as the Young Lords would term the Puerto Rican "divided nation" and limited the scope of political contestation. Social and cultural difference in the rubric of ethnic pluralism was normalized as an interchangeable form of equivalence requiring liberal administration. Liberal government endeavored to be seen as the disinterested arbiter of formally comparable interest groups, which competed for power and resources within the established terms of government.

In 1970, Nathan Glazer and Daniel Patrick Moynihan reflected on the persistence of poverty among Puerto Ricans in New York City and concluded that "Puerto Ricans have to struggle between a conception of themselves as 'colonized' and, therefore, 'exploited,' and a conception of themselves as 'immigrants.' The first leads to bitterness, the second to hope."[85] Ethnicity as a category of social belonging was closely associated with the immigrant narrative. Conceptions of ethnicity in the US context potentially underwrote a version of pluralism that obscured the particularities and relational dynamics of inequality.[86] With ethnic succession as the conventional template, the fact that African Americans, Puerto Ricans, Mexican Americans, Asian Americans, and American Indians experienced distinct forms of dispossession and exclusion that were quite different from the historical experience of Jewish, Irish, or Italian immigrants could be minimized. The slippage between race and ethnicity allowed for a historical narrative that simultaneously championed American pluralism and rendered inequality as the failing of the dispossessed and excluded. According to the historian Nikhil Pal Singh, the term "ethnicity" emerged in response to a particular problem: "In a country supposedly marked by unprecedented diversity and universal tolerance, it was an acute, unresolved question as to whether people of color could be folded into what was cast as a revolutionary drama of ethnic succession in which immigrants became . . . 'Americans all.' " Ethnicity thus provided "a type of intranational difference *different* from 'race,' the kind of difference, in other words, that supplements the national narrative of tolerance, inclusion, and global promise without disturbing it."[87] Nonetheless, there remained a paradox between ethnicity's foreign origins and its defining intranational character. It was necessary for this nation of nations to be domesticated and—at least partially—disengaged from its multiple trajectories of belonging in order to substantiate claims to a uniquely American pluralist society.

During the 1960s, it was precisely ethnicity's redeployment within the framework of nationalism by African Americans, Chicanos, Puerto Ricans, and Asian Americans that reasserted modes of belonging apart from the US nation-state and challenged the premise of integrationist pluralism. Michael Omi and Howard Winant have argued that "many blacks (and, later, many Latinos, Indians, and Asian Americans as well) rejected *ethnic* identity in favor of a more radical *racial* identity which demanded group rights and recognition." Omi and Winant further suggest but do not substantively elaborate on the argument that "despite the wide range of specific approaches, nation-based theory is fundamentally rooted in the dynamics of *colonialism*."[88] The assertion of self-determination and specific historical and material differences between groups threatened to depose the US state as the disinterested arbiter of multiple and equivalent constituents. Nevertheless, as will be evident in the Diné (Navajo) use of OEO funding, initiatives to affirm national status and cultural sovereignty through local antipoverty programs could also target the dynamics of colonialism in ways that did not appear to undermine the liberal pluralist model.

Nations Indivisible

In May 1964, the American Indian Capital Conference on Poverty convened in Washington, D.C., to lobby for Indian inclusion in programs to be funded by the Economic Opportunity Act (EOA), which the Johnson administration was then in the midst of drafting. With few exceptions, Congress had not included American Indians as beneficiaries of legislation aimed at the national population. Federal appropriations for Indian programs were historically the purview of the Bureau of Indian Affairs (BIA). Nevertheless, statistics showed that Native Americans were the most impoverished people in the United States, and Indian lobbying persuaded Sargent Shriver and the other members of the President's Task Force in the War against Poverty to recommend the inclusion of tribal groups in the EOA funding guidelines. Shriver agreed to accept Community Action Program proposals for pilot demonstration programs from sixteen tribes. The OEO was thus the first federal agency to grant funds directly to local programs designed by tribal members.[89]

The Navajo Tribal Council was one of the first tribal governments to take advantage of this development in federal Indian policy and apply for funds to the OEO. The largest tribe in the United States, during the mid-1960s the Navajo Nation comprised nearly 25 percent of the total American Indian population, with approximately 105,000 tribal members living on a reservation of almost twenty-five thousand square miles (a size equivalent to West Virginia) spanning Arizona, Utah, and New Mexico. At the time of the OEO application, the median income on the reservation (including public assistance contributions) was $1,900 for a family of 5.4, as compared to the national average of $7,700 for a family of 2.8.[90] The federal government awarded the Tribal Council an initial grant of $920,000 to establish the Office of Navajo Economic Opportunity (ONEO) in 1965. By the end of 1967, the ONEO included programs on local community development, home improvement training, alcoholism treatment, migrant and agricultural placement and assistance, and recreation and physical fitness, as well as a local branch of Head Start, a Navajo cultural center, legal services, a Neighborhood Youth Corps, and a small business development center.[91] The OEO also funded the Lukachukai Navaho Demonstration School in 1965, which—after an initial conflict between BIA teaching staff and OEO-sponsored Diné groups—was reorganized under OEO-Diné control as the Rough Rock Demonstration School.[92]

The Local Community Development Program (LCDP), as its name suggests, provides significant evidence of the ways in which the ONEO sought to capitalize on the OEO emphasis on community. The Tribal Council's original proposal for the LCDP appeared closely aligned in form, function, and rhetoric to the postwar community development model. The program would aim to overcome apathy and isolation through the collective work of community problem solving. The council's proposal explained: "The Community Development Program is intended to develop a feeling of hopefulness in the isolated communities which cover the Navajo reservation. This feeling of hopefulness is to be realized through the process of a community uniting, identifying, and solving its own problems." Working together would instill a sense of purpose and agency: "One of the greatest needs existing today on the Navajo Reservation lies in creating a feeling that the people in the isolated areas are important and that they do have an important role in determining their own future and destiny." But most of all, in order to persevere, the plans and projects of the LCDP had to provide a sense of autonomy and ownership for participants: "Community Development principles conclusively demonstrate that for a program to be maximally successful and enduring, it must come from within and be accepted by the community."[93] Success, from the standpoint of the LCDP, was not to be measured by reductions in material inequalities but by the inner transformation and increased feeling of self-worth achieved by participants. In contrast to claims made by welfare rights activists, participants were encouraged not to apply for public assistance and instead to develop self-help strategies. For example, one LCDP account described "a family in the Tuba City Chapter which has been receiving Welfare Assistance for several years and has become totally dependent upon it," but who, with encouragement and resources from the LCDP, were able to build their own home and move toward self-sufficiency.[94] Although reiterating the most conservative version of assisted self-help, LCDP narratives such as this were also intended to convey the prospect of an independent Navajo Nation with legitimate claims on federal subsidies.

Similar to the way in which the División de Educación de la Comunidad (Division of Community Education), as discussed in chapter 1, built on the Puerto Rican schools of the 1920s, the development of the LCDP was closely tied to the chapter organization of the Navajo Nation. Chapters were local political units with elected officials that operated through monthly or bimonthly community meetings and submitted recommendations on local and reservation-wide issues to the Tribal Council. The idea of the chapter system was modeled on the New England town meeting and was introduced in 1927 by John G. Hunter, BIA Superintendent of the Leupp Agency on the Navajo Nation. The anthropologist Aubrey Williams observes that, unlike the Tribal Council, whose structure and procedure were set by the US government, "local groups were allowed to use their traditional way of selecting leaders for the chapters, and decisions made by a chapter were to be enforced only by Navajos within their traditional patterns of maintaining social and political control." Moreover, Williams observes that as Navajos established chapters of their own volition, the US government strongly advised its agents "to remain in the background and to adopt the role of a guest at meetings rather than that of a political supervisor."[95] By 1934, there were more than sixty chapters across the reservation. In fact, chapters proved such an effective forum for local political organization that their role in Diné resistance to the Indian Reorganization Act and the BIA's program for livestock reduction prompted the federal government to officially withdraw support for them in that year. More than half of the existing chapters continued to meet regularly until 1955, when the Tribal Council passed a resolution to institutionalize and revitalize the chapter system.[96]

Before the sixteenth-century Spanish conquest, the Navajo tribe had maintained no centralized authority. The Diné shared a common language, customs, beliefs, and territory. Matrilineal kinship networks, cosmology, and a ceremonial system united the society. In her study of Navajo governance, the anthropologist Mary Shepardson argued: "Navajo authority was ultimately validated by the myths and by an appeal to Old Navajo Ways . . . [It] was personal, personally defined in particular situations; a Navajo owed loyalty to persons rather than to the community or the tribe as an abstract idea."[97] Such authority was based on respect and consent, rather than obligation or hierarchy. Shepardson notes:

> Early white observers described the Navajo authority system as "anarchy." Authority, however, was never completely diffuse, nor was it appropriated at random. The locus of authority was in the various functional groups, the biological family, the extended family[,] . . . the local group, the raiding party, the hunting party, and the ceremonial gathering. In so far as the authority for decision-making control in these groups was ultimate, that is, subject to no higher authority, it was political. The highest authority lay in the agreement achieved within the group after matters had been "talked over."[98]

Even after the brutal US military campaign against the Navajos in the mid-nineteenth century and the vicious conditions of their incarceration at the Bosque Redondo prison camp between 1864 and 1868 had decimated the tribe's population, the structure of Diné authority remained dispersed and based on consensus. Only in 1968, during the centennial year of the Bosque Redondo experience and the Treaty of 1868, would the official Navajo narrative proclaim a "Century of Progress" and ascribe to these events the making of the Diné as a modern nation.[99]

The primacy of autonomy and decentralized political authority for the Diné posed certain problems for US colonial management, but it was the imperatives of capitalism and legal contract that prompted political intervention. The consolidation of Navajo political representation was precipitated by the discovery of oil near Shiprock, New Mexico, in 1921. As a number of oil conglomerates scrambled to secure leases in order to proceed with surveying and drilling, there was contention both within the Diné and the BIA as to whether the San Juan Navajo, who lived in the area where the oil was found, should have control over the oil leases and profits, or whether these more properly belonged to the tribe as a whole. Acting Indian Commissioner E. B. Meritt drafted regulations in 1923 to establish a Navajo Tribal Council "in order to promote better administration of the affairs of the Navajo Tribe of Indians in conformity to law."[100] This early incarnation of the Tribal Council operated almost entirely at the discretion of the commissioner of the Navajo Tribe, who was appointed by the secretary of the interior.

Across Indian Country the role of the tribal council was transformed with BIA Commissioner John Collier's 1934 Indian Reorganization Act, which aimed at promoting traditional cultural practices and recognizing Indian tribes as political entities. Even as the act advocated what it called "re-tribalization," it sought to reproduce within Indian reservations the institutions and values of Euro-American capitalist society. It shifted Indian policy from an emphasis on individual acculturation to a program for community incorporation by supporting the development of dominant political and economic institutions in the reservation context. The act promoted representative government, market-oriented economic organization, and corporate associational models.[101] Although the Navajo Tribal Council was not established by the act, it was not altogether dissimilar from those tribal governments that were. At the same time, ironically, federal recognition of

Navajo community meeting, Torreon, New Mexico, circa mid-1950s. PHOTOGRAPH BY THEODORE
B. HETZEL, COURTESY OF THE THEODORE HETZEL PHOTOGRAPH COLLECTION, CENTER OF SOUTHWEST
STUDIES, FORT LEWIS COLLEGE, DURANGO, COLORADO.

tribes as political entities and the consolidation of tribal political authority
provided the Diné with a federally acknowledged institutional forum for
contesting other Collier-era programs, such as the reviled plan for livestock
reduction. This contestation, however, was partial—the Navajo Tribal
Council itself established livestock quotas in 1952 based largely on the BIA
plan.[102] OEO-sponsored community action produced similar tensions between recognition and self-determination.

Between 1950 and 1958, the Navajo Nation launched a series of preliminary community development projects in Round Rock, Arizona, followed
by others in Low Mountain, Arizona. The Low Mountain venture was
successful enough to attract visitors from the United Nations and the Ford
Foundation. In proposing the LCDP to the OEO, the Tribal Council cited
these earlier projects as evidence that community development initiatives
were both feasible and successful. The council used calculated language to
report to the OEO that "not all of the reaction was favorable. Vested interest
groups were not impressed with an uneducated and heretofore dependent

community beginning to do things for themselves and beginning to succeed and throw off the shackles of dependency." Efforts to expand and institutionalize these projects had proven financially implausible. The council's application observed that an already existing community development division of the tribal government, assigned to work closely with chapter officers, had been rendered inoperable due to lack of funding.[103]

With OEO sponsorship, the Tribal Council argued, the LCDP would be able to build on the lessons of these earlier endeavors and use community development workers as catalysts for community-based self-help projects. Noting that previous efforts had failed to develop local leadership to carry on projects after the departure of community workers, the council proposed staffing the local projects with community development aides who would be Navajos from the chapter area and who would serve with an exceptional "faith in and knowledge of their own people."[104] Aides were to be recruited from the poor. But since 96 percent of Navajos living on the reservation at the time earned an annual income of less than $3,000, this meant that almost everyone qualified.[105] OEO money would be used to hire and train both the community development workers (specialists) and aides (local residents), and to support their activities. Again using community development idiom, the Tribal Council pledged: "The emphasis throughout the program will be on the process rather than the projects." In this respect, "the community development worker would not tell the people what they ought to do or how they ought to act. Rather he would work quietly with the people using his skills to get the Navajo to identify their problems and select their programs."[106]

Once in operation, the LCDP coordinated its activities through the ninety-seven chapter organizations within the Tuba City, Fort Defiance, Chinle, Shiprock, and Crownpoint Diné subagencies. In each locality, one or two community development aides were selected by area residents under the aegis of the chapter organization. Aides were supervised and given support by community development specialists, many of whom were not Diné but who qualified for the position as a result of higher education (some had a master's degree, and others had completed at least two years of college-level course work in community organization). Eventually, an effort was made to promote aides, so that by the end of 1966, LCDP Director Leo Haven, himself Diné, could claim that "one third of the present specialists were promoted to that position from the ranks of the aides."[107] Vice President Hubert Humphrey, Sargent Shriver, and community development professionals from Africa and Asia were among the many early visitors to the reservation to observe the ONEO's 98 percent Navajo staff in action.[108]

Limited funds and staff affected program operations. There were approximately five aides for every specialist. Because of the great distance between chapter communities and dilapidated, unpaved reservation roads, this ratio meant that the specialists were often unable to maintain close contact with or provide support for the aides. Aides themselves spent most of their time traveling from home to home, interviewing and reaching out to families. A 1967 LCDP OEO grant application notes: "Transportation is expensive for the Community Development Aides . . . [In addition to the high cost of gasoline, aides] need a vehicle for transportation on their job. They have old vehicles that are constantly breaking down because of the rough roads."[109] An OEO evaluation adds: "Telephone service is often not available, and communication must be maintained by travel."[110] Indeed, the LCDP spent most of its OEO funding on salaries and transportation costs, leaving very little with which to directly finance local projects initiated by the chapter Community Action Committees (CACS).

By the end of 1966, all ninety-seven Navajo chapters had selected an aide, and most had established CACs of six to sixteen members, which met regularly in conjunction with the aide to plan and administer projects. Charley Long—a community development aide from Thoreau, New Mexico—described the function of the CAC in the following way:

> The CAC is like a team . . . they talk together, pull at the same time; they don't break the string; they go even; they discuss things in an even way; they make it balance, just the right balance; they don't make one side low, one side high, they make it balance. This is what we call Economic Opportunity, to fix things right, to make it balance right . . . We are trying to pull the poor ones to the top and make it even[,] balanced.[111]

Another aide, at a meeting in Fort Wingate, New Mexico, explained: "The chapter house is your kiva [a traditional sacred chamber for ceremonies and collective deliberation], you talk about things in your kiva room, in your chapter house there is a discussion and the community action committee talks in your kiva."[112] Consequently, OEO community self-help ideology seemed to harmonize with Diné consensus building and the traditional emphasis on cooperation.

OEO imperatives and Diné values, however, were not in fact so well aligned. As transcriptions of numerous meetings in 1969 throughout the Navajo Nation indicate, more than three years after the ONEO's launch, local representatives were still working to translate the terms of the OEO program language in a way that was both comprehensible and appealing to people living on the reservation. Noting that since the Diné "emerged from Kit Carson's concentration camp at Fort Sumner, New Mexico, a hundred years ago, the Navajo mistrusts the white man and patronizing government, imposing its values and culture upon him," an OEO evaluation observed: "The self-determination aspects of the community action program were—and still are, to some extent—unbelievable to him."[113] The evaluation's critical synopsis of US colonialism is striking, even as its objective remained Navajo participation in what it presumed was a more enlightened context of administration.[114]

An OEO-sponsored Indian Community Action Center publication also offers evidence of the OEO's self-critique necessary for the premise of self-determination. To an extent, the perpetual research and evaluation embedded into the OEO administration performed this same function at a structural level, putting potential criticism into the service of the OEO itself and protecting OEO programs from hostile federal legislators. In this case, the written comments of a community development specialist during an action center training session provide one of the most incisive—albeit ambivalent—critiques of the LCDP. Reflecting on community development doctrine, the specialist asked: "Under the conditions that exist on the reservation, is it practical . . . that we are interested in *process* and not project?"[115] He extended this question to the premise of the LCDP itself, observing:

> At this point my CD [community development] aides and, I guess, myself, seem to be at a loss as to how to stimulate the people to continue in our idea of community development—process instead of project emphasis. We seem to be in a slump in our area. At first, when we started, we were told that it would be important to talk with the people, to visit them, and, in the survey questionnaires, to help them talk about their problems. But now the surveys and visits are completed, and most of the Community Action Committees are formed, and, to tell the truth, we are facing the question "where do we go from here?" The aides and I understand what we should be emphasizing, but the people need, and are only interested in getting, projects accomplished.[116]

With the inexorable deprivations of poverty unassuaged, it was difficult to get people to respond to calls for inner transformation and democratic participation. Acknowledging this, the specialist nonetheless rationalized that perhaps the underlying philosophy of community development would gradually become apparent to at least a few participants, and concluded, "isn't this better than nothing?"[117] But clearly participation was motivated by the concrete benefits that the LCDP offered, rather than the intangible principle of process.

The LCDP did manage to provide support for local initiatives and to help link local projects to a variety of government and tribal sources capable of providing funding and other forms of assistance.[118] It produced tangible, if modest, results that directly benefited local groups and individuals. It was also closely tied to other ONEO components, such as the Home Improvement Training Program, which not only offered instruction in carpentry and masonry but also furnished building supplies. By the end of 1967, almost three thousand housing units had been built or repaired through this program.[119] Addressing a meeting in Fort Wingate, New Mexico, a speaker from the program emphasized that participating in it provided technical skills and could also function indirectly as a way to learn applied mathematics: "If you learn you can build your own home . . . You learn every measurement on your ruler, every number . . . just like you learn [when] you are going to school . . . In school maybe you just have to read about it, but that don't [sic] help you much."[120] Occasionally the ostensible benefits of the program would be challenged. During one chapter meeting, a Red Rock, New Mexico, resident asked whether after trainees have completed instruction, "will there be a job for them anywhere, where can they work on houses?"[121]

Nevertheless, ONEO programs did provide jobs and income. The LCDP compensated participants in the Community Action Committees. Members of the committees were often promoted to chapter officer positions.[122] The income and mobility that the LCDP provided for the aides was significant. An OEO evaluation commented: "Because of the extreme poverty, community development aide salaries put aides in upper-income brackets, wielding influence far greater than that of non-pros in urban programs (10 have been forced to resign because they became candidates for the Tribal Council)."[123]

These benefits, however, were overshadowed in the end by the essential purpose of community action on the reservation, which was to break the paternalistic stranglehold of the BIA. For the Diné, the ONEO was a demonstration of the viability of direct federal funding used at the tribe's own discretion for projects of its own design. The LCDP supplied material benefits with the capacity to recruit local support for what was an attempt to demonstrate tribal self-determination. One speaker remarked at a meeting in Fort Wingate: "We told the [OEO] Washington, DC that we Navajo can do it [ourselves] ... [W]e can run the OEO money ... So now we are running it the way we want."[124] LCDP efforts to build community were in the service of this broader goal.[125]

The ONEO motto *nááś 'ooldah* (forward together) thus suggested both the unification of the tribe through the harmony and cooperation of its communities, and a political equality between the Navajo Nation and the United States that nonetheless maintained federal support for Diné economic development. When ONEO's programs began, its leadership constituted another base for power in reservation politics. Heated conflicts between ONEO Executive Director Peter MacDonald, Tribal Chairman Raymond Nakai, and the Tribal Council's Advisory Committee were evidence of this changing political dynamic. However, this new force in tribal politics was also a conservative influence that channeled local activity into coordinated governmental and administrative networks. As an institution created by the Tribal Council, the ONEO was not politically incompatible with its progenitor. The council's early conflicts with the ONEO's Legal Services program and MacDonald's successful campaign for tribal chairman in 1970 were both in different ways evidence of this. The Tribal Council thus bequeathed to the ONEO a political form that it was already in certain ways predisposed to function in particular ways. "Like its white father, the U.S. Congress," Leslie Marmon Silko argues, "the tribal council form of government offers easy access to influence peddlers but fails to protect the local people most affected by its decisions."[126] Both the Tribal Council and the ONEO recognized, and were recognized by, the US state, while also transfiguring internal Diné political dynamics. As in the case of New York Puerto Ricans working to establish their autonomy from Puerto Rico, Diné uses of OEO funding reimagined the local in relation to the national. But in the Diné case, this funding also reasserted the integrity of the (Navajo) nation with respect to the United States.

The LCDP thus resonated with a familiar conception of local community in the service of nation building. A 1963 United Nations report on *Community Development and National Development* spelled out the terms of this broader agenda. The report argued: "Community development programmes aim at helping people to break the barriers of isolation and exclusion to serve the dual purpose of contributing to the achievement of national goals and of benefiting from the technical resources of government to which they are justly entitled." While emphasizing the importance of taking into account the particular circumstances of local communities, the report affirmed: "The basic point to be kept in mind is that community development makes use of and even creates those units of local action which seem most appropriate to the objective of linking people in with the national framework so that they can handle the additional and ever-expanding goals that modern life demands of them."[127] The substance of nation building for the Navajos, of course, was not the same as it was for the US government, not least because of the protracted circumstances of colonialism. Navajo community action may have trafficked in the same form and rhetoric, but Diné self-sufficiency and autonomy conveyed something far in excess of crafting individuals in the modern liberal sense. In fact, they communicated a mode of independent nationhood that recognized the necessity of claiming certain colonial debts as well as sovereign rights. But from the perspective of the OEO, perhaps unable to fully comprehend the stakes of tribal sovereignty, the terms of independence used by the Navajo and other native nations appeared to be a pluralist form of incorporation. Even with these fundamental discrepancies in mind, nation building required a normative and homogenizing imperative for the production and policing of boundaries.

While explaining the value of the OEO, the unidentified speaker at Fort Wingate quoted above tellingly juxtaposed Navajos and other American Indian nations with programs funded by the War on Poverty with African Americans. He asserted that the OEO "is not just for the Navajo people, but it is for all Nations in the United States. The OEO is trying to level up its people in the United States. The lowest income, they are going to build them as much as they can and I think . . . what the Negro people are fighting about is revolution . . . but revolution is a different problem."[128] Whether the statement represented a rejection of the predominant logic of revolution at the time—which, as María Josefina Saldaña-Portillo argues, relied on a developmentalist teleology that designated indigenous peoples as "traditional," "premodern," and awaiting progress[129]—or indifference to the insurgent transformation of US society from within, it insisted on the Diné context as appreciably dissimilar. The ONEO was not revolutionary, but a response to a very specific colonial predicament. In his 1962 epic account of the Southwest, the anthropologist Edward H. Spicer observed: "Anglo-American policy may be characterized generally as having moved from an indifference to Indian internal affairs to an intensive concern with them."[130] The political rationality of community in the ONEO was a way to externalize this intensive governance in the name of tribal self-determination.

Making Inequality Equivalent

The Puerto Rican Community Development Project and the Office of Navajo Economic Opportunity closely followed the procedural edicts of the Office of Economic Opportunity, even as each used the form and function of community action to attain distinct objectives. Federal legislation linking community and poverty as the object of policy resulted in the subordination of some differences and the accentuation of others in order for those named as a community to claim political power, recognition, and, to a limited extent, economic resources. In the case of both the PRCDP and the ONEO, a constitutive link between poverty and community—a link that obfuscated internal differences and inequalities—served as a requisite legitimating claim on political authority. The focus on local community served to consolidate a broader political entity, a distinctive imagined community with its own political horizon. Each program in its own way was animated by an understanding that community control did not diminish the systemic effect of the wider economic and political context. However, neither program promoted fundamental interventions into the political economy of US postwar capitalism or the modes of liberal governance. Instead, they sought to use this dominant logic in the service of their own agendas. This accomodationist strategy occasionally threatened to transgress the parameters of liberal governance, but more often than not the most visible conflicts were the result of competing interests or factional struggles that replicated the normative ideologies of political pluralism.

Poverty served as the "commonality of interest" that bridged newly reconfigured forms of local community and the interests of national governance, and that provided the cause for decentralized governmental action, which operated in tandem with what the Johnson administration called creative federalism. Whether particular community program goals managed to alleviate poverty was, in the end, largely incidental. Racial and ethnic divisions and the amplification of conflict—as long as this conflict was channeled toward normative arenas of competition—served the ultimate goal of governance. Liberal pluralism circumscribed the heterogeneity and internal tensions of the populations it rendered as competing interest groups, just as it muddled forms of affiliation and antagonism that might challenge the overarching frame of conventional political institutions. At the same time, pluralism was used to secure new forms of power and belonging, a purpose that had little to do with the concerns and protocols of the political establishment. The overall effect, however, was to remake community first and foremost as *constituency*—a discernible and internally coherent interest group—and, thus, to reinforce the prevailing terms of political representation rather than redistributing political power or economic security. The irony is that this was done in the name of expanded community participation, which made politics rather than poverty (in the systemic sense) the object of community action.

This process partially failed in Appalachia because the transposition from poverty to the normative regime of politics proved elusive and thus highlighted the political dimensions of poverty. It may be that the Appalachian Committee for Full Employment's association with violent resistance in the coalfields or their alliance with the New Left disqualified them as candidates for federal reform, whereas—even after the break with the Council of Southern Mountains—the AVs' credentials seemed less threatening. But in either case, a focus on the political economy of poverty eventually rendered both the ACFE and the AVs beyond the reach of government inclusion under a "commonality of interest" and the purview of liberal democratic pluralism. However much liberalism and democracy were made to appear naturally conjoined, the promise of democracy remained an unstable foundation for liberal authority. Jacques Rancière argues: "The democratic scandal simply consists in revealing this: there will never be, under the name of politics, a single principle of community, legitimating the acts of governors based on laws inherent in the coming together of human communities."[131] The War on Poverty relied on liberal pluralism as the way to provisionally reconcile these antagonisms and redirect conflict into equivalent expressions of inequality and manageable forms of competition.

Although the Diné national project was not a revolutionary endeavor, during the late 1960s and early 1970s, US Indian policy was partially animated by what policymakers perceived as a threat of insurgency that seemed to be closing in on all fronts. What was at stake for American Indians and African Americans were two very different configurations of nationalism, but both were in a sense forged or unified through distinct histories of Euro-American colonialism and dispossession. Furthermore, in contrast to the Diné community-based initiatives discussed in this chapter, groups such as the National Indian Youth Council and the American Indian Movement embraced a revolutionary internationalism that asserted indigenous self-determination globally. I turn now to this expanded horizon of political identification and the concerted amalgamation of self-determination and antiracist anti-imperialism by numerous oppositional groups that sought—in stark contrast to the efforts of the PRCDP, and more far-reaching ways than those proposed by the ONEO or the ACFE—to build a social and political movement beyond the pale of liberal pluralism.

CHAPTER FIVE

THRESHOLDS OF OPPOSITION
Liberty, Liberation, and the Horizon of Incrimination

On the morning of February 3, 1967, Clyde Warrior, president of the National Indian Youth Council (NIYC), testified in Memphis, Tennessee, before the President's National Advisory Commission on Rural Poverty. He excoriated the cheerful narrative of community empowerment promoted by the Office of Economic Opportunity (OEO), and countered: "We are not free . . . Our choices are made for us; we are the poor. For those of us who live on reservations, these choices and decisions are made by federal administrators, bureaucrats, and their 'yes men,' euphemistically called tribal governments. Those of us who live in non-reservation areas . . . have many rulers. They are called social workers, 'cops,' school teachers, churches, etc., and now OEO employees." Objecting to liberal policy explanations for poverty that refused to address poverty as a social relation actively produced through expropriation, Warrior argued that mainstream debate on the struggle for "community control" was largely a farce: "We are unconcerned with that struggle because we know that no one is arguing that the dispossessed, the poor, be given any control over their own destiny. The local white power elites who protest the loudest against federal control are the very ones who would keep us poor in spirit and worldly goods in order to enhance their own personal and economic station in the world." Antipoverty programs, according to Warrior, only further impoverished poor people and so-called grass-roots democracy served as a cover for coerced assimilation and the norma-tive imperatives of liberal reform.[1] By insisting that "we are not free," War-rior contended that poverty and self-determination were antithetical and demanded substantive autonomy beyond the abstraction of liberal freedom. Contrary to the presumptions of Great Society policymaking, poverty could not be rendered a crucible for democratic self-improvement, but was instead the very condition through which external control was asserted and maintained.

For many of those engaged in grass-roots initiatives for social justice, liberal regimes of participation and incorporation for the poor came to seem increasingly disingenuous. Richie Perez, formerly deputy minister of infor-mation for the Young Lords, recollected that by the late 1960s, many young mainland Puerto Ricans "had gone through the so-called War on Poverty and had worked in antipoverty agencies, had seen this was a sham and a false solution—that there was no intention of really grappling with and con-fronting the issue of poverty directly and effectively." In breaking with federally funded antipoverty organizations such as the Puerto Rican Com-munity Development Project, Perez reflected: "We saw the need . . . to create new organizations, and didn't believe in taking money from the government and thought that organizations that did would be hopelessly co-opted."[2] During the late 1960s, the Lords and the Puerto Rican Student Union were among a number of newly established organizations that had been galvanized by the recently deceased nationalist leader Pedro Albizu Campos and that worked to articulate a joint agenda of national liberation for the island and self-determination for mainland Puerto Ricans. Inspired by the revolutionary nationalism and militant tactics of the Black Panther Party for Self-Defense, the Young Lords approached the problem of poverty as a dilemma bequeathed by US imperialism and what Cedric Robinson has called racial capitalism.[3]

Puerto Rican and American Indian activists were not alone in their disillusionment with the War on Poverty—although their demands for self-determination were in different ways specifically addressed to the enduring conditions of US colonialism. Many community organizers found their initial enthusiasm for OEO programs stunted by the tortuous politics of implementation and administration, as well as the OEO's timid reformist agenda and susceptibility to lobbying by local elites. While some organizers chose to continue to work within the constraints of these state-sponsored programs (either as a tactical decision to gain access to state-provided re-sources, or as a genuine belief in the viability of existing political institu-tions), others instead organized alternative or oppositional movements that foregrounded demands for self-determination, the legacies and entrenched realities of white racism, and the link between poverty and US imperialism. In many instances, federally supported programs that pursued a more overtly insurgent agenda, or had simply been targeted for controversy by groups hostile to their efforts, lost their OEO funding. The rancorous cam-paigns against Mobilization for Youth and the Appalachian Volunteers, dis-cussed in previous chapters, were prime examples. However, the fact that many activists had at one point worked in the Community Action Program, or similar OEO programs, is significant not only because their decision to look elsewhere exposed the failures and incapacities of these programs. Perhaps more important, their initial involvement in these programs makes the con-nection between the War on Poverty and oppositional social movements essential for understanding the multiple politics that used the idea of commu-nity as a response to the conditions of poverty during the 1960s and 1970s.

On the Verge of Revolt

This chapter provisionally distinguishes between "liberty" and "liberation" so as to expand on the ideological tension between Great Society policy and grass-roots militancy. At stake in this distinction is the difference between the liberal investment in community as a way to ensure individual freedom and social order, on the one hand, and a radical conception of community as a means of achieving social solidarity and collective emancipation, on the other hand. "Liberty" denotes the substance of freedom itself, whereas "lib-eration" implies circumstances of subjugation to be overcome. As with the contrast between self-help and self-determination, liberty and liberation each convey a distinct politics of belonging, as well as competing notions of politics as such. Attending to these differences, as well as to their frictions and mutual entanglements, I analyze the political horizons of affiliation and conflict that resulted from liberationist versus liberal politics of poverty. Eldridge Cleaver, for instance, wrote in 1968 of new oppositional align-ments, declaring: "A community of interest began to emerge, dripping with blood, out of the ashes of Watts. The blacks in Watts and all over America could now see the Viet Cong's point: both were on the receiving end of what the armed forces were dishing out."[4] In light of the discussion in the previous chapter, Cleaver's invocation of "community of interest" suggests a tension between interest as the liberal abstraction of equivalence—interest as an instrument—and a political affinity shaped by common circumstances of oppression—interest as a condition of possibility. Whereas chapter 4 focused on political claims for recognition and the ways in which community was configured in order to gain access to political power and resources, this chapter examines fundamental differences in how social belonging and collectivity were imagined and acted on.

My focus in this chapter is thus on the ways that activists and community organizers worked with or confronted the instabilities and constraints of liberalism from the mid-1960s to the mid-1970s in order to redefine the substance and purpose of political community. I begin with an examination of the precarious outer limits of liberal reclamation by looking at the War on Poverty's initiatives aimed at gangs. A comparison between the Real Great Society, established by Puerto Rican gang members turned entrepreneurial social reformers, and the Blackstone Rangers, an African American gang that cultivated relations with both the Black Panther Party and the OEO, serves to address the elasticity and discord of liberal incorporation. Opponents of the Johnson administration's antipoverty programs, such as Senator John McClellan, denounced the gang initiatives as evidence that the OEO was a slush fund for criminals and revolutionaries. Where Great Society initiatives sought to ensure social order through incorporation and remediation, McClellan aimed to enforce governmental authority through exclusion and criminalization.

Turning to community-based antipoverty initiatives established beyond the pale of liberal reform, the chapter proceeds to an analysis of the Black Panther Party (BPP). Here I focus specifically on Huey P. Newton's notion of "revolutionary intercommunalism," the Panthers' "serve the people" community survival programs, and the local organizing efforts of the Illinois BPP chairman Fred Hampton (especially Hampton's political work with gangs in the Chicago area, including the Blackstone Rangers and the Young Lords). The Panthers' emphasis on building bridges between local African American self-defense and survival initiatives and global antiimperialist and antiracist struggles—as well as their focus on the *lumpenproletariat*—served as an influential alternative to liberal strategies that portrayed community as a means of delimiting and neutralizing the politics of poverty. The Young Lords built on the Panther model as a way to challenge

US colonialism and mobilize the divided Puerto Rican nation, which had been fragmented by the colonialist economy. In order to address the limits of community-based anti-imperial initiatives, I study how the Lords' efforts to build a national liberation movement that united mainland and island-based Puerto Ricans ran aground with their Ofensiva Rompe Cadenas (Break the Chains Offensive). Examining their mainland urban activism together with Ofensiva Rompe Cadenas foregrounds the problem of who and what they considered to be the nation or the people, as well as suggesting some of the unresolved problems posed by the imagined form and function of decolonization in this context.

Faced with the intransigence of the US imperial nation-state, the Black Panthers, the Young Lords, and indigenous coalitions such as the International Indian Treaty Council (an organization established by the American Indian Movement in the aftermath of the 1973 clash at Wounded Knee) petitioned the United Nations, hoping to make the United States accountable for violations of international law. Their UN campaigns convey how liberty and liberation became entangled at the scale of international governance.[5] Indeed, the gradual articulation of national self-determination by European diplomats as a principle of liberal internationalism[6] during the nineteenth century, the prominence of national self-determination as a universal standard at the 1919 Paris Peace Conference, and the rearticulation of self-determination attached to the still more expansive definition of "peoples" by the UN Charter in 1945 all remained intimately bound up with the shifting dimensions of modern colonialism and the conditions for neocolonial reconfiguration.[7] The international order after the Second World War both consolidated the prevalence of the nation-state and promised the enforceability of universal norms such as human rights that qualified the principle of national sovereignty. This chapter's last section, "A Global Arena," focuses on the constraints and consequences of seeking redress—or at least recognition—within the postwar international arena. Strategies and goals for appealing to international forums such as the United Nations varied from one oppositional movement to another according to a number of factors, the most obvious of which were the substantive differences between the circumstances of American Indians, Puerto Ricans, and African Americans (to mention only the groups discussed in this chapter) with respect to US colonialism.

The resemblance between federal War on Poverty rhetoric and countermovement community programs was partially a result of the calculated appeal that liberal policy made for incorporation. However, as with the Black Panthers' Maoist rendition of Head Start breakfast programs, specific oppositional tactics were also adapted from liberal initiatives. Akin to US propaganda directed toward former colonies during the postwar period and the embedded contradictions of liberal internationalism more broadly, government promotion of community control and democratic participation for poor people within the United States necessarily sustained a tension between promises of institutional reform and aspirations for more fundamental redistributions of power. But it was precisely a heightened awareness of the global dynamics at work, and the decision to challenge what they perceived as the racialized and mercenary dimensions of both US domestic and foreign policy, that motivated many activists to focus on the parallels between community self-determination and anti-imperialism.

BPP Chairman Huey P. Newton's article "We Are Nationalists and Internationalists," for instance, denounced the combined endeavors of domestic and international counterinsurgency, as well as linking military aggression to ostensibly benign liberal agencies. In the essay, written while he was incarcerated in the Alameda County Jail in 1968, Newton maintained: "The police in our ghettos are the foot soldiers in Vietnam. The AID [Agency for International Development] and Peace Corps men in Santo Domingo are the state and federal War-on-Poverty bureaucrats here."[8] From his perspective, it was the reciprocity between a nationalist platform—a belief in collective autonomy and self-defense—and a commitment to an international revolt against racial capitalism that determined the parameters of belonging and solidarity. Whereas the Puerto Rican Community Development Project and the Office of Navajo Economic Opportunity, discussed in the previous chapter, were convenient mechanisms for consolidating scarce economic resources and new political identities within the framework or at the limit of liberal pluralism, other horizons of affiliation and social transformation threatened to be irrepressible. Yet these oppositional alliances were likewise encumbered by the contradictions and entanglements that served as their conditions of political possibility.

By the late 1960s, a combined emphasis on global decolonization, antiracism, self-determination, and armed self-defense increasingly appealed to many activists as an alternative to the gradualist institutionalism of the mainstream civil rights movement and to the palliative reforms of the War on Poverty.[9] The Vietnam War made US imperialism a ubiquitous and visceral presence even for those people living in the United States who might not otherwise be inclined to make a connection between oppression at home and militarism abroad. For those disposed to more closely scrutinize US foreign policy during the 1960s, covert operations in Cambodia, Laos, Haiti, Guatemala, Ecuador, Congo, Peru, the Dominican Republic, Cuba, Indonesia, Ghana, Uruguay, Chile, Greece, and Bolivia made apparent the gruesome realities of US preponderance.[10]

Precarious Recuperations

As incorporation and containment were central to liberal governance, a pressing issue was the extent to which the excesses potentially set in motion by such a strategy—activism encouraged by the promise of overcoming poverty and disenfranchisement, but reluctant to settle for reformist compromise—could be salvaged and made useful for social regulation. The War on Poverty's treatment of street gangs reveals the tolerable threshold of liberal reform. Ostensibly it was poor youth who were likely to participate in urban riots and the most susceptible to the recruiting efforts of revolutionary nationalist organizations and other treacherous agents of social disorder.[11]

The prospect of transforming young gang members not only into respectable members of society but also into street-level leaders of socially constructive community action held immense appeal for liberal reformers. Projects developed and run by reformed gang members epitomized the idea that positive social change in the ghetto must be self-motivated and internally directed. Gang leaders appeared to represent an untapped reservoir of authority that, when they were remade as responsible citizens, might promote understanding between the world of the ghetto and the larger society. Youth summer job programs and the Neighborhood Youth Corps were among the earliest OEO projects of this sort.[12] Subsequently, the OEO also sponsored programs with groups including the Blackstone Rangers and Devil's Disciples in Chicago, the Mission Rebels in Action in San Francisco, and the Real Great Society in New York City, as well as underwriting regional initiatives such as the Street Scene Social Action Project in California's San Fernando Valley. One after another, however, gang-directed initiatives were caught up in scandal. Often highly sensationalized transgressions were simply the outcome of administrative and fiscal incompetence. Evidence for many of the more egregious charges against OEO-supported gang members often failed to materialize, but cases such as the 1968 Blackstone Rangers' indictment for defrauding the OEO and using federal money to stockpile weapons attracted national attention and proved the potential liability of such policy ventures.[13]

The apogee of 1960s mainstreamed gang self-reform was Youth Organizations United (YOU), a national coalition of street gangs eventually headquartered in Washington, D.C., whose acronym was intended to suggest identification and commonality with potential benefactors. The Conservative Vice Lords in Chicago, Thugs United in New Orleans, Sons of Watts in Los Angeles, and the Mission Rebels in San Francisco were among the members of YOU. The organization was established during the fall of 1967 by a group of gang leaders who, as their promotional booklet later explained, had "gone conservative and incorporated." YOU members were "trying their best to act as a constructive alternative to revolution in urban communities."[14] YOU's politics were unequivocally procapitalist and their projects market-oriented. As an umbrella organization, YOU provided youth leadership training and promoted the establishment-friendly activities of its members, which included education and recreation programs, services for school dropouts, and helping young people start small businesses. Within two years, YOU had also capitalized on the "insider" status of its membership and established the General Metropolitan Communications Corporation, a joint stock company specializing in consumer surveys and marketing campaigns within poor, inner-city neighborhoods.[15]

The Real Great Society (RGS), a Puerto Rican youth group from New York City, had been one of the principal forces behind the development of YOU. Established in 1964, RGS did not originate with OEO funding but instead was initially sponsored by the Vincent Astor and Ford Foundations.[16] Chino Garcia and Angelo Gonzalez, veteran Lower East Side gang leaders of the Dragons and the Assassins, respectively, were among the founders of RGS. Their first rather quixotic idea for organized youth reform was to use their street-fighting skills to form a commando unit called the Spartican Army, which would invade Cuba to aid in the US overthrow of Fidel Castro. The availability of War on Poverty funds encouraged them to shift their focus to battles closer at hand. With the support of a former social worker, his brother, and a former Harvard psychology professor, they assembled a group of Puerto Rican youth dedicated to redirecting their energies from gang warfare to local antipoverty and crime-reduction projects. An intense schedule of speaking events on college campuses, where they promoted the importance of self-directed programs by and for poor urban youth, helped generate publicity for their endeavors. During 1966 and 1967, leaders of the RGS traveled throughout the United States, promoting the idea that gangs should redirect their talents toward legitimate business ventures and provide services for their communities. As they explained in their OEO proposal, the RGS mission was to "proceed to the next stage of the war on poverty[,] which is to develop the permanent community-based institutions which will provide the resources and services necessary to bring about the needed changes in the socio-economic conditions in the ghetto."[17] These institutions would direct the ambitions of local youth toward legitimate enterprises and develop a social-service economy under local control.

By late 1968, the RGS had split into two semi-autonomous, mutually antagonistic organizations, although each faction attempted to capitalize on the widespread media attention that the original group had received— such as the September 1967 *Life* story "The Real Great Society: Some Tough New York Slum Kids Team Up to Fight Poverty Instead of Themselves."[18] The first major success of the RGS was its University of the Streets project, which provided a variety of classes for young people, including preparation for the general educational development (GED) exam. An uptown branch of the university was founded in 1967 and, in conjunction with the Division of Urban Planning at Columbia University, sponsored The First East Harlem Youth Conference. The conference established a series of education projects for school dropouts that ultimately became the East Harlem Prep School at the RGS/Town House Project. *Life* reported on the conference, describing "some 200 kids from East Harlem who had led and participated in the riots . . . They began by banning the press and screaming about black power. But by the end of the first day, the biggest applause went to the speaker who declared, 'Hey, we have to stop running everybody down. I dig people. People are where it's at.'"[19] This trajectory from unruly delinquents to civic-minded citizens was precisely the normative gist of the RGS's promotional narrative—a narrative that reaffirmed the potentially wayward, antisocial behavior of urban youth so as to claim authority for reformist remediation.

During the summer of 1968, RGS/Uptown began the East Harlem Urban Design and Planning Studio. Although administered in partnership with Columbia University's School of Architecture, the Urban Planning Studio foregrounded the notion of community self-determination in architectural design and urban planning. In a grant proposal submitted to the Ford and Astor Foundations, RGS/Uptown asserted: "East Harlem is an underdeveloped country . . . The people have become aware, as a part of a nationwide movement, that they must control their own environment in order to determine their own future, and that control begins at the planning level through the utilization of the community's own environmentalists."[20] As with the strategic deployment of foreignness discussed in chapter 2 and the pluralist notions of community leadership addressed in chapter 4, in this statement "underdeveloped country" signaled both a provisional difference that planned "development" can begin to remedy and a demand for the recognition of the RGS as an authoritative intermediary. RGS/Uptown Urban Planning Studio projects were conducted by teams consisting of an architect, an urban planner, an attorney, a community organizer, and an area specialist. By the end of 1969, the studio had worked on a number of small local park projects, contributed to the design of the Urban Coalition's Afro-Latin Unity Council Headquarters, submitted proposals for a series of cooperative housing projects and the East Harlem Triangle Urban Renewal Project, and helped to conduct a series of neighborhood planning studies. Like the Puerto Rican Community Development Project, RGS/ Uptown operations emphasized local Puerto Rican professionalization, and the group's rhetoric of community control focused on the upward mobility of Puerto Rican youth who might serve as mediators with the planning establishment.[21]

Throughout its endeavors, across each of its separate branches, the RGS advocated increased inclusion in the existing economic and political system. As the group stated in one OEO proposal: "Given the prevailing anti-establishment attitude among youth today, particularly minority youth, it is imperative that the government continue to support to completion a youth program with an organization of youth who are still willing to attempt to work from within the system."[22] RGS projects encouraged economic development that capitalized on minority niche markets and provided ghetto residents with "the opportunity for the realization of their full potentials in . . . a nation where private property was one of the most important founding ideals." Their insistence on private property as a cherished American value deliberately distinguished them from militant radicals and the spontaneous insurrection of urban rioters. "The underlying idea of this approach," the group explained, "is that the ghetto will become a highly desirable place to live and shop. As the Black, Puerto Rican, and Mexican communities develop their own pride and awareness, the manufacture and retail enterprises will be places which provide alternatives to shopping in alien downtown stores." The RGS focus on consumption as a way to promote self-esteem and civic consciousness was distinct from undertakings such as the National Welfare Rights Organization's campaign for consumers' rights for the poor during the same time. Whereas the NWRO advocated economic citizenship as a fundamental social right, the RGS's promotion of entrepreneurialism and consumption was dedicated to expanding the marketplace and opportunities for capitalizing on new markets. In terms reminiscent of reminders to the US State Department by Governor Luis Muñoz Marín's administration of the strategic significance of Puerto Rico a decade earlier, the RGS represented its members as mediators between the two mutually hostile societies that the Kerner Commission declared the United States had become. The RGS thus explicitly proposed to "bridge the gap between the ghetto and the 'outside world.'"[23]

Criminal Convictions

The Blackstone Rangers, in contrast, made no such promise to reconcile this hostile divide through reformist acquiescence. They did, however, as a matter of their own interest and evolving politicization, pursue federal antipoverty funding as a potential source of prestige and income. In certain respects, this placed them in closer ideological proximity to the Real Great Society, or the early incarnation of SDS's Economic Research and Action Project, than to the Black Panther Party (with whom they were briefly affiliated) and the Young Lords. First organized in the late 1950s by Jeff Fort and Eugene Hairston in the Woodlawn section of Chicago, the Rangers began to expand rapidly during the mid-1960s in response to territory battles with the Disciples, during which time they became one of the three largest youth gangs in Chicago. By the end of 1966, they had reconfigured themselves into a confederation of chapters under the umbrella of the Black P. Stone Nation, with twenty-one leaders who acted as the group's "board of directors."[24] The Chicago Police Department began to take a special interest in the Rangers when they met with Martin Luther King Jr. and his colleagues in the spring of 1966. The Southern Christian Leadership Conference was in the process of launching its Chicago Freedom Movement and had become convinced of the importance of gang participation.[25] As noted in chapter 3, this initial contact with the SCLC would subsequently lead to the group's participation in the Poor People's Campaign. Police interest in the Rangers intensified when it became apparent that the gang was indeed devoting its attention to manifestly legitimate community work and political organizing. It was precisely the coordinated law-abiding activities of thousands of poor African American youth that most troubled the city's law enforcement and political establishment.

Despite antagonisms between the Rangers and more reputable Woodlawn neighborhood residents, the gang maintained close relations with the First Presbyterian Church. The church served as a safe haven and meeting center for the Rangers, as well as facilitating the employment of fifty-five Rangers in the OEO's Neighborhood Youth Corps. Their connection to First Presbyterian also helped mediate interactions with The Woodlawn Organization (TWO). Originally established by the Industrial Areas Foundation, TWO was the conduit for federal antipoverty funds in the area, and the neighborhood-backed alternative to the Urban Progress Center supported by the administration of Mayor Richard J. Daley. The relationship between TWO and the Rangers eventually led to a TWO-administered contract for youth leadership and job training with the OEO. The youth program involved not only the Rangers but also their longtime rival gang the Disciples, both of whom agreed to a truce in order to implement the program.

At the very moment when OEO funding for the TWO program appeared likely to materialize, the Chicago Police Department took active measures to undermine the legitimacy of the Rangers and other youth gang organizations throughout the city, announcing in March 1967 the creation of a separate division targeting gangs.[26] In the department's words, which seem especially ironic given their timing, the Gang Intelligence Unit (GIU) was inaugurated "for eliminating the anti-social and criminal activities of groups of minors and young adults."[27] After the OEO-sponsored program began, the GIU routinely entered the four training centers and interrogated participants. Top Ranger leaders were arrested for alleged murders, with charges subsequently dropped for lack of evidence. To make matters worse, the *Chicago Tribune*, with the Daley administration as its accomplice, ran a series of incendiary articles charging that the program employed rapists and murderers, was forcing young people to quit school in order to participate in its classes, and was deliberately misappropriating federal funds. Despite the fact that an OEO investigation absolved TWO and the Rangers of these allegations, Roman Pucinski, an Illinois congressman and Daley loyalist, was able to use the media scandal to prompt hearings by Senator John McClellan's Permanent Subcommittee on Investigations the following summer.

Motivated initially by an interest in implicating the OEO's Community Action Program in the urban riots, the subcommittee's expansive mandate is especially interesting for the alleged connections and categorical associations it made between violent revolt in poor urban neighborhoods, student campus protests, and what it called "domestic terrorism." Conducting a single investigation of such disparate actions and events effectively condemned all of them as manifestations of anarchy aimed at the destruction of American society. McClellan later warned that, based on the evidence presented during the subcommittee's investigation, "no citizen can . . . be complacent about this problem or be under any illusion that there is not an underground effort or revolutionary effort to destroy this government."[28] The Chicago hearings provided further evidence for McClellan to use in his attempts to discredit the OEO. One newspaper headline read: "Gang Hearings Draw Full House; Best Capitol Hill Show in Years."[29] As with the Senate subcommittee investigations on the urban riots discussed in chapter 3, the specter of menacing and irredeemable youth of color provided McClellan with a sensationalized means of vilifying the OEO.

The Blackstone Ranger inquiry created a synergy of municipal interests and McClellan's national agenda. Although the subcommittee's investigators had initially traveled to Chicago looking for a follow-up to its Nashville and Houston inquiries and further confirmation that the OEO was funding or fomenting urban riots, the city's GIU told the investigators tantalizing stories of gangs arming for revolution and law breaking paid for by the federal dime. The GIU also provided an ample roster of witnesses to testify against the TWO-administered Rangers youth project. The hearings allowed the GIU to stage depositions in a high-profile, public forum with immunity from libel suits and free from the inconvenience of cross-examination.[30] The formal request by the Ranger leader Jeff Fort to question the parade of witnesses was summarily dismissed by McClellan.[31] In response, Fort refused to answer the subcommittee's questions, walked out of the hearings, and was subsequently cited for contempt of Congress.[32] Making the Rangers out to be scheming criminals intent on manipulating a permissive and ineffective system was to the advantage of both congressional opponents of the OEO and Chicago's power brokers.

There was public acknowledgment, nevertheless, that the Blackstone Rangers had played an important role in keeping the Woodlawn area from erupting following Martin Luther King Jr.'s assassination.[33] Two further Ranger actions brought widespread attention to the group's ideology and political orientation. The first, much to the consternation of the Daley administration, was their "no vote" campaign during the 1968 elections.[34] Many in the neighborhood initially balked at participating, given the still recent triumph of the 1965 Voting Rights Act, but a substantial number of residents eventually saw abstention as a way to vent their frustrations with Chicago machine politics. The campaign targeted a long-held tenet of politics in the city, which presupposed that 90 percent of the registered voters in poor black precincts would vote the Democratic Party line. In a calculated affront to Daley, the "no vote" campaign produced enough abstentions to deny presidential candidate Hubert Humphrey the needed plurality in Chicago to counteract the downstate vote and cost him Illinois. The "no vote" campaign was immediately followed by the considerable expansion of the city's GIU.[35]

The second action focused on discrimination in the construction trade unions. In 1969, the Rangers joined a coalition that included SCLC's Operation Breadbasket, to draw attention to the exclusionary hiring practices of the building trades in Chicago. Although the majority of the groups in the coalition planned to picket union and contractors' offices and engage union officials and contractors in dialogue, the Rangers decided that the best tactic was to close down the construction projects themselves. They did this by storming the work sites and literally chasing the construction workers off.[36] In less than a week, they succeeded in closing "one hundred million dollars' worth of construction, and it wasn't about to be started up again."[37] The campaign culminated by shutting down the University of Chicago's enormous Campus Circle construction project, which was to demolish low-income housing and displace poor residents.[38] The Rangers' tactics were confrontational and unapologetically militant, and they did not comply with established protocols of deferential negotiation.

Although the Rangers worked with more mainstream groups such as Operation Breadbasket and The Woodlawn Organization, they were quite clear that their primary affiliation was with the neighborhood poor. One young Ranger—in language rendered stereotypical by the transcriber's urge to replicate street vernacular—explained:

> We ain't givin' 'em some oily-mouth snake talk like them leeches at [the Urban Progress Center] . . . , always comin' around with program this and project that . . . They's parasites livin' *off* the peoples insteada helpin' 'em. They make their bread by takin' down the peoples' names and puttin' the names on papers and passin' the papers around and down to the loop so more parasites down there put the names on *their* papers and pass 'em back down here so's the parasites down here can read about 'em and go have a look if they still be the same peoples . . . No help atall. Detective's that way, too, layin' five dollar on some dude to get 'im to tell lies on a brother. We gonna protect the peoples from all that kinda shit.[39]

Indeed, antipoverty funding was never fully free from the surveillance mechanisms of law enforcement agencies. According to John Fry, the pastor at the First Presbyterian Church and a long-time advocate for the Rangers, the "peoples" in this statement meant a very particular group. It was not the Woodlawn "community" in general, but those presumably "dangerous classes" of which the Rangers were a part; precisely the people reputed not to be respectable and well-behaved members of the neighborhood.[40] They were situated in opposition to both normative propriety and the regulatory interplay of the welfare and police state, and were economically deprived and vulnerable.

The media frenzy and congressional outcry triggered by accusations that the Blackstone Rangers were using OEO money for weapons and parties had immediate repercussions for War on Poverty funding for gangs more broadly. Although YOU, the Real Great Society, and the Mission Rebels each briefly had their funding restored by President Richard Nixon's administration, the aftermath of the McClellan investigations proved insurmountable.[41] The FBI went so far as to raid RGS University of the Streets offices in 1969.[42] As public funding disappeared, the brush of criminality discredited even those most reform-oriented former gang organizations, driving private funding away from their programs as well. The prospect of recruiting gangs to the task of liberal reform proved too much of a political liability at a time when the entire edifice of Great Society policy seemed increasingly imperiled and its future uncertain.

During the late 1960s and 1970s, the Black Panther Party offered an influential countermodel to the federally sanctioned community-based strategies of the War on Poverty that was adapted by such groups as the Young Lords, the Brown Berets, and the American Indian Movement. Situating community in a frame that was both decisively local and purposefully international, an undated Black Panther flyer conveys how the BPP sought to disarticulate the notion of community from Johnson's Great Society. The leaflet proclaimed: "Ours is a struggle against community imperialism. Our black communities are colonized and controlled from the outside, and it is that control that has to be smashed, broken, shattered, by whatever means necessary." According to this account, the spatial dynamics of urban inequality reproduced the classic geopolitical economy of imperialism and gave contemporary form to the aftermath of slavery and colonial expropriation. If the Panthers advocated "national liberation"—the political independence and self-determination of colonized peoples—they also perceived the struggle for African American liberation as distinct from national struggles for decolonization outside the United States. The leaflet asserted: "In our struggle for national liberation, we are now in the phase of community liberation, to free our black communities from the imperialistic control exercised over them by the racist exploiting cliques within white communities, to free our people, locked up as they are in Urban Dungeons, from the imperialism of the white suburbs."[43] Panther philosophy defined community in primarily oppositional terms, as a scale of collective insurrection arising from the existing conditions of racial oppression and economic exploitation in the United States, and as a requisite building block in the making of revolution and national liberation. This approach was especially evident in their declared focus on the lumpenproletariat as the front line in the mobilization of the black poor into collective defiance of their racial subjugation and economic disposability.

The poor as the object of the War on Poverty and the lumpenproletariat as the foundational cadre for the Panthers were not equivalent. The distance between the two is evident in Eldridge Cleaver's remark that "we don't need a war on poverty. What we need is a war on the rich."[44] In the pamphlet *On the Ideology of the Black Panther Party*, Cleaver defined the lumpenproletariat as a class that had "no secure relationship or vested interest in the means of production and the institutions of capitalist society."[45] Moreover, as those who had been cast off and excluded, they were comprised of

> the so-called "Criminal Element," those who live by their wits, existing off that which they rip off, who stick guns in the faces of businessmen . . . Those who don't even want a job, who hate to work and can't relate to punching some pig's time clock, who would rather punch a pig in the mouth and rob him than punch that same pig's time clock and work for him . . . In short, all those who simply have been locked out of the economy and robbed of their rightful social heritage . . . [T]he very conditions of life of the Lumpen dictates the so-called spontaneous reactions against the system, and because the Lumpen is in this extremely oppressed condition, it therefore has an extreme reaction against the system as a whole.[46]

Cleaver also argued that Marxism provided an inadequate analysis of race and racism. He rejected Marx's contention that the lumpenproletariat was inevitably counterrevolutionary and instead claimed that it was precisely this group that directed the BPP to the specificities of race and class struggle in the context of the mid-twentieth-century United States.

The Panthers championed what they saw as the most bereft of the subaltern classes in a way that distinguished their approach from civil rights liberalism and the US Cold War suppression of class analysis. Their emphasis on the lumpenproletariat was partially derived from Malcolm X and Frantz Fanon.[47] For Fanon, the lumpenproletariat was closely associated with the tactical force of anticolonial guerrilla warfare. In *The Wretched of the Earth*, widely read by the Panthers, Fanon writes: "It is within this mass of humanity, this people of shantytowns, at the core of the *lumpenproletariat*, that the rebellion will find its urban spearhead. For the *lumpenproletariat*, that horde of starving men, uprooted from their tribe and from their clan, constitutes one of the most spontaneous and most radically revolutionary forces of a colonized people."[48] Despite the centrality of the lumpenproletariat for an anticolonial front, Fanon nonetheless argued that their position also made them susceptible to recruitment by counterrevolutionary forces. He cautioned that colonialists readily exploit this potential liability: "The enemy discovers the existence, side by side with the disciplined and well-organized advance guard of rebellion, of a mass of men whose participation is constantly at the mercy of their being for too long accustomed to physiological wretchedness, humiliation, and irresponsibility." The allegiance of the lumpenproletariat could be bought and thus would provide inroads for colonial control.[49] The Black Panthers' community survival programs were conceived with the capriciousness of mass desperation in mind, as well as in an attempt to practice the Maoist directive to "serve the people." The survival programs acknowledged that insurgency required sustenance as a prerequisite to anticolonial discipline.

Like Fanon, the Panthers did not consider the lumpenproletariat to be synonymous with "the people." Whereas the former was seen as the insurgent vanguard, the latter—the dispossessed majority—was the general social category on whose behalf the Panthers claimed revolutionary agency. Yet the people remained a more problematic referent than BPP rhetoric often suggested, ultimately expressing a political tension rather than providing an unproblematic means of asserting authority. The Panthers' claim to be servants of the people reinscribed this gap between the subject of politics and the class that is always already excluded from politics, while appearing to collapse the distinction completely.[50] To the extent that the Panthers' activities focused on the structural conditions of exploitation and violence, and had more to do with the transformation of these circumstances than with defining and defending a fixed constituency as the people, their understanding of the people resembled the view of the political philosopher Sofia Näsström: "The people is no longer the source, but the *object*, of legitimacy . . . people-making is what legitimacy is all about." According to Näsström, "the criteria of legitimacy make the people into a site of perpetual contestation . . . The constitution of the people is not a historical event. It is an ongoing claim that we make."[51] The Panthers' definition of the people as characterized by ongoing struggle and oppositionality operated in continual tension with their claim to serve the people as its vanguard, to act on behalf of a self-evident and irrefutably righteous constituency.

The survival programs exemplified the BPP's understanding of community as constituted in adversarial terms.[52] Distinguishing Panther programs from reformist measures, Huey Newton explained: "We called them survival programs pending revolution . . . [They] are emergency services. In themselves they do not change social conditions, but they are life saving vehicles until conditions change."[53] The first of these programs were the armed neighborhood self-defense patrols, launched in 1966 to discourage

Students from the Samuel Napier Intercommunal Youth Institute at the Black Panther Party's Black Community Survival Conference—which also featured free testing for sickle cell anemia and the distribution of two thousand bags of free groceries—in Bobby Hutton Memorial Park, Oakland, California, March 1972. PHOTOGRAPH BY STEPHEN SHAMES; COURTESY OF POLARIS IMAGES.

police harassment and police violence. After these, the best known and most widely implemented community undertaking was the Free Breakfast for Children program, started in 1968. Survival programs in various Panther area branches also included free health clinics, testing for sickle cell anemia, and a free ambulance service; free clothing programs; education programs, including liberation schools, community political education classes, and the Intercommunal Youth Institute (later renamed the Oakland Community School); Seniors Against a Fearful Environment (SAFE) programs for the elderly; and a program providing free busing to prisons for the families and friends of those incarcerated, a free commissary program for prison inmates, and free legal support and legal educational programs. JoNina Abron, a former Panther, describes this network of community survival programs as "designed to improve the life chances of African American people" otherwise cut short by institutional racism.[54]

The significance of the survival programs was not lost on J. Edgar Hoover, then head of the Federal Bureau of Investigation, who instructed his operatives to "destroy what the [BPP] stands for" and "eradicate its 'serve the people' programs."[55] The FBI's COINTELPRO initiative—a covert counterintelligence program in operation from 1956 to 1971 that targeted what it deemed to be "subversive" political organizations—waged a sustained offensive against Panther leaders and programs.[56] The free breakfast programs and liberation schools were the subject of constant police harassment. Venues for the programs were frequently charged with building code violations. Not only did municipal police and federal agents routinely disrupt these programs, but a nationwide misinformation campaign aimed to discredit them and encouraged parents to keep their children away.[57] As with the Chicago police department's targeted assault on the Blackstone Rangers' youth training programs, the relentless campaign against the BPP's community work was at the margins of legality and permissible coercion, supplementing allowable measures with covert infiltration and attempted entrapment. All the while, the BPP was made to appear culpable for the extremes of state violence, portrayed as the primary agent of its own aggressive undoing. Law enforcement agencies treated the BPP as a revolutionary movement with potential international consequences.

Indeed, for the Panthers, the struggle for community self-determination by the black poor was intended to be part of a worldwide struggle against imperialism.[58] By 1970, Huey Newton had reconfigured the BPP's anticolonial internationalism into what he called "revolutionary intercommunalism" based on readings of Mao Zedong, Frantz Fanon, and Ernesto "Che" Guevara.[59] Newton argued that individual sovereign nation-states were less important than the world system of racial capitalism and the forms of economic interdependence produced by US imperialism and organized under US monopoly control of the world's resources. He called this oppressive, interdependent system "reactionary intercommunalism" in order to emphasize a global capitalist elite without any national allegiance. In opposition to this formation, he described revolutionary intercommunalism as the struggle against the US empire, during which oppressed people throughout the world would seize the means of production and equitably redistribute wealth. Newton's terminology is notable for the ways in which "community" is defined by its specific forms of engagement, rather than as an immutable affiliation that exists before political antagonisms.

This enlarged analytic frame projected the Panthers' revolutionary nationalism outward. In a 1970 statement to the National Liberation Front and Provisional Revolutionary Government in South Vietnam, Newton elaborated on his vision of solidarity, declaring: "We cannot be nationalists, when our country is not a nation, but an empire." He advocated a revolutionary internationalism aimed at "the destruction of statehood itself," contending that the United States was "a government of international capitalists and inasmuch as they have exploited the world to accumulate wealth this country belongs to the world."[60] He explained the evolution of the BPP platform in the following terms: "We said that we are not only revolutionary nationalists—that is, nationalists who want revolutionary changes in everything, including the economic system the oppressor inflicts upon us—but we are also individuals deeply concerned with the other people of the world and their desire for revolution." From this position, the Panthers eventually concluded: "We say that the world today is a dispersed collection of communities. A community is different from a nation. A community is a small unit with a comprehensive collection of institutions that exist to serve a small group of people. And we say further that the struggle in the world today is between the small circle that administers and profits from the empire of the United States, and the peoples of the world who want to determine their own destinies."[61] Revolutionary intercommunalism, in Newton's formulation, was a precondition for the possibility of a socialist society. In this sense, Newton did what many leaders of decolonization worldwide did not: he attempted to theorize political community beyond the form of the nation-state. Whereas decolonization tended to work through the further universalization and consolidation of the nation-state, Newton suggested an interdependent radical localism and self-determination not derived from the hegemony of the nation-state that was then so central to the postwar liberal world order. This solidarity relied on the alignment of mutual interests in opposition to the colonial and imperialist powers to anchor the strictly negative force of resistance, rather than constituting positive forms of affiliation. Liberation as promise and struggle gave form to this oppositional collectivity, but liberation as an event would dissolve the bonds of oppression that constituted "the people."

Even before Newton had formulated the theory of intercommunalism, elements of this analysis informed the Panthers' coalition-building "People's Diplomacy" initiatives and were taken up by other revolutionary nationalist groups and the Marxist-Leninist organizations of the burgeoning New Communist Movement. Local community work was central to the liberation projects of such diverse groups as the Brown Berets, La Raza Unida Party, Crusade for Justice, Red Guard Party, I Wor Kuen, Yellow Brotherhood, and American Indian Movement. Although self-determination held distinct meanings for each, all these organizations shared a focus on the political mobilization of specific groups of poor people and translocal anti-imperialism, as well as political alliances that challenged the planetary reach of racial capitalism.[62] Although ultimately still invested in the seemingly self-evident capacity of self-determination, these groups also opposed what Denise Ferreira da Silva calls the "logic of obliteration"—that is, the presumed movement toward the annihilation of racialized others as requisite to the full realization of the Enlightenment subject.[63]

Since the publication of *The Communist Manifesto* in 1848 and the founding of the International Workingmen's Association in 1864, communism had sought to develop an explicitly global countermovement to the ever-expanding capitalist world system and to unite a working class artificially divided by nations—if nonetheless also reinscribing its own Eurocentric teleology. The US Third World Left rejected Stalin's "socialism in one country" thesis that had been Soviet policy since the 1920s, arguing instead that Leninism offered a more suitable anticapitalist framework for community liberation, and that revolutionary class agency emerged in collective opposition to imperialist war and racism. During the late 1960s and early 1970s, many activists increasingly considered the coordination of an overarching Marxist-Leninist revolutionary alliance to challenge the US imperial nation-state to be achievable and desirable. By the mid to late 1970s, an emphasis on party building and ideological purity, as well as the relentless offensive of government counterinsurgency, led to insurmountable divisions between revolutionary nationalists, socialists, and New Communist Movement organizations.[64] But before this debacle, the Panthers were a crucial force in establishing the grass-roots foundation of these expansive collaborations.

Fugitive Allies

In Chicago, the BPP leader Fred Hampton focused coalition-building energies on fostering relations with street gangs and promoting their political realignment. Between the founding of the Panthers' Illinois Chapter in the fall of 1968 and the early summer of 1969, during the brief time when he was not incarcerated and before his FBI-assisted assassination by the Chicago Police Department, Hampton sought to build an alliance with the Blackstone Rangers and nearly consummated a citywide gang truce.[65] The Daley administration viewed the potential affiliation of the Panthers and the Rangers as a threat. Indeed, a union of the Illinois BPP and the Rangers—who by various estimates claimed between two thousand and five thousand members—would have dramatically increased the size of the BPP nationally and decisively tipped the balance of power within Chicago in the Panthers' favor. The local police GIU and the FBI worked quickly and succeeded in fomenting mistrust and hostility between the Panthers and the Blackstone Rangers, prompting violence and unraveling the still-tentative nonaggression pact among the city's gangs.[66]

During the spring of 1969, Hampton organized a multiracial Rainbow Coalition between the Panthers, a group of poor white youth called the Young Patriots, and the Puerto Rican Young Lords Organization. Both the Patriots and the Lords were comprised largely of former gang members, although the Patriots were also closely aligned with the JOIN-Community Union, initiated by Students for a Democratic Society. Together they asserted: "The Rainbow Coalition understands that serving oppressed people in their communities must start immediately . . . Every successful example of fulfilling the real needs of oppressed people teaches thousands of others that they can transform their lives by demanding the state power that belongs to them."[67] Although the coalition remained largely a symbolic gesture toward interracial revolutionary unity, official representatives did attend the Students for a Democratic Society national convention in June in Chicago. The following month, members of both the Patriots and the Young Lords were featured speakers at the much-publicized and widely attended United Front against Fascism conference. In contrast to the liberal pluralist model in which interest groups act and are mediated through ostensibly disinterested institutions of establishment politics, alliances such as the Rainbow Coalition forged oppositional political solidarities and shared a commitment to organizing against state violence, racism, and US imperialism that disclaimed the narrow attribution of "interests" as well as challenging the establishment's claim to impartiality.

Internecine gang warfare had plagued the poor neighborhoods of Chicago for quite some time, but it was Hampton's political organizing—and the political work of the Blackstone Rangers—that prompted Mayor Daley to declare an "all-out war against street gangs" on May 19, 1969.[68] Alleged gang members were singled out for arrest, and the GIU worked diligently to factionalize and destabilize local gangs. With a calculated nod to the Blackstone Ranger–OEO scandal, Captain Edward L. Buckney, head of the GIU, claimed in a newspaper interview: "These gangs are living off federal and private payrolls. They shake down businessmen by threatening violence and riots. And they are constantly on the lookout for federal programs."[69] The journalist Guy Halverson reported that "in contrast to the Chicago Police Department's gang intelligence unit—which views the gangs solely as apolitical and 'terrorist organizations'—. . . sociologists believe that many of the black youth gangs are gradually becoming 'quasi-political' organizations."[70] Much to the chagrin of the GIU, the view of gangs as "legitimate" political organizations was not limited to academics, but was an increasingly widespread perception. Not only was the Daley administration intent on denying the emerging political claims of certain gangs, but it sought to impugn by association the Black Panther Party, which it was quick to suggest was nothing more than an opportunistic criminal organization.

While the Daley administration sought to conflate the Panthers with street gangs, members of the Illinois Chapter of the BPP countered: "We are not a gang!!! We are a revolutionary organization, an armed political party, a Black liberation army." They described the conditions that necessitated intervention and self-defense: "We realize that the people of the Black Community are oppressed and that they are being murdered daily by this racist system of capitalism and exploitation. People die every day from starvation, from indecent delapidated [sic], roach infested rat holes called houses, from poor health conditions therein. Or people are shot down on the streets of our community by fascist pigs who call themselves policemen."[71] Against the depoliticizing rhetoric of the Daley administration, the Panthers insisted that their organization and the community of which they were a part were defensive formations necessitated by the onslaught of racialized state and capitalist violence.

The Panthers were quick to point to the repercussions of establishment discourse on gangs. An article addressed to "parents" cautioned: "You let them call us gangs and when the gangs are wiped out you will have stood by and let the pigs wipe out the BLACK YOUTH! Let the Black Community deal with the gangs, NOT THE PIGS!!! It is an insult to the Black Community that we should call our own black youth 'GANGS.' YOUTH MAKES THE REVOLUTION!"[72] If the BPP felt compelled to respond to criticism that depoliticized their activities by depicting them as common criminals, they were equally adamant in their efforts to define gangs as political entities produced by specific conditions of poverty, exploitation, and social marginalization. By identifying youth as a revolutionary force and gangs as an organizational vehicle for revolution, the Panthers' approach to working with gangs was at odds with War on Poverty efforts to remake gang leaders as reformers who facilitated communication and cooperation between poor communities of color and establishment institutions. For the Panthers and other radical political groups, the goal was decidedly not such intermediation—which, from their perspective, would merely reinforce the dominant political, economic, and social arrangements—but political power.

Police and federal harassment of the BPP rapidly escalated during 1969, and culminated with the murder of Hampton by the Chicago police, during a midnight raid coordinated with William O'Neal, an undercover informant.[73] Before his assassination, speaking at the Olivet Church, Hampton reworked King's parable of the mountaintop. The Panthers, he said, "understand that you people and your problems are right here in the valley...[We] went into the valley knowing that the people are in the valley, knowing that our plight is the same plight as the people in the valley, knowing that our enemies are on the mountaintop."[74] The people of the valley were shaped by the conditions of subjugation perpetrated by those on the mountaintop. According to Hampton, the mountaintop evoked by King as a goal was in fact a way of maintaining the uneven terrain of class hierarchy and substituted the misguided prospect of upward mobility for a more fundamental aim: the leveling of material and racial inequality. Hampton's perspective was evident in the coalition building he initiated and his influence on groups such as the Young Patriots and the Young Lords Organization. Although the life of the Young Patriots—a group that began during the early 1960s as a gang of Southern and Appalachian migrant youth called the Peacemakers in Chicago's Uptown area and later led a neighborhood-wide campaign against police brutality in association with JOIN-Community Union—was cut short by the FBI's counterintelligence program after the group sought to expand nationally as the Patriot Party, the Young Lords became a widely acknowledged force in late 1960s radicalism.[75]

Nations Apart

The Young Lords Organization was established by Orlando Davila amid the escalating gang violence of 1950s Chicago. In the ethnically mixed Lincoln Park area, Puerto Rican youth formed gangs such as the Black Eagles, the

Paragons, and the Young Lords to defend themselves and retaliate against the white street gangs that dominated the neighborhood. Jose "Cha Cha" Jimenez joined the Lords in 1959. Like other young Puerto Rican so-called delinquents, Jimenez had not only spent time in jail and juvenile homes, as well as on probation, he had also been exiled to Puerto Rico for close to a year by court order. In 1964, at the age of seventeen, he became president of the Lords. His political education began in 1968, while he was incarcerated in a maximum security prison. There a Muslim inmate lent him literature, and he met Fred Hampton. After his release, Jimenez founded a group called Concerned Puerto Rican Youth. When this organization was absorbed into and immobilized by the local YMCA, he went on to form the Puerto Rican Progressive Movement, a Puerto Rican nationalist study group that soon became part of the Young Lords after Jimenez convinced the latter group to focus on community activism.[76]

Unlike organizations such as the Real Great Society, the Young Lords' turn to community work did not entail a complete renunciation of their former gang posture. A member of the Lords argued: "You have to understand, man, that even *before*, we were in some ways already revolutionary. Dig? It's not that we were a gang one minute and the next we were all Communists. What we had to realize was that it wasn't no good fightin' each other, but that what we were doing as a gang had to be against the capitalist institutions that are oppressing us."[77] The spring 1969 murder of Manuel Ramos, another member of the Lords, by an off-duty police officer further radicalized the group. Jimenez later recalled: "I think it was at that point that I became a real revolutionary . . . Instead of going out and killing a pig, I saw the need to sit down and analyze the ways of getting even . . . We have to educate the people before we think about guns."[78] Refusing to renounce their former gang activity, the Lords made their political work a consequence rather than a repudiation of their past endeavors. From this perspective, collective survival of structural violence was a potentially revolutionary act, rather than criminal and antisocial behavior.

The Young Lords' activities in Chicago focused on increasing neighborhood control of social service institutions, overseeing law enforcement activities, and restraining the onslaught of urban renewal. In November 1968, with the support of the church's minister, the Lords occupied the Armitage Street Methodist Church to protest the refusal of a faction of the congregation to allow them to use the church's basement for a day-care center. Following the occupation of the building and the subsequent retreat of the opposition, the Lords worked with the congregation to establish the first People's Church, which became their base of operations for community programs. In February 1969, the Lords organized a takeover of the Police-Community Relations Council of the 18th District by community residents to protest ongoing police harassment and the council's unwillingness to address this issue. Three months later, the Lords occupied the McCormick Theological Seminary, run by the Presbyterian Church, for five days to demand support for community programs under neighborhood control.[79] In June 1969, the Lords and a number of small neighborhood organizations formed the Poor People's Coalition to fight the Hartford Company's plan to build a middle-income housing complex in Lincoln Park, as an urban renewal project. The Lords' commandeering of spaces ostensibly devoted to community well-being publicized the group's frustration with establishment institutions and demonstrated their confrontational tactics in pursuit of a new, and more ethical, social collectivity.

Political organizing by the Lords in Chicago attracted the attention of a number of young Puerto Ricans in New York City. A small contingent of mainland Puerto Rican youth—members of La Sociedad de Albizu Campos at the State University of New York in Old Westbury and a group from East Harlem—traveled to Chicago after reading an interview with Cha Cha Jimenez published in the June 7, 1969, issue of the *Black Panther*.[80] Jimenez gave the visitors permission to jointly establish a New York chapter of the Young Lords, which they did in July 1969.[81] The Young Lords' "13 Point Program and Platform" linked self-determination, community control of institutions, armed self-defense, socialism, and Puerto Rican, Latino, and Third World liberation—and, eventually, women's rights. The group in New York quickly adopted the performative and confrontational tactics of the Chicago Lords.

The first collective action of the New York branch was the July 1969 garbage offensive. Targeting the everyday negligence of the city's sanitation department, the Lords successfully rallied East Harlem residents around this visible symbol of neglect and called attention to the uneven distribution of city services and the oppressive living conditions this fostered. Soon after this inaugural action, the New York Lords helped organize a welfare mothers' demonstration.[82] Their activities expanded quickly, encompassing a broad array of "serve the people" programs—which, following the Panthers' model, included such ongoing initiatives as free breakfast programs for children, day-care programs, clothing giveaways, health clinics, community dinners, cultural events, and political education classes. The group established the First People's Church in December 1969 by temporarily taking over the First Spanish Methodist Church on 111th Street and using the space to house the Young Lords' community programs. Iris Morales explained: "We believed that the most disenfranchised segment of our community, the most oppressed—the street people—would play a revolutionary role because they had nothing to lose."[83] The Young Lords understood their purpose to be directing the poorest of the poor to work together against the violence of impoverishment and toward the revolutionary transformation of the world from which they had been systematically and brutally excluded.

The New York chapter split with the original Chicago Lords in May 1970, ostensibly because the Chicago group was losing its political focus.[84] The New York contingent changed its name to the Young Lords Party (YLP) and continued to stage actions that closely resembled earlier activities by the Chicago Lords. In October, the YLP once again seized the First Spanish Methodist Church and established the Second People's Church to publicize demands for prisoners' rights in the city's jails after the suspicious death of Young Lord Julio Roldán while incarcerated in the Tombs (the Manhattan House of Detention). Following this action, the YLP devoted substantial energy to prison organizing, forming a Prisoner Solidarity Committee within the New York State prison system and, at the request of prisoners, sending representatives as official mediators during the 1971 Attica Prison uprising. In a leaflet titled "Prisons Are Concentration Camps for the Poor," the YLP charged:

> 85% of all the prisoners in U.S. prisons here come from oppressed nations and although most of them are not charged with so-called political crimes, they are political prisoners, prisoners of a system which drives them to commit "crimes" that are really only acts of survival against the oppressive conditions of racism and poverty. 100% of all the prisoners in U.S. prisons abroad come from oppressed nations and all of them are political prisoners because they are fighting the same war as the op-

pressed are fighting here: they are fighting for political freedom, they are fighting against racism, genocide, starvation, exploitation.[85]

The group's message asserted the continuum of the US matrix of incarceration and indicted the imperatives of the market economy. Activities of putative legality served the purposes of exploitation and dispossession. The YLP asserted: "The hands of billionaires and corporations are dripping with the blood of people all over the world, so when these capitalists scream 'law and order' they are screaming for War Against the Poor!"[86] The murder of George Jackson, a leader of the radical prison movement, in San Quentin Prison, ignited the Attica uprising.[87] The attempts of YLP representatives Juan "Fi" Ortiz and Jose Paris to act as negotiators at Attica, as well as the YLP's close association with the Inmates Liberation Front, built on the work that the Lords had begun after Roldán's death to confront the impunity of the state's punitive apparatus and to demonstrate the collateral damage of so-called law-and-order campaigns.

With these and other activities, the Lords fashioned an insurgent movement that began with the commonplace inequities, racism, and violence experienced by mainland Puerto Ricans and linked them to the systemic conditions of which such everyday adversities were symptomatic. The abysmal state of healthcare services for poor Puerto Ricans in New York led the Lords to work closely with the Health Revolutionary Unity Movement and stage an occupation of Lincoln Hospital in the South Bronx to protest the city's downsizing of the hospital's already inadequate facilities. The Young Lords developed programs targeting drug addiction and, with the help of volunteer medical students, conducted screening for lead poisoning, tuberculosis, and anemia (each significant problems among the city's poor). Responding to complaints from East Harlem, the Lords even unsuccessfully attempted to purge the neighborhood of drug dealers and eradicate the local heroin economy. In these ways the YLP worked against—and sought to define as manifestly political—the uneven distribution of disease, addiction, and other conditions that prematurely ended or devastated the lives of many impoverished Puerto Ricans.

Similarly, a number of YLP women underscored the routine chauvinism and political character of gender relations in the party itself. In response to the women's demands, the Central Committee redrafted the YLP's thirteen-point platform, replacing an affirmation of "revolutionary" machismo with the statement: "We want equality for women. Down with machismo and male chauvinism."[88] The committee also pledged that all levels of leadership should include women and warned that sexist behavior was grounds for a YLP member's suspension or expulsion from the organization. Moreover, the Lords established child-care services to allow for the full participation of women in the party, as well as forming a Women's Union addressed to the specific needs and concerns of Latina workers and campaigning against the mass sterilization of Puerto Rican women. Iris Morales recalled: "With these principles in place, more women joined the organization. The internal struggle strengthened the participation of women and gave voice to Latinas across the movement." Although asserting feminist principles, Morales also emphasized the specificity of this struggle for women of color, comparing them to some white feminists who sought to privilege gender inequality without attending to how gender and sexuality remained bound up with racial and economic relations.[89] The YLP's "Position Paper on Women" thus asserted: "Puerto Rican, Black, and other Third World (colonized) women . . . are suffering from three different types of oppression under capitalism. First, they are oppressed as Puerto Ricans or Blacks. Second, they are op-pressed as women. Third, they are oppressed by their own men."[90] This perspective also had direct consequences for rethinking the traditional ten-ets of revolutionary nationalism.

The YLP's version of nationalism advocated an ethics of collective com-mitment, shared obligations, and social reciprocity. Minister of Informa-tion Pablo "Yoruba" Guzmán explained: "We have to turn around the order of things, the capitalist order of things, and create a socialist order . . . We're brought up to be individuals who look out solely for themselves. In school we're taught that the first law of nature is self-preservation. We say that's bullshit—the first law of nature is preservation of the group, because as long as the group exists, as long as your nation exists, then you exist."[91] Guzmán thus contended:

> We've seen how the Black colony in America has been divided in terms of culture versus politics. We don't want to see the Puerto Rican colony divided that way . . . We're not gonna go into a trip glorifying the *pava*, which is a straw hat, or the *guayabera*, which is a kind of shirt, 'cause there ain't no hat or no shirt gonna free anybody. But the fact that our people, when put up against the wall, have managed to kick ass for centuries—

that is good, that is part of our culture, right. That's why we say that the most cultural thing we can do is pick up the gun to defend ourselves.[92]

"Our people" had gained coherence and cultural form under siege. From the perspective of YLP ideology, social belonging was historically determined by oppression and, under these conditions, the content of "our people"—with the proper political education and in opposition to what the YLP called Puerto Rican "lombrices" (parasitic worms) or the "capitalist and traitor" class—was immanently revolutionary. Whereas "the amerikkkan enemy . . . tell[s] us that we ain't got no history, no roots, no nothing," the YLP insisted that "in a national liberation struggle like ours, a movement must be built from the people, from our experiences, sorrows, joys."[93] According to the Lords' analysis, "the one major thing that holds us back in our fight to liberate Puerto Rico and all oppressed people is a lack of unity . . . [A] divided nation is a weak nation . . . To be stronger we must unite. But even this unification will not be enough if we still fight each other . . . [We] have been taught to fight against each other. Capitalism is a system that forces us to climb over our brothers and sisters' backs to get to the top."[94] The Lords similarly renounced the competitive relations of ethnic pluralism and interest group liberalism.

The first point in the YLP's thirteen-point program proclaimed: "We want self-determination for Puerto Ricans, liberation on the island and inside the United States." Their platform also specified the "Afro-Indio" cultural history of Puerto Ricans. In another context, Pablo Guzmán described the Young Lords' conception of "revolutionary nationalism" in terms distinct from Huey Newton: "It's ridiculous to say you're an internationalist and you're going to struggle for all oppressed people, without picking a particular segment of people you're gonna work in. Because the people, you know, are divided along nation and class lines, and we have to recognize both. In this country, for example, racism is like a stick that the pigs are clubbing you on the head with. Now you got to grab the other end and hit them back with it—and the other end of the stick is nationalism."[95] Nationalism was a reply to and a consequence of racial oppression. For the Lords, revolutionary nationalism thus combined the mobilization for Puerto Rican national liberation, the struggle against the uneven economic conditions of US colonialism, and the global fight against imperialism and racial capitalism. The necessary response to the imperial mechanisms that render "the people" divided and exploitable was, to the YLP, the affective political community supposed by nationalism. One problem for the Lords, however, was that although they vigorously framed as political the conditions and context of struggle within which Puerto Ricans lived, they did little to question the terms through which "the people" were constituted as multifaceted political subjects. Divisions in Puerto Rican society were treated as clearly aligned with either national liberation or the "amerikkkan enemy." Nowhere were the consequences of this simplification more evident than with the rift between island and mainland Puerto Ricans.

The YLP's Ofensiva Rompe Cadenas (Break the Chains Offensive) was a pivotal moment for the organization. In January 1971, the Lords announced plans to organize, with the Nationalist Party in Puerto Rico, a demonstration in commemoration of the 1937 Ponce Massacre, holding simultaneous marches on the island in Ponce and on the mainland in Philadelphia, New York City, and Bridgeport, Connecticut. The campaign signaled the YLP's intention to unite the divided nation of Puerto Rico—with one-third of its population on the US mainland and two-thirds on the island, split by the forces of colonial rule and capitalist labor exploitation—and to expand the group's community organizing to the island. Following the Ponce Massacre action, the YLP established branches on the island in Aguadilla and El Caño, working primarily on local housing and healthcare issues.[96] The Lords declared: "For the Puerto Rican nation this is another stage in our protracted war for liberation. To achieve our liberation we need a revolutionary Party, representative of all the people with one sole objective, national liberation. In that way we will give our largest contribution to the other oppressed people's [sic] of the world, as the people of Vietnam have done for us."[97] The island campaign proved difficult, however, not only because it spread the group's limited resources thin, but also because the Lords encountered considerable resistance to their presence on the island.

Juan "Fi" Ortiz and Juan Gonzalez had traveled to Puerto Rico the previous summer to assess the possibilities of the Lords' organizing on the island. They observed the dismal conditions of innumerable shantytowns and concluded: "We believe that the people that are forced to live in these areas will understand the need for revolutionary change and will be easy to organize because of the extent of their oppression."[98] But once the Lords' organizing efforts began, the group encountered a largely intractable division between Puerto Ricans on and off the island. Richie Perez recollected

The cover of an issue
of the Young Lords
Party's newspaper,
Palante, announcing
the Ofensiva Rompe
Cadenas (Break the
Chains Offensive),
March 1971.

that although "we received a warm welcome from the Nationalist Party,"
many members of the island-based Puerto Rican Left were hostile to the
Lords' efforts and "resented these Nuyoricans coming to tell them how to
conduct revolution on their island."[99] Some of the trouble the Lords experienced on the island had to do with factionalism and with ideological differences between the YLP and two local groups, the Partido Independentista
Puertorriqueño and the Movimiento Pro Independencia. According to the
YLP, "the origin of these groups was either from the petty or upper bourgeoisie," and the Lords would provide "more revolutionary leadership."[100]
But the ideological differences were also partly the result of the fact that the
Partido Independentista Puertorriqueño had been active on the island since
1946, and the Movimiento Pro Independencia since 1959. Although some

islanders welcomed the Lords, Perez concluded: "There were differences between those who had been shaped in the conditions of the American ghettos and those that had been shaped by the direct conditions of colonialism on the island."[101] Committed to mobilizing around the idea of the divided nation, the Young Lords may not have anticipated the extent of these differences. In July 1972, with inadequate resources and the YLP's internal ideological divisions becoming more pronounced, the Central Committee shut down Ofensiva Rompe Cadenas. The end of the campaign precipitated a substantial rethinking of tactics and ideology for the YLP, as well as a decision to forgo the divided nation thesis in favor of theorizing mainland Puerto Ricans as an "oppressed national minority"[102] that should join together with others similarly subjugated in a Marxist-Leninist revolutionary movement.

The failure of Ofensiva Rompe Cadenas also magnified an essential problem with the YLP's conception of community organizing, their notion of "democratic centralism."[103] Like the Panthers, even though the YLP actively recruited poor people as members, the group was organized on the principles of revolutionary vanguardism, centralized control, and strategic action as the work of a political party along the lines specified by Lenin in *What Is to Be Done?* Whereas for Marx the proletariat was predisposed as a class to be revolutionary agents, Lenin claimed that the party was a necessary mechanism for cultivating this revolutionary potential. The political philosopher Sylvain Lazarus argues that, from Lenin's perspective in 1902, "revolutionary consciousness, the appearance of revolutionary militants, is not a spontaneous phenomenon," but that political consciousness is realized through the apparatus of the party.[104] Beyond the Central Committee, there was little that was collective in the decision-making process of either the Panthers or the Lords. Both parties were explicitly organized on a military model because both believed this was necessary for armed self-defense in the face of the concerted and relentless violence of the state. Incessant law enforcement infiltration and coercion successfully fomented internal distrust and undermined both groups' capacity for open deliberation. But while the Panthers tended to subordinate Leninist models to their own particular needs, influential leaders among the Young Lords became increasingly rigid in asserting the so-called correct party line of interpretation.

Ofensiva Rompe Cadenas produced what proved to be an irrevocable split within the YLP. Soon after the branches in Aguadilla and El Caño were closed, the Young Lords held their first and only congress and announced their transformation into the Puerto Rican Revolutionary Workers Organization (PRRWO). Former PRRWO members later described this development as "part of a nation-wide break with the old eclectic period, and the rise of the Marxist-Leninist trend within the broad revolutionary movement."[105] With the name change, and the accompanying internal purges, the organization adopted a more strictly Marxist-Leninist line and redirected its efforts from community-based strategies to organizing at the point of production (inside factories). The "serve the people" programs ended, and even the Women's Union eventually closed. Whereas the "old eclectic period" had permitted coalitions across strategic and ideological differences, the "broad revolutionary movement" fragmented into sectarian turf wars.

Following the collapse of Ofensiva Rompe Cadenas, the retreat of the PRRWO into internecine factionalism and doctrinaire Marxist-Leninism had more to do with vanguardist "democratic centralism" than it did with the failure to galvanize a united struggle for national liberation. The subsequent renunciation of community mobilization in favor of factory organizing was most significant in that it signaled an effort—after the abortive attempt to create a unified national liberation movement—to grasp hold of a constituency (the working class) presumed to be an immanently revolutionary force. Ofensiva Rompe Cadenas made visible competing political imaginaries. It revealed the durability of the particularities and divisions produced through the historical management and segmentation of colonial incorporation and the ethnic and class-based strategies that emerged in response to this history. If the Puerto Rican Forum (discussed in chapter 4) had been anxious to establish an independent mainland identity, its efforts had increased the separation of social identities of island-based Puerto Ricans from Puerto Ricans living on the US mainland. In contrast, at the global scale, such internal particularities and differences appeared less pronounced. It was at this scale of international community—through the precedents of international law and the conventions of multilateral institutions—that a number of oppositional movements sought to call attention to and seek restitution for the historical conditions of colonialism.

A Global Arena

The Black Panthers, Young Lords, and the International Indian Treaty Council each turned to the international arena—in varying degrees and with distinct emphases—to make the United States liable for its violations of international law, to build global solidarity in opposition to Euro-American imperialism, and to assert the significance of colonial difference within the United States. But even as self-determination as a universal standard during the mid-twentieth century promised to delegitimize imperial prerogative, the specific rubric of sovereignty comprised its own troubling genealogies. This had partly to do with the absolutist organization of violence and the state of exception conveyed by sovereign power, but it was also a question of who should be recognized as rightful agents of decolonization and where the boundaries of emerging political communities should be drawn. These questions were further complicated by the fact that the most readily discernible spaces of political community were so often the consequence of colonialism itself—whether, in the United States, the legal parameters of tribal membership, the Mexican territory conquered by Spain and surrendered to the United States in the Treaty of Guadalupe Hidalgo, or, less literally, the so-called ghetto, circumscribed and held captive by politicians' gerrymandering and financial institutions' redlining. Appealing to internationally established principles and institutions was a way to circumvent or temper the authority of the US state. Demanding recognition of and redress for state-sanctioned illegalities also reversed the ascription of illegitimacy that so often branded the poor as undeserving and fraudulent, if not outright criminal. As with attempts to foreground the violence of the state, such as those discussed in chapter 3, these appeals to international forums sought to brand the United States as a global outlaw, a rogue state to be brought in line with international norms. Such an indictment cast the US imperial nation-state as an instrument of the capitalist class, culpable for the racially overdetermined conditions of poverty—instead of blaming poor people themselves, as Great Society policies implied.

How colonialism mattered and what self-determination meant varied substantially for oppositional groups within the United States during the 1960s and 1970s. For the Black Panthers, African Americans were a people whose historical experience was colonization and brutalization under the Atlantic slave trade and chattel slavery. Following the demise of slavery, colonial regimes of racial subordination continued, first in the redeployment of the plantation system through such arrangements as sharecropping and convict labor, and later in the spatial marginalization and racialized exploitation of urban ghettos by white economic interests. Thus, although

African Americans did not live under the conditions of traditional colonial rule, their situation was analogous to the predicament of the colonized in Africa and Asia, having historical roots in European colonial expropriation and with similar prospects for liberation from the economic and ideological tyranny of white privilege. For the Young Lords, US colonialism was an enduring condition complicated by migration and the schism between island and mainland Puerto Ricans. The failure of Ofensiva Rompe Cadenas forced the Young Lords to reassess who and where was the political community that comprised the people they sought to liberate, but even this dilemma appeared to be a consequence of US colonialism. The situations of Mexican Americans living in what was once northern Mexico, Chamorros and Samoans living under virtual military occupation, Kānaka Maoli dispossessed by the US seizure of Hawai'i, Filipinos who had moved to the US mainland in the wake of US colonization, and Caribbean migrants who arrived in the United States following the neocolonial reconfiguration of the Antilles suggest the multiple circumstances of US colonialism.

In this chapter, I have focused on how the localized politics of poverty articulated the sometimes figurative, sometimes empirical assertion of the international dimension within the United States. Although liberal reformers deployed universalized categories—poverty and community, in particular—to contain and localize challenges to prevailing social and economic conditions, organizations such as the Black Panthers and Young Lords insisted on the colonial character of seemingly domestic inequities while also identifying those universal categories as symptomatic of shared conditions of insurgent possibility. For many of the activists who had participated in and become disaffected by War on Poverty initiatives, their frustration was precisely that these programs refused to confront the expansive structural violence of racial capitalism. In the wake of nineteenth-century industrialization, international doctrines of capitalist development extended their rationalized calculus of market expansion and labor discipline in a manner that fostered antagonisms along the lines of race, gender, and region, but that also reproduced a particular structure of class relations. In the mid-twentieth century, oppositional groups and activists turned to the artificially unified category of poverty as precisely the global bond that facilitated resistance to uneven capitalist incursion worldwide.

The revolutionary internationalism of the Black Panther Party and the Young Lords proposed both a strategically united Third World front and a radical pluralism that contested the integrationist perspective of liberalism. This radical pluralism demanded going beyond liberalism's inability to comprehend the formation of collective identities and the contentious disposition of the political itself. The political philosopher Chantal Mouffe argues: "While politics aims at constructing a political community and creating a final unity, a fully inclusive political community and a final unity can never be realized since there will permanently be a 'constitutive outside,' an exterior to the community that makes its existence possible." According to Mouffe, in opposition to the integrationist pluralist narrative, democratic politics is not a homogeneous space of competing interests and a framework for consensus, but rather multiplies antagonisms and differences. Thus, she points out that "antagonistic forces will never disappear and politics is characterized by conflict and division. Forms of agreement can be reached but they are always partial and provisional since consensus is by necessity based on acts of exclusion."[106] This was not only a problem for liberalism. Although revolutionary internationalist endeavors clearly identified the structural and historical forces of racial capitalism as the principal agent of poverty, dispossession, and organized violence, coming to terms with the processes of contingency and exclusion that were inherent in the political proved far more difficult.

Decolonization and anti-imperial social movements after the Second World War changed the dynamics of the international arena. The influence of former colonies within international institutions such as the United Nations increased as their numbers grew after successful national independence movements. The new nations shared certain economic and political concerns that, at least in the UN General Assembly, could at times counterbalance Euro-American viewpoints. Since the 1919 Paris Peace Conference, the principle of national self-determination had been part of the liberal vision of a multilateral institutional infrastructure. This principle was reaffirmed in the 1945 UN Charter—in Chapter XI, Article 73, Declaration Regarding Non-Self-Governing Territories—and in Article 2 of the UN General Assembly's 1960 Declaration on the Granting of Independence to Colonial Countries and Peoples. Moreover, the principle of self-determination was applied even more expansively with the 1948 UN Universal Declaration of Human Rights, and in recognition of the rights of indigenous peoples in Article 2.1 of the International Labor Organization (ILO) Convention No. 107 of 1957 and, following the period discussed here, ILO

Convention No. 169 in 1989 and the UN Declaration on the Rights of Indigenous Peoples in 2007.

The Black Panthers' call for a UN plebiscite as one of the primary demands in the groups' ten-point program followed these developments, as well as African American appeals to the United Nations that included the NAACP's 1947 "An Appeal to the World" and the Harlem-based activist Jesse Gray's announcement in 1964 that he would lead a demonstration at the UN Plaza "to ask the UN to intervene in the 'police terror in the United States.' "[107] "Our major political objective," wrote Huey Newton and Bobby Seale, is "a United Nations-supervised plebiscite to be held throughout the black colony in which only black colonial subjects will be allowed to participate for the purpose of determining the will of black people as to their national destiny."[108] The BPP also petitioned the United Nations directly, asserting that "the Genocide Convention has been flagrantly violated by the Government of the United States" and that "the racist planned and unplanned terror suffered by more than 40 millions [sic] of black, brown, red, and yellow citizens of the United States cannot be regarded solely as a domestic issue."[109] Although the Panthers' efforts to pursue these charges through UN channels never went further than a petition, the BPP developed anticolonial alliances that suggested a future for their revolutionary intercommunalism on a world scale.[110]

The international diplomacy of American Indian peoples preexisted European contact and continued to be formally recognized until the US government officially—in the Indian Appropriation Act of 1871—ceased making treaties with native peoples. Following the global denunciation of colonial rule after the Second World War, renewed indigenous international initiatives gained increasing support during the 1970s. In the wake of the bloody confrontation at Wounded Knee in 1973, the American Indian Movement (AIM), Sioux tribal leaders, and representatives from ninety-five other indigenous nations convened in Aberdeen, South Dakota, in June 1974. At the conference, delegates began to formulate a strategy and agenda for seeking redress through the United Nations. Conference participants established the International Indian Treaty Council (IITC) and drafted the "Declaration of Continuing Independence."[111] The declaration stated: "We the sovereign Native Peoples charge the United States with gross violations of our International Treaties," noting that although "all Native Nations wish to avoid violence, . . . the United States government has always used force and violence to deny Native Nations basic human and treaty rights." The declaration also underscored the solidarities forged as a consequence of US colonialism that extended beyond tribal nations by asserting an alliance "with the colonized Puerto Rican people in their struggle for Independence of the same United States of America."[112] The US insistence on the subordinate sovereignty of tribal nations and deliberate use of repression (recently on display at Wounded Knee) made multilateral oversight a practical necessity.

At the inaugural meeting of the IITC, participants discussed the purpose and tactics of the new organization. John Trudell, AIM's national chairman, noted the incongruity of "going to the criminals (US government) and asking them to punish themselves for their acts toward us."[113] Jimmie Durham, then of AIM's International Division and soon to be the executive director of the IITC, recalled meeting Amilcar Cabral in Geneva before his murder by Portuguese agents and hearing about Cabral's African Party for the Independence of Guinea and the Cape Verde Islands. Durham emphasized how Cabral "learned to work with the UN, to make speeches and use 'white' ideals and pretensions" on behalf of national liberation.[114] Addressing the United Nations in 1972, Cabral had eloquently linked his party to the principles of the international organization, arguing: "We are not struggling only for the achievement of our aspirations for freedom and national independence. We are struggling, and will struggle till victory, in order that the resolutions of the UN Charter should be respected." Cabral explained that Portuguese colonialism was not only the murderous repression of the Guinean people, but an intolerable affront to UN doctrine: "In struggling and dying for the liberation of our country, we are, in the current context of international legality, giving our life for the ideal which the UN itself defined in its Charter and . . . particularly in the resolution on decolonization."[115] As Roxanne Dunbar-Ortiz would later reflect with regard to the IITC, the question was how best to "build our liberation movement so that we can assert our independence and take our right place in the world community alongside other countries which have forged themselves in the resistance to colonialism."[116] Self-determination required a tactical articulation of political community—the measured use of the principles of liberal internationalism and anticolonial alliance—that would use the weight of world opinion against the criminal exploits of colonialism.

In 1977, the IITC was granted Non-Governmental Organization consultative status by the United Nations, becoming the first indigenous peoples' organization to gain formal multilateral recognition in the twentieth century. In the same year, the IITC sent delegates to the International NGO Conference on Discrimination against Indigenous Populations in the Americas, sponsored by the UN Special Committee of NGOs on Human Rights Subcommittee on Racism, Racial Discrimination, Apartheid, and Decolonization at the Palais des Nations in Geneva.[117] In a significant gesture of sovereign independence, and much to the bewilderment of both the US and Swiss customs agents, the twenty-four Iroquois delegates who traveled to the conference used Haudenosaunee (Six Nations of the Iroquois Confederacy) passports.[118] Altogether, 130 indigenous delegates from throughout the Americas attended the conference, with selected representatives giving formal testimony. Speaking against "planned genocide by the governments of the Western Hemisphere," the AIM activist Russell Means reasserted the terms of the 1974 declaration: "I'm [also] here to talk about . . . [the] liberation of our people as separate entities, separate nations . . . There is only one color of mankind that is not allowed to participate in the international community. And that color is red."[119] Marie Sanchez, a Northern Cheyenne tribal judge, took the United Nations to task for not having initiated the recognition of indigenous peoples. "Why did we have to travel this distance to come to you?" she demanded. Sanchez called attention to the persistent violence against native peoples, and indigenous women in particular, stating: "Indian women of the Western Hemisphere are the target of the genocide that is still on-going, that is still the policy of the United States of America. We are undergoing the modern form called sterilization."[120] Even as they pursued redress through the United Nations, Sanchez and the other IITC delegates remained skeptical of the degree to which liberal internationalism might provide a framework capable of recognizing indigenous peoples and a bulwark against the realities of colonial violence.

UN officials, seeking to offset such skepticism, did not permit the United States to make an official presentation at the final plenary session. Instead, the US government submitted a statement for the record after the conference. At the time of the Geneva meeting, Andrew Young, the former executive director of the Southern Christian Leadership Council, was the US ambassador to the United Nations, having been appointed by President Jimmy Carter. Many of the IITC delegates remarked on the unfortunate irony of Young's and Carter's indifference to American Indian issues while

International Indian Treaty Council delegates at the UN International NGO Conference on Discrimination Against Indigenous Populations in the Americas in Geneva, September 1977.
PHOTOGRAPH BY AND COURTESY OF R. C. BANCROFT.

the ambassador and president championed human rights internationally. Roxanne Dunbar-Ortiz, for instance, argued: "The 'human rights' focus of the Carter administration has a purpose: To support certain foreign and tribal governments and their links with the U.S., while at the same time influencing changes in their methods of control internally."[121] The US statement replicated this approach to insinuating authority and containment, insisting that the US government was "pleased that the original people of our country have gathered here in Geneva to discuss these matters of vital importance to human rights." According to the statement, "perhaps the single most important aspect" of the conference was that it "authentically represents the voices of the native peoples themselves." The United States was "committed to hearing the truth from the voices of the native peoples themselves" and would investigate such allegations as the sterilization of indigenous women without informed consent, but it "categorically" renounced "charges of genocide." Affirming the authenticity of such "voice" in the abstract sense of self-representation, the United States nevertheless rejected "hyperbole"—genocide—while remaining "concerned about" and "sensitive to any serious charges of human rights abuses committed against United States citizens."[122] The statement therefore at once denied US culpability for violence against indigenous peoples and proclaimed the United States as the guardian of American Indians—who had involuntarily been made US citizens in 1924—against what could only be external abuses or threats.

In this context, liberal internationalism was insufficient to the self-determination of American Indian nations. At the same time, international forums—the United Nations in particular, but also the World Court—were indispensable tools when pure force was not viable. Hence, Jimmie Durham observed: "The international work is important only if we do the real work of organizing ourselves in a united front back home. We are the people who will liberate ourselves, finally . . . The international work is a vital and necessary part of that but it's only a part. If the other parts, survival schools, community organizing, discipline, self reliance, and other aspects are not strong and together, then the international work doesn't mean anything. But all of these parts go together, and each makes the other stronger."[123] Durham's comments were not analogous to the Black Panthers' conception of revolutionary intercommunalism—most obviously because neither the community nor international work that Durham described was purpose-fully revolutionary. Yet in the sense that reaching beyond the US imperial nation-state was essential to both survival and self-determination, to the terms of belonging, to the convergence of the past and present in localized conditions of struggle that simultaneously demanded worldwide articulation, there is a political resonance between the IITC and the Panthers' intercommunalism. For both groups, liberation was a process that could not presume a pre-political unity or generic local circumstances, but that nevertheless required coming to terms with the artificial unity in difference (for example, Indian or black) produced as a consequence of settler colonial rule—a constitutive outside that at once disavowed and accentuated its own externality.

Two months after the meeting in Geneva, IITC staff members Durham, Dunbar-Ortiz, and Allene Goddard, as well as Edith Ballantyne, president of the UN NGO board, presented the conference resolutions and official reports to the UN General Assembly. The IITC delegation met with UN officials, including the chairman of the UN Committee on Decolonization, the chairman of the African Group of the General Assembly, and the Cuban ambassador, Ricardo Alarcon.[124] An editorial in the IITC's *Treaty Council News* commented: "Decolonization, or a better term, liberation, is a slow, painstaking process. What the colonists accomplished over the past four centuries cannot be overcome easily." The editorial cautioned: "The former colonies which have been able to achieve liberation and get UN recognition have done so only after decades of all out war. Some, like the Puerto Rican movement, are in about the same position as ourselves, though they began to approach the international community nearly 20 years ago." The editorial argued for the necessity of addressing the "world community" as "Indian people . . . one people" in order to "eventually triumph in the liberation of Indian people from bondage." This was not to deny the heterogeneity of indigenous peoples, but to act strategically: "Internally, among ourselves, in our own communities there are many issues to be discussed."[125] The tactical articulation of "one people" was simply the most expedient scale of action on the stage of world politics.

The IITC's use of the term "liberation" rather than "decolonization" is significant in describing the group's approach to anticolonialism. UN Secretary General U Thant had declared: "The United Nations stands for the self-government and independence of all peoples, and the abolition of racial discrimination without reservations."[126] Yet, according to the legal scholar James Anaya, "the regime of decolonization prescriptions that were developed and promoted through the international system [after 1945] . . . largely bypassed indigenous patterns of association and political ordering that originated prior to European colonization." This had the effect of making what Anaya calls the "UN Charter–based decolonization regime" a way to further consolidate the colonial territorial unit as the postcolonial nation-state.[127] In certain respects, this decolonization regime functioned in much the same way as antipoverty policies in the United States, by making self-determination a consequence of embodying colonial norms and the liberal political order. During the 1970s, with increasing global stagflation and a growing energy crisis, the UN compromise threatened to come apart as the industrialized nations balked at such initiatives as the New Economic International Order. But the United Nations' disciplinary mechanisms of global governance and broad mandate for inclusion nonetheless continued to be essential political supplements to the accelerated expansion of global capitalism and the periodic crises that accompanied the proliferation of market relations.

Appeals to the United Nations by groups such as the Black Panthers, Young Lords, and the International Indian Treaty Council did not go unnoticed by the domestic US champions of law and order. For instance, in 1976, the Senate subcommittee chaired by Senator James Eastland—previously on the front line of the campaign to discredit the OEO, described in chapter 3—led an investigation into the administration of the Internal Security Act. The subcommittee's inquiry focused on "revolutionary activities within the United States" such as the Puerto Rican Revolutionary Workers Organization and AIM, the IITC's parent organization. Much of the proceedings devoted to AIM were comprised of testimony by Douglas Durham, the FBI agent who had infiltrated AIM and served as a witness for the prosecution in the aftermath of Wounded Knee. Durham described the supposed national security threat posed by AIM's international ventures. He alleged extensive AIM contact with the Irish Republican Army, the Palestine Liberation Organization, the Peoples Republic of China, and the Iranian Student Association, as well as domestic groups such as the Weather Underground.[128] For social conservatives, right-wing policymakers, Cold War realists, and many self-proclaimed progressives, emerging oppositional alignments such as these were no less suspect than—and, in the case of these hearings, were manifestly conflated with—the OEO initiatives directed at gangs and community control. Under such circumstances, UN forums offered a global stage on which to call attention to the violence and illegal actions of US imperialism. But ultimately, as activists such as Jimmie Durham made clear, they also guaranteed that the final horizon of political liberation would remain within the acceptable bounds of their normative mandates. Consequently, for those seeking more radical transformations, UN mechanisms required the enduring pressure of oppositional alliances outside their institutional framework in order to force them beyond the limits of reconciliation and to use their liberal conventions toward other ends.

A PECULIAR FREEDOM
Community and Poverty, from New Federalism to Neoliberalism

Since the demise of the War on Poverty, a bipartisan majority of US policymakers has contributed to the upward redistribution of wealth, increasing economic polarization, fiscal insecurity, and mass destitution. Although the term "liberal" in the United States today is often pejorative shorthand for someone who supports public spending, permissive social policies, and government regulation—with the spending considered impractical and the regulation excessive—the liberalism of the past century was never simply a break with its classical commitment to individual liberties, the free market, and natural rights conceived in historical opposition to absolutism and inherited social status.[1] Nevertheless, during the late twentieth century, the conflation of New Deal social provisions, Great Society community initiatives, socialist planning, and totalitarianism served as a foil for neoliberal doctrine. This line of thinking built on Friedrich A. Hayek's contention in 1944 that "what in effect unites the socialists of the Left and the Right is this common hostility to competition and their common desire to replace it by a directed economy." According to Hayek, "it was the union of the anticapitalist forces of the Right and the Left, the fusion of radical and conservative socialism, which drove from Germany everything that was liberal" and resulted in the political ascendance of Nazism.[2] In view of the present crisis of neoliberalism, it is crucial to point out that the repertoires of liberal governance do not supply a viable alternative to our current predicament but instead remain to a large extent entangled in the making of these conditions. Contemporary circumstances are as they are in no small part because of the persistence of liberal doctrines. We must therefore critically assess just how past formations of liberalism, as well as social movement opposition to and engagement with liberal norms, matter today.

During the 1970s, a procapitalist and socially conservative reprisal, partly inspired by the global recession and accompanying crisis of the Fordist-Keynesian rapprochement, sought to reaffirm racial, gender, and sexual norms—increasingly through tropes such as "multiculturalism" and "family values"—in response to the proliferating challenges to conventionally privileged authority and social order.[3] Moving from defensive to proactive measures, political and economic elites embraced neoliberal approaches that intensified governmental intervention explicitly aimed at dismembering legislatively defined social protections, advancing privatization, deunionizing and casualizing the labor market, and promoting economic deregulation as a way to maximize transnational corporate profits.[4] Neoliberalism—as a historically specific ensemble of market-driven social imaginaries and governing practices—did not so much pose a return to an earlier era's laissez-faire practices as propose the aggressive dismantling of the regulative infrastructure and social compact of the mid-twentieth century in order to cannibalize public assets and diminish the costs of doing business. Over the past forty years, neoliberal policies have increasingly shifted the burden of economic risk from the wealthy to everyone else, spreading social insecurity and desocializing wage labor, rendering racialized and increasingly abject populations as disposable, accelerating the criminalization of poverty, and punitively reconstructing the semiwelfare state through the coercive matrix of workfare regimes, the police state, and the prison-probation-parole complex.[5] At the same time, financialization—through the restructuring and deregulation of global capital markets and the expansion of credit and debt—served to defer and seemingly depoliticize the consequences of economic decline, while market populism advanced the mythology of individual ownership and entrepreneurial opportunity embodied in shareholder value as the cornerstone of democracy.[6] In spite of the intensifying crises of neoliberalism over the past two decades, many of the principal liberal presumptions that sustain its popular legitimacy appear to remain intact.

In this conclusion, I consider two examples that provide a sense of the extraordinary resilience of the historical themes addressed in this book. These examples also serve to clarify some of the ways in which conceptions of poverty and community have changed during the past forty years. First, I give a brief overview of the subsequent career of community development and the rise of the community development corporation model. Second, I discuss the World Bank's gradual embrace of particular forms of grass-roots development and community participation as indicative of the explicit reincorporation of social conditions as a concern and deliberate field of intervention by neoliberal institutions. I look at these examples not as a measure of the "success" or "failure" of the initiatives studied in the preceding chapters, but in order to emphasize the substantial historical contingency of such endeavors and the ways in which particular aspects of these earlier approaches were subsequently reappropriated and redisposed.

From Economic Growth to the Entrepreneurial Poor

By the mid to late 1960s, enthusiasm for community development as official policy in the international arena had begun to wane.[7] In 1959, at the height of US foreign assistance support for community development initiatives, the United States directly funded community development programs in twenty-five countries, including India, Indonesia, Jordan, Korea, Pakistan, and the Philippines. As the terms of the Cold War shifted and the United States prepared to escalate its military involvement in Vietnam, US funds for community development abroad rapidly decreased. In 1963, the US Agency for International Development eliminated its Community Development Division in Washington, D.C., along with the majority of its community development field offices abroad. The UN Department of Economic and Social Affairs and the leading international philanthropic foundations involved in funding community development also gradually moved their focus away from community development during the 1960s. The disappointing results of India's high-profile Community Development Program further hastened the decline of the community development model during this time. According to one administrator at the US Agency for International Development, "political leaders in developing countries were disillusioned because their community development programs had not demonstrated, as promised, that the community development approach would build stable 'grass roots' democratic institutions and would improve the economic and social well-being of rural people while contributing to the attainment of national economic goals."[8] Technocratic schemes such as the Green Revolution, with its promise of ending hunger and promoting profitable economic growth, began to displace the ethereal rhetoric of community development. Ironically, the initial appeal of community development for policymakers—that it was narrowly focused on the local in the service of nation building—later became the rationale for its elimination. Community development failed to alleviate poverty, provide material security, or develop sustainable, long-term improvements. In other words, it was incapable of transforming the structural conditions that exceeded locality. During the 1980s, community development principles would be given a revived neoliberal lease on life, but at the beginning of the 1970s it seemed that their heyday in the international arena had passed.

However, the policy life of community development in the United States was not over. US community development after the Second World War had never been charged with nation building for economic growth, as had been the case internationally. In the United States, community development was first and foremost a political form—or, more precisely, a circumscribed route to formal politics often deployed in the service of depoliticizing poverty. It was primarily a reformist model addressed to poverty amidst affluence, and to mediating inequalities through localization. As a mode of ideological incorporation, it thus required minimal evidence of economic upward mobility for the people it was supposed to benefit. Efforts by the federal government to insinuate dominant social and political institutions at the community level during the mid-twentieth century were perhaps most obviously prompted first by the civil rights movement and, later, by the tremendous influence and attraction of black power for dispossessed groups. During the late 1960s, the discourse of community was caught in perpetual tension between radical and reformist models contingent on the precise context of their enunciation. Nixon's New Federalism deployed the rhetoric of community to promote transferring federal resources to the so-called silent majority. Nixon sought to mobilize an electoral majority built on white working-class hostility to what he referred to as the "special interests"—in other words, African Americans—supposedly courted by the Johnson administration's urban policies.

Federal commitment to maximum feasible participation of the poor in the War on Poverty's Community Action Program was substantially qualified only three years after the Economic Opportunity Act (EOA) became law. The 1967 Green Amendments transferred community action agencies to municipal control, effectively retracting the federal government's challenge to city and state authority embodied in the 1964 EOA and refortifying the channels of local participation within the status quo. An emphasis on community service had already been given priority over community organizing with the 1966 EOA Amendments, and the 1968 guidelines of the Office of Economic Opportunity excluded political activism from government-sponsored community action.

The Office of Economic Opportunity was abolished in 1975. Administrative oversight of community action agencies was transferred to the newly established Community Services Administration, which—until President Ronald Reagan's Omnibus Budget Reconciliation Act of 1981 ended it—was housed in the Department of Health and Human Services. Community services block grants were subsequently administered by the Department of Health and Human Services' Office of Community Affairs.

Both the Nixon and Ford administrations promoted the transfer of authority from the federal government to state and local polities through revenue sharing and block grants. As with Johnson's initiatives, deference to local community continued as a dominant political rhetoric. President Ford, for instance, characterized the community development block grant program as an effort "to return power from the banks of the Potomac to the people in their own communities."[9] Both Nixon and Reagan touted New Federalist platforms that ostensibly championed localism. However, while Nixon's New Federalism redirected many of the Great Society initiatives toward the white middle class, Reagan's version was a more thorough attempt at devolution and privatization. Reagan's New Federalist policies devolved fiscal and juridical authority to states and cities, but it also reasserted state and municipal authority over local grass-roots activities.[10] Revisions to the administration of community development block grants, renamed community services block grants, is a case in point. Under the aegis of these changes, funding that had been formerly allocated directly to Community Development Corporations (CDCs) was now awarded to municipalities, which in turn distributed the federal awards to local constituents.

Writing prior to the Reagan realignment, Rita Mae Kelly opens her *Community Participation in Directing Economic Development* with the following observation: "The war on poverty of the 1960s has left in its wake many unrealized or shattered programs. In the debate over maximum feasible participation, the proponents of community control by low-income residents of government funded programs lost and regrouped constantly. Only one major program area of the movement survives relatively intact. Community control of community economic development is still alive and thriving in numerous urban and rural communities."[11] By the 1970s, the program that Kelly refers to was largely the domain of the CDC. Although evident in local experiments throughout the 1960s, the 1967 creation of the Bedford-Stuyvesant Restoration Corporation was the first comprehensive implementation of the CDC model. Supported by the 1966 Special Impact Amendment to the Economic Opportunity Act, the first generation of CDCs emerged from within the same turbulent legislative framework that produced the Community Action Program. Special Impact program funding was further institutionalized and supplemented by the 1969 Community Self-Determination Act, and it operated in conjunction with the Model Cities Program's move to purge political mobilization from community development.

By definition CDCs are community-controlled nonprofit corporations with a volunteer board of directors, established for the purpose of improving the quality of life for poor residents of a specifically defined geographic area. Although CDCs initially embraced a broad spectrum of economic development strategies, by the 1970s most had narrowed the scope of their activities to housing development and low-interest business loans. The CDC model originally sought to correct the inadequacies of the market to provide for the poor, but as government funding disappeared during the 1980s, CDCs increasingly sought to accommodate themselves to the market, rather than redirect and redistribute its surplus.[12] A 1987 study on CDCs released by the Ford Foundation summarized the shift in CDC emphasis in the following terms: "During the 1960s and 1970s, CDCs focused largely on trying to start their own businesses. Many failed. Few ever became very profitable or produced the hoped-for levels of jobs. Today's CDCs, by contrast, are more likely to supply equity capital, loans, incubator space, and technical assistance in support of home-grown private entrepreneurs and businesses in their midst."[13] Likewise, the sociologist Randy Stoecker has argued: "Supply-side approaches of attracting capital are emphasized over demand-side approaches and political action. At best, poor neighborhoods are seen as weak markets requiring reinvestment rather than as oppressed communities requiring mobilization." Stoecker also notes that because their financial resource base often remains external to the areas they serve, CDCs in fact exhibit very limited if any form of "community control." Moreover, the CDC development process conventionally promotes a market-oriented depoliticizing effect that potentially disorganizes local political mobilization in poor communities by fomenting internal competition.[14]

The Social Ethics of Neoliberalism

In the early 1970s, policymakers and multilateral lending institutions began to reassess the correlation of economic development with economic growth. Until then, growth as the ultimate goal of development and lending policy had been calculated as the increase in aggregate macro-economic indicators, such as gross national product and per capita income. It was in the form of this universalized abstraction that the so-called Third World was set within an international hierarchy of wealth and a temporal continuum of development, and entire countries were categorized as poor. Growth-oriented policies, for instance, often promoted industrialization at the expense of rural areas. One UN report concluded: "As a result of these policies, the benefits of growth-oriented development have accrued to a relatively small number of workers, farmers, and entrepreneurial elites, while little radiates towards the rural areas where, in many developing countries, the majority of the people make their livings."[15]

The increasing use of the rhetoric of poverty and participation at the World Bank is indicative of how social and cultural formation has been reintegrated into the managerial vision of development institutions. Following the widely publicized speech in 1973 in Nairobi by the president of the World Bank, Robert McNamara, the principal multilateral development institutions began to emphasize poverty alleviation rather than modernization.[16] Widespread criticism of lending practices helped to propel poverty and participation to the forefront of policy. In turn, targeting the social and cultural dimensions of development gradually emerged as a primary mechanism to ensure that development projects avoid what was called "elite capture" and reach the poorest sections of a given country in the most efficient and cost-effective manner. The concepts of participatory development and, later, social capital highlighted the value of culture as a way to ensure that the poor take care of themselves, instead of relying on the state.

Since the 1980s, the World Bank has been explicitly developing programs to support particular forms of grass-roots development and participation.

Notably, this support parallels the bank's intensified imposition of structural adjustment programs. When the formal end of the Cold War cleared the way for market-based triumphalism, a renewed civic moralism turned to championing a so-called third way of governing. This third way, between state and market, promoted the role of civil society and the Tocquevillian ideals of voluntary association as a way to dismantle the final vestiges of the welfare state and attendant forms of economic regulation. According to this viewpoint, community provided the social cohesion or social capital requisite for freedom and personal responsibility.

By the early 1990s, economists and other social scientists had abstracted and modeled key aspects of the practices that vast sectors of the poor had traditionally used to sustain themselves, such as barter and under-the-table labor, into a program package geared toward the informal economy.[17] In contrast to preceding modernization paradigms, these programs did not aim to make so-called backward groups abandon their cultural practices in order to become modern, but instead used what had been labeled as antiquated cultural practices as a way for the poor to simultaneously help themselves and the overall economy. The increasing use of microfinancing to ostensibly democratize capital and promote the promise that the world's poorest people "will serve as a 'frontier market,' opening up new horizons of capital accumulation" and eradicating "poverty through profits" demonstrates the contradictions of this approach to inequality.[18]

In the new millennium, the rhetoric of poverty alleviation and the valorization of community participation within the international context are central to the terms of political legitimacy. In principle, neoliberalism historically jettisoned the social and political in favor of an idealized economism, but, increasingly, influential neoliberal institutions such as the World Bank have sought to reintegrate ostensibly noneconomic factors into their policy agendas. According to this perspective, participation not only improves the efficacy of a given development project but is also fundamental to long-term sustainability.

The manner in which World Bank programs incorporate noneconomic factors actually narrows the scope of social action, obscuring the social costs of the market system and appropriating the survival strategies of the poor to support the ongoing maintenance of the so-called free market. For instance, the social capital initiatives of the World Bank are evidence of the intensified financialization or economization of social relations. Thus, the World

Bank explains its interest in social capital by noting: "A growing body of evidence indicates the size and density of social networks and institutions, and the nature of interpersonal connections, significantly affect the efficiency and sustainability of development programs."[19] The economic metaphor of social capital suggests the complete enclosure of social possibility within the paradigm of the market.[20] However, it would be incorrect to suggest that the idea of social capital simply promotes the colonization of the social by economic logic.

Perhaps what is most interesting is how social relations, and particularly the unruly issues of inequality and poverty, are rendered central to the problem of constituting an unfettered and rational global market. The market must be socialized in a proper neoliberal form, which depends on responsible collective institutions. The vigor of these social networks and institutions underwrites "good governance," a phrase with which the World Bank brings the state back into the picture, although largely as a tool for the forces of civil society.[21] Especially after the East Asian market debacle in 1997 and the global economic disaster of 2008, World Bank policymakers turned to a notion of governing the market, envisioning the primacy of market forces buttressed by accountable state and social institutions.

Quite distinct from community development in the early Cold War era, where state oversight in the developing world elicited local knowledge and participation in order to secure the primacy of the state, millennial frameworks for participation recognize state administration as a viable support for the market economy, to the extent to which they are responsive to and stabilized by social and cultural association. In this current formulation, the World Bank's embrace of noneconomic factors limits the purview of social action not because the social is reduced to the economic, but because neoliberal policies now cast social relations as the principal and privileged support for the market economy. The rhetorics of empowerment and inclusion are at the forefront of disciplining and promoting a self-reliant, responsible social context for the marketplace.[22]

This version of the social in fact excludes actual political mobilization and severs potential continuities between local organizations and higher levels of governance. Like Robert Putnam's taxonomies of social capital, neoliberal policymakers definitively reject grass-roots political mobilization as an expression of community or an indication of the magnitude and vitality of social networks and institutions. It is community as social cohesion, not conflict, that can transform the poor into stakeholders working in partnership with the World Bank that promotes what it terms "country ownership" of development projects. Although its NGO Working Group is often held up as an example of the World Bank's increasing cooperation with and accountability to marginalized social groups, participating nongovernmental organizations have been increasingly compliant with World Bank protocols and disconnected from global movements for social justice.[23]

With the shift in the social ideologies of neoliberalism—evident both domestically and internationally—ideas about community and participation are central to a mode of governance that aims primarily to stabilize and maximize market forces. Within this reconfigured neoliberal ideology, community is presented as a depoliticized social collectivity that, when linked to the problem of inequality, allows for the participation of the poor as a way to invigorate and underwrite global governance. For multilateral neoliberal institutions, such as the World Bank, and for postwelfare states, such as the United States, a new manner of civic responsibility—constituted through self-reliance and informal social networks—has not so much displaced state administration as it has worked in partnership with the state to corroborate deregulated market exchange.[24] As with the conflicts within mid-twentieth-century liberal governance, there have been concerted efforts to seize unintended opportunities from within the neoliberal regime, as well as outright challenges to its legitimacy.[25]

This book has examined the ways in which conceptions of poverty and community were crucial to the practice, appropriation, and contestation of liberal governance within and in relation to the United States during the mid-twentieth century. I have argued that the forms of knowledge and techniques of power animating US social policy during this period operated in conjunction with the global prescription for modernization and political and economic development as antidotes to poverty. My focus has been on the reciprocities and tensions between liberal governance and those who have either sought to use these inclusionary procedures for their own ends or struggled to breach the confines of liberal containment.

In a variety of ways, poverty was indispensable to competing claims to political authority and recognition at this time. The federal government rendered "the poor" as a singular administrative category, even as it attributed the underlying causes of poverty to external deviations: a lack of opportunity or competence; being outside of or foreign to the norms of liberal democratic citizenship, an exclusion best remedied by formal inclusion; a residual or provisional condition. In contrast, oppositional coalitions —such as the Poor People's Campaign or the (original) Rainbow Coalition —affirmed the radical heterogeneity of their participants while using normative frameworks as a means of articulating collaborative strategies. Neither the tactics and emancipatory aspirations of oppositional movements nor the techniques and entrepreneurial prospects of liberal governance emerged independently. It is the mutually constitutive and perpetually uneven relationship between them during the thirty years following the Second World War—with their shared commitments to and diverging conceptions of autonomy and freedom—that has been the subject of this book. Addressing how these reciprocities and antagonisms have animated notions of community and poverty is a way to at once engage the present conditions of political possibility and evoke as yet unimagined horizons of political life.

NOTES

Introduction

1. Dorothy Perez, "The Need for JOIN" (statement presented at the Cleveland Community People's Conference, Cleveland, OH, February 19–21, 1965), in *Working with JOIN for a Democratic Movement*, 1, 2, JOIN Community Union, ephemeral materials, 1965–, Wilcox Collection of Contemporary Political Movements, Spencer Research Library, University of Kansas, Lawrence (hereafter JOIN/Wilcox Collection). See also Connie Brown, "Cleveland: Conference of the Poor," *Studies on the Left* 5.2 (1965).

2. Quoted in "City Awarded Poverty Funds," *Chicago Tribune*, December 17, 1964, 1. Also see "Anti-Poverty Centers Picketed at Dedication," *Chicago Tribune*, February 13, 1965.

3. "Statement on Urban Progress Centers: Presented to the Uptown Urban Progress Center on its opening day by JOIN—a Community Union in Uptown Chicago, February 12, 1965," 1, 4, JOIN/Wilcox Collection.

4. Peggy Terry, "Organizing Poor Whites in Uptown, Chicago: A History and Prospectus of JOIN Community Union," circa 1968, 1–3, Pamphlet 85–2374, Wisconsin Historical Society Library Pamphlet Collection, Madison.

5. I use the term "governance" to indicate the exercise of political power and social administration, whether or not linked directly to the state apparatus. Liberal governance in this sense also includes the ways in which individuals and groups consider self-administration as a practice of presumably relative independence and autonomy. My use of "governance" draws on elements of Michel Foucault's conception of government and "governmentality." My concern throughout this book with the political dynamics of inclusion and exclusion is related in this sense to Foucault's contention that "liberal thought does not start from the existence of the state, finding in the government the means for achieving that end

that the state would be for itself; it starts instead from society, which exists in a complex relation of exteriority and interiority vis-à-vis the state" (*The Birth of Biopolitics: Lectures at the Collège de France, 1978–1979*, ed. Michel Senellart, trans. Graham Burchell [New York: Palgrave Macmillan, 2008], 319). I focus not on the institutions of government per se, but on specific governing practices as they were shaped, challenged, and reoriented through particular conflicts and relations of force in the mid-twentieth century.

6. This was true of the administration's intergovernmental relations as well. See David M. Welborn and Jesse Burkehead, *Intergovernmental Relations in the American Administrative State: The Johnson Presidency* (Austin: University of Texas Press, 1989).

7. Mitchell Dean, *Governing Societies: Political Perspectives on Domestic and International Rule* (London: Open University Press, 2007), 110.

8. Michael Harrington, *The Other America: Poverty in the United States* (Baltimore: Penguin Books, 1962), 155, 164.

9. Fredric Jameson, *The Political Unconscious: Narrative as a Socially Symbolic Act* (Ithaca: Cornell University Press, 1981), 81, 82.

10. United States Information Agency, "Infoguide: The Great Society," October 6, 1965, 1–2, WE-9 Poverty Program (Great Society, 1964–1966), Box 98, Confidential File WE/MC, Lyndon B. Johnson Library, Austin, TX.

11. Galbraith criticized the notion that continuous growth was the solution to social problems. He argued that, rather than gradually alleviating the conditions of material deprivation and producing a classless society, economic growth had passed over a small but significant number of people who were now increasingly marginalized and whose poverty was more and more entrenched. According to Galbraith, the task was thus to ensure that the benefits of growth reached those who were still excluded. See John Kenneth Galbraith, *The Affluent Society* (Boston: Houghton Mifflin, 1958); Harrington, *The Other America*; Dwight MacDonald, "Our Invisible Poor," *New Yorker*, January 19, 1963, 82–132.

12. Lillian B. Rubin, "Maximum Feasible Participation: The Origins, Implications, and Present Status," *Annals of the American Academy of Political and Social Science* 385 (September 1969), 14.

13. Daniel P. Moynihan, "What Is 'Community Action'?," *Public Interest* 5 (Fall 1966), 3–8; and *Maximum Feasible Misunderstanding: Community Action in the War on Poverty* (New York: Free Press, 1969).

14. Anatole Shaffer, "The Cincinnati Social Unit Experiment, 1917–19," *Social Service Review* 45.2 (1971).

15. Sarvepalli Radhakrishnan, Foreword, in *Approaches to Community Development*, ed. Phillips Ruopp (The Hague: W. Van Hoeve, 1953), vii–viii.

16. Significant contributions in the history of community development include Clarence King, *Organizing for Community Action* (New York: Harper and Brothers, 1948); T. R. Batten, *Communities and their Development: An Introduc-*

tory Study with Special Reference to the Tropics (London: Oxford University Press, 1957); Richard Poston, *Democracy Speaks Many Tongues* (New York: Harper and Bros., 1962); William W. Biddle and Loureide J. Biddle, *The Community Development Process: The Rediscovery of Local Initiative* (New York: Holt, Rinehart and Winston, 1965). Also see US Federal Security Agency, Social Security Administration, International Unit, *An Approach to Community Development* (Washington: Government Printing Office, 1952); International Cooperation Administration, "The Community Development Guidelines of the International Cooperation Administration," *Community Development Review* 3 (December 1956); UK Colonial Office, *Community Development: A Handbook* (London: Her Majesty's Stationary Office, 1958); Ford Foundation, *American Community Development: Preliminary Reports by Directors of Projects Assisted by the Ford Foundation in Four Cities and a State: Twenty-ninth Annual National Conference, National Association of Housing and Redevelopment Officials. Denver, Colorado, October 1, 1963* (New York: Ford Foundation, 1964); Florence Heller Graduate School for Advanced Studies in Social Work at Brandeis University, *Community Development and Community Organization: An International Workshop* (New York: National Association of Social Workers, 1961); UN Bureau of Social Affairs, *Social Progress through Community Development* (New York: United Nations, 1955); UN Ad Hoc Group of Experts on Community Development, *Community Development and National Development* (New York: UN Department of Economic and Social Affairs, 1963).

17. Uday Singh Mehta, *Liberalism and Empire: A Study in Nineteenth-Century British Liberal Thought* (Chicago: University of Chicago Press, 1999), 191.

18. Alice O'Connor, *Poverty Knowledge: Social Science, Social Policy, and the Poor in Twentieth-Century U.S. History* (Princeton: Princeton University Press, 2001), 15, 12.

19. See James L. Sundquist, *Politics and Policy: The Eisenhower, Kennedy, and Johnson Years* (Washington: Brookings Institution, 1968), 111.

20. Arturo Escobar, *Encountering Development: The Making and Unmaking of the Third World* (Princeton: Princeton University Press, 1995), 41, 24.

21. On CAP in this context, see Ralph M. Kramer, *Participation of the Poor: Comparative Case Studies in the War on Poverty* (Englewood Cliffs, NJ: Prentice-Hall, 1969); Moynihan, *Maximum Feasible Misunderstanding*; Allen J. Matusow, *The Unraveling of America: A History of Liberalism in the 1960s* (New York: Harper and Row, 1984); Michael B. Katz, *The Undeserving Poor: From the War on Poverty to the War on Welfare* (New York: Pantheon, 1989); Jill Quadagno, *The Color of Welfare: How Racism Undermined the War on Poverty* (New York: Oxford University Press, 1994); Sidney M. Milkis and Jerome M. Mileur, eds., *The Great Society and the High Tide of Liberalism* (Amherst: University of Massachusetts Press, 2005); Kent Germany, *New Orleans after the Promises: Poverty, Citizenship, and the Search for the Great Society* (Athens: University of

Georgia Press, 2007); Susan Youngblood Ashmore, *Carry It On: The War on Poverty and the Civil Rights Movement in Alabama, 1964–1972* (Athens: University of Georgia Press, 2008).

22. Jill Quadagno notes: "The civil rights movement brought to the forefront of national politics not only the brutality of racial oppression but also the instability of the New Deal compromise. The sacrifice of African Americans for the support of Southern Democrats had ensnared the party in an unresolvable conflict. In 1935 black voters were irrelevant to Democratic Party fortunes. By 1960 the pattern of black settlement had altered the political landscape" (*The Color of Welfare*, 26).

23. For a further discussion, see Gareth Stedman Jones, *An End to Poverty? A Historical Debate* (New York: Columbia University Press, 2004).

24. Giorgio Agamben, for instance, suggests that "when, starting with the French Revolution, sovereignty is entrusted solely to the people, the *people* become an embarrassing presence, and poverty and exclusion appear for the first time as an intolerable scandal in every sense. In the modern age, poverty and exclusion are not only economic and social concepts but also eminently political categories" (*Means without End: Notes on Politics*, trans. Vincenzo Binetti and Cesare Casarino [Minneapolis: University of Minnesota Press, 2000], 33).

25. Henry George, *Poverty and Progress: An Inquiry into the Cause of Industrial Depressions and of Increase of Want with Increase of Wealth . . . The Remedy* (1879; New York: Robert Schalkenbach Foundation, 1990), 7.

26. Giovanna Procacci, "Governing Poverty: Sources of the Social Question in Nineteenth-Century France," in *Foucault and the Writing of History*, ed. Jan Goldstein (Cambridge: Blackwell, 1994); and "Social Economy and the Government of Poverty," in *The Foucault Effect: Studies in Governmentality*, ed. Graham Burchell, Colin Gordon, and Peter Miller (Chicago: University of Chicago Press, 1991). Also see Giovanna Procacci, *Gouverner la misère: La question sociale en France, 1789–1848* (Paris: Seuil, 1993); Mitchell Dean, *The Constitution of Poverty: Toward a Genealogy of Liberal Governance* (London: Routledge, 1991). The arguments of both Procacci and Dean are indebted to Karl Polanyi, *The Great Transformation: The Political and Economic Origins of Our Time* (1944; Boston: Beacon Press, 1957). Writing on nineteenth-century liberalism and the state, Polanyi states: "The figure of the pauper, almost forgotten since, dominated a discussion the imprint of which was as powerful as that of the most spectacular events in history" (83–84). Polanyi's critique of laissez-faire ideology argues that "the problem of poverty centered around two closely related subjects: pauperism and political economy . . . [which together] formed part of one indivisible whole: the discovery of society" (103).

27. Procacci, "Social Economy and the Government of Poverty," 164.

28. Procacci, "Governing Poverty," 212.

29. Daniel T. Rodgers, *The Work Ethic in Industrial America, 1850–1920* (Chicago: University of Chicago Press, 1978).

30. Procacci, "Governing Poverty," 212.

31. Procacci, "Social Economy and the Government of Poverty," 160.

32. Evelyn Nakano Glenn, *Unequal Freedom: How Race and Gender Shaped American Citizenship and Labor* (Cambridge: Harvard University Press, 2002), 90. Also see Eric Foner, *Free Soil, Free Labor, Free Men: The Ideology of the Republican Party before the Civil War* (New York: Oxford University Press, 1970); David Roediger, *The Wages of Whiteness: Race and the Making of the American Working Class* (New York: Verso, 1991); Jacqueline Jones, "The History and Politics of Poverty in Twentieth-Century America," in *Perspectives on Modern America*, ed. Harvard Sitkoff (New York: Oxford University Press, 2001); Seth Rockman, *Scraping By: Wage Labor, Slavery, and Survival in Early Baltimore* (Baltimore: Johns Hopkins University Press, 2009); Gunja SenGupta, *From Slavery to Poverty: The Racial Origins of Welfare in New York, 1840–1918* (New York: New York University Press, 2009).

33. On the settlement house movement, see Allen F. Davis, *Spearheads for Reform: The Social Settlements and the Progressive Movement, 1890–1914* (New York: Oxford University Press, 1967); Judith Ann Trolander, *Professionalism and Social Change: From the Settlement House Movement to Neighborhood Centers* (New York: Columbia University Press, 1987); Kathryn Kish Sklar, *Florence Kelley and the Nation's Work: The Rise of Women's Political Culture* (New Haven: Yale University Press, 1995); Daniel J. Walkowitz, *Working with Class: Social Workers and the Politics of Middle-Class Identity* (Chapel Hill: University of North Carolina Press, 1999).

34. Robert Fisher, *Let the People Decide: Neighborhood Organizing in America*, updated ed. (New York: Twayne, 1994), 6.

35. Daniel T. Rodgers, *Atlantic Crossings: Social Politics in a Progressive Age* (Cambridge: Harvard University Press, 1998); Michael E. McGerr, *A Fierce Discontent: The Rise and Fall of the Progressive Movement in America* (New York: Free Press, 2003); Robert D. Johnston, *The Radical Middle Class: Populist Democracy and the Question of Capitalism in Progressive Era Portland, Oregon* (Princeton: Princeton University Press, 2003); Shelton Stromquist, *Reinventing 'The People': The Progressive Movement, the Class Problem, and the Origins of Modern Liberalism* (Urbana: University of Illinois Press, 2006); Maureen Flanagan, *America Reformed: Progressives and Progressivisms, 1890s–1920s* (New York: Oxford University Press, 2007).

36. Quadagno, *The Color of Welfare*, 19–31. Also see Linda Gordon, *Pitied but Not Entitled: Single Mothers and the History of Welfare* (New York: Free Press, 1994); Mary Poole, *The Segregated Origins of Social Security: African Americans and the Welfare State* (Chapel Hill: University of North Carolina Press, 2006). On the New Deal more broadly, see Alan Brinkley, *The End of Reform: New Deal Liberalism in Recession and War* (New York: Random House, 1995); David Plotke, *Building a Democratic Political Order: Reshaping American Liberalism in*

the 1930s and 1940s (Cambridge: Cambridge University Press, 1996); Suzanne Mettler, *Dividing Citizens: Gender and Federalism in New Deal Public Policy* (Ithaca: Cornell University Press, 1998); Jennifer Klein, *For All These Rights: Business, Labor, and the Shaping of America's Public-Private Welfare State* (Princeton: Princeton University Press, 2003); Jason Scott Smith, *Building New Deal Liberalism: The Political Economy of Public Works, 1933–1956* (Cambridge: Cambridge University Press, 2006).

37. Quoted in James T. Patterson, *America's Struggle Against Poverty in the Twentieth Century* (Cambridge: Harvard University Press, 2000), 59.

38. Ben B. Seligman, ed., *Poverty as a Public Issue* (New York: Free Press, 1965).

39. W. Arthur Lewis, *The Theory of Economic Growth* (Homewood, IL: R. D. Irwin, 1955); W. W. Rostow, *The Stages of Economic Growth: A Non-Communist Manifesto* (Cambridge: Cambridge University Press, 1960); H. W. Arndt, *The Rise and Fall of Economic Growth: A Study in Contemporary Thought* (1978; Chicago: University of Chicago Press, 1984); David C. Engerman, Nils Gilman, Mark H. Haefele, and Michael E. Latham, eds., *Staging Growth: Modernization, Development, and the Global Cold War* (Amherst: University of Massachusetts Press, 2003).

40. Gary S. Becker, *Human Capital: A Theoretical and Empirical Analysis, with Special Reference to Education* (New York: National Bureau of Economic Research, 1964). Also see S. M. Amadae, *Rationalizing Capitalist Democracy: The Cold War Origins of Rational Choice Liberalism* (Chicago: University of Chicago Press, 2003).

41. Timothy Mitchell, "Origins and Limits of the Modern Idea of the Economy" (Paper presented at the Workshop on Positivism and Post-Positivism, University of Chicago, October 2001), 18–19, 20, 22. Also see Hugo Radice, "The National Economy: A Keynesian Myth?," *Capital and Class* 22 (Spring 1984).

42. Mollie Orshansky, "Counting the Poor: Another Look at the Poverty Profile," *Social Security Bulletin* 28 (January 1965); "Who's Who Among the Poor: A Demographic View of Poverty," *Social Security Bulletin* 28 (July 1965); and "Recounting the Poor: A Five Year Review," *Social Security Bulletin* 29 (April 1966). Also see A. O'Connor, *Poverty Knowledge*, 182–84.

43. Gunnar Myrdal, *The Challenge to Affluence* (New York: Pantheon, 1962); George H. Dunne, ed., *Poverty in Plenty* (New York: P. J. Kennedy and Sons, 1964); Robert E. Will and Harold G. Vatter, *Poverty in Affluence: The Social, Political, and Economic Dimensions of Poverty in the United States* (New York: Harcourt, Brace and World, 1965); Leo Fishman, ed., *Poverty and Affluence* (New Haven: Yale University Press, 1966); Oscar Ornati, *Poverty amid Affluence* (New York: Twentieth Century Fund, 1966); Hanna H. Meissner, ed., *Poverty in the Affluent Society* (New York: Harper and Row, 1966).

44. For a lucid account of the central debates guiding US policy domestically—such as the dispute between John Kenneth Galbraith and the economist Robert J.

Lampman over the structural character of poverty in a growth economy—see A. O'Connor, *Poverty Knowledge*, 139–65.

45. Council of Economic Advisers, *Annual Report* (Washington: Government Printing Office, 1964), 60–61.

46. Andrew Ross, *Real Love: In Pursuit of Cultural Justice* (New York: New York University Press, 1998), 165.

47. Barbara Cruikshank, *The Will to Empower: Democratic Citizens and Other Subjects* (Ithaca: Cornell University Press, 1999), 48, 68, 38, 7.

48. "We Have No Government," in *Black Protest: History, Documents, and Analyses*, ed. Joanne Grant (Greenwich, CT: Fawcett, 1968), 501, 505.

49. Popular literature on self-help was first published during the 1830s. Samuel Smiles's *Self-Help* (1859) was the most influential of these early writings.

50. Kevin K. Gaines, *Uplifting the Race: Black Leadership, Politics, and Culture in the Twentieth Century* (Chapel Hill: University of North Carolina Press, 1996), 3, 4. Also see Brian Kelly, "Beyond the 'Talented Tenth': Black Elites, Black Workers, and the Limits of Accommodation in Industrial Birmingham, 1900–1921," in *Time Longer Than Rope: A Century of African American Activism, 1850–1950*, ed. Charles M. Payne and Adam Green (New York: New York University Press, 2003); Cathryn Bailey, "Anna Julia Cooper: 'Dedicated in the Name of My Slave Mother to the Education of Colored Working People,'" *Hypatia* 19.2 (2004).

51. Nancy Fraser and Linda Gordon, "A Genealogy of 'Dependency': Tracing a Keyword of the U.S. Welfare State," in Nancy Fraser, *Justice Interruptus: Critical Reflections on the "Postsocialist" Condition* (New York: Routledge, 1997), 131, 129.

52. Scholars such as María Josefina Saldaña-Portillo (*The Revolutionary Imagination in the Americas and the Age of Development*, 59) and Ramón Grosfoguel ("Developmentalism, Modernity, and Dependency Theory in Latin America," *Nepantla* 1.2 [2000]) have persuasively argued that despite dependency theory's critique of development orthodoxies, the horizon of its inquiry nonetheless remained fixed by the very terms of development discourse that it sought to criticize.

53. Mimi Abramovitz, *Regulating the Lives of Women: Social Welfare Policy from Colonial Times to the Present*, rev. ed. (Boston: South End Press, 1996), 39. Also see Gwendolyn Mink, *The Wages of Motherhood: Inequality in the Welfare State, 1917–1942* (Ithaca: Cornell University Press, 1995); Joanne Goodwin, "'Employable Mothers' and 'Suitable Work': A Re-Evaluation of Welfare and Wage-Earning for Women in the Twentieth Century United States," *Journal of Social History* 29 (Winter 1995).

54. Frederic L. Kirgis, Jr., "The Degrees of Self-Determination in the United Nations Era," *American Journal of International Law* 88.2 (1994); Antonio Cassese, *Self-Determination of Peoples: A Legal Reappraisal* (Cambridge: Cambridge University Press, 1999); Erez Manela, *The Wilsonian Moment: Self-Determination and the International Origins of Anticolonial Nationalism* (New York: Oxford University Press, 2007).

55. For surveys of US policy toward the Third World after the Second World War, see Kathryn Statler and Andrew Johns, eds., *The Eisenhower Administration, the Third World, and the Globalization of the Cold War* (Lanham: Rowman and Littlefield, 2006); Peter L. Hahn and Mary Ann Heiss, eds., *Empire and Revolution: The United States and the Third World since 1945* (Columbus: Ohio State University Press, 2001); H. W. Brands, *The Specter of Neutralism: The United States and the Emergence of the Third World, 1947–1960* (New York: Columbia University Press, 1989); Christian G. Appy, ed., *Cold War Constructions: The Political Culture of United States Imperialism, 1945–1966* (Amherst: University of Massachusetts Press, 2000); Robert Latham, *The Liberal Moment: Modernity, Security, and the Making of the Postwar International Order* (New York: Columbia University Press, 1997); Odd Arne Westad, *The Global Cold War: Third World Interventions and the Making of Our Times* (Cambridge: Cambridge University Press, 2005), Richard Saull, *The Cold War and After: Capitalism, Revolution and Superpower Politics* (London: Pluto, 2007).

56. Grosfoguel, "Developmentalism, Modernity, and Dependency Theory in Latin America," 348.

57. Cary Fraser, "Understanding American Policy toward the Decolonization of European Empires, 1945–1964," *Diplomacy and Statecraft* 3.1 (1992); S. Neil MacFarlane, *Superpower Rivalry and Third World Radicalism: The Idea of National Liberation* (London: Croom Helm, 1985); David Ryan and Victor Pungong, eds., *The United States and Decolonization: Power and Freedom* (New York: St. Martin's Press, 2000); Prasenjit Duara, "Introduction: The Decolonization of Asia and Africa in the Twentieth Century," in *Decolonization: Perspectives from Now and Then*, ed. Prasenjit Duara (New York: Routledge, 2003).

58. Brenda Gayle Plummer, *Rising Wind: Black Americans and U.S. Foreign Affairs, 1935–1960* (Chapel Hill: University of North Carolina Press, 1996); Penny Von Eschen, *Race against Empire: Black Americans and Anticolonialism, 1937–1957* (Ithaca: Cornell University Press, 1997); Mary Dudziak, *Cold War Civil Rights: Race and the Image of American Democracy* (Princeton: Princeton University Press, 2000); Thomas Borstelmann, *The Cold War and the Color Line: American Race Relations in the Global Arena* (Cambridge: Harvard University Press, 2001); Nikhil Pal Singh, *Black Is a Country: Race and the Unfinished Struggle for Democracy* (Cambridge: Harvard University Press, 2004); Kevin Gaines, *American Africans in Ghana: Black Expatriates and the Civil Rights Era* (Chapel Hill: University of North Carolina Press, 2006).

59. For Quijano the "coloniality of power" is the historical effect of "the constitution of America and colonial/modern Eurocentered capitalism as a new global power. One of the fundamental axes of this model of power is the social classification of the world's population around the idea of race, a mental construction that expresses the basic experience of colonial domination and pervades the more important dimensions of global power, including its specific rationality: Eurocen-

trism. The racial axis has a colonial origin and character, but it has proven to be more durable and stable than the colonialism in whose matrix it was established. Therefore, the model of power that is globally hegemonic today presupposes an element of coloniality" (Anibal Quijano, "Coloniality of Power, Eurocentrism, and Latin America," *Nepantla* 1.3 [2000], 533). For further discussions on the "coloniality of power," see Walter D. Mignolo, *Local Histories/Global Designs: Coloniality, Subaltern Knowledges, and Border Thinking* (Princeton: Princeton University Press, 2000); Mabel Moraña, Enrique Dussel, and Carlos A. Jáuregui, eds., *Coloniality at Large: Latin America and the Postcolonial Debate* (Durham: Duke University Press, 2008). Also see Frederick Cooper's critique of "coloniality" in *Colonialism in Question: Theory, Knowledge, History* (Berkeley: University of California Press, 2005).

60. Vine Deloria Jr. and Clifford M. Lytle, *The Nations Within: The Past and Future of American Indian Sovereignty* (1984; Austin: University of Texas Press, 1998), 230, 216.

61. Quoted in Manning Marable, *Race, Reform, and Rebellion: The Second Reconstruction in Black America, 1945–1990*, 2nd ed. (Jackson: University Press of Mississippi, 1991), 98. However, see Devin Fergus, *Liberalism, Black Power, and the Making of American Politics, 1965–1980* (Athens: University of Georgia Press, 2009), on the ways in which conservatives such as Jesse Helms used the entente between liberalism and black power to galvanize the ascendancy of the New Right.

62. Denise Ferreira da Silva, *Toward a Global Idea of Race* (Minneapolis: University of Minnesota Press, 2007), xxiv, 42.

63. Ibid., 218.

64. Graham Burchell, "Liberal Government and Techniques of the Self," in *Foucault and Political Reason: Liberalism, Neo-Liberalism and Rationalities of Government*, ed. Andrew Barry, Thomas Osborne, and Nikolas Rose (Chicago: University of Chicago Press, 1996), 23. Also see Peter Miller and Nikolas Rose, *Governing the Present: Administering Economic, Social and Personal Life* (Malden, MA: Polity, 2008).

65. The term "Hispano" refers to people claiming direct descent from Spanish colonists in the Southwest prior to the 1848 Treaty of Guadalupe Hidalgo. As will be discussed in chapter 2, this claim has specific political and economic connotations.

66. For instance, Nancy writes: "Community is what takes place through others and for others . . . it assumes the impossibility of its own immanence, the impossibility of a communitarian being in the form of a subject" (*The Inoperative Community*, ed. and trans. Peter Connor [Minneapolis: University of Minnesota Press, 1991], 15). He thus argues that "what this community has 'lost'—the immanence and the intimacy of a communion—is lost only in the sense that such a 'loss' is constitutive of 'community' itself" (12). Moreover, Nancy contends that "there is no common understanding of community, that sharing does not constitute under-

standing (or a concept, or an intuition, or a schema) ... it does not constitute a knowledge ... it gives no one, including community itself, mastery over being-in-common" (69). Also see Jean-Luc Nancy, "Of Being-in-Common," in *Community at Loose Ends*, ed. Miami Theory Collective, trans. James Creech (Minneapolis: University of Minnesota Press, 1991). Nancy similarly insists that "politics is the place of an 'in common' as such—but only along the lines of an incommensurability that is kept open ... It does not subsume the 'in common' under any kind of union, community, subject, or epiphany ... neither the sphere of the 'in common' nor that of politics allows for the separation between 'society as exteriority' and 'community as interiority'" (Jean-Luc Nancy, *The Truth of Democracy*, trans. Pascale-Anne Brault and Michael Naas [New York: Fordham University Press, 2010], 50–51).

1. Freedom Between

1. Phillips Ruopp, "Approaches to Community Development," in *Approaches to Community Development*, ed. Phillips Ruopp (The Hague: W. Van Hoeve, 1953), 20 (emphasis added). See also UN Bureau of Social Affairs, *Social Progress through Community Development* (New York: United Nations, 1955).

2. División de Educación de la Comunidad, "La Voluntad que Ignacio no Tuvo," in *Los Casos de Ignacio y Santiago*, ed. René Marqués (San Juan, PR: Departamento de Instrucción Pública, 1953, 3–23; my translation).

3. René Marqués, "Literary Pessimism and Political Optimism" (1959), in *The Docile Puerto Rican: Essays*, trans. Barbara Bockus Aponte (Philadelphia: Temple University Press, 1976), 23. Also see René Marqués, "Writing for a Community Education Programme," *UNESCO Reports and Papers on Mass Communication* 24 (November 1957).

4. *Ignacio* (dir. Angel F. Rivera, 1956); my translation.

5. Quoted in Ellery Foster, "Planning for Community Development through Its People," *Human Organization* 12.2 (1953), 8, 9.

6. Ibid., 7.

7. Nancy Cohen, *The Reconstruction of American Liberalism, 1865–1914* (Chapel Hill: University of North Carolina Press, 2002); Doug Rossinow, *Visions of Progress: The Left-Liberal Tradition in America* (Philadelphia: University of Pennsylvania Press, 2008), 13–102; Brian Balogh, *A Government out of Sight: The Mystery of National Authority in Nineteenth-Century America* (Cambridge: Cambridge University Press, 2009), 352–99.

8. Quoted in Balogh, *A Government out of Sight*, 352.

9. Ibid., 353.

10. Maurice Parmelee, *Poverty and Social Progress* (New York: Macmillan, 1916), 454.

11. Mary Parker Follett, *The New State: Group Organization, The Solution of Popular Government* (New York: Longmans, Green, 1918), 190, 202. Likewise, in his

influential 1921 study of community organization, Eduard Lindeman envisioned that "the ideal Democratic Community would be completely articulated; all of its parts would be related to the community process." He cautioned, however, that "such communities do not exist, nor has the democratic idea been adequately applied to community action" (*The Community: An Introduction to the Study of Community Leadership and Organization* [New York: Association Press, 1921], 119).

12. Jesse F. Steiner, "An Appraisal of the Community Movement," *Social Forces* 7.3 (1929), 333.

13. Jesse F. Steiner, "Community Organization: A Study of Its Rise and Recent Tendencies," *Journal of Social Forces* 1.1 (1922), 12.

14. Robert Woods, a social settlement advocate and longtime head of the South End House in Boston, argued in this regard that "the neighborhood is large enough to include in essence all the problems of the city, the state, and the nation; and in a constantly increasing number of instances in this country it includes all the fundamental international issues. It is large enough to present these problems in a recognizable community form, with some beginnings of social sentiment with regard to them . . . On the other hand, it is small enough to be a comprehensible and manageable community unit . . . The neighborhood is concretely conceivable; the city is not, and will not be except as it is organically integrated through its neighborhoods" ("The Neighborhood in Social Reconstruction," *American Journal of Sociology* 19.5 [1914], 578–79).

15. Ronald Schaffer, *America in the Great War: The Rise of the War Welfare State* (New York: Oxford University Press, 1991); and Marc Stears, *Demanding Democracy: American Radicals in Search of a New Politics* (Princeton: Princeton University Press, 2010), 21–55.

16. Henry E. Jackson, "A Man without a Community," in *Rural Organization: Proceedings of the Third Annual National Country Life Conference, 1920* (Chicago: University of Chicago Press for the American Country Life Association, 1921), 78. See also Henry E. Jackson, *A Community Center: What It Is and How to Organize It* (New York: Macmillan, 1918).

17. "Community Centre as a War Council," *New York Times*, October 13, 1918.

18. "The Permanent Community Council," *Atlanta Constitution*, March 16, 1919.

19. "Community Council in After-War Work," *New York Times*, January 24, 1919.

20. Follett, *The New State*, 194–95.

21. Randolph S. Bourne, *War and the Intellectuals: Collected Essays, 1915–1919* (New York: Harper and Row, 1964), 39, 57.

22. John Collier, "Community Councils—Democracy Every Day," *Survey*, August 31, 1918; "Community Councils—Democracy Every Day II: The Growing-Up of the Community Councils of National Defense," *Survey*, September 21, 1918; and "Community Councils—Democracy Every Day III: Plans for Community Councils in the Great Cities," *Survey*, September 28, 1918.

23. Charles Sprague Smith, *Working with the People* (New York: A. Wessells, 1904), 60. Also see Charles Sprague Smith, "The Peoples' Institute of New York and Its Work for the Development of Citizenship along Democratic Lines," *Arena*, July 1907.
24. John Collier, "The People's Institute," *Independent*, May 30, 1912.
25. See, among innumerable examples from the *New York Times*, "Socialists out in Force," February 10, 1900; "Charter Revision Views," May 12, 1900; "900 Citizen-Voters Shout for Reprisals," February 24, 1906; "Arrest at Meeting in Cooper Union," April 8, 1908; "Free Speech," March 12, 1914.
26. C. Smith, *Working with the People*, 54–56.
27. "Rule of the Philippines: People's Institute Votes against the Administration's Policy," *New York Times*, January 6, 1900. For background information on the institute's position and earlier forum debates on the Philippines, see Ethel Osgood Mason, "Some Characteristics of a Cooper Union Audience," *New York Times*, December 27, 1898; and Charles Sprague Smith's reply, "The Cooper Union Audience," *New York Times*, January 1, 1899.
28. "Cooper Union Peace Vote," *New York Times*, February 12, 1917, 4.
29. Edward Sanderson, "The Cooper Union Vote," *New York Times*, February 13, 1917, 10.
30. Ibid. As Charles Sprague Smith put it, the institute's belief "in popular government holds that for America there is safety only in ever more and more democracy, provided only sound education and character building accompany every step forward." He further argued: "So far as the Socialist element in our audience is of value, it indicates that, as in Germany, so here intolerance, extreme radicalism, is losing ground and the movement is being transformed from a revolutionary to a radical-democratic party" (*Working with the People*, 61, 125).
31. Collier, "The People's Institute."
32. "Traction Meeting Winds Up in a Row: Audience at People's Institute Pass Resolutions over Chairman's Head," *New York Times*, April 14, 1909.
33. Ibid.
34. "Need of Individuality," *New York Times*, February 8, 1901, 7.
35. "Volley of Questions Shot at Dr. Slicer," *New York Times*, February 12, 1906, 7.
36. Collier, "The People's Institute," 1144, 1145, 1146. For a comprehensive account of these activities, see Nancy J. Rosenbloom, "In Defense of the Moving Pictures: The People's Institute, the National Board of Censorship, and the Problem of Leisure in Urban America," *American Studies* 33.2 (1992), and "From Regulation to Censorship: Film and Political Culture in New York in the Early Twentieth Century," *Journal of the Gilded Age and Progressive Era* 3.4 (2004).
37. John Collier, "Film Shows and Law Makers," *Survey*, February 8, 1913.
38. Quoted in Rosenbloom, "In Defense of the Moving Pictures," 50.
39. Collier, "The People's Institute," 1146.
40. Eleanor T. Glueck, *The Community Use of Schools* (Baltimore: Williams and Wilkins, 1927).

41. Robert B. Fisher, "The People's Institute of New York City, 1897–1934: Culture, Progressive Democracy, and the People" (PhD diss., New York University, 1974), 310–53.

42. "The First National Conference on Community Centers," *National Municipal Review* 5.3 (1916), 496–97. See also John Collier, "Definitions and Debates of the Community Center Conference," *The American City* 19.6 (1916).

43. John Collier, "The New York Training School for Community Center Workers; and the Community Center Movement," 1–2, Box 12 Folder 14, People's Institute Records, Manuscripts and Archives Division, New York Public Library, New York, NY (hereafter PI/NYPL).

44. "Community Work—The Local Community Will Save the Nation by Saving Itself," n.d., n.p., Box 12, Folder 14, PI/NYPL.

45. "Criticisms of the Training School as reported by Mrs. C., Mr. McB., etc.," Box 12, Folder 13, PI/NYPL.

46. John Collier, "The Crisis of Democracy: A Speech by John Collier, Secretary of the National Community Center Conference, Tuesday, April 17, at the Auditorium Hotel, Recital Hall," 2, 9, Box 12, Folder 2, PI/NYPL.

47. Fisher, "The People's Institute of New York City," 335.

48. John Collier, "Why Community Organization? A Statement of a Need, and Some Suggestions for Meeting It" (presentation at the National Social Unit Conference, Cincinnati, OH, October 23–25, 1919), 3, 2, Box 9, Folder 8, Wilbur C. and Elsie C. Phillips Papers, Social Welfare History Archives, University of Minnesota, Minneapolis, MN (hereafter Phillips Papers).

49. Wilbur C. Phillips, *Adventuring for Democracy* (New York: Social Unit Press, 1940), 59–60.

50. W. C. Phillips, "Replies to First Set of Questions: Final Copy Sent to Mr. Bookman," May 27, 1919, 8, Box 11, Folder 1, Phillips Papers.

51. W. C. Phillips, "Memo to C. M. Bookman: Replies to Second Set of Questions Submitted to Us," May 27, 1919, 1, Box 11, Folder 1, Phillips Papers.

52. Phillips, "Replies to First Set of Questions," 10–11.

53. Quoted in "Cincinnati's Social Welfare Scheme," *New York Times*, April 15, 1917.

54. "Seek to Centralize Social Activities," *New York Times*, April 12, 1916.

55. Phillips, "Replies to First Set of Questions," 9.

56. Patricia Mooney-Melvin, *The Organic City: Urban Definition and Community Organization, 1880–1920* (Lexington: University Press of Kentucky, 1987), 73–97.

57. Ibid., 82.

58. Courtenay Dinwiddie, "The Work Accomplished by the Social Unit Organization," *Proceedings of the National Conference of Social Work—at the 45th Annual Session, Held in Kansas City, Missouri, May 15–22, 1918* (Chicago: National Conference of Social Work, 1919), 497–98; and *Community Responsibility: A Review of the Cincinnati Social Unit Experiment* (New York: New York School of Social Work, 1921), 7.

59. Dinwiddie, "The Work Accomplished by the Social Unit Organization," 497. Similarly, the text accompanying a MBSUO publicity photograph states: "The district selected for the Social Unit experiment is a middle class district, large enough to include a representative population. The people who live in these homes [pictured in the photograph] are people of some means, but nevertheless glad to co-operate with the Social Unit which might well write over its doors 'not Charity—Justice'" (Cincinnati Social Unit photographs, Box 38, Folder 12, Phillips Papers).

60. Robert B. Fairbanks, *Making Better Citizens: Housing Reform and the Community Development Strategy in Cincinnati, 1890–1960* (Urbana: University of Illinois Press, 1988), 63.

61. In his evaluation of the social unit, the prominent reformer Edward T. Devine reaffirmed the NSUO perspective and praised the fact that the experiment's district "is a typical industrial population, mostly English-speaking, largely of German stock, with very few Negroes and comparatively few recent immigrants" ("The Social Unit in Cincinnati: An Experiment in Organization," *Survey*, November 15, 1919, 117).

62. Gertrude Matthews Shelby, "Extending Democracy: What the Cincinnati Social Unit Has Accomplished," *Harper's*, April 1920, 690.

63. Mooney-Melvin, *The Organic City*, 86.

64. Anatole Shaffer, "The Cincinnati Social Unit Experiment, 1917–19," *Social Service Review* 45.2 (1971), 168.

65. Mooney-Melvin's *The Organic City* is the most complete secondary source on the social unit. Also see Jesse F. Steiner, *Community Organization: A Study of Its Theory and Current Practice* (New York: Century, 1925), 239–53; Shaffer, "The Cincinnati Social Unit Experiment"; Neil Betten and Michael J. Austin, *The Roots of Community Organizing, 1917–1939* (Philadelphia: Temple University Press, 1990), 35–53.

66. "Democracy on the Social Unit Pattern," *Survey*, February 16, 1918, 551.

67. S. Gale Lowrie, "The Social Unit—An Experiment in Politics," *National Municipal Review* 9.9 (1920), 554, 566.

68. Dinwiddie, *Community Responsibility*, 24.

69. Mary L. Hicks and Roe S. Eastman, "Block Workers: As Developed under the Social Unit Experiment in Cincinnati," *Survey*, September 1, 1920.

70. Quoted in Shelby, "Extending Democracy," 691.

71. Hicks and Eastman, "Block Workers."

72. "Women Voters to Have Part in Fall Election," *Social Unit Bulletin*, September 11, 1920.

73. Quoted in Shelby, "Extending Democracy," 691.

74. Phillips, *Adventuring for Democracy*, 209–10.

75. Ibid., 232, 239.

76. Shelby, "Extending Democracy," 691.

77. "Self-Governed Neighborhoods: One Plan for Americanization," n.d., Cincinnati Social Unit Organization: Publicity, 1917–1920, Box 10, Folder 4, Phillips Papers.

78. Indeed, Phillips later wrote that he hoped to come up with "something which had an appeal for everybody . . . The needs of children! No controversy there. 'We're all for the children'" (*Adventuring for Democracy*, 165). His conception of democracy is similar.

79. Quoted in Dorothy Thompson, "The Unit Plan of Health Administration," *National Municipal Review* 7.11 (1918), 599.

80. George Rosen, *A History of Public Health* (New York: MD Publications, 1958), 472.

81. Abbie Roberts, "Report of the Nursing Service for 1918," Mohawk-Brighton Social Unit Organization, January 1919, Box 10, Folder 12, Phillips Papers.

82. Arthur G. Kreidler and Wilbur C. Phillips, "Medical Organization of the Social Unit and Work during the First Six Months of 1918," August 5, 1918; Medical Advisory Council of the National Social Unit Organization, "Special Report No. 2," September 1, 1918, and "A Plan for the Solution of Pressing National Health Problems," October 2, 1918, Box 10, Folder 12, Phillips Papers.

83. Phillips, "Replies to First Set of Questions," 13.

84. Quoted in Dinwiddie, *Community Responsibility*, 122–23.

85. Letter from John Landis to W. C. Phillips, June 24, 1918, Box 11, Folder 4, Phillips Papers.

86. William J. Norton, "The Social Unit Organization of Cincinnati," *Studies from the Helen S. Trounstine Foundation*, February 1, 1919, Box 11, Folder 4, Phillips Papers.

87. Quoted in "Cincinnati Mayor Raps 'Social Unit,'" *Washington Post*, March 11, 1919. Also see "Bolshevism or Democracy: Which Is Encouraged by the Social Unit?," *Social Unit Bulletin*, March 28, 1919.

88. Quoted in Mooney-Melvin, *The Organic City*, 133–34.

89. Letter from Mary L. Hicks to Mayor John Galvin, March 11, 1919, reprinted in *Social Unit Bulletin*, March 28, 1919.

90. Phillips, "To the Committee Appointed by the Council of Social Agencies to Investigate the Social Unit," 3.

91. Phillips, *Adventuring for Democracy*, 164.

92. Of 6,000 eligible voters, 4,154 ballots were cast, with 4,034 in favor of continuing the social unit and 120 against. "All Mohawk-Brighton Turns Out to Vote: Landslide Victory for the Social Unit," *Social Unit Bulletin*, April 16, 1919. Also see "Shall the Social Unit Experiment Be Continued?," *Social Unit Bulletin*, April 8, 1919.

93. William C. Ewing, "To the Committee on the Referendum"; Martin McGuinn, "To the Committee on the Referendum," reprinted in *Social Unit Bulletin*, April 4, 1919.

94. Special Committee of the Council of Social Agencies, "Investigation of Charges Against the Social Unit Organization," June 25, 1919, 13, Box 11, Folder 4, Phillips Papers.

95. Quoted in Shelby, "Extending Democracy," 695.

96. Phillips, *Adventuring for Democracy*, 112. Also see Robert Fisher, *Let the People Decide: Neighborhood Organizing in America*, updated ed. (New York: Twayne, 1994), 30.

97. Michael Denning, *The Cultural Front: The Laboring of American Culture in the Twentieth Century* (New York: Verso, 1996), 21–37.

98. Richard Saull, *The Cold War and After: Capitalism, Revolution and Superpower Politics* (London: Pluto, 2007), 16–48; David C. Engerman, "Ideology and the Origins of the Cold War, 1917–1962," in *The Cambridge History of the Cold War, Vol. I: Origins*, ed. Melvyn P. Leffler and Odd Arne Westad (Cambridge: Cambridge University Press, 2010).

99. On the legal history of Puerto Rico and US empire, see Christina Duffy Burnett and Burke Marshall, eds., *Foreign in a Domestic Sense: Puerto Rico, American Expansion, and the Constitution* (Durham: Duke University Press, 2001); Bartholomew H. Sparrow, *The Insular Cases and the Emergence of American Empire* (Lawrence: University Press of Kansas, 2006).

100. William W. Biddle, *The Cultivation of Community Leaders: Up from the Grass Roots* (New York: Harper and Brothers, 1953), 3, 8, 9, 39.

101. The historian Sugata Dasgupta describes the Institute of Rural Reconstruction as an effort to make the villagers "self-reliant and self-respectful, acquainted with the cultural tradition of their own country and competent to make an efficient use of modern resources for the fullest development of their physical, social, economic, and intellectual conditions" (*A Poet and a Plan: Tagore's Experiments in Rural Reconstruction* [Calcutta: Thacker Spink, 1962], 28). Also see C. B. Mamoria, *Co-Operation, Community Development, and Village Panchayats in India* (Allahabad, India: Kitab Mahal, 1966). On India's Community Development Program in the larger context of US policy see Dennis Merrill, *Bread and the Ballot: The United States and India's Economic Development, 1947–1963* (Chapel Hill: University of North Carolina, 1990).

102. Quoted in David Brokensha and Peter Hodge, *Community Development: An Interpretation* (San Francisco: Chandler, 1969), 27.

103. Among the voluminous literature on international development and modernization, outstanding critical studies include Arturo Escobar, *Encountering Development: The Making and Unmaking of the Third World* (Princeton: Princeton University Press, 1995); Michael P. Cowan and Robert W. Shenton, *Doctrines of Development* (New York: Routledge, 1996); Frederick Cooper and Randall Packard, eds., *International Development and the Social Sciences: Essays on the History and Politics of Knowledge* (Berkeley: University of California Press, 1997); Gilbert Rist, *The History of Development: From Western Origins to Global Faith*

(London: Zed, 1997); Timothy Mitchell, *Rule of Experts: Egypt, Techno-Politics, Modernity* (Berkeley: University of California Press, 2002); María Josefina Saldaña-Portillo, *The Revolutionary Imagination in the Americas and the Age of Development* (Durham: Duke University Press, 2003); Nils Gilman, *Mandarins of the Future: Modernization Theory in Cold War America* (Baltimore: Johns Hopkins University Press, 2003); David Ekbladh, *The Great American Mission: Modernization and the Construction of an American World Order* (Princeton: Princeton University Press, 2010).

104. John Foster Dulles, "Instruction from the Secretary of State to All Diplomatic Missions in the American Republics," in *Foreign Relations of the United States, 1955–1957* (Washington: Government Printing Office, 1987), 6:300.

105. Luis Muñoz Marín, "An America to Serve the World" (speech delivered at the Annual Convention of the Associated Harvard Clubs, Coral Gables, Florida, April 7, 1956), Pamphlet Collection, Centro de Estudios Puertorriqueños, Hunter College, City University of New York, New York, 11.

106. Although the sociologist Eduardo Seda has argued that the "success" of land reform was achieved in part because local PPD officials simply took the place of the expropriated *hacendados*, assuming the role of patron with little change in local structures of power, it is clear that such measures did cement widespread party loyalty among the rural poor, and thus the simple transposition of power fails to explain the dynamics of hegemony at work. See Eduardo Seda, *Social Change and Personality in a Puerto Rican Agrarian Reform Community* (Evanston, IL: Northwestern University Press, 1973). Also see P. B. Vázquez-Calcerrada, "A Research Project on Rural Communities in Puerto Rico," *Rural Sociology* 18.3 (1953).

107. Ian Roxborough, "Cold War, Capital Accumulation, and Labor Control in Latin America: The Closing of a Cycle, 1945–1990," in *Rethinking the Cold War*, ed. Allen Hunter (Philadelphia: Temple University Press, 1998), 124.

108. John Kenneth Galbraith and Carolyn Shaw Solo, "Puerto Rican Lessons in Economic Development," *Annals of the American Academy of Political and Social Science* 285 (January 1953), 57.

109. Muñoz Marín, "An America to Serve the World," 9. Also see Luis Muñoz Marín, "Puerto Rico Refutes Charges of U.S. Colonialism by Cuba and U.S.S.R.," in *U.S. Department of State Bulletin* 43 (October 24, 1960).

110. Quoted in Pedro Muñoz Amato, "Congressional Conservatism and Puerto Rican Democracy in the Commonwealth Relationship," *Revista Jurídica de la Universidad de Puerto Rico* 21.4 (1952), 323.

111. Sherman S. Hayden and Benjamin Rivlin, *Non-Self-Governing Territories: Status of Puerto Rico* (New York: Woodrow Wilson Foundation, 1954); Surendra Bhana, *The United States and the Development of the Puerto Rican Status Question, 1936–1968* (Lawrence: University of Kansas Press, 1975), 174–75.

112. See, for example, Millard Hansen and Henry Wells, eds., "Puerto Rico: A Study

in Democratic Development," special issue, *Annals of the American Academy of Political and Social Science* 285 (January 1953).

113. Carl J. Friedrich, *Puerto Rico: The Middle Road to Freedom* (New York: Rinehart, 1959); Earl Parker Hanson, *Puerto Rico: Ally for Progress* (New York: D. Van Nostrand, 1962), 132.

114. On Puerto Rican development during this period, see Emilio Pantojas-García, *Development Strategies as Ideology: Puerto Rico's Export-Led Industrialization Experience* (Boulder, CO: Lynne Rienner, 1990); Gordon K. Lewis, *Puerto Rico: Freedom and Power in the Caribbean* (New York: Monthly Review, 1963); Ramón Grosfoguel, "Puerto Rico's Exceptionalism: Industrialization, Migration, and Housing Development" (PhD diss., Temple University, 1992). Uncritical but useful studies include A. W. Maldonado, *Teodoro Moscoso and Puerto Rico's Operation Bootstrap* (Gainesville: University of Florida Press, 1997); William H. Stead, *Fomento: The Economic Development of Puerto Rico* (Washington: National Planning Association, 1958); Harvey Perloff, *Puerto Rico's Economic Future: A Study in Planned Development* (Chicago: University of Chicago Press, 1950). For an economic analysis extending into the period after Operation Bootstrap, see James Dietz, *Puerto Rico: Negotiating Development and Change* (Boulder, CO: Lynne Rienner, 2003).

115. The most comprehensive account of DIVEDCO is Catherine Marsh Kennerley, *Negociaciones culturales: Los intelectuales y el proyecto pedagógico del estado muñocista* (San Juan, PR: Callejón, 2009).

116. Willard W. Beatty, "The Nature and Purpose of Community Education," in *Community Education: Principles and Practices from World-Wide Experience— The Fifty-Eighth Yearbook of the National Society for the Study of Education*, ed. Nelson B. Henry (Chicago: University of Chicago Press, 1959), 11.

117. Quoted in *Un Programa de Educacion de la Communidad en Puerto Rico/Community Education Program in Puerto Rico* (New York: RCA International Division, n.d.), n.p.

118. Ismael García-Colón, "Hegemony, Land Reform, and Social Space in Puerto Rico: Parcelas, a Land Distribution Program for Landless Workers, 1940s–1960s" (PhD diss., University of Connecticut, 2002), 126–27. The dissertation was published in revised form as *Land Reform in Puerto Rico: Modernizing the Colonial State, 1941–1969* (Gainesville: University of Florida Press, 2009).

119. Fred Wale, *Report of the Division of Community Education of the Department of Education: From July 1, 1949 to October 15, 1951* (San Juan, PR: Department of Education, 1952), 35.

120. Kalervo Oberg, "Community Development Programs in Puerto Rico," *Community Development Review* 1 (January 1956), 59.

121. Marqués, "Writing for a Community Education Programme."

122. William W. Biddle and Loureide J. Biddle, *The Community Development Process: The Rediscovery of Local Initiative* (New York: Holt, Rinehart and Winston, 1965), 78–79.

123. Stephen B. Withey and Charles F. Cannell, Introduction, in "Community Change: An Action Program in Puerto Rico," ed. Charles F. Cannell, Fred G. Wale, and Stephen B. Withey, special issue, *Journal of Social Issues* 9.2 (1953), 2.

124. Fred Wale, "The Division of Community Education—An Overview," in "Community Change: An Action Program in Puerto Rico," ed. Charles F. Cannell, Fred G. Wale, and Stephen B. Withey, special issue, *Journal of Social Issues* 9.2 (1953), 12.

125. Zacarías Rodríguez, "A Village Becomes a Community," *Fundamental and Adult Education* 5.2 (1953), 63.

126. Carmen Isales and Fred Wale, "The Field Program," in "Community Change: An Action Program in Puerto Rico," ed. Charles F. Cannell, Fred G. Wale, and Stephen B. Withey, special issue, *Journal of Social Issues* 9.2 (1953), 23.

127. Fred Wale and Carmen Isales, *The Meaning of Community Development: A Report from the Division of Community Education* (San Juan, PR: Department of Education, 1967), 7–8.

128. Ibid., 26.

129. Quoted in Marjorie Page, "Out in the Field with an Organizer," *Island Times*, January 5, 1962.

130. Henry Wells, *The Modernization of Puerto Rico: A Political Study of Changing Values and Institutions* (Cambridge: Harvard University Press, 1969).

131. Antonio Lauria-Pericelli, "Images and Contradictions: DIVEDCO's Portrayal of Puerto Rican Life," *Centro Journal* 3.1 (1990–91).

132. Laura Briggs, *Reproducing Empire: Race, Sex, Science, and U.S. Imperialism in Puerto Rico* (Berkeley: University of California Press, 2002). Briggs's discussion of Puerto Rican feminist discourse on sterilization at the time is especially important in this regard.

133. Jorge Duany, *The Puerto Rican Nation on the Move: Identities on the Island and in the United States* (Chapel Hill: University of North Carolina Press, 2002). On the Creole propertied elite construction of cultural nationalism with respect to the dispossessed majority, also see Kelvin A. Santiago-Valles, "The Unruly City and the Mental Landscape of Colonized Identities: Internally Contested Nationality in Puerto Rico, 1945–1980," *Social Text* 38 (Spring 1994).

134. Robert W. Anderson, *Party Politics in Puerto Rico* (Stanford: Stanford University Press, 1965); Kenneth R. Farr, *Personalism and Party Politics: Institutionalization of the Popular Democratic Party of Puerto Rico* (Hato Rey, PR: Inter-American University Press, 1973); Jorge Heine, *The Last Cacique: Leadership and Politics in a Puerto Rican City* (Pittsburgh: University of Pittsburgh Press, 1993); Grosfoguel, "Puerto Rico's Exceptionalism."

135. Waldemar Perez Quintana, "An Oral History of the Division of Community Education of Puerto Rico from 1949 to the Present: The Perspective of Eight Puerto Rican Educators" (PhD diss., Pennsylvania State University, 1984), 426.

136. Ramón Grosfoguel, "The Divorce of Nationalist Discourses from the Puerto

Rican People: A Sociohistorical Perspective," in *Puerto Rican Jam: Rethinking Colonialism and Nationalism*, ed. Frances Negrón-Muntaner and Ramón Grosfoguel (Minneapolis: University of Minnesota Press, 1997), 67–70. Also see Richard Weisskoff, *Factories and Food Stamps: The Puerto Rican Model of Development* (Baltimore: Johns Hopkins University Press, 1985).

137. T. R. Batten, *Communities and Their Development: An Introductory Study with Special Reference to the Tropics* (London: Oxford University Press, 1957), 87–89, 26.

138. See, for instance, US International Cooperation Administration, *Report of the Interregional Conference on Community Development and Its Role in Nation Building, Seoul, Korea, May 6–12, 1961* (Washington: US International Cooperation Administration, 1961); UN Ad Hoc Group of Experts on Community Development, *Community Development and National Development* (New York: UN Department of Economic and Social Affairs, 1963).

139. Bonnie Honig, *Democracy and the Foreigner* (Princeton: Princeton University Press, 2001), 7, 76.

140. Rey Chow, *The Protestant Ethnic and the Spirit of Capitalism* (New York: Columbia University Press, 2002), 32, 34.

141. Julian Go, *American Empire and the Politics of Meaning: Elite Political Cultures in the Philippines and Puerto Rico during U.S. Colonialism* (Durham: Duke University Press, 2008), 25–54.

142. Puerto Rico as "foreign in a domestic sense" is a reference to the 1901 Supreme Court decision in *Downes v. Bidwell*, which was among the so-called *Insular Cases* (1901–1904) that determined the constitutional status of Hawai'i, Puerto Rico and the Philippines.

2. On the Internal Border

1. Peace Corps, *Second Annual Report* (Washington: Peace Corps Office of Public Affairs, 1963), 36.

2. Initially presented as the fourth policy objective in President Truman's 1949 inauguration speech, Point Four was the first extensive US foreign aid program outside Europe and a corollary to the 1947 Truman Doctrine aimed at winning the allegiance of the nonaligned countries. In 1950, the objectives of Point Four were the basis of the Act for International Development.

3. Walter Mignolo, *Local Histories/Global Designs: Coloniality, Subaltern Knowledges, and Border Thinking* (Princeton: Princeton University Press, 2000).

4. As noted in the introduction, the term "Hispano" refers to people who claim direct descent from Spanish colonists in the Southwest prior to the Treaty of Guadalupe Hidalgo.

5. Harry S. Truman, "Inaugural Address," in *Public Papers of the Presidents of the United States: Harry S. Truman, 1949* (Washington: Government Printing Office, 1964), 114. Also see Walter M. Daniels, ed., *The Point Four Program* (New York: H. W. Wilson, 1951).

6. Council of Economic Advisers, *Annual Report* (Washington: Government Printing Office, 1964), 55.

7. Alice O'Connor, *Poverty Knowledge: Social Science, Social Policy, and the Poor in Twentieth-Century U.S. History* (Princeton: Princeton University Press, 2001), 99–123.

8. Timothy Mitchell, "Origins and Limits of the Modern Idea of the Economy" (Paper presented at the Workshop on Positivism and Post-Positivism, University of Chicago, October 2001), 18, 22. Also see Hugo Radice, "The National Economy: A Keynesian Myth?" *Capital and Class* 22 (Spring 1984); Timothy Mitchell, "Economists and the Economy in the Twentieth Century," in *The Politics of Method in the Human Sciences: Positivism and Its Epistemological Others*, ed. George Steinmetz (Durham: Duke University Press, 2005).

9. Majid Rahnema, "Global Poverty: A Pauperizing Myth," *Interculture* 24.2 (1991). Also see Arturo Escobar, *Encountering Development: The Making and Unmaking of the Third World* (Princeton: Princeton University Press, 1995).

10. Nils Gilman, *Mandarins of the Future: Modernization Theory in Cold War America* (Baltimore: Johns Hopkins University Press, 2003), 92–94.

11. Lewis first proposed his "culture of poverty" thesis in *Five Families: Mexican Case Studies in the Culture of Poverty* (New York: Basic, 1959). For nuanced readings of the "culture of poverty" thesis and its subsequent uses, see Laura Briggs, *Reproducing Empire: Race, Sex, Science, and U.S. Imperialism in Puerto Rico* (Berkeley: University of California Press, 2002), 162–92; A. O'Connor, *Poverty Knowledge*; Karin Alejandra Rosemblatt, "Other Americas: Transnationalism, Scholarship, and the Culture of Poverty in Mexico and the United States," *Hispanic American Historical Review* 89.4 (2009).

12. On *Cherokee Nation v. Georgia* and the history of US-American Indian treaties, see Vine Deloria Jr., *Behind the Trail of Broken Treaties: An Indian Declaration of Independence*, 2nd ed. (Austin: University of Texas Press, 1985); Joanne Barker, "For Whom Sovereignty Matters," in *Sovereignty Matters: Locations of Contestation and Possibility in Indigenous Struggles for Self-Determination*, ed. Joanne Barker (Lincoln: University of Nebraska Press, 2005); Stuart Banner, *How the Indians Lost Their Land: Law and Power on the Frontier* (Cambridge: Harvard University Press, 2005); Robert A. Williams Jr., *Like a Loaded Weapon: The Rehnquist Court, Indian Rights, and the Legal History of Racism in America* (Minneapolis: University of Minnesota Press, 2005). On the disputed legacy of the Treaty of Guadalupe Hidalgo, see Richard Griswold del Castillo, *The Treaty of Guadalupe Hidalgo: A Legacy of Conflict* (Norman: University of Oklahoma Press, 1990). For insights into the racialized terms of the treaty, see María Josefina Saldaña-Portillo, " 'Wavering on the Horizon of Social Being': The Treaty of Guadalupe-Hidalgo and the Legacy of Its Racial Character in Paredes's *George Washington Gómez*," *Radical History Review* 89 (Spring 2004). On the *Insular Cases* and the legal construction of the unincorporation, see Christina Duffy

Burnett and Burke Marshall, eds., *Foreign in a Domestic Sense: Puerto Rico, American Expansion, and the Constitution* (Durham: Duke University Press, 2001); Bartholomew H. Sparrow, *The* Insular Cases *and the Emergence of American Empire* (Lawrence: University Press of Kansas, 2006).

13. D'Arcy McNickle, "A Ten-Point Program for American Indians" (Eighth Annual Convention of the National Congress of American Indians, July 24–27, 1951, St. Paul, Minnesota), 4, 9, 10, Conventions and Mid-Year Conferences, Speeches 1951; NCAI, Conventions, 1950–1953, Box 3; National Anthropological Archives, Smithsonian Institution, Washington (hereafter NAA). On federal termination policy, see Donald L. Fixico, *Termination and Relocation: Federal Indian Policy, 1945–1960* (Albuquerque: University of New Mexico Press, 1986); Vine Deloria Jr. and Clifford M. Lytle, *The Nations Within: The Past and Future of American Indian Sovereignty* (1984; Austin: University of Texas Press, 1998); Kenneth R. Philp, *Termination Revisited: American Indians and the Trail to Self-Determination, 1933–1953* (Lincoln: University of Nebraska Press, 1999); David E. Wilkins and K. Tsianina Lomawaima, *Uneven Ground: American Indian Sovereignty and Federal Law* (Norman: University of Oklahoma Press, 2001).

14. Daniel M. Cobb, *Native Activism in Cold War America: The Struggle for Sovereignty* (Lawrence: University Press of Kansas, 2008), 12–13.

15. For a history of the NCAI between 1944 and 1961, see Thomas W. Cowger, *The National Congress of American Indians: The Founding Years* (Lincoln: University of Nebraska Press, 1999).

16. D'Arcy McNickle, "U.S. Indian Affairs—1953," *América Indígena* 13 (October 1953): 273.

17. Cowger, *The National Congress of American Indians*, 108–9, 117.

18. Quoted in Harold E. Fey and D'Arcy McNickle, *Indians and Other Americans: Two Ways of Life Meet* (New York: Harper and Brothers, 1959), 198.

19. Cobb, *Native Activism in Cold War America*, 17–22.

20. In an effort to avoid characterizing the relationship of the United States to Puerto Rico as one of colonial occupation, the 1901 Supreme Court decision in *Downes v. Bidwell* described Puerto Rico as "foreign in a domestic sense." As noted earlier, this was one of the *Insular Cases* (1901–1904) on the constitutional status of Hawai'i, Puerto Rico, and the Philippines.

21. "Announcement of Opportunity to Study 'Operation Bootstrap' in Puerto Rico," February 12, 1958, National Congress of American Indians—Puerto Rico Study Trip (Operation Bootstrap 1956–1958); NCAI Fundraising, Box 6, NAA.

22. "Misión de los Pueblos Indios de Norteamérica en Puerto Rico," *El Mundo* (San Juan, Puerto Rico), March 6, 1958; Ramon M. Diaz, "Muñoz Va a Congreso de Indios," *El Imparcial*, March 6, 1958.

23. John Fahey, *Saving the Reservation: Joe Garry and the Battle to Be Indian* (Seattle: University of Washington Press, 2001), 123.

24. House Committee on Interior and Insular Affairs, *Operation Bootstrap for the*

American Indian: Hearings before the Subcommittee on Indian Affairs, H.R. 7701, 8803, and 8590, 86th Congress, 2nd Session (Washington: Government Printing Office, 1960), 27. Also see Cowger, *The National Congress of American Indians*, 122–23.

25. Ibid., 77.

26. Ibid., 81.

27. On American Indian activism during this period, see George Pierre Castile, *To Show Heart: Native American Self-Determination and Federal Indian Policy, 1960–1975* (Tucson: University of Arizona Press, 1998); Daniel M. Cobb and Loretta Fowler, eds., *Beyond Red Power: American Indian Politics and Activism since 1900* (Santa Fe: SAR Press, 2007); Cobb, *Native Activism in Cold War America*.

28. US Congress Joint Economic Committee, *Toward Economic Development for Native American Communities* (Washington: Government Printing Office, 1969), 1:236.

29. Roxanne Dunbar-Ortiz, ed., *Economic Development in American Indian Reservations* (Albuquerque: Native American Studies, University of New Mexico, 1979); Dean Howard Smith, *Modern Tribal Development: Paths to Self-Sufficiency and Cultural Integrity in Indian Country* (Walnut Creek, CA: AltaMira, 2000); Brian Hosmer and Colleen O'Neill, eds., *Native Pathways: Indian Culture and Economic Development in the Twentieth Century* (Boulder: University Press of Colorado, 2004).

30. Henry S. Reuss, "A Point Four Youth Corps," in *The Peace Corps*, ed. Pauline Madow (New York: H. W. Wilson, 1964), 12.

31. The phrase "shirt-sleeve diplomacy" was often used by US policymakers to describe the Point Four program. See, for example, Jonathan B. Bingham, *Shirt-Sleeve Diplomacy: Point 4 in Action* (New York: John Day, 1954).

32. Gerald T. Rice, *The Bold Experiment: JFK's Peace Corps* (Notre Dame, IN: University of Notre Dame Press, 1985), 10–12.

33. Indeed, the historian Elizabeth Cobbs Hoffman has commented: "The Peace Corps brought into the American lexicon a new term—culture shock—which it did not invent but certainly helped to popularize" (*All You Need Is Love: The Peace Corps and the Spirit of the 1960s* [Cambridge: Harvard University Press, 1998], 134).

34. Harlan Cleveland and Gerard J. Mangone, eds., *The Art of Overseasmanship* (Syracuse, NY: Syracuse University Press, 1957); Harlan Cleveland, Gerard J. Mangone, and John Clarke Adams, *The Overseas Americans* (New York: McGraw-Hill, 1960).

35. Kalervo Oberg, "Culture Shock: Adjustment to New Cultural Environments," *Practical Anthropology* 7.4 (July–August 1960). This article originally appeared in the State Department's *Technical Assistance Overseas Bulletin*.

36. Charles B. Arnold, "Culture Shock and a Peace Corps Field Mental Health

Program," *Community Mental Health Journal* 3.1 (1967). Also see Robert B. Textor, ed., *Cultural Frontiers of the Peace Corps* (Cambridge: MIT Press, 1966).

37. On the centrality of psychological thought as a normative framework in mid-twentieth-century US thought, see Steven C. Ward, *Modernizing the Mind: Psychological Knowledge and the Remaking of Society* (Westport, CT: Praeger, 2002).

38. Mitchell Ginsberg, "Short-Term Training for the Peace Corps," *Social Work* 9.1 (1964), 62–68; Gertrude Samuels, "Peace Corps Trains in New York," *New York Times*, October 21, 1962; "Peace Corps Trainees Work, Study in New York Slums," *Peace Corps Volunteer* 1.1 (1962).

39. Quoted in Ginsberg, "Short-Term Training for the Peace Corps," 65.

40. George Sullivan, *The Story of the Peace Corps* (New York: Fleet, 1964), 64–65. For how certain sectors of Hawai'i encouraged field training on the islands, see "Concurrent Resolution of Hawaii Legislature Relating to Peace Corps," *Congressional Record* 107.4 (1961): 4849; David L. Englund, "Peace Corps Training and the American University," *International Review of Education* 11.2 (1965).

41. Moritz Thomsen, *Living Poor: A Peace Corps Chronicle* (Seattle: University of Washington Press, 1969). This book is representative of a number of laudatory memoirs published by Peace Corps volunteers during the 1960s.

42. Michael Latham, *Modernization as Ideology: American Social Science and "Nation Building" in the Kennedy Era* (Chapel Hill: University of North Carolina Press, 2000), 144–46. Sargent Shriver, reiterating the conventional interpretation of Frederick Jackson Turner's frontier thesis, insisted: "The Peace Corps is truly a new frontier in the sense that it provides the challenge of self-reliance and independent action which the vanished frontier once provided on our own continent. Sharing in the progress of other countries helps us to rediscover ourselves at home" (quoted in Latham, *Modernization as Ideology*, 145).

43. Marshall Nason, "A Proposed Training Center for Peace Corps Personnel, The University of New Mexico, Albuquerque, New Mexico, April 10, 1961," 1–2, Box 1; and Tom L. Popejoy, President, UNM, letter to Dr. Joseph Kauffman, Chief, Training Program, Peace Corps, Washington, June 2, 1962, Colombia III Training Proposal 1962, Box 8, Peace Corps Collection, Center for Southwest Research, University Libraries, University of New Mexico, Albuquerque (hereafter PC/CSWR).

44. Margaret Mead, *Cultural Patterns and Technical Change* (New York: Mentor, 1955), 151–77. The text on the cover of this popular edition read: "An exciting voyage to *distant lands* where centuries-old methods of ancient people give way to the most modern machines and techniques mankind has devised" (my emphasis).

45. Clark S. Knowlton, "Area Development in New Mexico: Implications for Dependency and for Economic and Social Growth" (New Mexico Conference of Social Welfare, 1961–1962), 2, 4, Clark S. Knowlton Collection, Box 33, Folder 8, New Mexico State Records Center and Archives, Santa Fe, NM.

46. Erlinda Gonzales-Berry and David R. Maciel, eds., *The Contested Homeland: A Chicano History of New Mexico* (Albuquerque: University of New Mexico Press, 2000); Charles Montgomery, *The Spanish Redemption: Heritage, Power, and Loss on New Mexico's Upper Rio Grande* (Berkeley: University of California Press, 2002).

47. Suzanne Forrest, *The Preservation of the Village: New Mexico's Hispanics and the New Deal*, 2nd ed. (Albuquerque: University of New Mexico Press, 1998).

48. See, for instance, José A. Rivera, *Acequia Culture: Water, Land and Community in the Southwest* (Albuquerque: University of New Mexico Press, 1998).

49. On the extensive Native American presence in Albuquerque and the need to understand urban life and urbanization as a long-standing context for indigenous peoples, see Myla Vicenti Carpio, *Indigenous Albuquerque* (Lubbock: Texas Tech University Press, 2011).

50. See John H. Burma and David E. Williams, *An Economic, Social and Educational Survey of Rio Arriba and Taos Counties* (El Rito: Northern New Mexico College, 1960), for contemporary data on the complexity of class and ethnic relations in the area.

51. "The Entrance of C.D. into Northern New Mexico Communities," March–April 1963, Box 4, PC/CSWR.

52. Phillip B. Gonzales, "Struggle for Survival: The Hispanic Land Grants of New Mexico, 1848–2001," *Agricultural History* 77.2 (2003); David Correia, "'Retribution Will Be Their Reward': New Mexico's Las Gorras Blancas and the Fight for the Las Vegas Land Grant Commons," *Radical History Review* 108 (October 2010).

53. David Correia, "'Rousers of the Rabble' in the New Mexico Land Grant War: La Alianza Federal De Mercedes and the Violence of the State," *Antipode* 40.4 (2008), 562.

54. Reies López Tijerina, memo to President Adolfo López Mateos, January 14, 1964; "La Gran Caravana Internacional de los Herederos Reales," September 14, 1964, Reies Tijerina Papers, Box 31, Folder 16, Center for Southwest Research, University Libraries, University of New Mexico, Albuquerque.

55. Peter Nabokov, *Tijerina and the Courthouse Raid* (Albuquerque: University of New Mexico Press, 1969); Richard Gardner, *¡Grito! Tijerina and the New Mexico Land Grant War of 1967* (Indianapolis: Bobbs-Merrill, 1970); Reies López Tijerina, *They Called Me "King Tiger": My Struggle for the Land and Our Rights* (Houston: Arte Público, 2000).

56. Correia, "'Rousers of the Rabble' in the New Mexico Land Grant War." Also see Elizabeth "Betita" Martinez, "A View from New Mexico: Recollections of the *Movimiento* Left," *Monthly Review* 54.3 (2002).

57. "Phase I and II Lesson Plans," Community Development, Box 4, PC/CSWR.

58. "Manual for PCV's Field Work," Training—Community Development—Field Training, Box 5, PC/CSWR.

59. "Field Experience—Colombia XIII," Evaluations, October 1963; "Group Leaders' Report—Week of 'Field Utilization,' Colombia XIII," October 19, 1963, Training—Community Development—Field Training, Box 4, PC/CSWR.

60. Elliot V. Smith, "Peace Corps Training Center Evaluation, October 11, 1965," Training—Community Development—Evaluation of Program, Box 7, PC/CSWR.

61. Bill McKinstry, "Field Training Introduction," report reprinted in John Arango, "The Community Development Program of the University of New Mexico Peace Corps Training Center for Latin America" (June 1965), 134–45, Report—Community Development Program 1965, Box 3, PC/CSWR.

62. Bill McKinstry, "Field Experience—Purpose," n.d., 1, Training—Community Development—Training Plans in New Mexico 1965, Box 7, PC/CSWR.

63. John Arango, "The Community Development Program of the University of New Mexico Peace Corps Training Center for Latin America" (June 1965), 134, Report—Community Development Program 1965, Box 3, PC/CSWR.

64. Peace Corps, *Second Annual Report*, 36.

65. Arango, "The Community Development Program of the University of New Mexico Peace Corps Training Center for Latin America," 51.

66. John Arango, memo to David T. Benedetti, director of the UNM Peace Corps Training Center, April 14, 1965, 5–6, Correspondence—General 1965, Box 3, PC/CSWR.

67. John Arango, letter to Jules Pagano, February 8, 1965, Correspondence—General 1965, Box 3, PC/CSWR.

68. Jules Pagano, *Education in the Peace Corps: Evolving Concepts of Volunteer Training* (Boston: Boston University Center for the Study of Liberal Education for Adults, 1965), vii.

69. Ibid., 34.

70. "No Changes, Please," *New Mexican*, December 6, 1963.

71. Crisóforo Martínez, letter to Marshall Nason, director, UNM Peace Corps Training, March 28, 1964, El Llano, N.M., Training—Community Development, Box 7, PC/CSWR.

72. "Peace Corps Trainees Enroute [sic] to Villanueva," *Daily Optic*, April 22, 1964. Also see in the same newspaper: "New Peace Corps Members Arrive," May 8, 1964; "Peace Corps Work Continues," May 8, 1964; "Villanueva Area Development Group Elects [Officers]," June 16, 1964.

73. "U.S. Peace Corps Training Center to Close Jan. 21," *Albuquerque Journal*, January 5, 1967, Newspaper articles—1967, Box 3, PC/CSWR. Lack of university enthusiasm for the program was probably a contributing factor as well. Tom Popejoy, UNM president, wrote Peace Corps Training Center Director David Benedetti: "It seems to me that this is an appropriate time for us to give more attention to instructional and research programs which relate to South America," January 16, 1967, Correspondence—General—1967, Box 3, PC/CSWR.

74. Albert R. Wight and Mary Anne Hammons, *Guidelines for Peace Corps Cross-*

Cultural Training (Estes Park, CO: Center for Research and Education, 1970), 1:ix, x.

75. "Peace Corps: Negroes Play Vital Role in U.S. Quest for Friends Abroad," *Ebony*, November 1961; "Peace Corps Training at Howard: Negro University Prepares Interracial Group for U.S. Good-Will Missions Abroad," *Ebony*, November 1962; Juanita Thurston, "Valuable Job of Volunteer," *Christian Science Monitor*, June 16, 1971; Minority Activity in the Peace Corps," *Congressional Record*, July 6, 1971; Jonathan Zimmerman, "Beyond Double Consciousness: Black Peace Corps Volunteers in Africa, 1961–1971," *Journal of American History* 82.3 (1995); Julius A. Amin, "The Peace Corps and the Struggle for African American Equality," *Journal of Black Studies* 29.6 (1999).

76. Brent Ashabranner, *A Moment in History: The First Ten Years of the Peace Corps* (Garden City, NY: Doubleday, 1971), 259.

77. Sargent Shriver, memo to the president, July 27, 1965, "Weekly Report of Peace Corps Activities," Peace Corps 1965, Box 129, Confidential Files, Agency Reports, Lyndon B. Johnson Library, Austin, Texas.

78. Leon Ginsburg, "Project Peace Pipe" (report presented at the Oklahomans for Indian Opportunity board meeting, July 8, 1967), 3, Fred R. Harris Collection, Box 284, Folder 16; Carl Albert Congressional Research and Studies Center, Congressional Archives, University of Oklahoma, Norman.

79. LaDonna Harris, *LaDonna Harris: A Comanche Life*, ed. H. Henrietta Stockel (Lincoln: University of Nebraska Press, 2000), 59–64, 80–82.

80. Mrs. Fred R. Harris [LaDonna Harris] and Leon H. Ginsberg, "Project Peace Pipe: Indian Youth Pre-Trained for Peace Corps Duty," *Journal of American Indian Education* 7.2 (1968): 26.

81. Ibid., 23.

82. Fritz Fischer, *Making Them Like Us: Peace Corps Volunteers in the 1960s* (Washington: Smithsonian Institution, 1998), 102–3.

83. I'm alluding here to the "domestic dependent nation" status invented for American Indian tribes by Chief Justice John Marshall in his decision *Cherokee Nation v. Georgia*, 30 U.S. 1 (1831).

84. On this point, also see Ashabranner, *A Moment in History*, 268–70; Jack Anderson, "Peace Corps Indian Project Fails," *Washington Post*, November 4, 1970.

85. Interview with LaDonna Harris, June 6, 2006, Albuquerque, NM.

86. For discussions of the "internal border," see Étienne Balibar, *Masses, Classes, Ideas: Studies on Politics and Philosophy before and after Marx*, trans. James Swenson (New York: Routledge, 1994), 61–86; Marc Redfield, "Imagi-Nation: The Imagined Community and the Aesthetics of Mourning," in *Grounds of Comparison: Around the Work of Benedict Anderson*, ed. Jonathan Culler and Pheng Cheah (New York: Routledge, 2003).

87. Étienne Balibar, *Politics and the Other Scene*, trans. Christine Jones, James Swenson, and Chris Turner (London: Verso, 2002), 154. Balibar contrasts "real uni-

versality" with "fictive universality" and "ideal universality." Fictive universality has to do with the domain of institutions and representations. Ideal universality is intended to suggest "the fact that universality also exists as an ideal, in the form of absolute or infinite claims which are symbolically raised against the limits of any institution" (163–64).

88. Uday Singh Mehta, *Liberalism and Empire: A Study in Nineteenth-Century British Liberal Thought* (Chicago: University of Chicago Press, 1999), 46.

89. Ibid., 191.

90. Quoted in Hoffman, *All You Need Is Love*, 197.

91. "Address by Sargent Shriver before the American Society of Newspaper Editors, Washington, D.C., April 18, 1964," Aides Files—Richard N. Goodwin, Box 24, Poverty Speeches, Lyndon B. Johnson Library, Austin, TX.

92. "The Werner Report: Board Dissents with Report," *Navajo Times*, January 15, 1970, 19.

3. Civics and Civilities of Poverty

1. "Riots and Poverty," *New York Times*, August 4, 1964, 28.

2. US House Committee on Education and Labor, *Economic Opportunity Amendments of 1966: Report Together with Minority Views (to Accompany H.R. 15111)* (Washington: Government Printing Office, 1966); US Senate Committee on Labor and Public Welfare, Subcommittee on Employment, Manpower, and Poverty, *Hearings: Amendments to the Economic Opportunity Act of 1964* (Washington: Government Printing Office, 1966). The 1968 Civil Rights Act would similarly adopt antiriot measures.

3. Lyndon B. Johnson, "Special Message to the Congress Proposing a Nationwide War on the Sources of Poverty," in *Public Papers of the Presidents of the United States: Lyndon B. Johnson, 1963–1964* (Washington: Government Printing Office, 1965), 1:376.

4. US Senate Committee on Labor and Public Welfare, Select Subcommittee on Poverty, *The War on Poverty: The Economic Opportunity Act: A Compilation of Materials Relevant to S. 2642* (Washington: Government Printing Office, 1964), 53–54. For accounts of the "maximum feasible participation" policy in the War on Poverty, see "Participation of the Poor: Section 202(a) (3) Organization under the Economic Opportunity Act of 1964," *Yale Law Journal* 75.4 (1966), 599–629; Richard W. Boone, "What Is Meaningful Participation?," *Community Development* 1.5 (1966), 27–32; Lillian B. Rubin, "Maximum Feasible Participation: The Origins, Implications, and Present Status," *Annals of the American Academy of Political and Social Science* 385 (September 1969); Ralph M. Kramer, *Participation of the Poor: Comparative Community Case Studies in the War on Poverty* (Englewood Cliffs, NJ: Prentice-Hall, 1969); Daniel Patrick Moynihan, *Maximum Feasible Misunderstanding: Community Action in the War on Poverty* (New York: Free Press, 1969); J. David Greenstone and Paul E. Peterson, *Race*

and *Authority in Urban Politics: Community Participation and the War on Poverty* (Chicago: University of Chicago Press, 1973).

5. The third chapter of Gayatri Chakravorty Spivak's *A Critique of Postcolonial Reason: Toward a History of the Vanishing Present* (Cambridge: Harvard University Press, 1999) critically expands on her original essay "Can the Subaltern Speak?" in *Marxism and the Interpretation of Culture*, ed. Lawrence Grossberg and Cary Nelson (Urbana: University of Illinois Press, 1988). Spivak had initially planned to title the essay "Power, Desire, Interest," and each of these three terms remains constitutive of the injunction that the subaltern subject speak. For an exemplary analysis of the politics of sterilization in Puerto Rico that employs Spivak's theorization, see Laura Briggs, *Reproducing Empire: Race, Sex, Science, and U.S. Imperialism in Puerto Rico* (Berkeley: University of California Press, 2002), 142–61.

6. Gayatri Chakravorty Spivak, "In Response: Looking Back, Looking Forward," in *Can the Subaltern Speak? Reflections on the History of an Idea*, ed. Rosalind C. Morris (New York: Columbia University Press, 2010), 230.

7. Richard A. Cloward and Frances Fox Piven, "The Weight of the Poor: A Strategy to End Poverty," *Nation*, May 2, 1966, 510–17.

8. Carole Pateman, *Participation and Democratic Theory* (Cambridge: Cambridge University Press, 1970), 22–27.

9. Kramer, *Participation of the Poor*, 1–21.

10. Moynihan, *Maximum Feasible Misunderstanding*.

11. Barbara Cruikshank, *The Will to Empower: Democratic Citizens and Other Subjects* (Ithaca: Cornell University Press, 1999), 67–86.

12. Michel Crozier, Samuel P. Huntington, and Joji Watanuki, *The Crisis of Democracy: Report on the Governability of Democracies to the Trilateral Commission* (New York: New York University Press, 1975), 114.

13. Ralph M. Kramer notes: "The use of military terminology in the war on poverty was as pervasive as it was inappropriate. References to social services as 'weapons' in an 'arsenal,' to staff members as 'poverty warriors,' and programs as an 'assault' or 'attack' conjure up false images of a concerted, planned, and massive program" (*Participation of the Poor*, 2).

14. Lyndon B. Johnson, "Special Message to the Congress Proposing a Nationwide War on the Sources of Poverty," 1:380.

15. Michael S. Sherry, *In the Shadow of War: The United States since the 1930s* (New Haven: Yale University Press, 1995), 262.

16. Both examples are discussed in Michael Latham, *Modernization as Ideology: American Social Science and "Nation Building" in the Kennedy Era* (Chapel Hill: University of North Carolina Press, 2000). On the "strategic hamlet" program in Vietnam, also see Philip E. Catton, *Diem's Failure: Prelude to America's War in Vietnam* (Lawrence: University Press of Kansas, 2002).

17. National Action/Research on the Military-Industrial Complex, *Police on the*

Homefront: They're Bringing It All Back (Philadelphia: National Action/Research on the Military-Industrial Complex, 1971); Tracy Tullis, "A Vietnam at Home: Policing the Ghettos in the Counterinsurgency Era" (PhD diss., New York University, 1999); Jennifer Light, *From Warfare to Welfare: Defense Intellectuals and Urban Problems in Cold War America* (Baltimore: Johns Hopkins University Press, 2003); Michael W. Flamm, *Law and Order: Street Crime, Civil Unrest, and the Crisis of Liberalism in the 1960s* (New York: Columbia University Press, 2005), 113–19.

18. Flamm, *Law and Order*, 112.

19. Julie Skurski and Fernando Coronil, "States of Violence and the Violence of States," in *States of Violence*, ed. Fernando Coronil and Julie Skurski (University of Michigan Press, 2006).

20. Slavoj Žižek, *Violence* (New York: Picador, 2008), 13.

21. See, for instance, Ford Foundation, *American Community Development: Preliminary Reports by Directors of Projects Assisted by the Ford Foundation in Four Cities and a State: Twenty-ninth Annual National Conference, National Association of Housing and Redevelopment Officials. Denver, Colorado, October 1, 1963* (New York: Ford Foundation, 1964); Alice O'Connor, "Community Action, Urban Reform, and the Fight against Poverty: The Ford Foundation's Gray Areas Program," *Journal of Urban History* 22 (July 1996); Charles F. Grosser, "Neighborhood Community-Development Programs for Serving the Poor," in *Community Action against Poverty: Readings from the Mobilization Experience*, ed. George A. Brager and Francis P. Purcell (New Haven, CT: College and University Press, 1967); Harold H. Weissman, ed., *Community Development in the Mobilization for Youth Experience* (New York: Association Press, 1969); Frances Fox Piven, "The New Urban Programs: The Strategy of Federal Intervention," in *The Politics of Turmoil* (New York: Pantheon, 1974).

22. Malcolm M. Feeley and Austin Sarat, *The Policy Dilemma: Federal Crime Policy and the Law Enforcement Assistance Administration, 1968–1978* (Minneapolis: University of Minnesota Press, 1980), 39–40; John E. Moore, "Controlling Delinquency: Executive, Congressional, and Juvenile, 1961–1964," in *Congress and Urban Problems*, ed. Frederic N. Cleaveland (Washington: Brookings Institution, 1969).

23. Richard A. Cloward and Lloyd E. Ohlin, *Delinquency and Opportunity: A Theory of Delinquent Gangs* (Glencoe, IL: Free Press, 1960), 150–52.

24. Daniel Knapp and Kenneth Polk, *Scouting the War on Poverty: Social Reform Politics in the Kennedy Administration* (Lexington, MA: Heath Lexington, 1971); Peter Marris and Martin Rein, *Dilemmas of Social Reform: Poverty and Community Action in the United States*, 2nd ed. (Chicago: University of Chicago Press, 1973).

25. Cloward and Ohlin, *Delinquency and Opportunity*. Ohlin and Cloward argued against the prevailing behaviorist, therapeutic consensus on juvenile delinquency

of the 1950s. In particular, they drew on Clifford Shaw's ideas on "cultural transmission" and Leonard S. Cottrell's notion of "community competence," both concepts that deliberately shifted the scale of analysis from the individual to the interactions of a local population. See Clifford R. Shaw, *The Jack-Roller: A Delinquent Boy's Own Story* (Chicago: University of Chicago Press, 1930); Nelson N. Foote and Leonard S. Cottrell, *Identity and Interpersonal Competence: A New Direction in Family Research* (Chicago: University of Chicago Press, 1955). Also see Noel A. Cazenave, "Chicago Influences the War on Poverty," *Journal of Policy History* 5 (January 1993); Knapp and Polk, *Scouting the War on Poverty,* 25–52.

26. Joseph Helfgot, *Professional Reforming: Mobilization for Youth and the Failure of Social Science* (Lexington, MA: Lexington, 1981), 18; Eric C. Schneider, *Vampires, Dragons, and Egyptian Kings: Youth Gangs in Postwar New York* (Princeton: Princeton University Press, 1999), 211.

27. Ernest W. Burgess, Joseph D. Lohman, and Clifford R. Shaw, "The Chicago Area Project," in *Coping with Crime: Yearbook of the National Probation Association,* ed. Marjorie Bell (New York: National Probation Association, 1937); Solomon Kobrin, "The Chicago Area Project—A 25-Year Assessment," *Annals of the American Academy of Political and Social Science* 322 (March 1959); David Wolcott and Steven Schlossman, "In the Voices of Delinquents: Social Science, the Chicago Area Project, and a Boys' Culture of Casual Crime and Violence in the 1930s," in *When Science Encounters the Child,* ed. Barbara Beatty, Emily D. Cahan, and Julia Grant (New York: Teachers College Press, 2006); Andrew J. Diamond, *Mean Streets: Chicago Youths and the Everyday Struggle for Empowerment in the Multiracial City, 1908–1969* (Berkeley: University of California Press, 2009). The most in-depth secondary source on the Chicago Area Project remains Steven Schlossman and Michael Sedlak, *The Chicago Area Project Revisited* (Santa Monica, CA: RAND, 1983).

28. Clifford R. Shaw, with Frederick M. Zorbaugh, Henry D. McKay, and Leonard S. Cottrell, *Delinquency Areas: Study of the Geographical Distribution of School Truants, Juvenile Delinquents, and Adult Offenders in Chicago* (Chicago: University of Chicago Press, 1929).

29. Edwin Stoll, "Use Democratic Idea as Brake on Delinquency: Russell Square Checks Arrests of Boys," *Chicago Daily Tribune,* November 27, 1938.

30. See Schlossman and Sedlak, *The Chicago Area Project Revisited,* 16–17.

31. Ibid., 61–62.

32. Southside Community Committee, *Bright Shadows in Bronzetown: The Story of the Southside Community Committee* (Chicago: Southside Community Committee, 1949), 57, 26, 65. Also see Billie M. Hamilton, "Roadblock to Delinquency: Fresh Approach Includes Helping Individuals Work Out Their Own Problems," *Christian Science Monitor,* September 25, 1948.

33. Southside Community Committee, *Bright Shadows in Bronzetown,* 88.

34. Robert M. Mennel, "Attitudes and Policies toward Juvenile Delinquency in the United States," *Crime & Justice* 4 (1983): 191–224; James Gilbert, *A Cycle of Outrage: America's Reaction to the Juvenile Delinquent in the 1950s* (New York: Oxford University Press, 1986). On delinquency as a category for social intervention during the Progressive Era, see Anthony M. Platt, *The Child Savers: The Invention of Delinquency*, 2nd ed. (Chicago: University of Chicago Press, 1977); Mary Odem, *Delinquent Daughters: Protecting and Policing Adolescent Female Sexuality in the United States, 1885–1920* (Chapel Hill: University of North Carolina Press, 1995); David Tanenhaus, *Juvenile Justice in the Making* (New York: Oxford University Press, 2004). Platt argues that "unlike earlier specialists in social control," Progressive Era reformers "viewed the criminal justice apparatus as an institution for *preventing* disorder and *harmonizing* social conflicts, as well as simply *reacting* with brute force" (xxvii). This perspective was further refined by reformers in the 1960s with their emphasis on community and participation.

35. Flamm, *Law and Order*, 14–22.

36. Initially Ohlin and Cloward were selected as co-directors of the research, but Ohlin left MFY in 1960 when he was appointed to the newly formed President's Committee on Juvenile Delinquency and Youth Crime.

37. Noel Cazenave provides a superbly detailed analysis of these conflicts in *Impossible Democracy: The Unlikely Success of the War on Poverty Community Action Programs* (Albany: State University of New York Press, 2007).

38. Sections of the 1961 MFY proposal that refer to "organizing the unaffiliated" are concerned with unaffiliated organizations, not individuals, though the latter would eventually become the focus of MFY organizing. See Mobilization for Youth, *A Proposal for the Prevention and Control of Delinquency by Expanding Opportunities* (New York: Mobilization for Youth, December 9, 1961), 132–37.

39. Ibid., 126.

40. Harold H. Weissman, "Overview of the Community Development Program," in *Community Development in the Mobilization for Youth Experience*, ed. Harold H. Weissman (New York: Association Press, 1969), 26.

41. Quoted in Helfgot, *Professional Reforming*, 119.

42. Telephone interview with Frank Espada, August 26, 2008.

43. Cazenave, *Impossible Democracy*, 209.

44. Quoted in Bernard Weintraub, "Lower East Side Vexed by Housing," *New York Times*, July 7, 1963.

45. Premilla Nadasen, *Welfare Warriors: The Welfare Rights Movement in the United States* (New York: Routledge, 2005), 26; Felicia Kornbluh, *The Battle for Welfare Rights: Politics and Poverty in Modern America* (Philadelphia: University of Pennsylvania Press, 2007), 25–26.

46. George A. Brager and Francis P. Purcell, eds., *Community Action against Poverty: Readings from the Mobilization Experience* (New Haven, CT: College and Uni-

versity Press, 1967); Weissman, "Overview of the Community Development Program"; Helfgot, *Professional Reforming*, 81–87; Cazenave, *Impossible Democracy*, 117–21.

47. Quoted in "Report on Principals' Dispute with Mobilization for Youth," February 19, 1964, 1, Box 55, Folder 9, Frances Fox Piven Papers, Sophia Smith Collection, Smith College, Amherst, MA (hereafter Piven Papers). The most thorough published account of the controversy remains Alfred Fried, "The Attack on Mobilization," in *Community Development in the Mobilization for Youth Experience*, ed. Harold H. Weissman (New York: Association Press, 1969). In addition to Fried's essay, see Marris and Rein, *Dilemmas of Social Reform*, 176–81; Knapp and Polk, *Scouting the War on Poverty*, 157–67; Larry R. Jackson and William A. Johnson, *Protest by the Poor: The Welfare Rights Movement in New York City* (Lexington, MA: Lexington, 1974), 53–60; Helfgot, *Professional Reforming*, 69–105; Cazenave, *Impossible Democracy*, 65–83, 116–35.

48. Quoted in Fried, "The Attack on Mobilization," 140. Much of the principals' fury was aimed at the MFY-sponsored Mobilization of Mothers, a group of neighborhood mothers of children in public schools. For an account of MFY's interaction with the New York City school system, see the file marked "confidential," Mobilization of Mothers, n.d., Box 55, Folder 9, Piven Papers.

49. On the March on Washington, see James E. McCarthy letter to Bernard Russell, director, Juvenile Delinquency and Youth Development, Department of Health, Education and Welfare, December 4, 1963, Box 55, Folder 9, Piven Papers.

50. Quoted in Fried, "The Attack on Mobilization," 142.

51. Quoted in Ibid., 142.

52. Quoted in Ibid., 147.

53. Quoted in ibid., 149. Also see "City Investigating Agency for Youth on the East Side," *New York Times*, August 16, 1964; "Probe Youth Agency for Alleged Red Link," *Chicago Tribune*, August 17, 1964; Homer Bigart, "City Hunts Reds in Youth Project on East Side," *New York Times*, August 17, 1964.

54. A review panel for the President's Committee on Juvenile Delinquency and Youth Crime, chaired by Leonard Cottrell, issued a report praising MFY and recommending continued federal support for the organization. Attorney General Nicholas Katzenbach and Secretary of Labor Willard Wirtz also publicly affirmed federal approval of MFY. Furthermore, as became clear from Screvane's public claims, the city's intention was not to do away with MFY but to take it over, an arrangement explicitly recommended in Screvane's official report on the city's investigation of MFY. In December 1964, speaking before a conference of social workers sponsored by the United Neighborhood Houses, Mayor Wagner proclaimed: "Our intention and determination is to continue this demonstration program and to utilize it as an important weapon in the War Against Poverty" (quoted in Fried, "The Attack on Mobilization," 156). Also see Joseph Zullo, "Youth Project Makes Comeback," *Chicago Tribune*, December 9, 1965.

55. Richard A. Cloward and Frances Fox Piven, *The Politics of Turmoil* (New York: Pantheon, 1974), 69.

56. Ibid., 70–71.

57. Richard A. Cloward and Frances Fox Piven, "The Weight of the Poor: A Strategy to End Poverty," *Nation*, May 2, 1966; Joseph Loftus, "Guaranteed Income Backers Hope to Provoke Welfare Crisis," *New York Times*, June 5, 1966; Julius Horwitz, "In One Month, 50,000 Persons Were Added to the City's Welfare Roles," *New York Times Magazine*, January 26, 1969, 22, 44–48, 54. Also see Richard A. Cloward and Frances Fox Piven, *Poor People's Movements: Why They Succeed, How They Fail* (New York: Vintage, 1977); Sanford F. Schram, *Praxis for the Poor: Piven and Cloward and the Future of Social Science in Social Welfare* (Minneapolis: University of Minnesota Press, 2002), 49–108; "Symposium: Poor People's Movements," *Perspectives on Politics* 1.4 (2003).

58. Quoted in Nick Kotz and Mary Lynn Kotz, *A Passion for Equality: George Wiley and the Movement* (New York: W. W. Norton, 1977), 220.

59. Guida West, *The National Welfare Rights Movement: The Social Protest of Poor Women* (New York: Praeger, 1981), 22–24; Nadasen, *Welfare Warriors*, 1–43; Kornbluh, *The Battle for Welfare Rights*, 14–38. Also see Annelise Orleck, *Storming Caesars Palace: How Black Mothers Fought Their Own War on Poverty* (Boston: Beacon Press, 2005). The Ohio Steering Committee for Adequate Welfare, the Milwaukee Welfare Rights Organization, Mothers for Adequate Welfare in Boston, and the Barry Homes Welfare Committee in Washington were among other early local welfare rights organizations.

60. Quoted in Kotz and Kotz, *A Passion for Equality*, 185.

61. Quoted in ibid.

62. Although the National Welfare Rights Organization and its local affiliates operated more as a network than as a mass-based organization at the national level, Wiley and the group's National Coordinating Committee did place a premium on building membership. This emphasis on formal membership was at odds with Piven and Cloward's contention that such a focus ran counter to a mobilization strategy. In their account of the welfare rights movement, Piven and Cloward explicitly point to "the development of an elaborate organizational structure, and the constraining influence of this structure on NWRO's leadership" as a principal factor in the collapse of welfare rights organizing (Cloward and Piven, *Poor People's Movements*, 307–17). Indeed, following the pattern analyzed by Piven and Cloward, the height of the organization's influence was during this formative period of coordinated action. Despite significant continued formal membership, its political power waned after 1969.

63. Nadasen, *Welfare Warriors*, 31–33, 140–46, 165–68.

64. Poverty/Rights Action Center, "Summary Report: Welfare Action Meeting, May 21, 1966, YMCA Hotel, Chicago, Illinois," May 27, 1966; Poverty/Rights Action Center, "Round-Up of June 30th Welfare Demonstrations," June 28,

1966; and Poverty/Rights Action Center, "Summary Report on National Welfare Rights Meeting Held in Chicago, Illinois on August 6th and 7th, 1966," August 11, 1966, Box 54, Folder 7, Piven Papers. Also see West, *The National Welfare Rights Movement*; Cloward and Piven, *The Politics of Turmoil*, 127–40; Kotz and Kotz, *A Passion for Equality*, 189–93.

65. West, *The National Welfare Rights Movement*, 56.

66. "The Tangle of Pathology" is the title of the fourth chapter in the so-called "Moynihan Report," US Department of Labor, Office of Policy Planning and Research, *The Negro Family: The Case for National Action* (Washington: Government Printing Office, 1965). Senator Russell B. Long's "brood mares" slur was directed at welfare rights activists when he refused to let them testify before the Senate Finance Committee that he chaired. See Morton Mintz, " 'Wait-In' Group Described as 'Brood Mares,' " *Washington Post*, September 22, 1967, A2.

67. "Rep. Ford Cites Riots, Urges Ouster of LBJ," *Washington Post*, August 24, 1966; John Herbers, "G.O.P. Will Press Racial Disorders as Election Issue," *New York Times*, October 4, 1966.

68. *Administrative History of the Office of Economic Opportunity*, 1:579–90, Lyndon B. Johnson Library, Austin, TX (hereafter LBJ Library); US Senate Committee on Government Operations, Permanent Subcommittee on Investigations, *Hearings: Riots, Civil and Criminal Disorders, 90th Congress, 1st Session* (Washington: U.S. Government Printing Office, 1968), part 8.

69. US House Committee on Education and Labor, *Economic Opportunity Act Amendments of 1967: Hearings, 90th Congress, 1st, on H.R. 8311* (Washington: Government Printing Office, 1967), part 4, 3577.

70. Quoted in "Behind the Riots," *Wall Street Journal*, July 26, 1967, 1.

71. Quoted in Arlen J. Large, "Riot Repercussions," *Wall Street Journal*, July 27, 1967, 1. Also see Jill Quadagno, *The Color of Welfare: How Racism Undermined the War on Poverty* (New York: Oxford University Press, 1994), 48–52; David Zarefsky, *President Johnson's War on Poverty: Rhetoric and History* (Tuscaloosa: University of Alabama Press, 1986), 113–15; John Herbers, "Newark Jailer Says Poverty Aides Stirred Riots," *New York Times*, August 8, 1967.

72. Quoted in Kenneth O'Reilly, "The FBI and the Politics of the Riots, 1964–1968," *Journal of American History* 75.1 (1988), 110.

73. US Senate Committee on Government Operations, Permanent Subcommittee on Investigations, *Hearings: Riots, Civil and Criminal Disorders, 90th Congress, 1st Session* (Washington: U.S. Government Printing Office, 1967), parts 1–4; US Senate, Committee on the Judiciary, *Antiriot Bill—1967: Hearings on H.R. 421, 90th Congress, 1st Session* (Washington: Government Printing Office, 1967), Part 1, 135–224.

74. "Semper Paratus," *Newsweek*, August 28, 1967; "Strange Case of the Telescopic Sights," *Houston Tribune*, August 17, 1967; "Panel Bars Rifle Scope Testimony," *Houston Chronicle*, December 4, 1967; *Administrative History of the Office of Economic Opportunity*, Box 1, 1:590–592, LBJ Library.

75. "OEO and the Riots: A Summary," n.d., 5, *Administrative History of the Office of Economic Opportunity*, Box 2, Vol. II, Documentary Supplement, Chapter III–IV, LBJ Library.

76. William Raspberry, "Officials Must Reach Militants, Give Them Roles in Poverty War," *Washington Post*, September 1, 1967.

77. Marjorie Hunter, "Revisions in Poverty Law Sought to Abate Criticism," *New York Times*, April 10, 1967.

78. Edith Green, one of the congressional sponsors of the 1961 Juvenile Delinquency and Youth Offenses Control Act, had quickly become an outspoken critic of the direction of programs initiated under the legislation. Her antipathy was easily extended to CAP, although some scholars argue that Shriver covertly supported her 1967 amendment as the only politically feasible way of salvaging the OEO in the face of congressional hostility. See Allen J. Matusow, *The Unraveling of America: A History of Liberalism in the 1960s* (New York: Harper and Row, 1984), 113–14, 269.

79. Quoted in Sargent Shriver, "Bi-Weekly Report to the President," July 27, 1967, 1, Confidential File, Agency Reports, Office of Economic Opportunity, 1967–; LBJ Library.

80. Donald M. Baker, Memorandum, "Power to suspend and terminate personnel in OEO-assisted programs," August 19, 1967, 2, OEO Community Action Programs; Aides Files, James Gaither, Box 29, LBJ Library.

81. Statement of Theodore M. Berry before the National Advisory Commission on Civil Disorders, October 6, 1967, 1, 9, 10, 11, Folder: "Riots [1 of 2]," OEO Office of Operations, Policy Development and Review Division, Program Subject Files 1967–72, Box 25; National Archives and Records Administration, College Park, MD.

82. "Statement of Martin Luther King, Jr., . . . before the National Advisory Commission on Civil Disorders on October 23, 1967," 1, Speeches, Sermons, etc. August 2, 1967–December 24, 1967, Martin Luther King, Jr. Papers, the Martin Luther King, Jr. Center Library and Archives, Atlanta, GA (hereafter MLK Papers). Also see Martin Luther King Jr., "The Crisis in America's Cities: An Analysis of Social Disorder and a Plan of Action Against Poverty, Discrimination and Racism in Urban America," August 15, 1967, Box 178, Folder 37, Southern Christian Leadership Conference Papers, the Martin Luther King, Jr. Center Library and Archives, Atlanta, GA (hereafter SCLC Papers).

83. Martin Luther King, Jr., Press conference, Washington, D.C., October 23, 1967, 1, Speeches, Sermons, etc. August 2, 1967–December 24, 1967, MLK Papers.

84. Quoted in David J. Garrow, *Bearing the Cross: Martin Luther King, Jr., and the Southern Leadership Conference* (New York: Vintage, 1986), 581–82.

85. For an excellent account of King's life in general that explicitly situates his work in the context of global struggles, see Thomas F. Jackson, *From Civil Rights to Human Rights: Martin Luther King, Jr., and the Struggle for Economic Justice* (Philadelphia: University of Pennsylvania Press, 2007).

86. Ben A. Franklin, "Dr. King to Start March on the Capital April 22—Links Antipoverty Protest to Vietnam Peace Drive," *New York Times*, March 5, 1968.

87. King, "The Crisis in America's Cities," n.p. King is quoting here from his December 15, 1966 testimony to the US Senate Subcommittee on Executive Reorganization during a series of hearings on the urban crisis.

88. Charles V. Pratt, "Poor Americans Wake Up," SCLC *News: Trenton N.J.*, June 1968.

89. Southern Christian Leadership Conference, "Statement of Purpose: Washington, D.C. Poor People's Campaign," January 1968, 2, Box 179, Folder 18, SCLC Papers.

90. "National Statement of Purpose," included in a pamphlet for a Poor People's Campaign "Southern Leg" mass meeting in Norfolk, Virginia, May 17, 1968, n.p., Box 178, Folder 19, SCLC Papers.

91. For instance, speaking at a rally for the Poor People's Campaign, George Wiley warned: "The Southern Christian Leadership Conference and the Poor People's Campaign offers to the country more than it does to poor people, for it is white America, the middle-class, the affluent and the rich to which the Campaign offers the last peaceful alternative to the chaos which is about to beset us in our cities and indeed in rural areas as well" ("Speech by Dr. George A. Wiley, Executive Director, National Welfare Rights Organization, Poor People's Campaign Rally," April 29, 1968, n.p., 1968 Poor People's Campaign, Box 33, Folder 1, George Wiley Papers, State Historical Society of Wisconsin, Madison [hereafter Wiley Papers]).

92. "National Statement of Purpose," n.p.

93. Quoted in Walter Rugaber, "Dr. King Planning to Disrupt Capital in Drive for Jobs," *New York Times*, December 5, 1967, 1.

94. Garrow, *Bearing the Cross*, 578–602.

95. Quoted in Kotz and Kotz, *A Passion for Equality*, 252.

96. "Participants of Minority Group Conference," March 14, 1968, Box 179, Folder 11, SCLC Papers.

97. T. Jackson, *From Civil Rights to Human Rights*, 329–58; Ernesto B. Vigil, *The Crusade for Justice: Chicano Militancy and the Government's War on Dissent* (Madison: University of Wisconsin Press, 1999), 54–63; Robert T. Chase, "Class Resurrection: The Poor People's Campaign of 1968 and Resurrection City," *Essays in History* 40 (1998).

98. Quoted in Kornbluh, *The Battle for Welfare Rights*, 102.

99. NWRO, Press Release, April 23, 1968, n.p., 1968 Poor People's Campaign, Box 33, Folder 1, Wiley Papers.

100. NWRO, "Proposals for a Living Memorial," n.p., n.d., Southern Christian Leadership Conference, 1968–1972, Box 33, Folder 14, Wiley Papers.

101. "Statements of Demands for Rights of the Poor, Presented to Agencies of the U.S. Government by the Poor People's Campaign and Its Committee of 100,

April 29–30, May 1, 1968," 2, Declaration Committee, April–May 1968, Box 177, Folder 24, SCLC Papers.

102. Mel Thom, "The Poor People's Campaign Speaks to: [the] Department of the Interior," 46, 48, May 1, 1968, Box 177, Folder 28, SCLC Papers.

103. "Statements of Demands for Rights of the Poor," 12.

104. Quoted in Ben A. Franklin, "Abernathy Declares 'Poor Power' Will Change Policies and Priorities of U.S.," *New York Times*, May 2, 1968.

105. "Statements of Demands for Rights of the Poor," 15–17.

106. "Poor People's Campaign Caravan Chronicle, April-May 1968," Box 177, Folder 8, SCLC Papers.

107. "March Leaders Are Hip To Gang Control," *Chicago Daily Defender*, May 23, 1968.

108. Gerald D. McKnight, *The Last Crusade: Martin Luther King, Jr., the FBI, and the Poor People's Campaign* (Boulder, CO: Westview Press, 1998), 93–106.

109. "Poor People's Campaign Caravan Chronicle, April-May 1968," 10.

110. Bertrand M. Harding, Memorandum for the President, May 17, 1968, 2, Office of Economic Opportunity 1967–, Confidential File, Agency Reports, OEO, Box 129, LBJ Library.

111. Bernadette Carey, "U.S. to Deny Park Use for March," *Washington Post*, April 18, 1968; Ben A. Franklin, "Bills Speeded to Check Poor People's Campaign," *New York Times*, May 3, 1968; Ben A. Franklin, "Southerners Seek Laws to Bar 'Mob Rule' in Campaign of Poor," *New York Times*, May 7, 1968.

112. Quoted in William C. Selover, "Congress Blows Hot and Cold over Washington March," *Christian Science Monitor*, May 15, 1968, 7.

113. Quoted in Charles Fager, *Uncertain Resurrection: The Poor People's Washington Campaign* (Grand Rapids, MI: William B. Eerdmans, 1969), 36.

114. Fager, *Uncertain Resurrection*; Walter E. Afield and Audrey B. Gibson, *Children of Resurrection City* (Washington: Association for Childhood Education International, 1970).

115. Walter E. Fauntroy, Memo to Washington Ad Hoc Committee, May 3, 1968, 1968 Poor People's Campaign, Box 33, Folder 1, Wiley Papers.

116. Quoted in William C. Selover, "The Poor Settle on Washington," *Christian Science Monitor*, May 14, 1968, 3.

117. "NWRO Demands for the Poor People's Campaign," n.d.; George A. Wiley, memorandum to All NWRO Affiliated Groups, "Plans for Mothers Day," May 3, 1968; George A. Wiley, memorandum to the National Steering Committee of the Poor People's Campaign, June 10, 1968; Records of the National Welfare Rights Organization, Box 2101, Manuscript Division, Moorland-Spingarn Research Center, Howard University, Washington, D.C.

118. Quoted in Martin Weil, "West's Poor: A Proud People," *Washington Post*, May 28, 1968, B8; "Demands of the Indo-Hispano to the Federal Government as read by Mr. Rafael Duran to Mr. Dean Rusk at the Poor People's Campaign Hearing," unpaginated, n.d., Box 179, Folder 9, SCLC Papers.

119. Quoted in Bernadette Carey, "What Brings the Poor People to the Capital?," *Washington Post*, May 24, 1968, A14.

120. A fascinating document in this respect is Albert E. Gollin, *The Demography of Protest: A Statistical Profile of Participants in the Poor People Campaign* (Washington: Bureau of Social Science Research, 1968).

121. Nationwide Welfare Rights Organization, "Proposed Demands for the Poor People's Campaign," n.d., 1968 Poor People's Campaign, Box 33, Folder 1, Wiley Papers.

122. "Poor People's Campaign Answer to the Response of the Department of Health, Education, and Welfare," June 12, 1968, 5, Box 177, Folder 27, SCLC Papers.

123. "Answers of the Poor People's Campaign to Response of the Department of State," June 14, 1968, 2, Box 177, Folder 31, Declaration Committee, Department of State, June 1968, SCLC Papers.

124. McKnight's *The Last Crusade* provides an extensive account of the government and military mobilization against the campaign.

125. Ben A. Franklin, "Law Enforcement Men to Outnumber Protestors at March of Poor in Capital," *New York Times*, March 4, 1968. Notably, such counterinsurgency measures preceded the violence that accompanied King's march in Memphis in support of the city's striking black sanitation workers on March 28, which the SCLC worried would prompt doubts about the nonviolent character of the campaign.

126. "The Responsibility of Dissent," *New York Times*, December 6, 1967.

127. US Senate, Committee on Government Operations, Permanent Subcommittee on Investigations, *Conference on Problems Involved in the Poor People's March on Washington, D.C.* (Washington: Government Printing Office, 1968).

128. Quoted in McKnight, *The Last Crusade*, 92.

129. Quoted in Fager, *Uncertain Resurrection*, 32.

130. The FBI followed up on McClellan's charges, but his accusations turned out to be so lacking in evidence that Hoover called off further investigation and the bureau informed McClellan that it would be best for him not to publicly pursue this line of indictment (McKnight, *The Last Crusade*, 87–88).

131. Poor People's Campaign Information Center, untitled report, June 23, 1968, 4, Box 178, Folder 35, SCLC Papers.

132. Nadasen documents receptivity to the campaign's demands on the part of the Department of Health, Education, and Welfare, but it remains difficult to gauge the extent to which the agency's support for a more substantive role for the poor in welfare policy translated into agency policy and practice (*Welfare Warriors*, 72–74).

133. On the 1932 Bonus March, see Franklin Folsom, *Impatient Armies of the Poor: The Story of Collective Action of the Unemployed, 1808–1942* (Niwot: University Press of Colorado, 1991).

134. Joy James, *Resisting State Violence: Radicalism, Gender, and Race in U.S. Culture* (Minneapolis: University of Minnesota Press, 1996).

135. National Advisory Commission on Civil Disorders, *Report of the National Advisory Commission on Civil Disorders* (New York: E. P. Dutton, 1968), 299, 301.

136. President's Commission on Law Enforcement and the Administration of Justice, *National Survey of Police and Community Relations* (Washington: Government Printing Office, 1967).

137. On Project PACE, see Terry Eisenberg, Robert H. Fosen, and Albert S. Glickman, *Police-Community Action: A Program for Change in Police-Community Behavior Patterns* (New York: Praeger, 1973).

138. Ben W. Gilbert, *Ten Blocks from the White House: Anatomy of the Washington Riots of 1968* (New York: Praeger, 1968).

139. Reverend Ralph D. Abernathy, letter to Bertrand Harding, OEO acting director, June 17, 1968, 1, Box 179, Folder 17, SCLC Papers.

140. Rita Mae Kelly, *On Improving Police-Community Relations: Findings from the Conduct and Evaluation of an OEO-Funded Experiment in Washington, D.C.* (Kensington, MD: American Institutes for Research, 1972); Carol Honsa, "UPO Reluctantly Agrees to Pilot Police Project," *Washington Post*, September 11, 1968.

141. Quoted in Jonathan I. Z. Agronsky, *Marion Barry: The Politics of Race* (Latham, NY: British American, 1991), 120.

142. For a discussion of the Washington home rule issue framed as a question of internal colonialism, see Sam Smith, *Captive Capital: Colonial Life in Modern Washington* (Bloomington: Indiana University Press, 1974).

143. Gabriel A. Almond and Sidney Verba, *The Civic Culture: Political Attitudes and Democracy in Five Nations* (Princeton: Princeton University Press, 1963).

144. In addition to Fager, *Uncertain Resurrection*, and Afield and Gibson, *Children of Resurrection City*, see Charlayne Hunter, "On the Case in Resurrection City," in *The Transformation of Activism*, ed. August Meier (Chicago: Aldine, 1970).

145. A transcription of King's speech on January 11, 1968, is available on Ohio Northern University's website (http://www.onu.edu/node/28509/).

146. In retrospect, many critics have suggested that Piven and Cloward's strategy was an outright failure, and largely responsible for precipitating the backlash against welfare. However, not only was this backlash to an extent parallel to their endeavors, but this criticism obscures the successes of the crisis strategy. The journalists Nick and Mary Lynn Kotz note: "Late in 1968, Governor Nelson Rockefeller of New York called for a federalization of welfare that would provide uniform benefits across the country. Rockefeller was responding to the economic predicament in which New York found itself. The New York City welfare rolls had doubled to more than a million people between 1966 and 1968. New York City and New York State could no longer afford their share of the costs. To some extent, the Cloward-Piven theory was beginning to work" (*A Passion for Equality*, 260). Cloward and Piven discuss the waning of the movement subsequently precipitated by changing political circumstances in *Poor People's Movements*, 335–59.

4. The Surplus of Inclusion

1. "Miners Protest at Whitehouse," *New York Times*, January 8, 1964; Lyndon B. Johnson, "Annual Message to the Congress on the State of the Union," in *Public Papers of the Presidents of the United States: Lyndon B. Johnson, 1963–1964* (Washington: Government Printing Office, 1965), 1:114; "Kentucky's Miners See Johnson Aide," *New York Times*, January 10, 1964; "Appointment Schedule of Miners Delegation," n.d., Everette Tharp Collection, Box 1, Folder 3, Special Collections and Digital Programs, University of Kentucky Libraries, Lexington, KY (hereafter cited as the Tharp Collection).

2. Everette Tharp, "The Appalachian Committee for Full Employment: Background and Purpose," *Appalachian South* 1 (Summer 1965): 45.

3. [Appalachian Committee for Full Employment Mission Statement], *Voice for Jobs and Justice*, November 20, 1964, 1. Also see Kate Black, "The Roving Picket Movement and the Appalachian Committee for Full Employment, 1959–1965: A Narrative," *Journal of the Appalachian Studies Association* 2 (1990); Appalachian Committee for Full Employment [Charter], January 1964, Box 1, Folder 3, Tharp Collection.

4. Tharp, "The Appalachian Committee for Full Employment," 46.

5. " 'Washington' Meets with ACFE," *Voice for Jobs and Justice*, December 11, 1964, 1.

6. See especially Judith Russell, *Economics, Bureaucracy, and Race: How Keynesians Misguided the War on Poverty* (New York: Columbia University Press, 2004). Even job training programs such as the Neighborhood Youth Corps were more concerned with inculcating values than with facilitating employment. See, for example, Dennis Ekberg and Claude Ury, "Education for What? A Report on an MDTA Program," *Journal of Negro Education* 37.1 (1968); Gerald D. Robin, "Anti-Poverty Programs and Delinquency," *Journal of Criminal Law, Criminology, and Police Science* 60.3 (1969).

7. Quoted in James T. Patterson, *America's Struggle against Poverty in the Twentieth Century* (Cambridge: Harvard University Press, 2000), 129–30.

8. Despite the multiracial composition of Appalachia, the region served to personify white poverty. Yarmolinsky's statement is all the more ironic given that historically the US semiwelfare state has served supposedly deserving white people while systematically excluding people of color. Yarmolinsky similarly recalled: "We were busy telling people it wasn't just racial because we thought it'd be easier to sell that way, and we thought it was less racial than it turned out to be" (quoted in Jill Quadagno, *The Color of Welfare: How Racism Undermined the War on Poverty* [New York: Oxford University Press, 1994], 31). Also see Susan Youngblood Ashmore, *Carry It On: The War on Poverty and the Civil Rights Movement in Alabama, 1964–1972* (Athens: University of Georgia Press, 2008), 28.

9. Marjorie Hunter, "President Hailed on 5-State Tour of Poverty Areas," *New York Times*, April 25, 1964. Johnson's attention to Appalachia followed Ken-

nedy's decisive victory in West Virginia during the 1960 presidential primary campaign, as well as Harry Caudill's popular 1962 *Night Comes to the Cumberlands: A Biography of a Depressed Area*, the journalist Homer Bigart's fall 1963 series on the region in the *New York Times*, and the January 1964 special issue of *Life* magazine on Appalachian poverty.

10. David E. Whisnant, *Modernizing the Mountaineer: People, Power, and Planning in Appalachia*, rev. ed. (Knoxville: University of Tennessee Press, 1994), 94–98.

11. Gregory S. Wilson, *Communities Left Behind: The Area Redevelopment Administration, 1945–1960* (Knoxville: University of Tennessee Press, 2009).

12. *Economic Opportunity Act of 1964, As Amended* (Washington: Government Printing Office, 1970), 28.

13. See, for instance, Nelson W. Polsby, *Community Power and Political Theory* (New Haven: Yale University Press, 1963); Robert A. Dahl, *Pluralist Democracy in the United States: Conflict and Consent* (Chicago: Rand McNally, 1967). Also see Theodore J. Lowi's critique, *The End of Liberalism: The Second Republic of the United States*, 2nd ed. (New York: W. W. Norton, 1979).

14. Michel Foucault, *The Birth of Biopolitics: Lectures at the Collège de France, 1978–1979*, ed. Michel Senellart, trans. Graham Burchell (New York: Palgrave Macmillan, 2008), 44–45. The most influential mid-twentieth-century account of government as a political logic of interests is David B. Truman, *The Governmental Process: Political Interests and Public Opinion* (New York: Knopf, 1951).

15. Patchen Markell theorizes recognition in ways especially significant for my study of liberal governance and its relation to the state. Markell contends that contemporary multiculturalism "creates incentives for people to frame claims about justice *as* claims for recognition on behalf of identifiable groups. That mode of address, after all, furthers the state's project of rendering the social world 'legible' and governable: to appeal to the state *for* recognition of one's own identity—to present oneself as knowable—is already to offer the state the reciprocal recognition of its sovereignty that it demands" (*Bound by Recognition* [Princeton: Princeton University Press, 2003], 31). In his account of the politics of recognition, Markell writes: "Rather than treating the state as an already-sovereign institution that can transcend struggles for recognition, I suggest that the modern state is instead one of the central objects of identification onto which persons displace, and through which they pursue, the desire for independence and masterful agency" (125). Thus, "while states may be disproportionately powerful actors in many respects, they can no more achieve the sovereignty they seek, and that others seek through them, than can individuals. (This impossibility is already manifest in the fact that states depend upon their subjects, as well as other states, to recognize their sovereignty—a dependence that ironically undercuts the very condition of *in*dependence it is supposed to sustain)" (31).

16. Quoted in Peter Kihss, "Overhauling of Poverty Groups Asked," *New York Times*, February 12, 1968, 78.

17. Chad Montrie, *To Save the Land and People: A History of Opposition to Surface Coal Mining in Appalachia* (Chapel Hill: University of North Carolina Press, 2003), 61–126.

18. Black, "Roving Picket Movement and the Appalachian Committee for Full Employment"; Richard Greenberg, "Problems Relating to Unemployment in the Vicinity of Hazard, Kentucky," September 1964, Student Nonviolent Coordinating Committee Papers, 1959–1972, Reel 68, File 382, Page 0824, the Martin Luther King, Jr. Center Library and Archives, Atlanta, GA.

19. "The Facts of Life," *Time*, December 28, 1962.

20. The phrase is in reference to Jack E. Weller, *Yesterday's People: Life in Contemporary Appalachia* (Lexington: University of Kentucky Press, 1965).

21. Everette Tharp, "The History, Goals and Objectives of the Appalachian Committee for Full Employment," January 1965, Box 1, Folder 3, Tharp Collection; "Hazard, KY: Committee for Miners," *Studies on the Left* 5.3 (1965); Hamish Sinclair, "Hazard, KY: Document of the Struggle," *Radical America* 2.1 (January–February, 1968).

22. Peter B. Levy, *The New Left and Labor in the 1960s* (Urbana: University of Illinois Press, 1994), 35; Sinclair, "Hazard, KY," 1.

23. On the War on Poverty in Appalachia, see John M. Glen, "The War on Poverty in Appalachia—A Preliminary Report," *Register of the Kentucky Historical Society* 87 (Winter 1989); John M. Glen, "The War on Poverty in Appalachia: Oral History from the 'Top Down' and the 'Bottom Up,'" *Oral History Review* 22.1 (1995); Whisnant, *Modernizing the Mountaineer*, 92–125; Ronald Eller, *Uneven Ground: Appalachia since 1945* (Lexington: University Press of Kentucky, 2008), 53–176; Thomas Kiffmeyer, *Reformers to Radicals: The Appalachian Volunteers and the War on Poverty* (Lexington: University Press of Kentucky, 2008). An excellent firsthand account is Huey Perry, *"They'll Cut Off Your Project": A Mingo County Chronicle* (New York: Praeger, 1972).

24. Stanley Aronowitz et al., *Working Papers for Nyack Conference on Unemployment and Social Change* (New York: Students for a Democratic Society, 1963), 2.

25. Jennifer Frost, *"An Interracial Movement for the Poor": Community Organizing and the New Left in the 1960s* (New York: New York University Press, 2001); Richard Rothstein, "ERAP: Evolution of the Organizers," *Radical America* 2.2 (1968).

26. James O'Connor, "Towards a Theory of Community Unions," *Studies on the Left* 4.2 (1964), 146, 147. Also see James O'Connor, "Towards a Theory of Community Unions II," *Studies on the Left* 4.3 (1964). Vanessa Tait points out that "his theory would have supported CORE's activities, as well, but unlike the black-initiated CORE union projects, the mostly white-run ERAP enjoyed wide support from the trade unions, churches, and foundations" (*Poor Workers' Unions: Rebuilding Labor from Below* [Cambridge, MA: South End Press, 2005], 34).

27. Todd Gitlin, "The Radical Potential of the Poor," in *The New Left: A Documentary History*, ed. Massimo Teodori (New York: Bobbs-Merrill, 1969), 137.

28. Rennie Davis, "The War on Poverty: Notes on Insurgent Response," in *The New Student Left: An Anthology*, ed. Mitchell Cohen and Dennis Hale (Boston: Beacon, 1966), 158.

29. Carl Wittman and Thomas Hayden, "An Interracial Movement of the Poor?," in *The New Student Left: An Anthology*, ed. Mitchell Cohen and Dennis Hale (Boston: Beacon, 1966), 215.

30. Norm Fruchter and Robert Kramer, "An Approach to Community Organizing," *Studies on the Left* 6.2 (1966), 37.

31. Clayborne Carson, *In Struggle: SNCC and the Black Awakening of the 1960s*, rev. ed. (Cambridge: Harvard University Press, 1995), 100–103; Wesley C. Hogan, *Many Minds, One Heart: SNCC's Dream for a New America* (Chapel Hill: University of North Carolina Press, 2007), 133–40.

32. Rothstein, "ERAP: Evolution of the Organizers," 9.

33. Carl Wittman, "Students and Economic Action," in *The New Student Left: An Anthology*, ed. Mitchell Cohen and Dennis Hale (Boston: Beacon, 1966), 172.

34. Sinclair, "Hazard, KY," 4.

35. "Statement of the Appalachian Committee for Full Employment, Hazard, KY, to the Student-Miners Conference on Poverty and Unemployment," March 1964, 1, Box 1, Folder 3, Tharp Collection.

36. Levy, *The New Left and Labor in the 1960s*, 35–36; Rothstein, "ERAP: Evolution of the Organizers."

37. Sinclair, "Hazard, KY," 8–20; Hamish Sinclair, "Appalachian Project: Hazard Field Report," August 14, 1964, Box 1, Folder 3, Tharp Collection.

38. ACFE, "Application for Community Organizing Program in the four counties of the Upper Kentucky River Area Development Council," n.d. (1964), Box 1, Folder 3, Tharp Collection; " 'Washington' Meets with ACFE," 1–2.

39. Tom Gish, "This Is the War That Is," Whitesburg (KY) *Mountain Eagle*, November 26, 1964, reprinted in *Voice for Jobs and Justice*, December 11, 1964, 5–8.

40. "Hazard, KY: Committee for Miners," 105.

41. Sinclair, "Hazard, KY," 8.

42. Ibid., 12.

43. Quoted in Kiffmeyer, *Reformers to Radicals*, 86.

44. Appalachian Volunteers, "Quarterly Report: October 1967," Appalachian Volunteers Records, Box 8, Folder 9, Special Collections and Archives, Hutchins Library, Berea College, Berea, KY (hereafter AV Records).

45. See, for instance, Kiffmeyer, *Reformers to Radicals*, 113; Robert Coles, "An Evaluation of the Appalachian Volunteers," n.d. (fall 1966), Box 12, Folder 8, AV Records.

46. Albert Whitehouse, "Statement on Appalachian Volunteers Situation in Kentucky," September 11, 1967, 1, 4, 6, Box 13, Folder 4, AV Records.

47. Joseph Mulloy interview, November 10, 1990, 9, 5, 12, APP288, War on Poverty in Appalachia Oral History Project, Louie B. Nunn Center for Oral History, University of Kentucky Libraries, Lexington, KY (hereafter WOP OHP).

48. Sue Ella Easterling Kobak interview, January 2, 1991, 25, APP299, WOP OHP.

49. Roslea Johnson interview, June 24, 1991, 23, 26 APP314, WOP OHP.

50. Quoted in Kiffmeyer, *Reformers to Radicals*, 189.

51. "A Special Report to Governor Edward T. Breathitt on the Program of the Appalachian Volunteers in Eastern Kentucky," October 2, 1967, Box 8, Folder 9, AV Records; Montrie, *To Save the Land and People*, 91–94; Mulloy interview, 12–14.

52. Kiffmeyer, *Reformers to Radicals*, 195–200.

53. Phillip J. Obermiller, "The Question of Appalachian Ethnicity," in *The Invisible Minority: Urban Appalachians*, ed. William W. Philliber and Clyde B. McCoy (Lexington: University Press of Kentucky, 1981); Roger Guy, *From Diversity to Unity: Southern and Appalachian Migrants in Uptown Chicago, 1950–1970* (Lanham, MD: Lexington, 2007).

54. Barbara Ellen Smith, "De-Gradations of Whiteness: Appalachia and the Complexities of Race," *Journal of Appalachian Studies* 10.1–2 (2004). Also see John Hartigan Jr., *Odd Tribes: Toward a Cultural Analysis of White People* (Durham: Duke University Press, 2005).

55. Helen M. Lewis, Linda Johnson, and Don Askins, eds., *Colonialism in Modern America: The Appalachian Case* (Boone, NC: Appalachian Consortium, 1978).

56. C. Vann Woodward, *Origins of the New South, 1877–1913* (Baton Rouge: Louisiana State University Press, 1951).

57. Quoted in Henry Raymont, "Mayor Will Seek More Advice Here on Puerto Ricans," *New York Times*, January 23, 1967, 1, 38. Also see Paul Hofmann, "Mayor Criticized by Puerto Ricans," *New York Times*, February 5, 1966.

58. James Jennings, *Puerto Rican Politics in New York City* (Washington: University Press of America, 1977); Sherrie Baver, "Puerto Rican Politics in New York City: The Post-World War II Period," in *Puerto Rican Politics in Urban America*, ed. James Jennings and Monte Rivera (Westport, CT: Greenwood, 1984).

59. Peter Kihss, "Lindsay Promises Aid for Programs of Puerto Ricans," *New York Times*, April 16, 1967.

60. Manuel Díaz, in "Part IV: Strategy for Community Development: Challenge to the Puerto Rican Community," in *Puerto Ricans Confront Problems of the Complex Urban Society: A Design for Change* (New York: High School of Art and Design, 1967), 167, 172, 173.

61. On the early history of Puerto Ricans in New York City, see Virginia Sánchez Korrol, *From Colonia to Community: The History of Puerto Ricans in New York City, 1917–1948* (Westport, CT: Greenwood, 1983); Gabriel Haslip-Viera, Angelo Falcón, and Félix V. Matos-Rodríguez, ed., *Boricuas in Gotham: Puerto Ricans in the Making of New York City* (Princeton, NJ: Markus Wiener, 2004); Carmen Teresa Whalen and Víctor Vázquez-Hernández, eds., *The Puerto Rican Diaspora: Historical Perspectives* (Philadelphia: Temple University Press, 2005).

62. On Puerto Rican migration during this period, see History Task Force, Centro

de Estudios Puertorriqueños, *Labor Migration under Capitalism: The Puerto Rican Experience* (New York: Monthly Review, 1979); Vilma Ortiz, "Changes in the Characteristics of Puerto Rican Migrants from 1955 to 1980," *International Migration Review* 20.3 (1986); Laura Briggs, *Reproducing Empire: Race, Sex, Science, and U.S. Imperialism in Puerto Rico* (Berkeley: University of California Press, 2002), 162–92; Jorge Duany, *The Puerto Rican Nation on the Move: Identities on the Island and in the United States* (Chapel Hill: University of North Carolina Press, 2002), 166–235.

63. History Task Force, *Labor Migration under Capitalism*, 127.

64. Antonia Pantoja, "Puerto Ricans in New York: A Historical and Community Development Perspective," *Centro Journal* 2.5 (1989); Carlos Rodriguez-Fraticelli and Amilcar Tirado, "Notes towards a History of Puerto Rican Community Organizations in New York City," *Centro Journal* 2.6 (1989); Michael Lapp, "Managing Migration: The Migration Division of Puerto Rico and Puerto Ricans in New York City, 1948–1968" (PhD diss., Johns Hopkins University, 1990).

65. Josephine Nieves, audiotaped interview, May 24, 1988, side A, Centro de Estudios Puertorriqueños, Hunter College, City University of New York, NY.

66. Quoted in Stephen Price, "The Effect of Federal Anti-Poverty Programs and Policies on the Hasidic and Puerto Rican Communities of Williamsburg" (PhD diss., Brandeis University, 1979), 164.

67. On the Puerto Rican Community Development Project and its context, see John W. Gotsch, "Puerto Rican Leadership in New York" (master's thesis, New York University, 1966); Judith F. Herbstein, "Rituals and Politics of the Puerto Rican 'Community' in New York City" (PhD diss., City University of New York, 1978); Rosa Estades, *Patterns of Political Participation of Puerto Ricans in New York City* (San Juan, PR: Editorial Universitaria, Universidad de Puerto Rico, 1978); Joseph P. Fitzpatrick, *Puerto Rican Americans: The Meaning of Migration to the Mainland*, 2nd ed. (Englewood Cliffs, NJ: Prentice-Hall, 1987); Antonia Pantoja, *Memoir of a Visionary* (Houston: Arte Público, 2002), 109–19.

68. Puerto Rican Forum, *The Puerto Rican Community Development Project: A Proposal for a Self-Help Project to Develop the Community by Strengthening the Family, Opening Opportunities for Youth, and Making Full Use of Education* (1964; New York: Arno, 1975), 76–77, 84–85.

69. Gotsch, "Puerto Rican Leadership in New York," 14.

70. Quoted in Edward C. Burks, "Split Emphasized by Puerto Ricans," *New York Times*, March 16, 1965.

71. Alfredo Lopez, *The Puerto Rican Papers: Notes on the Re-Emergence of a Nation* (New York: Bobbs-Merrill, 1973), 275.

72. Human Resources Administration, "Evaluation Summary of Findings of the Community Development Agency, Human Resources Administration, City of New York, of the Puerto Rican Community Development Project," May 12,

1967, unpaginated, Frank Torres Papers, Box 21, Folder 6, Centro de Estudios Puertorriqueños, Hunter College, City University of New York, NY (hereafter Torres Papers).

73. See, for instance, Stephen M. David, "Welfare: The Community-Action Program Controversy," in *Race and Politics in New York City*, ed. Jewel Bellush and Stephen M. David (New York: Praeger, 1971); Bertram M. Beck, "Organizing Community Action," *Proceedings of the Academy of Political Science* 29.4 (1969); Jack Krauskopf, "New York City's Antipoverty Program," *City Almanac* 7.4 (1972). For historical context, also see Martha Biondi, *To Stand and Fight: The Struggle for Civil Rights in Postwar New York City* (Cambridge: Harvard University Press, 2003).

74. Manuel Díaz Jr., "Outline of the Puerto Rican Community Development Project," n.d., 1, Box 21, Folder 3, Torres Papers. For more on the Block Organization Program, see also Puerto Rican Community Development Project, "Block Approach Program . . . a Guide for Community Workers," November 17, 1966, Box 21, Folder 3, Torres Papers; Human Resources Administration, "Summary of Findings: Puerto Rican Community Development Project," n.d. (May 12, 1967), Box 21, Folder 3, Torres Papers; Puerto Rican Community Development Project, "Block Organization Program: Achievement Report, 1966–1967," Box 21, Folder 4, Torres Papers; Program Development Department, PRCDP, "Puerto Rican Community Development Project Annual Report, 1969," n.d., Series 10, Subseries 1, Box 103, Puerto Rican Community Development Project, 1969–1970, Senator Jacob K. Javits Collection, Frank Melville Jr. Memorial Library, Stony Brook University, Stony Brook, NY.

75. Although the overall implication of the statistics provided on program operations is unclear, they do give a general sense of the program's volume and growth over its first several years. During the first year, while staff positions were still being filled and community workers recruited, a total of 28,914 individuals, the vast majority of whom were Puerto Rican, "sought and received aid" from the program. In 1968, that number increased to 42,535; it was 65,119 in 1969. This would mean that in 1969, each community worker was in contact with approximately twenty-seven new individuals, groups, or families every weekday. None of the reports gives any sense of what extent of interaction constituted a "contact," other than to note that only "new" contacts were counted. They were, however, categorized by theme. The top three categories for individual contacts were housing, welfare, and employment. Education, housing, and consumer action topped the list for group meetings that the program organized. See Puerto Rican Community Development Project, "Block Organization Program: Achievement Report, 1966–1967," 1; Program Development Department, "Puerto Rican Community Development Project Annual Report, 1969," 5.

76. Manuel Díaz, for instance, cites the definition of "community development" in the UN Bureau of Social Affairs' *Social Progress through Community Development*

in a paper he presented during the initial workshops organized to design the PRCDP ("Planning and the Puerto Rican Community Development Project," presented at the PRCDP Institute, Hotel Biltmore, New York City, August 8, 1964 [Centro Library Vertical Files, Centro de Estudios Puertorriqueños, Hunter College, City University of New York, NY]). The UN-defined role of community development was also presented as the framework for discussions on community development at the 1967 conference Puerto Ricans Confront Problems of the Complex Urban Society (see Julio Sabater, "Discussion Group Report," in *Puerto Ricans Confront Problems of the Complex Urban Society*, 181).

77. PRCDP, "Block Approach Program . . . a Guide for Community Workers," 1–2.

78. Human Resources Administration, "Evaluation Summary of Findings of the Community Development Agency, Human Resources Administration, City of New York, of the Puerto Rican Community Development Project," unpaginated.

79. Ibid.

80. Ibid.

81. Quoted in Gotsch, "Puerto Rican Leadership," 22–23.

82. Judith Herbstein, "The Politicization of Puerto Rican Ethnicity in New York, 1955–1975," *Ethnic Groups* 5 (July 1983), 36, 38–39.

83. William W. Sales and Rod Bush, "The Political Awakening of Blacks and Latinos in New York City: Competition or Cooperation?" *Social Justice* 27.1 (2000), 19. Also see Andrés Torres, *Between Melting Pot and Mosaic: African Americans and Puerto Ricans in the New York Political Economy* (Philadelphia: Temple University Press, 1995).

84. Telephone interview with Frank Espada, August 26, 2008.

85. Nathan Glazer and Daniel Patrick Moynihan, "How the Catholics Lost Out to the Jews in New York Politics," *New York*, August 10, 1970, 47.

86. For example, Stephen Steinberg opens his classic appraisal of theories of ethnicity with the following claim: "Ethnic pluralism in America has its origins in conquest, slavery, and exploitation of foreign labor" (*The Ethnic Myth: Race, Ethnicity, and Class in America* [New York: Atheneum, 1981], 5). He also argues: "The trouble with this current celebration of ethnicity [during the 1970s] is that it ignores the essentially negative basis on which pluralism developed historically" (4).

87. Nikhil Pal Singh, *Black Is a Country: Race and the Unfinished Struggle for Democracy* (Cambridge: Harvard University Press, 2004), 113, 254.

88. Michael Omi and Howard Winant, *Racial Formation in the United States: From the 1960s to the 1980s* (New York: Routledge, 1986), 20, 39.

89. Valuable overviews of this history include Christopher Riggs, "Indians, Liberalism, and Johnson's Great Society, 1963–1969" (PhD diss., University of Colorado, 1997); George Pierre Castile, *To Show Heart: Native American Self-Determination and Federal Indian Policy, 1960–1975* (Tucson: University of Arizona

Press, 1998); Thomas Clarkin, *Federal Indian Policy in the Kennedy and Johnson Administrations, 1961–1969* (Albuquerque: University of New Mexico Press, 2001); Daniel M. Cobb, *Native Activism in Cold War America: The Struggle for Sovereignty* (Lawrence: University Press of Kansas, 2008).

90. Thomas Atcitty, "Poverty on the Navajo Reservation," *Navajo Times*, April 20, 1967.

91. "Navajos Ask for Aid" and "A Proposed Community Action Plan," *Navajo Times*, October 8, 1964; "A Six-Month Progress Report on the Navajo Indian War on Poverty," *Navajo Times*, December 2, 1965. Also see Peter Iverson, *The Navajo Nation* (Albuquerque: University of New Mexico Press, 1981), 89–100; Peter MacDonald, with Ted Schwarz, *The Last Warrior: Peter MacDonald and the Navajo Nation* (New York: Orion, 1993); Peter Iverson, *Diné: A History of the Navajos* (Albuquerque: University of New Mexico Press, 2002), 236–52.

92. Broderick H. Johnson, *Navaho Education at Rough Rock* (Rough Rock, AZ: Rough Rock Demonstration School, 1968); Robert A. Roessel, *Navajo Education in Action* (Chinle, AZ: Navajo Curriculum Center, 1977); Teresa L. McCarty, *A Place to be Navajo: Rough Rock and the Struggle for Self-Determination in Indigenous Schooling* (Mahwah, NJ: Lawrence Erlbaum Associates, 2002).

93. "Application for Community Action Program by the Navajo Tribe; Submitted to Office of Economic Opportunity," June 11, 1965, 1, Component Project No. 7–1, Office of Economic Opportunity, Office of Operations, Indian Division, Grant Files, 1965–1969, Arizona/Hualapai, Navajo, Box 6; National Archives and Records Administration, College Park, MD (hereafter NARA).

94. Quoted in Office of Navajo Economic Opportunity, *A History and a Semi-Annual Report* (Fort Defiance, AZ: Office of Navajo Economic Opportunity, 1968), 73.

95. Aubrey Willis Williams, Jr., "The Function of the Chapter House System in Contemporary Navajo Political Structure" (PhD diss., University of Arizona, 1965), xii.

96. Williams, "The Function of the Chapter House System in Contemporary Navajo Political Structure"; Sam Bingham and Janet Bingham, *Navajo Chapters*, rev. ed. (Tsaile, AZ: Navajo Community College Press, 1987).

97. Mary Shepardson, *Navajo Ways in Government: A Study in Political Process* (Menasha, WI: American Anthropological Association, 1963), 47.

98. Ibid.

99. Jennifer Nez Denetdale, "Discontinuities, Remembrances, and Cultural Survival: History, Diné/Navajo Memory, and the Bosque Redondo Memorial," *New Mexico Historical Review* 82.3 (2007), 306–7. Also see Jennifer Nez Denetdale, *Reclaiming Diné History: The Legacies of Navajo Chief Manuelito and Juanita* (Tucson: University of Arizona Press, 2007).

100. Quoted in Shepardson, *Navajo Ways in Government*, 79.

101. Edward H. Spicer, *Cycles of Conquest: The Impact of Spain, Mexico, and the*

United States on the Indians of the Southwest, 1533–1960 (Tucson: University of Arizona Press, 1962), 351–53.

102. On Diné political history and organization during this period, see Shepardson, *Navajo Ways in Government*, 78–82; Robert W. Young, "The Rise of the Navajo Tribe," in *Plural Society in the Southwest*, ed. Edward H. Spicer and Raymond H. Thompson (Albuquerque: University of New Mexico Press, 1972); Iverson, *Diné*, 133–36; David E. Wilkins, *The Navajo Political Experience*, rev. ed. (Lanham, MD: Rowman and Littlefield, 2003).

103. "Application for Community Action Program by the Navajo Tribe," 2.

104. Ibid., 4.

105. Paul Weeks memo to Edgar May, October 7, 1966, 5 [OEO Navajo Inspection Report] "Correspondence [2 of 5]," Office of Economic Opportunity, Office of Operations, Indian Division, Grant Files, 1965–1969, Arizona/Hualapai, Navajo, Box 6, NARA.

106. "Application for Community Action Program by the Navajo Tribe," 5, 6.

107. Quoted in Paul Weeks memo to Edgar May, Inspection of the Office of Navajo Economic Opportunity, November 21, 1966, 34, Office of Economic Opportunity, Office of Operations, Indian Division, Grant Files, 1965–1969, Arizona/Navajo, Papago, Office of Inspection (Part 1 of 2), Box 9, NARA.

108. Office of Navajo Economic Opportunity, *A History and a Semi-Annual Report*, 48–49.

109. "Local Community Development Program," 3, n.d. [1967], Office of Economic Opportunity, Office of Operations, Indian Division, Grant Files, 1965–1969, Arizona/Navajo, Papago, Office of Inspection (Part 1 of 2), Box 9, NARA.

110. Paul Weeks memo to Edgar May, Inspection of the Office of Navajo Economic Opportunity, November 21, 1966, 4, Office of Economic Opportunity, Office of Operations, Indian Division, Grant Files, 1965–1969, Arizona/Navajo, Papago, Office of Inspection (Part 1 of 2), Box 9, NARA.

111. Charley Long, Tribal Leaders Workshop, Kaibeta, Arizona, June 1969, 13, transcript of tape #409, American Indian Oral History Project, Center for Southwest Research, University Libraries, University of New Mexico, Albuquerque, NM (hereafter cited as AIOHP, CSWR).

112. Howard Leonard, Bi-monthly meeting, Fort Wingate, New Mexico, June 1969 3, transcript of tape #400, AIOHP, CSWR.

113. Paul Weeks memo to Edgar May, October 7, 1966, 3.

114. Similarly, the Diné historian Jennifer Nez Denetdale critically notes how the Navajo Long Walk and the Bosque Redondo concentration camp have been represented by non-Indian scholars and some Navajos as tragedies that ultimately achieved the greater good of transforming "Navajos into model American citizens who willingly embraced the benefits of white civilization," and that served as "the catalyst for founding the modern Navajo Nation" ("Discontinuities, Remembrances, and Cultural Survival," 301). Denetdale observes: "Accord-

ing to this type of history, after surviving U.S. genocidal policies, Navajos agreed to become both American and Navajo citizens, their choice affirming America's story as a liberal nation that embraces multiculturalism" (306).

115. Quoted in Benjamin A. Bennett, Keith Pearson, and Abe Plummer, "Community Development Training on the Navaho Reservation," in Robert A. Roessel, Jr., *Indian Communities in Action*, ed. Broderick H. Johnson (Tempe: Bureau of Publications, Arizona State University, 1967), 194.

116. Ibid., 194–95.

117. Ibid., 196.

118. In 1972, the LCDP remained one of the most integral components of the ONEO. With a total staff of 120, it was second in size only to the Child Development Program (the preschool program, which had 334 employees) and equal to the Navajo Pre-Vocational Training Program, a later incarnation of the Home Improvement Training Program. Moreover, LCDP staff worked closely with these other two programs as well the Community Action Committees. The staff of all ten ONEO programs and administrative personnel in 1972 numbered 898 (Office of Navajo Economic Opportunity, *ONEO Handbook* [Fort Defiance, AZ: Office of Navajo Economic Development, 1972]).

119. Office of Navajo Economic Opportunity, *A History and a Semi-Annual Report*, 21.

120. Richard Mariano, Bi-monthly meeting, Fort Wingate, New Mexico, June 1969, 8, transcript of Tape #400, AIOHP, CSWR.

121. Jimmy Mason, Bi-monthly meeting, Fort Wingate, New Mexico, June 1969, 26, transcript of Tape #399, Side One, AIOHP, CSWR.

122. Office of Navajo Economic Opportunity, *A History and a Semi-Annual Report*, 75.

123. Paul Weeks memo to Edgar May, November 21, 1966, 2.

124. Unidentified speaker, Bi-monthly meeting, Fort Wingate, New Mexico, June 1969, 2, transcript of Tape #403, AIOHP, CSWR.

125. A revealing contrast to the LCDP was Diné Be'iiná 'Náhiilnah Bee Agha'diit'aahii (Attorneys Who Contribute to the Economic Revitalization of the People, or DNA). Under the direction of Ted Mitchell, the DNA was probably the most controversial ONEO program. Although the DNA provided services that directly benefited a very substantial number of Diné, it also came into conflict with both the Tribal Council and its Advisory Committee. The council and the committee used the fact that the DNA was disproportionately comprised of non-Navajo attorneys to claim that the DNA did not represent the interests of the community. See Mary Shepardson, "Navajo Tribe Factionalism and the Outside World," in *Apachean Culture History and Ethnology*, ed. Keith H. Basso and Morris E. Opler (Tucson: University of Arizona Press, 1971); Iverson, *The Navajo Nation*, 91–100.

126. Leslie Marmon Silko, *Yellow Woman and a Beauty of the Spirit* (New York: Simon and Schuster, 1996), 94.

127. UN Ad Hoc Group of Experts on Community Development, *Community Development and National Development* (New York: UN Department of Economic and Social Affairs, 1963), 30, 6.

128. Unidentified speaker, Bi-monthly meeting, Fort Wingate, June 1969, 1.

129. María Josefina Saldaña-Portillo, *The Revolutionary Imagination in the Americas and the Age of Development* (Durham: Duke University Press, 2003).

130. Spicer, *Cycles of Conquest*, 352.

131. Jacques Rancière, *Hatred of Democracy*, trans. Steve Corcoran (New York: Verso, 2006), 51.

5. Thresholds of Opposition

1. Clyde Warrior, "Testimony of Clyde Warrior," in *Rural Poverty: Hearings before the National Advisory Committee on Rural Poverty: Memphis, Tennessee, February 2 and 3, 1967* (Washington: Government Printing Office, 1967), 144.

2. Richie Perez, audiotaped interview with Carlos Rodríguez-Fraticelli, June 28, 1988, Tape 1, Side A, Centro de Estudios Puertorriqueños, Hunter College, City University of New York, NY.

3. Cedric J. Robinson argues that the development of capitalism has been historically inextricable from processes of racialization. He provides an account of the "emergence of racial order in feudal Europe and delineates its subsequent impact on the organization of labor under capitalism" in order to argue that racism "was not simply a convention for the ordering of relations of European to non-European peoples but has its genesis in the 'internal' relations of European peoples . . . The development, organization, and expansion of capitalist society pursued essentially racial directions, so too did social ideology. As a material force, then it could be expected that racialism would inevitably permeate the social structures emergent from capitalism." Robinson uses "the term 'racial capitalism' to refer to this development and to the subsequent structure as a historical agency" (*Black Marxism: The Making of the Black Radical Tradition* [1983; Chapel Hill: University of North Carolina Press, 2000], 2).

4. Eldridge Cleaver, *Soul on Ice* (New York: McGraw-Hill, 1968), 132.

5. Robert Latham, *The Liberal Moment: Modernity, Security, and the Making of Postwar International Order* (New York: Columbia University Press, 1997), 97–102. Also see Craig N. Murphy, *Global Institutions, Marginalization, and Development* (New York: Routledge, 2005).

6. "Liberal internationalism," as it has been embodied during the twentieth century first by the League of Nations and then by the United Nations, is a project dedicated to the creation of international institutions as necessary instruments for the prevention and management conflict between states and the promotion of market relations as the most effective means of advancing and realizing individual liberty. This project is based on the Enlightenment belief in human freedom and progress as universal values, as well as the Kantian conception of a

world federation working to ensure international peace. It is important to note also that although liberal internationalism works to establish international conditions that minimize war, it is by no means a pacifist doctrine. Rather, liberal internationalism sanctions particular forms of intervention in defense of what its sponsors perceive as order and security.

7. Balakrishnan Rajagopal, *International Law from Below: Development, Social Movements, and Third World Resistance* (Cambridge: Cambridge University Press, 2003); Antony Anghie, *Imperialism, Sovereignty, and the Making of International Law* (Cambridge: Cambridge University Press, 2005).

8. Huey P. Newton, "We Are Nationalists and Internationalists," in *The Coming of the New International*, ed. John Gerassi (New York: World, 1971), 567.

9. Harold Cruse describes the dimensions of a reinvigorated black nationalism as a fundamental constituent of the worldwide anticolonial movement. Cruse argues that, in contrast to an orthodox Marxist focus on the Euro-American proletariat, anticolonial uprisings around the world and African Americans in the United States had become the leading forces for revolutionary change ("Revolutionary Nationalism and the Afro-American," 1962, in Harold Cruse, *Rebellion or Revolution?* [New York: William Morrow, 1968]). Robert F. Williams, Malcolm X, and the Revolutionary Action Movement were also important in this regard. See Timothy B. Tyson, *Radio Free Dixie: Robert F. Williams and the Roots of Black Power* (Chapel Hill: University of North Carolina Press, 1999); William W. Sales Jr., *From Civil Rights to Black Liberation: Malcolm X and the Organization of Afro-American Unity* (Boston: South End, 1994); Robin D. G. Kelley, *Freedom Dreams: The Black Radical Imagination* (Boston: Beacon, 2003); Nikhil Pal Singh, *Black Is a Country: Race and the Unfinished Struggle for Democracy* (Cambridge: Harvard University Press, 2004); Cynthia Young, *Soul Power: Culture, Radicalism, and the Making of a U.S. Third World Left* (Durham: Duke University Press, 2006); Kevin K. Gaines, *American Africans in Ghana: Black Expatriates and the Civil Rights Era* (Chapel Hill: University of North Carolina Press, 2006), 179–209.

10. William Blum, *Killing Hope: U.S. Military and CIA Interventions since World War II*, updated ed. (Monroe, ME: Common Courage, 2003); Greg Grandin, *Empire's Workshop: Latin America, the United States, and the Rise of the New Imperialism* (New York: Metropolitan, 2006).

11. See, for instance, Robert C. Maynard, "Police—Symbol of Oppression," *Washington Post*, September 26, 1967, and "Nationalists Woo Young," *Washington Post*, September 28, 1967.

12. Will Lissner, "Teen-Agers Find Summer Jobs Here through Youth Program," *New York Times*, July 28, 1965.

13. John Hall Fish, *Black Power/White Control: The Struggle of the Woodlawn Organization in Chicago* (Princeton: Princeton University Press, 1973); Richard W. Poston, *The Gang and the Establishment* (New York: Harper and Row, 1971);

Joseph Loftus, "Antipoverty Office Suspends Coast Project for Rehabilitation of Gang Youths," *New York Times*, September 28, 1967.

14. Warren Gilmore, *Y.O.U.* (Washington: Youth Organizations United, 1970), 1.

15. National Conference of Youth Organizations United, *A Report by the Center for the Study of Crime, Delinquency, and Corrections, Southern Illinois University* (Edwardsville: Southern Illinois University, 1968); Ellen Ferber, "Thugs United," *Social Service Outlook* 5.4 (1970); Poston, *The Gang and the Establishment*, 111–44; Kent Germany, *New Orleans after the Promises: Poverty, Citizenship, and the Search for the Great Society* (Athens: University of Georgia Press, 2007), 211–45.

16. On the Real Great Society, see Poston, *The Gang and the Establishment*; Syeus Mottel, *Charas: The Improbable Dome Builders* (New York: Drake, 1973); Luis Aponte-Parés, "Lessons from *el Barrio*—The East Harlem Real Great Society/Urban Planning Studio: A Puerto Rican Chapter in the Fight for Urban Self-Determination," in *Latino Social Movements: Historical and Theoretical Perspectives*, ed. Rodolfo D. Torres and George Katsiaficas (New York: Routledge, 1999).

17. Application from Real Great Society to the Office of Economic Opportunity, ca. 1968, 4, General Counsel, Subject and Litigation Files, 1967–1974, Box 12, RGS CG-8531, Grants (2 of 2), National Archives and Records Administration, College Park, MD (hereafter NARA).

18. Roger Vaughn, "The Real Great Society: Some Tough New York Slum Kids Team Up to Fight Poverty Instead of Themselves," *Life*, September 15, 1967.

19. Ibid., 76.

20. Quoted in Aponte-Parés, "Lessons from *el Barrio*," 56.

21. Carlos (Chino) Garcia, chairman/president RGS, letter to Senator Jacob K. Javits, June 2, 1969; Senator Jacob K. Javits, letter to Frederick W. Richmond, the Richmond Foundation, September 5, 1969, Series 10, Subseries 1, Box 106, Real Great Society, 1969–1970; Carol M. Khosrovi, OEO associate director for congressional and governmental relations, memorandum regarding Real Great Society Project to John Scales, Minority Counsel, US Senate Subcommittee on Employment, Manpower, and Poverty, October 31, 1969, Series 4, Subseries 4, Box 22, Poverty Correspondence and Memos, 1969–1972, Senator Jacob K. Javits Collection, Frank Melville Jr. Memorial Library, Stony Brook University, Stony Brook, NY. Also see Peter Kihss, "Ex-Gang Leaders Obtain U.S. Funds," *New York Times*, February 27, 1968.

22. Application from Real Great Society to the Office of Economic Opportunity, October 1967, 15, General Counsel, Subject and Litigation Files, 1967–1974, Box 12, RGS CG-8531, Grants (1 of 2), NARA.

23. Application from Real Great Society to the Office of Economic Opportunity, ca. 1968, 26, 2.

24. Richard T. Sale, *The Blackstone Rangers: A Reporter's Account of Time Spent with*

the Street Gang on Chicago's South Side (New York: Random House, 1971); John R. Fry, *Locked-Out Americans: A Memoir* (New York: Harper and Row, 1973); Fish, *Black Power/White Control*, 115–74; Nicholas von Hoffman, "Chicago 'Super-Gang' Boasts 'Mighty Nation,'" *Washington Post*, December 18, 1966; Andrew J. Diamond, *Mean Streets: Chicago Youths and the Everyday Struggle for Empowerment in the Multiracial City, 1908–1969* (Berkeley: University of California Press, 2009), 261–300.

25. James R. Ralph Jr., *Northern Protest: Martin Luther King, Jr., Chicago, and the Civil Rights Movement* (Cambridge: Harvard University Press, 1993), 94–95; Jon F. Rice, "Black Radicalism on Chicago's West Side: A History of the Illinois Black Panther Party" (PhD diss., Northern Illinois University, 1998); Betty Washington, "SCLC Organizing Youth Gangs City Wide," *Chicago Daily Defender*, June 13, 1966.

26. D. J. R. Bruckner, "Chicago Police Launch Teen Gang Operation," *Los Angeles Times*, March 6, 1967.

27. Quoted in Fish, *Black Power/White Control*, 140.

28. In his opening remarks to the final session of hearings, McClellan cautioned: "The bombers have as their objectives the breakdown of the democratic process and the destruction of our society. They seek to prevent due process of law, and if they continue in their nefarious deeds with any degree of success, they can hinder and do great damage to our opportunities to improve race relations. They cause tremendous overreaction and repression" (US Senate Committee on Government Operations, Permanent Subcommittee on Investigations, *Hearings: Riots, Civil and Criminal Disorders* [Washington: Government Printing Office, 1970], 5741). The line of causation here was clear: the bombers, and by extension all those involved in confrontational or unruly challenges to governmental authority, were themselves the cause of reaction and repression; they were responsible for state violence, excusing any and all acts of repression and excessive force by the state.

29. Aldo Beckman, "Gang Hearings Draw Full House; Best Capitol Hill Show in Years," *Chicago Tribune*, July 7, 1968.

30. Fish, *Black Power/White Control*, 161; Rowland Evans and Robert Novak, "Chicago Police behind Probe into Blackstone Rangers Affair," *Washington Post*, July 12, 1968.

31. McClellan's dismissal was all the more insidious given the fact that the Illinois attorney general initiated a grand jury investigation into the activities of the Blackstone Rangers the day after Fort's aborted testimony. Donald Mosby, "Launch Grand Jury Probe into Activities of Blackstone Rangers," *Chicago Daily Defender*, July 11, 1968.

32. Jeff Fort, "Testimony of Jeff Fort, Accompanied by Counsel, Marshall Patner," in US Senate, Committee on Government Operations, Permanent Subcommittee on Investigations, *Hearings: Riots, Civil and Criminal Disorders* (Washing-

ton: Government Printing Office, 1968), 2545–50; Arthur M. Brazier, *Black Self-Determination: The Story of the Woodlawn Organization* (Grand Rapids, MI: William B. Eerdmans, 1969), 108–15; Betty Washington, "Fort Faces a Contempt Charge for His Walkout," *Chicago Daily Defender*, July 10, 1968.

33. Irving A. Spergel, "Youth Gangs and Urban Riots," in *Riots and Rebellion: Civil Violence in the Urban Community*, ed. Louis H. Masotti and Don R. Bowen (Beverly Hills, CA: Sage, 1968).

34. Lucia Mouat, "Vote Boycott?," *Christian Science Monitor*, October 9, 1968; Lloyd Hogan, "Rangers Plan 'No Vote' Drive," *Chicago Daily Defender*, November 4, 1968.

35. The GIU's force was increased from thirty-eight to two hundred officers. Patricia Leeds, "Conlisk Tells Plans to Enlarge Gang Unit," *Chicago Tribune*, November 8, 1968.

36. John Kifner, "Chicago Blacks Resume Protest in Bid for Building Trade Jobs," *New York Times*, August 22, 1969.

37. Fry, *Locked-Out Americans*, 133.

38. Fish, *Black Power/White Control*, 75–78.

39. Quoted in Fry, *Locked-Out Americans*, 43.

40. Ibid.

41. Colman McCarthy, "OEO and Poverty Are Still with Us," *Washington Post*, August 15, 1969.

42. Aponte-Parés, "Lessons from *el Barrio*."

43. Black Panther Party, "Defend the Ghetto," in *The Black Panthers Speak*, ed. Philip S. Foner (Philadelphia: J. B. Lippincott, 1970), 180.

44. Eldridge Cleaver, *Post-Prison Writings and Speeches* (New York: Random House, 1969), 22.

45. Eldridge Cleaver, *On the Ideology of the Black Panther Party* (San Francisco: Ministry of Information, Black Panther Party, 1968), 7, Pamphlet 71–596, Wisconsin Historical Society Library Pamphlet Collection, Madison, WI.

46. Ibid., 11.

47. Errol A. Henderson, "The Lumpenproletariat as Vanguard? The Black Panther Party, Social Transformation, and Pearson's Analysis of Huey Newton," *Journal of Black Studies* 28.2 (1997); Chris Booker, "Lumpenization: A Critical Error of the Black Panther Party," in *The Black Panther Party (Reconsidered)*, ed. Charles E. Jones (Baltimore: Black Classic, 1998); Jeffrey O. G. Ogbar, *Black Power: Radical Politics and African American Identity* (Baltimore: Johns Hopkins University Press, 2005), 93–110.

48. Frantz Fanon, *The Wretched of the Earth*, trans. Constance Farrington (1961; New York: Grove, 1968), 129.

49. Ibid., 137.

50. This was taken to quasireligious stature with Huey Newton's official designation as "Supreme Servant of the People." For a critical discussion of this attribution

see Kathleen Neal Cleaver, "Back to Africa: The Evolution of the International Section of the Black Panther Party (1969–1972)," in *The Black Panther Party (Reconsidered)*, ed. Charles E. Jones (Baltimore: Black Classic, 1998), 236.

51. Sofia Näsström, "The Legitimacy of the People," *Political Theory* 35.5 (2007), 641, 644–45.

52. JoNina M. Abron, " 'Serving the People': The Survival Programs of the Black Panther Party," in *The Black Panther Party (Reconsidered)*, ed. Charles E. Jones (Baltimore: Black Classic, 1998); Rod Bush, *We Are Not What We Seem: Black Nationalism and Class Struggle in the American Century* (New York: New York University Press, 1999), 200–204; Paul Alkebulan, *Survival Pending Revolution: The History of the Black Panther Party* (Tuscaloosa: University of Alabama Press, 2007), 27–45; Alondra Nelson, *Body and Soul: The Black Panther Party and the Fight against Medical Discrimination* (Minneapolis: University of Minnesota Press, 2011).

53. Quoted in Abron, " 'Serving the People,' " 179.

54. Ibid., 178.

55. Quoted in Ward Churchill and Jim Vander Wall, *Agents of Repression: The FBI's Secret Wars against the Black Panther Party and the American Indian Movement*, corrected ed. (Boston: South End Press, 1990), 68.

56. Churchill and Vander Wall, *Agents of Repression*; US Senate, *Final Report of the Select Committee to Study Governmental Operations with Respect to Intelligence Activities* (Washington: Government Printing Office, 1976).

57. For example, see in *Black Panther*: "Three Students Suspended for Attending Free Breakfast Program," June 14, 1969; "Free Breakfast for Children about to Be Vamped On," July 19, 1969; "San Diego Breakfast Moves Ahead," 26 July 1969; "San Jose Liberation School," August 9, 1969; Donald Campbell, "Serving the People: Fascist Power Structure Copies Panther Breakfast Program," August 16, 1969; "L.A. Pigs Vamp on Free Breakfast Program," September 13, 1969.

58. On BPP internationalism, see Michael L. Clemons and Charles E. Jones, "Global Solidarity: The Black Panthers in the International Arena," in *Liberation, Imagination, and the Black Panther Party*, ed. Kathleen Cleaver and George Katsiaficas (New York: Routledge, 2001); Jennifer B. Smith, *An International History of the Black Panther Party* (New York: Garland, 1999); Max Elbaum, *Revolution in the Air: Sixties Radicals Turn to Lenin, Mao and Che* (New York: Verso, 2002); Black Panther Party, "Petition to the United Nations," in *The Black Panthers Speak*; Singh, *Black Is a Country*, 193–211.

59. For a further discussion of Huey Newton's conception of intercommunalism, see Bush, *We Are Not What We Seem*, 198–200; Singh, *Black Is a Country*, 198–99; Huey P. Newton, "Intercommunalism," in Erik H. Erikson and Huey P. Newton, *In Search of Common Ground* (New York: W. W. Norton, 1973). On the critical reception of "intercommunalism" by Eldridge Cleaver, and how this precipitated divisions within the BPP, see Kathleen Neal Cleaver, "Back to Af-

rica: The Evolution of the International Section of the Black Panther Party (1969–1972)."

60. Huey P. Newton, "Message to the Vietnamese," in *The Coming of the New International*, ed. John Gerassi (New York: World, 1971), 594–95.

61. Newton, "Intercommunalism," 28, 30.

62. William Wei, *The Asian American Movement* (Philadelphia: Temple University Press, 1993); Ernesto B. Vigil, *The Crusade for Justice: Chicano Militancy and the Government's War on Dissent* (Madison: University of Madison Press, 1999); Fred Ho, ed., with Carolyn Antonio, Diane Fujino, and Steve Yip, *Legacy to Liberation: Politics and Culture of Revolutionary Asian Pacific America* (San Francisco: AK Press, 2000); Ernesto Chávez, *"¡Mi Raza Primero!": Nationalism, Identity, and Insurgency in the Chicano Movement in Los Angeles, 1966–1978* (Berkeley: University of California Press, 2002); Kelley, *Freedom Dreams*; Singh, *Black Is a Country*; Kimberly Springer, *Living for the Revolution: Black Feminist Organizations, 1968–1980* (Durham: Duke University Press, 2005); Laura Pulido, *Black, Brown, Yellow, and Left: Radical Activism in Los Angeles* (Berkeley: University of California Press, 2006); Young, *Soul Power*; Fred Ho and Bill V. Mullen, eds., *Afro Asia: Revolutionary Political and Cultural Connections between African Americans and Asian Americans* (Durham: Duke University Press, 2008); Daryl J. Maeda, *Chains of Babylon: The Rise of Asian America* (Minneapolis: University of Minnesota Press, 2009).

63. Denise Ferreira da Silva, *Toward a Global Idea of Race* (Minneapolis: University of Minnesota Press, 2007), 154.

64. Elbaum, *Revolution in the Air*.

65. C. Clark Kissinger, "'Serve the People,'" *Guardian* (US), May 17, 1969.

66. Rice, "Black Radicalism on Chicago's West Side"; Churchill and Vander Wall, *Agents of Repression*, 65–66; Diamond, *Mean Streets*, 303–12.

67. The Rainbow Coalition, "The Rainbow Food Program," in *From the Movement toward Revolution*, ed. Bruce Franklin (New York: Van Nostrand Reinhold, 1971), 112.

68. "Daley Asks War on Street Gangs," *Chicago Tribune*, May 20, 1969.

69. Quoted in Guy Halverson, "Critics Snipe at Chicago's War against Street Gangs," *Christian Science Monitor*, July 30, 1969, 11.

70. Ibid.

71. Illinois Chapter, Black Panther Party, "Serving the People," *Black Panther*, September 6, 1969, 11.

72. Mama Jewell and Babatunde, "An Open Letter to Parents," *Black Panther*, September 6, 1969, 11.

73. Eugene Charles, "Harassment of Illinois Panthers," *Black Panther*, June 21, 1969; Churchill and Vander Wall, *Agents of Repression*, 64–77.

74. Fred Hampton, "Three Speeches by Fred Hampton," *Vita Wa Watu* 11 (August 1987), 7.

75. Clarus Backes, "Poor People's Power in Uptown," *Chicago Tribune*, September 29, 1968; Todd Gitlin and Nanci Hollander, *Uptown: Poor Whites in Chicago* (New York: Harper and Row, 1970), 375–97; Amy Sonnie and James Tracy, "Uptown's JOIN Community Union from 1964–1966," *AREA Chicago 7*, December 2008; Virgil Reed, "White Folks Gotta Get Together," *Firing Line*, January 16, 1968; and James Tracy, "Rising Up: Poor, White, and Angry in the New Left," in *The Hidden 1970s: Histories of Radicalism*, ed. Dan Berger (New Brunswick, NJ: Rutgers University Press, 2010).

76. On the Chicago branch of the Young Lords, see "Interview with Cha Cha Jimenez, Chairman—The Young Lords Organization," *Black Panther*, June 7, 1969; Cha-Cha Jimenez Defense Committee, *"Que Viva El Pueblo": A Biographical History of Jose Cha-Cha Jimenez, General Secretary of the Young Lords Organization* (Chicago: Cha-Cha Jimenez Defense Committee, 1973); Frank Browning, "From Rumble to Revolution: The Young Lords," in *The Puerto Rican Experience: A Sociological Sourcebook*, ed. Francesco Cordasco and Eugene Bucchioni (Totowa, NJ: Rowman and Littlefield, 1973).

77. Quoted in Browning, "From Rumble to Revolution," 233.

78. Quoted in ibid., 234.

79. Felix M. Padilla, *Puerto Rican Chicago* (Notre Dame, IN: University of Notre Dame Press, 1987), 120–23; "Community Relates to Cops," *Guardian* (US), March 1, 1969; Cha-Cha Jimenez Defense Committee, *"Que Viva El Pueblo,"* 17–18.

80. "Interview with Cha Cha Jimenez, Chairman—The Young Lords Organization."

81. The group included Denise Oliver, Mickey Melendez, and Iris Morales—each of whom had been involved with the Real Great Society. See Miguel "Mickey" Melendez, *We Took the Streets: Fighting for Latino Rights with the Young Lords* (New York: St. Martin's Press, 2003), 73–77; Iris Morales, "¡Palante, Siempre Palante! The Young Lords," in *The Puerto Rican Movement: Voices from the Diaspora*, ed. Andrés Torres and José E. Velázquez (Philadelphia: Temple University Press, 1998).

82. On the New York branch of the Young Lords, see The Young Lords Party and Michael Abramson, *Palante: Young Lords Party* (New York: McGraw-Hill, 1971); Alfredo Lopez, *The Puerto Rican Papers: Notes on the Re-Emergence of a Nation* (New York: Bobbs-Merrill Company, 1973), 209–353; Roberto P. Rodríguez-Morazzani, "Puerto Rican Political Generations in New York: Pioneros, Young Turks, and Radicals," *Centro Journal* 4.1 (1992); Agustín Laó, "Resources of Hope: Imagining the Young Lords and the Politics of Memory," *Centro Journal* 7.1 (1994–1995); Pablo "Yoruba" Guzmán, "Puerto Rican Barrio Politics in the United States," in *Historical Perspectives on Puerto Rican Survival in the United States*, ed. Clara E. Rodríguez and Virginia Sánchez Korrol (Princeton, NJ: Markus Weiner, 1996); Roberto P. Rodríguez-Morazzani, "Political Cultures

of the Puerto Rican Left in the United States," Carmen Teresa Whalen, "Bridging Homeland and Barrio Politics: The Young Lords in Philadelphia," Pablo Guzmán, "*La Vida Pura*: A Lord of the Barrio," and Morales, "¡Palante, Siempre Palante! The Young Lords," in *The Puerto Rican Movement: Voices from the Diaspora*, ed. Andrés Torres and José E. Velázquez (Philadelphia: Temple University Press, 1998); Matthew Gandy, "Between Borinquen and the Barrio: Environmental Justice and New York City's Puerto Rican Community, 1969–1972," *Antipode* 34.4 (September 2002); Melendez, *We Took the Streets*. Also see "Analysis of 3-Year History of YLP," in Puerto Rican Revolutionary Workers Organization (Young Lords Party), *Resolutions and Speeches, First Congress* (New York: Puerto Rican Revolutionary Workers Organization, November 1972), Lourdes Torres Papers, Box 11, Folder 11, Centro de Estudios Puertorriqueños, Hunter College, City University of New York, NY.

83. Morales, "¡Palante, Siempre Palante!," 214.

84. Guzmán, "*La Vida Pura*: A Lord of the Barrio," 157.

85. Young Lords Party, "Prisons Are Concentration Camps for the Poor," n.d., n.p., Publications relating to the Young Lords Party, Vertical Files, Tamiment Library and Robert F. Wagner Labor Archives, New York University, New York, NY.

86. Ibid.

87. The role of the YLP in the Attica negotiations is documented, among other places, in New York State Special Commission on Attica, *Attica: The Official Report* (New York: Praeger, 1972).

88. Young Lords Party, "13 Point Program and Platform," in Young Lords Party and Michael Abramson, *Palante: Young Lords Party*, 150.

89. Morales, "¡Palante, Siempre Palante!," 218–19. Also see Jennifer Nelson, *Women of Color and the Reproductive Rights Movement* (New York: New York University Press, 2003), 113–32.

90. Young Lords Party, "Position Paper on Women," *NACLA Newsletter* 14 (October 1970), 14.

91. Pablo "Yoruba" Guzmán, "We're Trying to Make a Society Where Opportunity Is the Rule for Everybody," in *Palante: Young Lords Party*, 57.

92. Ibid.

93. Pablo "Yoruba" Guzmán, "On History and Dialectics," in *The Ideology of the Young Lords Party* (Bronx, NY: National Headquarters of the Young Lords Party, 1972), 5.

94. Denise Oliver, "Colonized Mentality and Non-Conscious Ideology," in *The Ideology of the Young Lords Party* (Bronx, NY: National Headquarters of the Young Lords Party, 1972), 26.

95. Pablo "Yoruba" Guzmán, "Before People Called Me a Spic, They Called Me a Nigger," in *Palante: Young Lords Party*, 83.

96. See from *Palante*: "Ofensiva Rompe Cadenas," January 29, 1971; "Ofensiva Rompecadenas [sic]," March 5–19, 1971; Richie Perez, "Que Viva Puerto Rico

Libre!," Benjy Cruz, "Toa Baja, Puerto Rico," and Gloria Gonzalez, "Nueva Rama en Aguadilla," April 2–19, 1971; Carmen Mercado, "Aguadilla: Y Pronto No Tendremos Hospital," June 1971. Also see Eneid Routte, "The Young Lords in El Caño," *San Juan Star*, August 15, 1971; "Analysis of 3-Year History of YLP," 8–16.

97. Gloria Gonzalez, "Protracted War in Puerto Rico," in *The Ideology of the Young Lords Party* (Bronx, NY: National Headquarters of the Young Lords Party, 1972), 19.

98. Juan "Fi" Ortiz and Juan Gonzalez, "Letter from Puerto Rico," *Palante*, September 11, 1970, 4.

99. Richie Perez, audiotaped interview with Carlos Rodrigúez-Fraticelli, Tape 1, Side A.

100. Gonzalez, "Protracted War in Puerto Rico," 17, 18.

101. Richie Perez, audiotaped interview with Carlos Rodrigúez-Fraticelli, Tape 1, Side A.

102. "Our Tasks," in Puerto Rican Revolutionary Workers Organization (Young Lords Party), *Resolutions and Speeches, First Congress*, 31.

103. See especially "Analysis of 3-Year History of YLP," 10–17. On "democratic centralism" more broadly, see V. I. Lenin, "What Is to Be Done?," in *Essential Works of Lenin*, ed. Henry M. Christman (New York: Dover, 1987).

104. Sylvain Lazarus, "Lenin and the Party, 1902–November 1917," in *Lenin Reloaded: Toward a Politics of Truth*, ed. Sebastian Budgen, Stathis Kouvelakis, and Slavoj Žižek (Durham: Duke University Press, 2007), 259.

105. Former PRRWO Cadres, *The Degeneration of the PRRWO: From Revolutionary Organization to Neo-Trotskyite Sect* (New York: Former PRRWO Cadres, 1977), 19.

106. Chantal Mouffe, *The Return of the Political* (New York: Verso, 1993), 69.

107. Quoted in a footnote by Philip S. Foner to Black Panther Party, "Petition to the United Nations," in *The Black Panthers Speak*, 274.

108. Black Panther Party, "What We Want, What We Believe," in *The Black Panthers Speak*, 3–4. This Black Panther Party Platform and Program was written by Huey Newton and Bobby Seale in October 1966.

109. Black Panther Party, "Petition to the United Nations," 255.

110. See especially Clemons and Jones, "Global Solidarity."

111. "How It Is with Us," *Akwesasne Notes*, December 31, 1977; Roxanne Dunbar-Ortiz, *Indians of the Americas: Human Rights and Self-Determination* (New York: Praeger, 1984), 32–35.

112. "Declaration of Continuing Independence by the First International Indian Treaty Council at Standing Rock Indian Country June 1974," Roger A. Finzel American Indian Movement Papers, 1965–1995, Box 2, Folder 21, Center for Southwest Research, University Libraries, University of New Mexico, Albuquerque, NM (hereafter Finzel/CSWR).

113. "Meeting of the International Workgroup on Treaties," June 10, 1974, 1, Box 2, Folder 21, Finzel/CSWR.

114. Ibid.

115. Amilcar Cabral, *Unity and Struggle: Speeches and Writings*, trans. Michael Wolfers (New York: Monthly Review, 1979), 265.

116. Roxanne Dunbar-Ortiz, "What Is 'Human Rights?,'" *Treaty Council News*, July–August 1977, 4–5.

117. Jimmie Durham, "United Nations Conference on Indians," *Treaty Council News*, April 1977; Paul Smith, "Indians Prepare for Geneva," *Treaty Council News*, July–August 1977; "Native Americans before the U.N.," *American Indian Journal*, 3.9 (September 1977), 3–4.

118. "Geneva: A Report," *Akwesasne Notes*, December 31, 1977, 4.

119. "Indian Delegates Speak," *Treaty Council News*, October 1977, 5. In the 1974 declaration, the sentences paraphrased by Means are immediately followed by the statement: "We recognize this lack of representation in the United Nations comes from the genocidal policies of the colonial power of the United States" ("Declaration of Continuing Independence by the First International Indian Treaty Council at Standing Rock Indian Country June 1974," n.p.).

120. "Indian Delegates Speak," 12.

121. Dunbar-Ortiz, "What Is 'Human Rights'?," 4–5.

122. "U.S. Statement," *American Indian Journal*, 3:11 (November 1977), 7.

123. Jimmie Durham, "Where We Go from Here," *Treaty Council News*, October 1977, 34.

124. "Geneva Resolutions Presented at UN," *Treaty Council News*, December 1977; "The Work beyond Geneva," *Akwesasne Notes*, December 31, 1977.

125. "Decolonization, Liberation, and the International Community," *Treaty Council News*, December 1977, 3.

126. Quoted in UN Office of Public Information, *The United Nations and Decolonization: Summary of the Work of the Special Committee of Twenty-Four* (New York: United Nations, 1965), 1.

127. S. James Anaya, *Indigenous Peoples in International Law*, 2nd ed. (New York: Oxford University Press, 2004), 53–54. Also see William Roger Louis and Ronald Robinson, "The Imperialism of Decolonization," in William Roger Louis, *Ends of British Imperialism: The Scramble for Empire, Suez, and Decolonization; Collected Essays* (London: I. B. Tauris, 2006).

128. US Senate Committee on the Judiciary, *Revolutionary Activities within the United States: The American Indian Movement: Hearing before the Subcommittee to Investigate the Administration of the Internal Security Act and Other Internal Security Laws* (Washington: Government Printing Office, 1976); US Senate, Committee on the Judiciary, Subcommittee to Investigate the Administration of the Internal Security Act and Other Internal Security Laws, *The Puerto Rican Revolutionary Workers Organization: A Staff Study* (Washington: Government Printing Office, 1976).

Conclusion

1. On the early configurations of liberal thought, see Andreas Kalyvas and Ira Katznelson, *Liberal Beginnings: Making a Republic for the Moderns* (Cambridge: Cambridge University Press, 2008); Domenico Losurdo, *Liberalism: A Counter-History* (New York: Verso, 2011).

2. Friedrich A. Hayek, *The Road to Serfdom* (1944; Chicago: University of Chicago Press, 2007), 88, 182. Hayek thus claims that liberalism "has the distinction of being the doctrine most hated by Hitler" (81).

3. See especially Lisa Duggan, *The Twilight of Equality: Neoliberalism, Cultural Politics, and the Attack on Democracy* (Boston: Beacon, 2003); Sanford F. Schram, *Welfare Discipline: Discourse, Governance, and Globalization* (Philadelphia: Temple University Press, 2006); Jodi Melamed, "The Spirit of Neoliberalism: From Racial Liberalism to Neoliberal Multiculturalism," *Social Text* 89 (Winter 2006); Anna Marie Smith, *Welfare Reform and Sexual Regulation* (Cambridge: Cambridge University Press, 2007); Marisa Chappell, *The War on Welfare: Family, Poverty, and Politics in Modern America* (Philadelphia: University of Pennsylvania Press, 2010); Kaaryn S. Gustafson, *Cheating Welfare: Public Assistance and the Criminalization of Poverty* (New York: NYU Press, 2011).

4. Bill Fletcher Jr. and Fernando Gapasin, *Solidarity Divided: The Crisis of Organized Labor and a New Path toward Social Justice* (Berkeley: University of California Press, 2008).

5. See, for instance, Ruth Wilson Gilmore, *Golden Gulag: Prisons, Surplus, Crisis, and Opposition in Globalizing California* (Berkeley: University of California Press, 2007); Jonathan Simon, *Governing through Crime: How the War on Crime Transformed American Democracy and Created a Culture of Fear* (New York: Oxford University Press, 2007).

6. Greta R. Krippner, *Capitalizing on Crisis: The Political Origins of the Rise of Finance* (Cambridge: Harvard University Press, 2011); Jamie Peck, *Constructions of Neoliberalism* (New York: Oxford University Press, 2010); Karen Ho, *Liquidated: An Ethnography of Wall Street* (Durham: Duke University Press, 2009).

7. Lane E. Holdcraft, "The Rise and Fall of Community Development in Developing Countries, 1950–65," Michigan State University Rural Development Papers, No. 2 (East Lansing: Department of Agricultural Economics, Michigan State University, 1978).

8. Ibid., 19.

9. Quoted in William A. Schambra, "Is New Federalism the Wave of the Future?," in *The Great Society and Its Legacy*, ed. Marshall Kaplan and Peggy L. Cuciti (Durham: Duke University Press, 1986), 24.

10. Timothy Conlan, *From New Federalism to Devolution: Twenty-Five Years of Intergovernmental Reform* (Washington, D.C.: Brookings Institution Press, 1998).

11. Rita Mae Kelly, *Community Participation in Directing Economic Development* (Cambridge, MA: Center for Community Economic Development, 1976), 1.

12. William H. Simon, *The Community Economic Development Movement: Law, Business, and the New Social Policy* (Durham: Duke University Press, 2001); James DeFilippis, *Unmaking Goliath: Community Control in the Face of Global Capital* (New York: Routledge, 2004). As celebrated public-private partnerships and examples of grass-roots entrepreurialism, CDCs closely approximate the nongovernmental organizations championed in neoliberal aid discourse. For insightful accounts of such organizations with respect to neoliberalism, see George Yúdice, *The Expediency of Culture: Uses of Culture in the Global Era* (Durham: Duke University Press, 2003); Julia Elyachar, *Markets of Dispossession: NGOs, Economic Development, and the State in Cairo* (Durham: Duke University Press, 2005).

13. Neal R. Peirce and Carol F. Steinbach, *Corrective Capitalism: The Rise of America's Community Development Corporations* (New York: Ford Foundation, 1987), 31.

14. Randy Stoecker, "The CDC Model of Urban Redevelopment: A Critique and an Alternative," *Journal of Urban Affairs* 19:1 (1997), 5.

15. UN Department of International Economic and Social Affairs, *Popular Participation as a Strategy for Promoting Community-Level Action and National Development* (New York: United Nations, 1981), 3.

16. Robert L. Ayers, *Banking on the Poor: The World Bank and World Poverty* (Cambridge: MIT Press, 1983).

17. Paul Francis, "Participatory Development at the World Bank: The Primacy of Process," in *Participation: The New Tyranny?*, ed. Bill Cooke and Uma Kothari (London: Zed, 2001); Elyachar, *Markets of Dispossession*.

18. Ananya Roy, *Poverty Capital: Microfinance and the Making of Development* (New York: Routledge, 2010), 5.

19. Christiaan Grootaert and Thierry van Bastelaer, "Understanding and Measuring Social Capital: A Synthesis of Findings and Recommendations from the Social Capital Initiative," *Social Capital Initiative Working Paper* 24 (Washington: World Bank, Social Development Department, 2001), 1.

20. John Harriss, *Depoliticizing Development: The World Bank and Social Capital* (London: Anthem, 2002); Margit Mayer, "The Onward Sweep of Social Capital: Causes and Consequences for Understanding Cities, Communities, and Urban Movements," *International Journal of Urban and Regional Research* 27.1 (2003).

21. Thandike Mkandawire, "'Good Governance': The Itinerary of an Idea," *Development in Practice* 17.4–5 (2007).

22. Mick Moore, "Empowerment at Last?," *Journal of International Development* 13.3 (2001); Suzanne Bergeron, "Challenging the World Bank's Narrative of Inclusion," in *World Bank Literature*, ed. Amitava Kumar (Minneapolis: University of Minnesota Press, 2003).

23. Catherine Eschle, "Globalizing Civil Society? Social Movements and the Challenge of Global Politics from Below," in *Globalization and Social Movements*, ed. Pierre Hamel, Henri Lustiger-Thaler, Jan Nederveen Pieterse, and Sasha Roseneil (New York: Palgrave, 2001).

24. Susan Brin Hyatt, "From Citizen to Volunteer: Neoliberal Governance and the Erasure of Poverty," in *The New Poverty Studies: The Ethnography of Power, Politics, and Impoverished People in the United States*, ed. Judith Goode and Jeff Maskovsky (New York: New York University Press, 2001); DeFilippis, *Unmaking Goliath*; Helga Leitner, Jamie Peck, and Eric Sheppard, eds., *Contesting Neoliberalism: Urban Frontiers* (New York: Guilford, 2007). For rather stark examples of this neoliberal approach to governance and community, see Douglas Henton, John Melville, and Kim Walesh, *Civic Revolutionaries: Igniting the Passion for Change in America's Communities* (San Francisco: Jossey-Bass, 2004); Peter Block, *Community: The Structure of Belonging* (San Francisco: Berrett-Koehler, 2008).

25. For an excellent study that elaborates on these tensions, see Nancy Grey Postero, *Now We Are Citizens: Indigenous Politics in Postmulticultural Bolivia* (Stanford: Stanford University Press, 2007).

BIBLIOGRAPHY

Abramovitz, Mimi. *Regulating the Lives of Women: Social Welfare Policy from Colonial Times to the Present.* Rev. ed. Boston: South End Press, 1996.

Abron, JoNina M. " 'Serving the People': The Survival Programs of the Black Panther Party." In *The Black Panther Party (Reconsidered)*, edited by Charles E. Jones, 177–92. Baltimore: Black Classic, 1998.

Afield, Walter E., and Audrey B. Gibson. *Children of Resurrection City.* Washington, D.C.: Association for Childhood Education International, 1970.

Agamben, Giorgio. *Means without End: Notes on Politics.* Translated by Vincenzo Binetti and Cesare Casarino. Minneapolis: University of Minnesota Press, 2000.

Agronsky, Jonathan I. Z. *Marion Barry: The Politics of Race.* Latham, NY: British American, 1991.

Alkebulan, Paul. *Survival Pending Revolution: The History of the Black Panther Party.* Tuscaloosa: University of Alabama Press, 2007.

Almond, Gabriel A., and Sidney Verba. *The Civic Culture: Political Attitudes and Democracy in Five Nations.* Princeton: Princeton University Press, 1963.

Amadae, S. M. *Rationalizing Capitalist Democracy: The Cold War Origins of Rational Choice Liberalism.* Chicago: University of Chicago Press, 2003.

Amin, Julius A. "The Peace Corps and the Struggle for African American Equality." *Journal of Black Studies* 29.6 (1999): 809–26.

Anaya, S. James. *Indigenous Peoples in International Law.* 2nd ed. New York: Oxford University Press, 2004.

Anderson, Robert W. *Party Politics in Puerto Rico.* Stanford: Stanford University Press, 1965.

Anghie, Antony. *Imperialism, Sovereignty, and the Making of International Law.* Cambridge: Cambridge University Press, 2005.

Aponte-Parés, Luis. "Lessons from *el Barrio*—The East Harlem Real Great Society/

Urban Planning Studio: A Puerto Rican Chapter in the Fight for Urban Self-Determination." In *Latino Social Movements: Historical and Theoretical Perspectives*, edited by Rodolfo D. Torres and George Katsiaficas, 43–78. New York: Routledge, 1999.

Appy, Christian G., ed. *Cold War Constructions: The Political Culture of United States Imperialism, 1945–1966*. Amherst: University of Massachusetts Press, 2000.

Arndt, H. W. *The Rise and Fall of Economic Growth: A Study in Contemporary Thought*. 1978. Chicago: University of Chicago Press, 1984.

Arnold, Charles B. "Culture Shock and a Peace Corps Field Mental Health Program." *Community Mental Health Journal* 3.1 (1967): 53–60.

Aronowitz, Stanley, et al. *Working Papers for Nyack Conference on Unemployment and Social Change*. New York: Students for a Democratic Society, 1963.

Ashabranner, Brent. *A Moment in History: The First Ten Years of the Peace Corps*. Garden City, NY: Doubleday, 1971.

Ashmore, Susan Youngblood. *Carry It On: The War on Poverty and the Civil Rights Movement in Alabama, 1964–1972*. Athens: University of Georgia Press, 2008.

Ayers, Robert L. *Banking on the Poor: The World Bank and World Poverty*. Cambridge: MIT Press, 1983.

Bailey, Cathryn. "Anna Julia Cooper: 'Dedicated in the Name of My Slave Mother to the Education of Colored Working People.'" *Hypatia* 19.2 (2004): 56–73.

Balibar, Étienne. *Masses, Classes, Ideas: Studies on Politics and Philosophy before and after Marx*. Translated by James Swenson. New York: Routledge, 1994.

——. *Politics and the Other Scene*. Translated by Christine Jones, James Swenson, and Chris Turner. London: Verso, 2002.

Balogh, Brian. *A Government out of Sight: The Mystery of National Authority in Nineteenth-Century America*. Cambridge: Cambridge University Press, 2009.

Banner, Stuart. *How the Indians Lost Their Land: Law and Power on the Frontier*. Cambridge: Harvard University Press, 2005.

Barker, Joanne. "For Whom Sovereignty Matters." In *Sovereignty Matters: Locations of Contestation and Possibility in Indigenous Struggles for Self-Determination*, edited by Joanne Barker, 1–31. Lincoln: University of Nebraska Press, 2005.

Batten, T. R. *Communities and Their Development: An Introductory Study with Special Reference to the Tropics*. London: Oxford University Press, 1957.

Baver, Sherrie. "Puerto Rican Politics in New York City: The Post-World War II Period." In *Puerto Rican Politics in Urban America*, edited by James Jennings and Monte Rivera, 43–59. Westport, CT: Greenwood, 1984.

Beatty, Willard W. "The Nature and Purpose of Community Education." In *Community Education: Principles and Practices from World-Wide Experience—The Fifty-Eighth Yearbook of the National Society for the Study of Education*, edited by Nelson B. Henry, 3–37. Chicago: University of Chicago Press, 1959.

Beck, Bertram M. "Organizing Community Action." *Proceedings of the Academy of Political Science* 29.4 (1969): 162–78.

Becker, Gary S. *Human Capital: A Theoretical and Empirical Analysis, with Special Reference to Education.* New York: National Bureau of Economic Research, 1964.

Bennett, Benjamin A., Keith Pearson, and Abe Plummer. "Community Development Training on the Navaho Reservation." In Robert A. Roessel Jr., *Indian Communities in Action,* edited by Broderick H. Johnson, 180–203. Tempe: Bureau of Publications, Arizona State University, 1967.

Bergeron, Suzanne. "Challenging the World Bank's Narrative of Inclusion." In *World Bank Literature,* edited by Amitava Kumar, 157–71. Minneapolis: University of Minnesota Press, 2003.

Betten, Neil, and Michael J. Austin. *The Roots of Community Organizing, 1917–1939.* Philadelphia: Temple University Press, 1990.

Bhana, Surendra. *The United States and the Development of the Puerto Rican Status Question, 1936–1968.* Lawrence: University of Kansas Press, 1975.

Biddle, William W. *The Cultivation of Community Leaders: Up from the Grass Roots.* New York: Harper and Brothers, 1953.

Biddle, William W., and Loureide J. Biddle. *The Community Development Process: The Rediscovery of Local Initiative.* New York: Holt, Rinehart and Winston, 1965.

Bingham, Jonathan B. *Shirt-Sleeve Diplomacy: Point 4 in Action.* New York: John Day, 1954.

Bingham, Sam, and Janet Bingham. *Navajo Chapters.* Rev. ed. Tsaile, AZ: Navajo Community College Press, 1987.

Biondi, Martha. *To Stand and Fight: The Struggle for Civil Rights in Postwar New York City.* Cambridge: Harvard University Press, 2003.

Black, Kate. "The Roving Picket Movement and the Appalachian Committee for Full Employment, 1959–1965: A Narrative." *Journal of the Appalachian Studies Association* 2 (1990): 110–27.

Black Panther Party. "Defend the Ghetto." In *The Black Panthers Speak,* edited by Philip S. Foner, 180. Philadelphia: J. B. Lippincott, 1970.

——. "Petition to the United Nations." In *The Black Panthers Speak,* edited by Philip S. Foner, 254–55. Philadelphia: J. B. Lippincott, 1970.

——. "What We Want, What We Believe." In *The Black Panthers Speak,* edited by Philip S. Foner, 2–4. Philadelphia: J. B. Lippincott, 1970.

Block, Peter. *Community: The Structure of Belonging.* San Francisco: Berrett-Koehler, 2008.

Blum, William. *Killing Hope: U.S. Military and CIA Interventions since World War II.* Updated ed. Monroe, ME: Common Courage, 2003.

Booker, Chris. "Lumpenization: A Critical Error of the Black Panther Party." In *The Black Panther Party (Reconsidered),* edited by Charles E. Jones, 337–62. Baltimore: Black Classic, 1998.

Boone, Richard W. "What Is Meaningful Participation?" *Community Development* 1.5 (1966): 27–32.

Borstelmann, Thomas. *The Cold War and the Color Line: American Race Relations in the Global Arena.* Cambridge: Harvard University Press, 2001.

Bourne, Randolph S. *War and the Intellectuals: Collected Essays, 1915–1919.* New York: Harper and Row, 1964.

Brager, George A., and Francis P. Purcell, eds. *Community Action against Poverty: Readings from the Mobilization Experience.* New Haven, CT: College and University Press, 1967.

Brands, H. W. *The Specter of Neutralism: The United States and the Emergence of the Third World, 1947–1960.* New York: Columbia University Press, 1989.

Brazier, Arthur M. *Black Self-Determination: The Story of the Woodlawn Organization.* Grand Rapids, MI: William B. Eerdmans, 1969.

Briggs, Laura. *Reproducing Empire: Race, Sex, Science, and U.S. Imperialism in Puerto Rico.* Berkeley: University of California Press, 2002.

Brinkley, Alan. *The End of Reform: New Deal Liberalism in Recession and War.* New York: Random House, 1995.

Brokensha, David, and Peter Hodge. *Community Development: An Interpretation.* San Francisco: Chandler, 1969.

Brown, Connie. "Cleveland: Conference of the Poor." *Studies on the Left* 5.2 (1965): 71–74.

Browning, Frank. "From Rumble to Revolution: The Young Lords." In *The Puerto Rican Experience: A Sociological Sourcebook,* edited by Francesco Cordasco and Eugene Bucchioni, 231–45. Totowa, NJ: Rowman and Littlefield, 1973.

Burchell, Graham. "Liberal Government and Techniques of the Self." In *Foucault and Political Reason: Liberalism, Neo-Liberalism and Rationalities of Government,* edited by Andrew Barry, Thomas Osborne, and Nikolas Rose, 19–36. Chicago: University of Chicago Press, 1996.

Burgess, Ernest W., Joseph D. Lohman, and Clifford R. Shaw. "The Chicago Area Project." In *Coping with Crime: Yearbook of the National Probation Association,* edited by Marjorie Bell, 8–28. New York: National Probation Association, 1937.

Burma, John H., and David E. Williams. *An Economic, Social and Educational Survey of Rio Arriba and Taos Counties.* El Rito: Northern New Mexico College, 1960.

Burnett, Christina Duffy, and Burke Marshall, eds. *Foreign in a Domestic Sense: Puerto Rico, American Expansion, and the Constitution.* Durham: Duke University Press, 2001.

Bush, Rod. *We Are Not What We Seem: Black Nationalism and Class Struggle in the American Century.* New York: NYU Press, 1999.

Cabral, Amilcar. *Unity and Struggle: Speeches and Writings.* Translated by Michael Wolfers. New York: Monthly Review, 1979.

Carpio, Myla Vicenti. *Indigenous Albuquerque.* Lubbock: Texas Tech University Press, 2011.

Carson, Clayborne. *In Struggle: SNCC and the Black Awakening of the 1960s.* Rev. ed. Cambridge: Harvard University Press, 1995.

Cassese, Antonio. *Self-Determination of Peoples: A Legal Reappraisal.* Cambridge: Cambridge University Press, 1999.

Castile, George Pierre. *To Show Heart: Native American Self-Determination and Federal Indian Policy, 1960–1975.* Tucson: University of Arizona Press, 1998.

Catton, Philip E. *Diem's Failure: Prelude to America's War in Vietnam.* Lawrence: University Press of Kansas, 2002.

Cazenave, Noel A. "Chicago Influences the War on Poverty." *Journal of Policy History* 5.1 (January 1993): 52–68.

——. *Impossible Democracy: The Unlikely Success of the War on Poverty Community Action Programs.* Albany: State University of New York Press, 2007.

Cha-Cha Jimenez Defense Committee. *"Que Viva El Pueblo": A Biographical History of Jose Cha-Cha Jimenez, General Secretary of the Young Lords Organization.* Chicago: Cha-Cha Jimenez Defense Committee, 1973.

Chappell, Marisa. *The War on Welfare: Family, Poverty, and Politics in Modern America.* Philadelphia: University of Pennsylvania Press, 2010.

Chase, Robert T. "Class Resurrection: The Poor People's Campaign of 1968 and Resurrection City." *Essays in History* 40 (1998).

Chávez, Ernesto. *"¡Mi Raza Primero!": Nationalism, Identity, and Insurgency in the Chicano Movement in Los Angeles, 1966–1978.* Berkeley: University of California Press, 2002.

Chow, Rey. *The Protestant Ethnic and the Spirit of Capitalism.* New York: Columbia University Press, 2002.

Churchill, Ward, and Jim Vander Wall. *Agents of Repression: The FBI's Secret Wars against the Black Panther Party and the American Indian Movement.* Corrected ed. Boston: South End Press, 1990.

Clarkin, Thomas. *Federal Indian Policy in the Kennedy and Johnson Administrations, 1961–1969.* Albuquerque: University of New Mexico Press, 2001.

Cleaver, Eldridge. *Post-Prison Writings and Speeches.* New York: Random House, 1969.

——. *Soul on Ice.* New York: McGraw-Hill, 1968.

Cleaver, Kathleen Neal. "Back to Africa: The Evolution of the International Section of the Black Panther Party (1969–1972)." In *The Black Panther Party (Reconsidered)*, edited by Charles E. Jones, 211–54. Baltimore: Black Classic, 1998.

Clemons, Michael L., and Charles E. Jones. "Global Solidarity: The Black Panthers in the International Arena." In *Liberation, Imagination, and the Black Panther Party*, edited by Kathleen Cleaver and George Katsiaficas, 20–39. New York: Routledge, 2001.

Cleveland, Harlan, and Gerard J. Mangone, eds. *The Art of Overseasmanship.* Syracuse, NY: Syracuse University Press, 1957.

Cleveland, Harlan, Gerard J. Mangone, and John Clarke Adams. *The Overseas Americans.* New York: McGraw-Hill, 1960.

Cloward, Richard A., and Lloyd E. Ohlin. *Delinquency and Opportunity: A Theory of Delinquent Gangs.* Glencoe, IL: Free Press, 1960.

Cloward, Richard A., and Frances Fox Piven. *The Politics of Turmoil: Essays on Poverty, Race, and the Urban Crisis.* New York: Pantheon, 1974.

——. *Poor People's Movements: Why They Succeed, How They Fail.* New York: Vintage, 1977.

——. "The Weight of the Poor: A Strategy to End Poverty." *Nation*, May 2, 1966, 510–17.

Cobb, Daniel M. *Native Activism in Cold War America: The Struggle for Sovereignty.* Lawrence: University Press of Kansas, 2008.

Cobb, Daniel M., and Loretta Fowler, eds., *Beyond Red Power: American Indian Politics and Activism since 1900.* Santa Fe: SAR Press, 2007.

Cohen, Nancy. *The Reconstruction of American Liberalism, 1865–1914.* Chapel Hill: University of North Carolina Press, 2002.

Collier, John. "Definitions and Debates of the Community Center Conference." *American City* 19.6 (1916): 572–74.

"Concurrent Resolution of Hawaii Legislature Relating to Peace Corps." *Congressional Record* 107.4 (1961): 4849.

Conlan, Timothy. *From New Federalism to Devolution: Twenty-Five Years of Intergovernmental Reform.* Washington, D.C.: Brookings Institution Press, 1998.

Cooper, Frederick. *Colonialism in Question: Theory, Knowledge, History.* Berkeley: University of California Press, 2005.

Cooper, Frederick, and Randall Packard, eds. *International Development and the Social Sciences: Essays on the History and Politics of Knowledge.* Berkeley: University of California Press, 1997.

Correia, David. "'Retribution Will Be Their Reward': New Mexico's Las Gorras Blancas and the Fight for the Las Vegas Land Grant Commons." *Radical History Review* 108 (October 2010): 49–72.

——. "'Rousers of the Rabble' in the New Mexico Land Grant War: *La Alianza Federal de Mercedes* and the Violence of the State." *Antipode* 40.4 (2008): 561–83.

Council of Economic Advisers. *Annual Report.* Washington, D.C.: Government Printing Office, 1964.

Cowan, Michael P., and Robert W. Shenton. *Doctrines of Development.* New York: Routledge, 1996.

Cowger, Thomas W. *The National Congress of American Indians: The Founding Years.* Lincoln: University of Nebraska Press, 1999.

Crozier, Michel, Samuel P. Huntington, and Joji Watanuki. *The Crisis of Democracy: Report on the Governability of Democracies to the Trilateral Commission.* New York: NYU Press, 1975.

Cruikshank, Barbara. *The Will to Empower: Democratic Citizens and Other Subjects.* Ithaca: Cornell University Press, 1999.

Cruse, Harold. "Revolutionary Nationalism and the Afro-American." In Harold Cruse, *Rebellion or Revolution?*, 74–96. 1962. New York: William Morrow, 1968.

Dahl, Robert A. *Pluralist Democracy in the United States: Conflict and Consent.* Chicago: Rand McNally, 1967.

Daniels, Walter M., ed. *The Point Four Program.* New York: H. W. Wilson, 1951.

Dasgupta, Sugata. *A Poet and a Plan: Tagore's Experiments in Rural Reconstruction.* Calcutta: Thacker Spink, 1962.

David, Stephen M. "Welfare: The Community-Action Program Controversy." In *Race and Politics in New York City,* edited by Jewel Bellush and Stephen M. David, 25–58. New York: Praeger, 1971.

Davis, Allen F. *Spearheads for Reform: The Social Settlements and the Progressive Movement, 1890–1914.* New York: Oxford University Press, 1967.

Davis, Rennie. "The War on Poverty: Notes on Insurgent Response." In *The New Student Left: An Anthology,* edited by Mitchell Cohen and Dennis Hale, 154–69. Boston: Beacon, 1966.

Dean, Mitchell. *The Constitution of Poverty: Toward a Genealogy of Liberal Governance.* London: Routledge, 1991.

——. *Governing Societies: Political Perspectives on Domestic and International Rule.* London: Open University Press, 2007.

DeFilippis, James. *Unmaking Goliath: Community Control in the Face of Global Capital.* New York: Routledge, 2004.

Deloria, Vine, Jr. *Behind the Trail of Broken Treaties: An Indian Declaration of Independence.* 2nd ed. Austin: University of Texas Press, 1985.

Deloria, Vine, Jr., and Clifford M. Lytle. *The Nations Within: The Past and Future of American Indian Sovereignty.* 1984. Austin: University of Texas Press, 1998.

Denetdale, Jennifer Nez. "Discontinuities, Remembrances, and Cultural Survival: History, Diné/Navajo Memory, and the Bosque Redondo Memorial." *New Mexico Historical Review* 82.3 (2007): 295–316.

——. *Reclaiming Diné History: The Legacies of Navajo Chief Manuelito and Juanita.* Tucson: University of Arizona Press, 2007.

Denning, Michael. *The Cultural Front: The Laboring of American Culture in the Twentieth Century.* New York: Verso, 1996.

Diamond, Andrew J. *Mean Streets: Chicago Youths and the Everyday Struggle for Empowerment in the Multiracial City, 1908–1969.* Berkeley: University of California Press, 2009.

Díaz, Manuel. "Part IV: Strategy for Community Development: Challenge to the Puerto Rican Community," in *Puerto Ricans Confront Problems of the Complex Urban Society: A Design for Change,* 165–176. New York: High School of Art and Design, 1967.

Dietz, James. *Puerto Rico: Negotiating Development and Change.* Boulder, CO: Lynne Rienner, 2003.

Dinwiddie, Courtenay. *Community Responsibility: A Review of the Cincinnati Social Unit Experiment.* New York: New York School of Social Work, 1921.

——. "The Work Accomplished by the Social Unit Organization." In *Proceedings of the National Conference of Social Work—at the 45th Annual Session, Held in Kansas City, Missouri, May 15–22, 1918,* 495–507. Chicago: National Conference of Social Work, 1919.

División de Educación de la Comunidad. "La Voluntad que Ignacio no Tuvo." In *Los Casos de Ignacio y Santiago*, edited by René Marqués, 3–23. San Juan, PR: Departamento de Instrucción Pública, 1953.

Duany, Jorge. *The Puerto Rican Nation on the Move: Identities on the Island and in the United States*. Chapel Hill: University of North Carolina Press, 2002.

Duara, Prasenjit. "Introduction: The Decolonization of Asia and Africa in the Twentieth Century." In *Decolonization: Perspectives from Now and Then*, edited by Prasenjit Duara, 1–18. New York: Routledge, 2003.

Dudziak, Mary. *Cold War Civil Rights: Race and the Image of American Democracy*. Princeton: Princeton University Press, 2000.

Duggan, Lisa. *The Twilight of Equality: Neoliberalism, Cultural Politics, and the Attack on Democracy*. Boston: Beacon, 2003.

Dulles, John Foster. "Instruction from the Secretary of State to All Diplomatic Missions in the American Republics." In *Foreign Relations of the United States, 1955–1957*, 6:300–303. Washington, D.C.: Government Printing Office, 1987.

Dunbar-Ortiz, Roxanne, ed. *Economic Development in American Indian Reservations*. Albuquerque: Native American Studies, University of New Mexico, 1979.

——. *Indians of the Americas: Human Rights and Self-Determination*. New York: Praeger, 1984.

Dunne, George H., ed. *Poverty in Plenty*. New York: P. J. Kennedy and Sons, 1964.

Economic Opportunity Act of 1964, As Amended. Washington, D.C.: Government Printing Office, 1970.

Eisenberg, Terry, Robert H. Fosen, and Albert S. Glickman. *Police-Community Action: A Program for Change in Police-Community Behavior Patterns*. New York: Praeger, 1973.

Ekberg, Dennis, and Claude Ury. "Education for What? A Report on an MDTA Program." *Journal of Negro Education* 37.1 (1968): 15–22.

Ekbladh, David. *The Great American Mission: Modernization and the Construction of an American World Order*. Princeton: Princeton University Press, 2010.

Elbaum, Max. *Revolution in the Air: Sixties Radicals Turn to Lenin, Mao and Che*. New York: Verso, 2002.

Eller, Ronald. *Uneven Ground: Appalachia since 1945*. Lexington: University Press of Kentucky, 2008.

Elyachar, Julia. *Markets of Dispossession: NGOs, Economic Development, and the State in Cairo*. Durham: Duke University Press, 2005.

Engerman, David C. "Ideology and the Origins of the Cold War, 1917–1962." In *The Cambridge History of the Cold War, Vol. I: Origins*, edited by Melvyn P. Leffler and Odd Arne Westad, 20–43. Cambridge: Cambridge University Press, 2010.

Engerman, David C., Nils Gilman, Mark H. Haefele, and Michael E. Latham, eds. *Staging Growth: Modernization, Development, and the Global Cold War*. Amherst: University of Massachusetts Press, 2003.

Englund, David L. "Peace Corps Training and the American University." *International Review of Education* 11.2 (1965): 209–17.

Eschle, Catherine. "Globalizing Civil Society? Social Movements and the Challenge of Global Politics from Below." In *Globalization and Social Movements*, edited by Pierre Hamel, Henri Lustiger-Thaler, Jan Nederveen Pieterse, and Sasha Roseneil, 61–85. New York: Palgrave, 2001.

Escobar, Arturo. *Encountering Development: The Making and Unmaking of the Third World*. Princeton: Princeton University Press, 1995.

Estades, Rosa. *Patterns of Political Participation of Puerto Ricans in New York City*. San Juan, PR: Editorial Universitaria, Universidad de Puerto Rico, 1978.

Fager, Charles. *Uncertain Resurrection: The Poor People's Washington Campaign*. Grand Rapids, MI: William B. Eerdmans, 1969.

Fahey, John. *Saving the Reservation: Joe Garry and the Battle to Be Indian*. Seattle: University of Washington Press, 2001.

Fairbanks, Robert B. *Making Better Citizens: Housing Reform and the Community Development Strategy in Cincinnati, 1890–1960*. Urbana: University of Illinois Press, 1988.

Fanon, Frantz. *The Wretched of the Earth*. Translated by Constance Farrington. 1961. New York: Grove, 1968.

Farr, Kenneth R. *Personalism and Party Politics: Institutionalization of the Popular Democratic Party of Puerto Rico*. Hato Rey, PR: Inter-American University Press, 1973.

Feeley, Malcolm M., and Austin Sarat. *The Policy Dilemma: Federal Crime Policy and the Law Enforcement Assistance Administration, 1968–1978*. Minneapolis: University of Minnesota Press, 1980.

Ferber, Ellen. "Thugs United." *Social Service Outlook* 5.4 (1970): 5–7.

Fergus, Devin. *Liberalism, Black Power, and the Making of American Politics, 1965–1980*. Athens: University of Georgia Press, 2009.

Fey, Harold E., and D'Arcy McNickle. *Indians and Other Americans: Two Ways of Life Meet*. New York: Harper and Brothers, 1959.

"The First National Conference on Community Centers," *National Municipal Review* 5.3 (1916): 496–98.

Fischer, Fritz. *Making Them Like Us: Peace Corps Volunteers in the 1960s*. Washington, D.C.: Smithsonian Institution, 1998.

Fish, John Hall. *Black Power/White Control: The Struggle of the Woodlawn Organization in Chicago*. Princeton: Princeton University Press, 1973.

Fisher, Robert. *Let the People Decide: Neighborhood Organizing in America*. Updated ed. New York: Twayne, 1994.

——. "The People's Institute of New York City, 1897–1934: Culture, Progressive Democracy, and the People." PhD diss., New York University, 1974.

Fishman, Leo, ed. *Poverty and Affluence*. New Haven: Yale University Press, 1966.

Fitzpatrick, Joseph P. *Puerto Rican Americans: The Meaning of Migration to the Mainland*. 2nd ed. Englewood Cliffs, NJ: Prentice-Hall, 1987.

Fixico, Donald L. *Termination and Relocation: Federal Indian Policy, 1945–1960*. Albuquerque: University of New Mexico Press, 1986.

Flamm, Michael W. *Law and Order: Street Crime, Civil Unrest, and the Crisis of Liberalism in the 1960s*. New York: Columbia University Press, 2005.

Flanagan, Maureen. *America Reformed: Progressives and Progressivisms, 1890s–1920s*. New York: Oxford University Press, 2007.

Fletcher, Bill, Jr., and Fernando Gapasin. *Solidarity Divided: The Crisis of Organized Labor and a New Path toward Social Justice*. Berkeley: University of California Press, 2008.

Florence Heller Graduate School for Advanced Studies in Social Work at Brandeis University. *Community Development and Community Organization: An International Workshop*. New York: National Association of Social Workers, 1961.

Follett, Mary Parker. *The New State: Group Organization, the Solution of Popular Government*. New York: Longmans, Green, 1918.

Folsom, Franklin. *Impatient Armies of the Poor: The Story of Collective Action of the Unemployed, 1808–1942*. Niwot: University Press of Colorado, 1991.

Foner, Eric. *Free Soil, Free Labor, Free Men: The Ideology of the Republican Party before the Civil War*. New York: Oxford University Press, 1970.

Foote, Nelson N., and Leonard S. Cottrell. *Identity and Interpersonal Competence: A New Direction in Family Research*. Chicago: University of Chicago Press, 1955.

Ford Foundation, *American Community Development: Preliminary Reports by Directors of Projects Assisted by the Ford Foundation in Four Cities and a State: Twenty-ninth Annual National Conference, National Association of Housing and Redevelopment Officials. Denver, Colorado, October 1, 1963*. New York: Ford Foundation, 1964.

Former PRRWO Cadres. *The Degeneration of the PRRWO: From Revolutionary Organization to Neo-Trotskyite Sect*. New York: Former PRRWO Cadres, 1977.

Forrest, Suzanne. *The Preservation of the Village: New Mexico's Hispanics and the New Deal*. 2nd ed. Albuquerque: University of New Mexico Press, 1998.

Foster, Ellery. "Planning for Community Development through Its People." *Human Organization* 12.2 (1953): 5–9.

Foucault, Michel. *The Birth of Biopolitics: Lectures at the Collège de France, 1978–1979*. Edited by Michel Senellart. Translated by Graham Burchell. New York: Palgrave Macmillan, 2008.

Francis, Paul. "Participatory Development at the World Bank: The Primacy of Process." In *Participation: The New Tyranny?*, edited by Bill Cooke and Uma Kothari, 72–87. London: Zed, 2001.

Fraser, Cary. "Understanding American Policy toward the Decolonization of European Empires, 1945–1964." *Diplomacy & Statecraft* 3.1 (1992): 105–25.

Fraser, Nancy, and Linda Gordon. "A Genealogy of 'Dependency': Tracing a Keyword of the U.S. Welfare State." In Nancy Fraser, *Justice Interruptus: Critical Reflections on the "Postsocialist" Condition*, 121–50. New York: Routledge, 1997.

Fried, Alfred. "The Attack on Mobilization." In *Community Development in the Mobilization for Youth Experience*, edited by Harold H. Weissman, 137–62. New York: Association Press, 1969.

Friedrich, Carl J. *Puerto Rico: The Middle Road to Freedom*. New York: Rinehart, 1959.

Frost, Jennifer. *"An Interracial Movement for the Poor": Community Organizing and the New Left in the 1960s*. New York: NYU Press, 2001.

Fruchter, Norm, and Robert Kramer. "An Approach to Community Organizing." *Studies on the Left* 6.2 (1966): 31–61.

Fry, John R. *Locked-Out Americans: A Memoir*. New York: Harper and Row, 1973.

Gaines, Kevin K. *American Africans in Ghana: Black Expatriates and the Civil Rights Era*. Chapel Hill: University of North Carolina Press, 2006.

——. *Uplifting the Race: Black Leadership, Politics, and Culture in the Twentieth Century*. Chapel Hill: University of North Carolina Press, 1996.

Galbraith, John Kenneth. *The Affluent Society*. Boston: Houghton Mifflin, 1958.

Galbraith, John Kenneth, and Carolyn Shaw Solo. "Puerto Rican Lessons in Economic Development." *Annals of the American Academy of Political and Social Science* 285 (January 1953): 55–59.

Gandy, Matthew. "Between Borinquen and the Barrio: Environmental Justice and New York City's Puerto Rican Community, 1969–1972." *Antipode* 34.4 (2002): 730–61.

García-Colón, Ismael. "Hegemony, Land Reform, and Social Space in Puerto Rico: Parcelas, a Land Distribution Program for Landless Workers, 1940s–1960s." PhD diss., University of Connecticut, 2002.

——. *Land Reform in Puerto Rico: Modernizing the Colonial State, 1941–1969*. Gainesville: University of Florida Press, 2009.

Gardner, Richard. *¡Grito! Tijerina and the New Mexico Land Grant War of 1967*. Indianapolis: Bobbs-Merrill, 1970.

Garrow, David J. *Bearing the Cross: Martin Luther King, Jr., and the Southern Christian Leadership Conference*. New York: Vintage, 1986.

George, Henry. *Poverty and Progress: An Inquiry into the Cause of Industrial Depressions and of Increase of Want with Increase of Wealth . . . The Remedy*. 1879. New York: Robert Schalkenbach Foundation, 1990.

Germany, Kent. *New Orleans after the Promises: Poverty, Citizenship, and the Search for the Great Society*. Athens: University of Georgia Press, 2007.

Gilbert, Ben W. *Ten Blocks from the White House: Anatomy of the Washington Riots of 1968*. New York: Praeger, 1968.

Gilbert, James. *A Cycle of Outrage: America's Reaction to the Juvenile Delinquent in the 1950s*. New York: Oxford University Press, 1986.

Gilman, Nils. *Mandarins of the Future: Modernization Theory in Cold War America*. Baltimore: Johns Hopkins University Press, 2003.

Gilmore, Ruth Wilson. *Golden Gulag: Prisons, Surplus, Crisis, and Opposition in Globalizing California*. Berkeley: University of California Press, 2007.

Gilmore, Warren. *Y.O.U.* Washington, D.C.: Youth Organizations United, 1970.

Ginsberg, Mitchell. "Short-Term Training for the Peace Corps." *Social Work* 9.1 (1964): 62–68.

Gitlin, Todd. "The Radical Potential of the Poor." In *The New Left: A Documentary History*, edited by Massimo Teodori, 136–49. New York: Bobbs-Merrill, 1969.

Gitlin, Todd, and Nanci Hollander. *Uptown: Poor Whites in Chicago*. New York: Harper and Row, 1970.

Glazer, Nathan, and Daniel Patrick Moynihan. "How the Catholics Lost Out to the Jews in New York Politics." *New York*, August 10, 1970, 39–49.

Glen, John M. "The War on Poverty in Appalachia—A Preliminary Report." *Register of the Kentucky Historical Society* 87 (Winter 1989): 40–57.

——. "The War on Poverty in Appalachia: Oral History from the 'Top Down' and the 'Bottom Up.'" *Oral History Review* 22.1 (1995): 67–93.

Glenn, Evelyn Nakano. *Unequal Freedom: How Race and Gender Shaped American Citizenship and Labor*. Cambridge: Harvard University Press, 2002.

Glueck, Eleanor T. *The Community Use of Schools*. Baltimore: Williams and Wilkins, 1927.

Go, Julian. *American Empire and the Politics of Meaning: Elite Political Cultures in the Philippines and Puerto Rico during U.S. Colonialism*. Durham: Duke University Press, 2008.

Gollin, Albert E. *The Demography of Protest: A Statistical Profile of Participants in the Poor People Campaign*. Washington, D.C.: Bureau of Social Science Research, 1968.

Gonzales, Phillip B. "Struggle for Survival: The Hispanic Land Grants of New Mexico, 1848–2001." *Agricultural History* 77.2 (2003): 293–324.

Gonzales-Berry, Erlinda, and David R. Maciel, eds. *The Contested Homeland: A Chicano History of New Mexico*. Albuquerque: University of New Mexico Press, 2000.

Gonzalez, Gloria. "Protracted War in Puerto Rico." In *The Ideology of the Young Lords Party*, 13–19. Bronx, NY: National Headquarters of the Young Lords Party, 1972.

Goodwin, Joanne. "'Employable Mothers' and 'Suitable Work': A Re-Evaluation of Welfare and Wage-Earning for Women in the Twentieth Century United States." *Journal of Social History* 29.2 (Winter 1995): 253–74.

Gordon, Linda. *Pitied but Not Entitled: Single Mothers and the History of Welfare*. New York: Free Press, 1994.

Gotsch, John W. "Puerto Rican Leadership in New York." Master's thesis, New York University, 1966.

Grandin, Greg. *Empire's Workshop: Latin America, the United States, and the Rise of the New Imperialism*. New York: Metropolitan, 2006.

Greenstone, J. David, and Paul E. Peterson. *Race and Authority in Urban Politics: Community Participation and the War on Poverty*. Chicago: University of Chicago Press, 1973.

Griswold del Castillo, Richard. *The Treaty of Guadalupe Hidalgo: A Legacy of Conflict*. Norman: University of Oklahoma Press, 1990.

Grootaert, Christiaan, and Thierry van Bastelaer. "Understanding and Measuring Social Capital: A Synthesis of Findings and Recommendations from the Social

Capital Initiative." *Social Capital Initiative Working Paper* 24. Washington, D.C.: World Bank, Social Development Department, 2001.

Grosfoguel, Ramón. "Developmentalism, Modernity, and Dependency Theory in Latin America." *Nepantla* 1.2 (2000): 347–74.

——. "The Divorce of Nationalist Discourses from the Puerto Rican People: A Sociohistorical Perspective." In *Puerto Rican Jam: Rethinking Colonialism and Nationalism*, edited by Frances Negrón-Muntaner and Ramón Grosfoguel, 57–76. Minneapolis: University of Minnesota Press, 1997.

——. "Puerto Rico's Exceptionalism: Industrialization, Migration, and Housing Development." PhD diss., Temple University, 1992.

Grosser, Charles F. "Neighborhood Community-Development Programs for Serving the Poor." In *Community Action against Poverty: Readings from the Mobilization Experience*, edited by George A. Brager and Francis P. Purcell, 243–52. New Haven, CT: College and University Press, 1967.

Gustafson, Kaaryn S. *Cheating Welfare: Public Assistance and the Criminalization of Poverty*. New York: NYU Press, 2011.

Guy, Roger. *From Diversity to Unity: Southern and Appalachian Migrants in Uptown Chicago, 1950–1970*. Lanham, MD: Lexington, 2007.

Guzmán, Pablo "Yoruba." "Before People Called Me a Spic, They Called Me a Nigger." In Young Lords Party and Michael Abramson, *Palante: Young Lords Party*, 73–83. New York: McGraw-Hill, 1971.

——. "On History and Dialectics." In *The Ideology of the Young Lords Party*, 5–12. Bronx, NY: National Headquarters of the Young Lords Party, 1972.

——. "Puerto Rican Barrio Politics in the United States." In *Historical Perspectives on Puerto Rican Survival in the United States*, edited by Clara E. Rodríguez and Virginia Sánchez Korrol, 143–52. Princeton, NJ: Markus Weiner, 1996.

——. "*La Vida Pura*: A Lord of the Barrio." In *The Puerto Rican Movement: Voices from the Diaspora*, edited by Andrés Torres and José E. Velázquez, 155–72. Philadelphia: Temple University Press, 1998.

——. "We're Trying to Make a Society Where Opportunity Is the Rule for Everybody." In Young Lords Party and Michael Abramson, *Palante: Young Lords Party*, 56–58. New York: McGraw-Hill, 1971.

Hahn, Peter L., and Mary Ann Heiss, eds. *Empire and Revolution: The United States and the Third World since 1945*. Columbus: Ohio State University Press, 2001.

Hampton, Fred. "Three Speeches by Fred Hampton." *Vita Wa Watu* 11 (August 1987): 1–23.

Hansen, Millard, and Henry Wells, eds. "Puerto Rico: A Study in Democratic Development." Special issue, *Annals of the American Academy of Political and Social Science* 285 (January 1953).

Hanson, Earl Parker. *Puerto Rico: Ally for Progress*. New York: D. Van Nostrand, 1962.

Harrington, Michael. *The Other America: Poverty in the United States*. Baltimore: Penguin, 1962.

Harris, LaDonna. *LaDonna Harris: A Comanche Life*. Edited by H. Henrietta Stockel. Lincoln: University of Nebraska Press, 2000.

Harris, Mrs. Fred R. [LaDonna Harris], and Leon H. Ginsberg. "Project Peace Pipe: Indian Youth Pre-Trained for Peace Corps Duty." *Journal of American Indian Education* 7.2 (1968): 21–26.

Harriss, John. *Depoliticizing Development: The World Bank and Social Capital*. London: Anthem, 2002.

Hartigan, John, Jr. *Odd Tribes: Toward a Cultural Analysis of White People*. Durham: Duke University Press, 2005.

Haslip-Viera, Gabriel, Angelo Falcón, and Félix V. Matos-Rodríguez, eds. *Boricuas in Gotham: Puerto Ricans in the Making of New York City*. Princeton, NJ: Markus Wiener, 2004.

Hayden, Sherman S., and Benjamin Rivlin. *Non-Self-Governing Territories: Status of Puerto Rico*. New York: Woodrow Wilson Foundation, 1954.

Hayek, Friedrich A. *The Road to Serfdom*. 1944. Chicago: University of Chicago Press, 2007.

"Hazard, KY: Committee for Miners." *Studies on the Left* 5.3 (1965): 87–107.

Heine, Jorge. *The Last Cacique: Leadership and Politics in a Puerto Rican City*. Pittsburgh: University of Pittsburgh Press, 1993.

Helfgot, Joseph. *Professional Reforming: Mobilization for Youth and the Failure of Social Science*. Lexington, MA: Lexington, 1981.

Henderson, Errol A. "The Lumpenproletariat as Vanguard? The Black Panther Party, Social Transformation, and Pearson's Analysis of Huey Newton." *Journal of Black Studies* 28.2 (1997): 171–99.

Henton, Douglas, John Melville, and Kim Walesh. *Civic Revolutionaries: Igniting the Passion for Change in America's Communities*. San Francisco: Jossey-Bass, 2004.

Herbstein, Judith. "The Politicization of Puerto Rican Ethnicity in New York, 1955–1975." *Ethnic Groups* 5 (July 1983): 31–54.

——. "Rituals and Politics of the Puerto Rican 'Community' in New York City." PhD diss., City University of New York, 1978.

History Task Force, Centro de Estudios Puertorriqueños. *Labor Migration under Capitalism: The Puerto Rican Experience*. New York: Monthly Review, 1979.

Ho, Fred, ed., with Carolyn Antonio, Diane Fujino, and Steve Yip. *Legacy to Liberation: Politics and Culture of Revolutionary Asian Pacific America*. San Francisco: AK Press, 2000.

Ho, Fred, and Bill V. Mullen, eds. *Afro Asia: Revolutionary Political and Cultural Connections between African Americans and Asian Americans*. Durham: Duke University Press, 2008.

Ho, Karen. *Liquidated: An Ethnography of Wall Street*. Durham: Duke University Press, 2009.

Hoffman, Elizabeth Cobbs. *All You Need Is Love: The Peace Corps and the Spirit of the 1960s*. Cambridge: Harvard University Press, 1998.

Hogan, Wesley C. *Many Minds, One Heart: SNCC's Dream for a New America.* Chapel Hill: University of North Carolina Press, 2007.

Holdcraft, Lane E. "The Rise and Fall of Community Development in Developing Countries, 1950–65." Michigan State University Rural Development Papers, No. 2. East Lansing: Department of Agricultural Economics, Michigan State University, 1978.

Honig, Bonnie. *Democracy and the Foreigner.* Princeton: Princeton University Press, 2001.

Hosmer, Brian, and Colleen O'Neill, eds. *Native Pathways: Indian Culture and Economic Development in the Twentieth Century.* Boulder: University Press of Colorado, 2004.

Hunter, Charlayne. "On the Case in Resurrection City." In *The Transformation of Activism,* edited by August Meier, 5–28. Chicago: Aldine, 1970.

Hyatt, Susan Brin. "From Citizen to Volunteer: Neoliberal Governance and the Erasure of Poverty." In *The New Poverty Studies: The Ethnography of Power, Politics, and Impoverished People in the United States,* edited by Judith Goode and Jeff Maskovsky, 201–35. New York: NYU Press, 2001.

Isales, Carmen, and Fred Wale. "The Field Program." In "Community Change: An Action Program in Puerto Rico," edited by Charles F. Cannell, Fred G. Wale, and Stephen B. Withey, special issue, *Journal of Social Issues* 9.2 (1953): 23–42.

Iverson, Peter. *Diné: A History of the Navajos.* Albuquerque: University of New Mexico Press, 2002.

———. *The Navajo Nation.* Albuquerque: University of New Mexico Press, 1981.

Jackson, Henry E. *A Community Center: What It Is and How to Organize It.* New York: Macmillan, 1918.

———. "A Man without a Community." In *Rural Organization: Proceedings of the Third Annual National Country Life Conference, 1920,* 78–81. Chicago: University of Chicago Press for the American Country Life Association, 1921.

Jackson, Larry R., and William A. Johnson. *Protest by the Poor: The Welfare Rights Movement in New York City.* Lexington, MA: Lexington, 1974.

Jackson, Thomas F. *From Civil Rights to Human Rights: Martin Luther King, Jr., and the Struggle for Economic Justice.* Philadelphia: University of Pennsylvania Press, 2007.

James, Joy. *Resisting State Violence: Radicalism, Gender, and Race in U.S. Culture.* Minneapolis: University of Minnesota Press, 1996.

Jameson, Fredric. *The Political Unconscious: Narrative as a Socially Symbolic Act.* Ithaca: Cornell University Press, 1981.

Jennings, James. *Puerto Rican Politics in New York City.* Washington, D.C.: University Press of America, 1977.

Johnson, Broderick H. *Navaho Education at Rough Rock.* Rough Rock, AZ: Rough Rock Demonstration School, 1968.

Johnson, Lyndon B. "Annual Message to the Congress on the State of the Union." In

Public Papers of the Presidents of the United States: Lyndon B. Johnson, 1963–1964, 1:112–18. Washington, D.C.: Government Printing Office, 1965.

——. "Special Message to the Congress Proposing a Nationwide War on the Sources of Poverty." In *Public Papers of the Presidents of the United States: Lyndon B. Johnson, 1963–1964*, 1:375–80. Washington, D.C.: Government Printing Office, 1965.

Johnston, Robert D. *The Radical Middle Class: Populist Democracy and the Question of Capitalism in Progressive Era Portland, Oregon*. Princeton: Princeton University Press, 2003.

Jones, Gareth Stedman. *An End to Poverty? A Historical Debate*. New York: Columbia University Press, 2004.

Jones, Jacqueline. "The History and Politics of Poverty in Twentieth-Century America." In *Perspectives on Modern America*, edited by Harvard Sitkoff, 125–44. New York: Oxford University Press, 2001.

Kalyvas, Andreas, and Ira Katznelson. *Liberal Beginnings: Making a Republic for the Moderns*. Cambridge: Cambridge University Press, 2008.

Katz, Michael B. *The Undeserving Poor: From the War on Poverty to the War on Welfare*. New York: Pantheon, 1989.

Kelley, Robin D. G. *Freedom Dreams: The Black Radical Imagination*. Boston: Beacon, 2003.

Kelly, Brian. "Beyond the 'Talented Tenth': Black Elites, Black Workers, and the Limits of Accommodation in Industrial Birmingham, 1900–1921." In *Time Longer Than Rope: A Century of African American Activism, 1850–1950*, edited by Charles M. Payne and Adam Green, 276–301. New York: NYU Press, 2003.

Kelly, Rita Mae. *Community Participation in Directing Economic Development*. Cambridge, MA: Center for Community Economic Development, 1976.

——. *On Improving Police-Community Relations: Findings from the Conduct and Evaluation of an OEO-Funded Experiment in Washington, D.C.* Kensington, MD: American Institutes for Research, 1972.

Kennerley, Catherine Marsh. *Negociaciones culturales: Los intelectuales y el proyecto pedagógico del estado muñocista*. San Juan, PR: Callejón, 2009.

Kiffmeyer, Thomas. *Reformers to Radicals: The Appalachian Volunteers and the War on Poverty*. Lexington: University Press of Kentucky, 2008.

King, Clarence. *Organizing for Community Action*. New York: Harper and Brothers, 1948.

Kirgis, Frederic L., Jr. "The Degrees of Self-Determination in the United Nations Era." *American Journal of International Law* 88.2 (1994): 304–10.

Klein, Jennifer. *For All These Rights: Business, Labor, and the Shaping of America's Public-Private Welfare State*. Princeton: Princeton University Press, 2003.

Knapp, Daniel, and Kenneth Polk. *Scouting the War on Poverty: Social Reform Politics in the Kennedy Administration*. Lexington, MA: Heath Lexington, 1971.

Kobrin, Solomon. "The Chicago Area Project—A 25-Year Assessment." *Annals of the American Academy of Political and Social Science* 322 (March 1959): 19–29.

Kornbluh, Felicia. *The Battle for Welfare Rights: Politics and Poverty in Modern America.* Philadelphia: University of Pennsylvania Press, 2007.

Kotz, Nick, and Mary Lynn Kotz. *A Passion for Equality: George Wiley and the Movement.* New York: W. W. Norton, 1977.

Kramer, Ralph M. *Participation of the Poor: Comparative Case Studies in the War on Poverty.* Englewood Cliffs, NJ: Prentice-Hall, 1969.

Krauskopf, Jack. "New York City's Antipoverty Program." *City Almanac* 7.4 (1972): 1–13.

Krippner, Greta R. *Capitalizing on Crisis: The Political Origins of the Rise of Finance.* Cambridge: Harvard University Press, 2011.

Laó, Agustín. "Resources of Hope: Imagining the Young Lords and the Politics of Memory," *Centro Journal* 7.1 (1994–95): 34–49.

Lapp, Michael. "Managing Migration: The Migration Division of Puerto Rico and Puerto Ricans in New York City, 1948–1968." PhD diss., Johns Hopkins University, 1990.

Latham, Michael. *Modernization as Ideology: American Social Science and "Nation Building" in the Kennedy Era.* Chapel Hill: University of North Carolina Press, 2000.

Latham, Robert. *The Liberal Moment: Modernity, Security, and the Making of the Postwar International Order.* New York: Columbia University Press, 1997.

Lauria-Pericelli, Antonio. "Images and Contradictions: DIVEDCO's Portrayal of Puerto Rican Life." *Centro Journal* 3.1 (1990–91): 92–96.

Lazarus, Sylvain. "Lenin and the Party, 1902–November 1917." In *Lenin Reloaded: Toward a Politics of Truth,* edited by Sebastian Budgen, Stathis Kouvelakis, and Slavoj Žižek, 255–68. Durham: Duke University Press, 2007.

Leitner, Helga, Jamie Peck, and Eric Sheppard, eds. *Contesting Neoliberalism: Urban Frontiers.* New York: Guilford, 2007.

Lenin, V. I. "What Is to Be Done?" In *Essential Works of Lenin,* edited by Henry M. Christman, 53–175. New York: Dover, 1987.

Levy, Peter B. *The New Left and Labor in the 1960s.* Urbana: University of Illinois Press, 1994.

Lewis, Gordon K. *Puerto Rico: Freedom and Power in the Caribbean.* New York: Monthly Review, 1963.

Lewis, Helen M., Linda Johnson, and Don Askins, eds. *Colonialism in Modern America: The Appalachian Case.* Boone, NC: Appalachian Consortium, 1978.

Lewis, Oscar. *Five Families: Mexican Case Studies in the Culture of Poverty.* New York: Basic, 1959.

Lewis, W. Arthur. *The Theory of Economic Growth.* Homewood, IL: R. D. Irwin, 1955.

Light, Jennifer. *From Warfare to Welfare: Defense Intellectuals and Urban Problems in Cold War America.* Baltimore: Johns Hopkins University Press, 2003.

Lindeman, Eduard. *The Community: An Introduction to the Study of Community Leadership and Organization.* New York: Association Press, 1921.

Lopez, Alfredo. *The Puerto Rican Papers: Notes on the Re-Emergence of a Nation.* New York: Bobbs-Merrill, 1973.

Losurdo, Domenico. *Liberalism: A Counter-History.* New York: Verso, 2011.

Louis, William Roger, and Ronald Robinson. "The Imperialism of Decolonization." In William Roger Louis, *Ends of British Imperialism: The Scramble for Empire, Suez, and Decolonization; Collected Essays,* 451–502. London: I. B. Tauris, 2006.

Lowi, Theodore J. *The End of Liberalism: The Second Republic of the United States.* 2nd ed. New York: W. W. Norton, 1979.

Lowrie, S. Gale. "The Social Unit—An Experiment in Politics." *National Municipal Review* 9.9 (1920): 553–66.

MacDonald, Dwight. "Our Invisible Poor." *New Yorker,* January 19, 1963, 82–132.

MacDonald, Peter, with Ted Schwarz. *The Last Warrior: Peter MacDonald and the Navajo Nation.* New York: Orion, 1993.

MacFarlane, S. Neil. *Superpower Rivalry and Third World Radicalism: The Idea of National Liberation.* London: Croom Helm, 1985.

Maeda, Daryl J. *Chains of Babylon: The Rise of Asian America.* Minneapolis: University of Minnesota Press, 2009.

Maldonado, A. W. *Teodoro Moscoso and Puerto Rico's Operation Bootstrap.* Gainesville: University of Florida Press, 1997.

Mamoria, C. B. *Co-Operation, Community Development, and Village Panchayats in India.* Allahabad, India: Kitab Mahal, 1966.

Manela, Erez. *The Wilsonian Moment: Self-Determination and the International Origins of Anticolonial Nationalism.* New York: Oxford University Press, 2007.

Marable, Manning. *Race, Reform, and Rebellion: The Second Reconstruction in Black America, 1945–1990.* 2nd ed. Jackson: University Press of Mississippi, 1991.

Markell, Patchen. *Bound by Recognition.* Princeton: Princeton University Press, 2003.

Marqués, René. "Literary Pessimism and Political Optimism." 1959. In René Marqués, *The Docile Puerto Rican: Essays,* 3–26. Translated by Barbara Bockus Aponte. Philadelphia: Temple University Press, 1976.

——. "Writing for a Community Education Programme." *UNESCO Reports and Papers on Mass Communication* 24 (November 1957): 5–11.

Marris, Peter, and Martin Rein. *Dilemmas of Social Reform: Poverty and Community Action in the United States.* 2nd ed. Chicago: University of Chicago Press, 1973.

Martinez, Elizabeth "Betita." "A View from New Mexico: Recollections of the Movimiento Left." *Monthly Review* 54.3 (2002): 79–86.

Matusow, Allen J. *The Unraveling of America: A History of Liberalism in the 1960s.* New York: Harper and Row, 1984.

Mayer, Margit. "The Onward Sweep of Social Capital: Causes and Consequences for Understanding Cities, Communities, and Urban Movements." *International Journal of Urban and Regional Research* 27.1 (2003): 110–32.

McCarty, Teresa L. *A Place to Be Navajo: Rough Rock and the Struggle for Self-Determination in Indigenous Schooling.* Mahwah, NJ: Lawrence Erlbaum Associates, 2002.

McGerr, Michael E. *A Fierce Discontent: The Rise and Fall of the Progressive Movement in America*. New York: Free Press, 2003.

McKnight, Gerald D. *The Last Crusade: Martin Luther King, Jr., the FBI, and the Poor People's Campaign*. Boulder, CO: Westview, 1998.

McNickle, D'Arcy. "U.S. Indian Affairs—1953." *América Indígena* 13 (October 1953): 263–73.

Mead, Margaret. *Cultural Patterns and Technical Change*. New York: Mentor, 1955.

Mehta, Uday Singh. *Liberalism and Empire: A Study in Nineteenth-Century British Liberal Thought*. Chicago: University of Chicago Press, 1999.

Meissner, Hanna H., ed. *Poverty in the Affluent Society*. New York: Harper and Row, 1966.

Melamed, Jodi. "The Spirit of Neoliberalism: From Racial Liberalism to Neoliberal Multiculturalism." *Social Text* 89 (Winter 2006): 1–24.

Melendez, Miguel "Mickey." *We Took the Streets: Fighting for Latino Rights with the Young Lords*. New York: St. Martin's, 2003.

Mennel, Robert M. "Attitudes and Policies toward Juvenile Delinquency in the United States." *Crime & Justice* 4 (1983): 191–224.

Merrill, Dennis. *Bread and the Ballot: The United States and India's Economic Development, 1947–1963*. Chapel Hill: University of North Carolina, 1990.

Mettler, Suzanne. *Dividing Citizens: Gender and Federalism in New Deal Public Policy*. Ithaca: Cornell University Press, 1998.

Mignolo, Walter D. *Local Histories/Global Designs: Coloniality, Subaltern Knowledges, and Border Thinking*. Princeton: Princeton University Press, 2000.

Milkis, Sidney M., and Jerome M. Mileur, eds. *The Great Society and the High Tide of Liberalism*. Amherst: University of Massachusetts Press, 2005.

Miller, Peter, and Nikolas Rose. *Governing the Present: Administering Economic, Social and Personal Life*. Malden, MA: Polity, 2008.

Mink, Gwendolyn. *The Wages of Motherhood: Inequality in the Welfare State, 1917–1942*. Ithaca: Cornell University Press, 1995.

Mitchell, Timothy. "Economists and the Economy in the Twentieth Century." In *The Politics of Method in the Human Sciences: Positivism and Its Epistemological Others*, edited by George Steinmetz, 126–41. Durham: Duke University Press, 2005.

——. "Origins and Limits of the Modern Idea of the Economy." Paper presented at the Workshop on Positivism and Post-Positivism, University of Chicago, October 2001.

——. *Rule of Experts: Egypt, Techno-Politics, Modernity*. Berkeley: University of California Press, 2002.

Mkandawire, Thandike. " 'Good Governance': The Itinerary of an Idea." *Development in Practice* 17.4–5 (2007): 679–81.

Mobilization for Youth. *A Proposal for the Prevention and Control of Delinquency by Expanding Opportunities*. New York: Mobilization for Youth, 1961.

Montgomery, Charles. *The Spanish Redemption: Heritage, Power, and Loss on New Mexico's Upper Rio Grande*. Berkeley: University of California Press, 2002.

Montrie, Chad. *To Save the Land and People: A History of Opposition to Surface Coal Mining in Appalachia*. Chapel Hill: University of North Carolina Press, 2003.

Mooney-Melvin, Patricia. *The Organic City: Urban Definition and Community Organization, 1880–1920*. Lexington: University Press of Kentucky, 1987.

Moore, John E. "Controlling Delinquency: Executive, Congressional, and Juvenile, 1961–1964." In *Congress and Urban Problems*, edited by Frederic N. Cleaveland, 110–72. Washington, D.C.: Brookings Institution, 1969.

Moore, Mick. "Empowerment at Last?" *Journal of International Development* 13.3 (2001): 321–29.

Morales, Iris. "¡Palante, Siempre Palante! The Young Lords." In *The Puerto Rican Movement: Voices from the Diaspora*, edited by Andrés Torres and José E. Velázquez, 210–27. Philadelphia: Temple University Press, 1998.

Moraña, Mabel, Enrique Dussel, and Carlos A. Jáuregui, eds. *Coloniality at Large: Latin America and the Postcolonial Debate*. Durham: Duke University Press, 2008.

Mottel, Syeus. *Charas: The Improbable Dome Builders*. New York: Drake, 1973.

Mouffe, Chantal. *The Return of the Political*. New York: Verso, 1993.

Moynihan, Daniel P. *Maximum Feasible Misunderstanding: Community Action in the War on Poverty*. New York: Free Press, 1969.

——. "What Is 'Community Action'?" *Public Interest* 5 (Fall 1966): 3–8.

Muñoz Amato, Pedro. "Congressional Conservatism and Puerto Rican Democracy in the Commonwealth Relationship." *Revista Juridica de la Universidad de Puerto Rico* 21.4 (1952): 321–36.

Murphy, Craig N. *Global Institutions, Marginalization, and Development*. New York: Routledge, 2005.

Myrdal, Gunnar. *The Challenge to Affluence*. New York: Pantheon, 1962.

Nabokov, Peter. *Tijerina and the Courthouse Raid*. Albuquerque: University of New Mexico Press, 1969.

Nadasen, Premilla. *Welfare Warriors: The Welfare Rights Movement in the United States*. New York: Routledge, 2005.

Nancy, Jean-Luc. *The Inoperative Community*. Edited and translated by Peter Connor. Minneapolis: University of Minnesota Press, 1991.

——. "Of Being-in-Common." In *Community at Loose Ends*, edited by the Miami Theory Collective, 1–12. Translated by James Creech. Minneapolis: University of Minnesota Press, 1991.

——. *The Truth of Democracy*. Translated by Pascale-Anne Brault and Michael Naas. New York: Fordham University Press, 2010.

Näsström, Sofia. "The Legitimacy of the People." *Political Theory* 35.5 (2007): 624–58.

National Action/Research on the Military-Industrial Complex. *Police on the Homefront: They're Bringing It All Back*. Philadelphia: National Action/Research on the Military-Industrial Complex, 1971.

National Advisory Commission on Civil Disorders. *Report of the National Advisory Commission on Civil Disorders*. New York: E. P. Dutton, 1968.

National Advisory Committee on Rural Poverty. *Rural Poverty: Hearings before the National Advisory Committee on Rural Poverty: Memphis, Tennessee, February 2 and 3, 1967*. Washington, D.C.: Government Printing Office, 1967.

National Conference of Youth Organizations United. *A Report by the Center for the Study of Crime, Delinquency, and Corrections, Southern Illinois University*. Edwardsville: Southern Illinois University, 1968.

Nelson, Alondra. *Body and Soul: The Black Panther Party and the Fight against Medical Discrimination*. Minneapolis: University of Minnesota Press, 2011.

Nelson, Jennifer. *Women of Color and the Reproductive Rights Movement*. New York: NYU Press, 2003.

New York State Special Commission on Attica. *Attica: The Official Report*. New York: Praeger, 1972.

Newton, Huey P. "Intercommunalism." In Erik H. Erikson and Huey P. Newton, *In Search of Common Ground*, 23–43. New York: W. W. Norton, 1973.

———. "Message to the Vietnamese." In *The Coming of the New International*, edited by John Gerassi, 593–95. New York: World, 1971.

———. "We Are Nationalists and Internationalists." In *The Coming of the New International*, edited by John Gerassi, 563–68. New York: World, 1971.

Oberg, Kalervo. "Community Development Programs in Puerto Rico." *Community Development Review* 1 (January 1956): 55–61.

———. "Culture Shock: Adjustment to New Cultural Environments." *Practical Anthropology* 7.4 (1960): 177–82.

Obermiller, Phillip J. "The Question of Appalachian Ethnicity." In *The Invisible Minority: Urban Appalachians*, edited by William W. Philliber and Clyde B. McCoy, 9–19. Lexington: University Press of Kentucky, 1981.

O'Connor, Alice. "Community Action, Urban Reform, and the Fight against Poverty: The Ford Foundation's Gray Areas Program." *Journal of Urban History* 22 (July 1996): 586–625.

———. *Poverty Knowledge: Social Science, Social Policy, and the Poor in Twentieth-Century U.S. History*. Princeton: Princeton University Press, 2001.

O'Connor, James. "Towards a Theory of Community Unions." *Studies on the Left* 4.2 (1964): 143–48.

———. "Towards a Theory of Community Unions II." *Studies on the Left* 4.3 (1964): 99–102.

Odem, Mary. *Delinquent Daughters: Protecting and Policing Adolescent Female Sexuality in the United States, 1885–1920*. Chapel Hill: University of North Carolina Press, 1995.

Office of Navajo Economic Development. *ONEO Handbook*. Fort Defiance, AZ: Office of Navajo Economic Development, 1972.

Office of Navajo Economic Opportunity. *A History and a Semi-Annual Report*. Fort Defiance, AZ: Office of Navajo Economic Opportunity, 1968.

Ogbar, Jeffrey O. G. *Black Power: Radical Politics and African American Identity*. Baltimore: Johns Hopkins University Press, 2005.

Oliver, Denise. "Colonized Mentality and Non-Conscious Ideology." In *The Ideology of the Young Lords Party*, 26–32. Bronx, NY: National Headquarters of the Young Lords Party, 1972.

Omi, Michael, and Howard Winant. *Racial Formation in the United States: From the 1960s to the 1980s*. New York: Routledge, 1986.

O'Reilly, Kenneth. "The FBI and the Politics of the Riots, 1964–1968." *Journal of American History* 75.1 (1988): 91–114.

Orleck, Annelise. *Storming Caesars Palace: How Black Mothers Fought Their Own War on Poverty*. Boston: Beacon, 2005.

Ornati, Oscar. *Poverty amid Affluence*. New York: Twentieth Century Fund, 1966.

Orshansky, Mollie. "Counting the Poor: Another Look at the Poverty Profile." *Social Security Bulletin* 28 (January 1965): 3–29.

———. "Recounting the Poor: A Five Year Review." *Social Security Bulletin* 29 (April 1966): 2–19.

———. "Who's Who among the Poor: A Demographic View of Poverty." *Social Security Bulletin* 28 (July 1965): 3–32.

Ortiz, Vilma. "Changes in the Characteristics of Puerto Rican Migrants from 1955 to 1980." *International Migration Review* 20.3 (1986): 612–28.

Padilla, Felix M. *Puerto Rican Chicago*. Notre Dame, IN: University of Notre Dame Press, 1987.

Pagano, Jules. *Education in the Peace Corps: Evolving Concepts of Volunteer Training*. Boston: Boston University Center for the Study of Liberal Education for Adults, 1965.

Pantoja, Antonia. *Memoir of a Visionary*. Houston: Arte Público, 2002.

———. "Puerto Ricans in New York: A Historical and Community Development Perspective." *Centro Journal* 2.5 (1989): 21–31.

Pantojas-García, Emilio. *Development Strategies as Ideology: Puerto Rico's Export-Led Industrialization Experience*. Boulder, CO: Lynne Rienner, 1990.

Parmelee, Maurice. *Poverty and Social Progress*. New York: Macmillan, 1916.

"Participation of the Poor: Section 202(a) (3) Organization under the Economic Opportunity Act of 1964." *Yale Law Journal* 75.4 (1966): 599–629.

Pateman, Carole. *Participation and Democratic Theory*. Cambridge: Cambridge University Press, 1970.

Patterson, James T. *America's Struggle against Poverty in the Twentieth Century*. Cambridge: Harvard University Press, 2000.

Peace Corps. *Second Annual Report*. Washington, D.C.: Peace Corps Office of Public Affairs, 1963.

"Peace Corps: Negroes Play Vital Role in U.S. Quest for Friends Abroad." *Ebony*, November 1961, 38–40.

"Peace Corps Training at Howard: Negro University Prepares Interracial Group for U.S. Good-Will Missions Abroad." *Ebony*, November 1962, 69–77.

Peck, Jamie. *Constructions of Neoliberalism*. New York: Oxford University Press, 2010.

Peirce, Neal R., and Carol F. Steinbach. *Corrective Capitalism: The Rise of America's Community Development Corporations*. New York: Ford Foundation, 1987.

Perez Quintana, Waldemar. "An Oral History of the Division of Community Education of Puerto Rico from 1949 to the Present: The Perspective of Eight Puerto Rican Educators." PhD diss., Pennsylvania State University, 1984.

Perloff, Harvey. *Puerto Rico's Economic Future: A Study in Planned Development*. Chicago: University of Chicago Press, 1950.

Perry, Huey. *"They'll Cut Off Your Project": A Mingo County Chronicle*. New York: Praeger, 1972.

Phillips, Wilbur C. *Adventuring for Democracy*. New York: Social Unit Press, 1940.

Philp, Kenneth R. *Termination Revisited: American Indians and the Trail to Self-Determination, 1933–1953*. Lincoln: University of Nebraska Press, 1999.

Piven, Frances Fox. "The New Urban Programs: The Strategy of Federal Intervention." In *The Politics of Turmoil: Essays on Poverty, Race, and the Urban Crisis*, 284–313. New York: Pantheon, 1974.

Platt, Anthony M. *The Child Savers: The Invention of Delinquency*. 2nd ed. Chicago: University of Chicago Press, 1977.

Plotke, David. *Building a Democratic Political Order: Reshaping American Liberalism in the 1930s and 1940s*. Cambridge: Cambridge University Press, 1996.

Plummer, Brenda Gayle. *Rising Wind: Black Americans and U.S. Foreign Affairs, 1935–1960*. Chapel Hill: University of North Carolina Press, 1996.

Polanyi, Karl. *The Great Transformation: The Political and Economic Origins of Our Time*. 1944. Boston: Beacon Press, 1957.

Polsby, Nelson W. *Community Power and Political Theory*. New Haven: Yale University Press, 1963.

Poole, Mary. *The Segregated Origins of Social Security: African Americans and the Welfare State*. Chapel Hill: University of North Carolina Press, 2006.

Postero, Nancy Grey. *Now We Are Citizens: Indigenous Politics in Postmulticultural Bolivia*. Stanford: Stanford University Press, 2007.

Poston, Richard W. *Democracy Speaks Many Tongues*. New York: Harper and Bros., 1962.

———. *The Gang and the Establishment*. New York: Harper and Row, 1971.

President's Commission on Law Enforcement and the Administration of Justice. *National Survey of Police and Community Relations*. Washington, D.C.: Government Printing Office, 1967.

Price, Stephen. "The Effect of Federal Anti-Poverty Programs and Policies on the Hasidic and Puerto Rican Communities of Williamsburg." PhD diss., Brandeis University, 1979.

Procacci, Giovanna. *Gouverner la misère: La question sociale en France, 1789–1848*. Paris: Seuil, 1993.

———. "Governing Poverty: Sources of the Social Question in Nineteenth-Century France." In *Foucault and the Writing of History*, edited by Jan Goldstein, 206–19. Cambridge: Blackwell, 1994.

——. "Social Economy and the Government of Poverty." In *The Foucault Effect: Studies in Governmentality*, edited by Graham Burchell, Colin Gordon, and Peter Miller, 151–68. Chicago: University of Chicago Press, 1991.

Un Programa de Educacion de la Communidad en Puerto Rico/Community Education Program in Puerto Rico. New York: RCA International Division, n.d.

Puerto Rican Forum. *The Puerto Rican Community Development Project: A Proposal for a Self-Help Project to Develop the Community by Strengthening the Family, Opening Opportunities for Youth, and Making Full Use of Education*. 1964. New York: Arno, 1975.

Puerto Rican Revolutionary Workers Organization (Young Lords Party). "Analysis of 3-Year History of YLP." In *Resolutions and Speeches, First Congress*, 3–17. New York: Puerto Rican Revolutionary Workers Organization, 1972.

——. "Our Tasks." In *Resolutions and Speeches, First Congress*, 30–33. New York: Puerto Rican Revolutionary Workers Organization, 1972.

Pulido, Laura. *Black, Brown, Yellow, and Left: Radical Activism in Los Angeles*. Berkeley: University of California Press, 2006.

Quadagno, Jill. *The Color of Welfare: How Racism Undermined the War on Poverty*. New York: Oxford University Press, 1994.

Quijano, Anibal. "Coloniality of Power, Eurocentrism, and Latin America." *Nepantla* 1.3 (2000): 533–80.

Radhakrishnan, Sarvepalli. Foreword. In *Approaches to Community Development*, edited by Phillips Ruopp, vii–viii. The Hague: W. Van Hoeve, 1953.

Radice, Hugo. "The National Economy: A Keynesian Myth?" *Capital and Class* 22 (Spring 1984): 111–40.

Rahnema, Majid. "Global Poverty: A Pauperizing Myth." *Interculture* 24.2 (1991): 4–51.

The Rainbow Coalition. "The Rainbow Food Program." In *From the Movement toward Revolution*, edited by Bruce Franklin, 112–13. New York: Van Nostrand Reinhold, 1971.

Rajagopal, Balakrishnan. *International Law from Below: Development, Social Movements, and Third World Resistance*. Cambridge: Cambridge University Press, 2003.

Ralph, James R., Jr. *Northern Protest: Martin Luther King, Jr., Chicago, and the Civil Rights Movement*. Cambridge: Harvard University Press, 1993.

Rancière, Jacques. *Hatred of Democracy*. Translated by Steve Corcoran. New York: Verso, 2006.

Redfield, Marc. "Imagi-Nation: The Imagined Community and the Aesthetics of Mourning." In *Grounds of Comparison: Around the Work of Benedict Anderson*, edited by Jonathan Culler and Pheng Cheah, 75–105. New York: Routledge, 2003.

Reuss, Henry S. "A Point Four Youth Corps." In *The Peace Corps*, edited by Pauline Madow, 10–16. New York: H. W. Wilson, 1964.

Rice, Gerald T. *The Bold Experiment: JFK's Peace Corps*. Notre Dame, IN: University of Notre Dame Press, 1985.

Rice, Jon F. "Black Radicalism on Chicago's West Side: A History of the Illinois Black Panther Party." PhD diss., Northern Illinois University, 1998.

Riggs, Christopher. "Indians, Liberalism, and Johnson's Great Society, 1963–1969." PhD diss., University of Colorado, 1997.

Rist, Gilbert. *The History of Development: From Western Origins to Global Faith*. London: Zed, 1997.

Rivera, José A. *Acequia Culture: Water, Land and Community in the Southwest*. Albuquerque: University of New Mexico Press, 1998.

Robin, Gerald D. "Anti-Poverty Programs and Delinquency." *Journal of Criminal Law, Criminology, and Police Science* 60.3 (1969): 323–31.

Robinson, Cedric J. *Black Marxism: The Making of the Black Radical Tradition*. 1983. Chapel Hill: University of North Carolina Press, 2000.

Rockman, Seth. *Scraping By: Wage Labor, Slavery, and Survival in Early Baltimore*. Baltimore: Johns Hopkins University Press, 2009.

Rodgers, Daniel T. *Atlantic Crossings: Social Politics in a Progressive Age*. Cambridge: Harvard University Press, 1998.

——. *The Work Ethic in Industrial America, 1850–1920*. Chicago: University of Chicago Press, 1978.

Rodríguez, Zacarías. "A Village Becomes a Community." *Fundamental and Adult Education* 5.2 (1953): 58–63.

Rodriguez-Fraticelli, Carlos, and Amilcar Tirado. "Notes towards a History of Puerto Rican Community Organizations in New York City." *Centro Journal* 2.6 (1989): 35–47.

Rodríguez-Morazzani, Roberto P. "Political Cultures of the Puerto Rican Left in the United States." In *The Puerto Rican Movement: Voices from the Diaspora*, edited by Andrés Torres and José E. Velázquez, 25–47. Philadelphia: Temple University Press, 1998.

——. "Puerto Rican Political Generations in New York: Pioneros, Young Turks, and Radicals." *Centro Journal* 4.1 (1992): 97–116.

Roediger, David. *The Wages of Whiteness: Race and the Making of the American Working Class*. New York: Verso, 1991.

Roessel, Robert A. *Navajo Education in Action*. Chinle, AZ: Navajo Curriculum Center, 1977.

Rosemblatt, Karin Alejandra. "Other Americas: Transnationalism, Scholarship, and the Culture of Poverty in Mexico and the United States." *Hispanic American Historical Review* 89.4 (2009): 603–41.

Rosen, George. *A History of Public Health*. New York: MD Publications, 1958.

Rosenbloom, Nancy J. "From Regulation to Censorship: Film and Political Culture in New York in the Early Twentieth Century." *Journal of the Gilded Age and Progressive Era* 3.4 (2004): 369–406.

——. "In Defense of the Moving Pictures: The People's Institute, the National Board of Censorship, and the Problem of Leisure in Urban America." *American Studies* 33.2 (1992): 41–60.

Ross, Andrew. *Real Love: In Pursuit of Cultural Justice.* New York: NYU Press, 1998.

Rossinow, Doug. *Visions of Progress: The Left-Liberal Tradition in America.* Philadelphia: University of Pennsylvania Press, 2008.

Rostow, W. W. *The Stages of Economic Growth: A Non-Communist Manifesto.* Cambridge: Cambridge University Press, 1960.

Rothstein, Richard. "ERAP: Evolution of the Organizers." *Radical America* 2.2 (1968): 1–18.

Roxborough, Ian. "Cold War, Capital Accumulation, and Labor Control in Latin America: The Closing of a Cycle, 1945–1990." In *Rethinking the Cold War*, edited by Allen Hunter, 117–32. Philadelphia: Temple University Press, 1998.

Roy, Ananya. *Poverty Capital: Microfinance and the Making of Development.* New York: Routledge, 2010.

Rubin, Lillian B. "Maximum Feasible Participation: The Origins, Implications, and Present Status." *Annals of the American Academy of Political and Social Science* 385 (September 1969): 14–29.

Ruopp, Phillips. "Approaches to Community Development." In *Approaches to Community Development*, edited by Phillips Ruopp, 1–20. The Hague: W. Van Hoeve, 1953.

Russell, Judith. *Economics, Bureaucracy, and Race: How Keynesians Misguided the War on Poverty.* New York: Columbia University Press, 2004.

Ryan, David, and Victor Pungong, eds. *The United States and Decolonization: Power and Freedom.* New York: St. Martin's, 2000.

Sabater, Julio. "Discussion Group Report." In *Puerto Ricans Confront Problems of the Complex Urban Society: A Design for Change*, 181–83. New York: High School of Art and Design, 1967.

Saldaña-Portillo, María Josefina. *The Revolutionary Imagination in the Americas and the Age of Development.* Durham: Duke University Press, 2003.

———. " 'Wavering on the Horizon of Social Being': The Treaty of Guadalupe-Hidalgo and the Legacy of Its Racial Character in Paredes's *George Washington Gómez*." *Radical History Review* 89 (Spring 2004): 135–64.

Sale, Richard T. *The Blackstone Rangers: A Reporter's Account of Time Spent with the Street Gang on Chicago's South Side.* New York: Random House, 1971.

Sales, William W., Jr. *From Civil Rights to Black Liberation: Malcolm X and the Organization of Afro-American Unity.* Boston: South End Press, 1994.

Sales, William W., Jr., and Rod Bush. "The Political Awakening of Blacks and Latinos in New York City: Competition or Cooperation?" *Social Justice* 27.1 (2000): 19–42.

Sánchez Korrol, Virginia. *From Colonia to Community: The History of Puerto Ricans in New York City, 1917–1948.* Westport, CT: Greenwood, 1983.

Santiago-Valles, Kelvin A. "The Unruly City and the Mental Landscape of Colonized Identities: Internally Contested Nationality in Puerto Rico, 1945–1985." *Social Text* 38 (Spring 1994): 149–63.

Saull, Richard. *The Cold War and After: Capitalism, Revolution and Superpower Politics*. London: Pluto, 2007.

Schaffer, Ronald. *America in the Great War: The Rise of the War Welfare State*. New York: Oxford University Press, 1991.

Schambra, William A. "Is New Federalism the Wave of the Future?" In *The Great Society and Its Legacy*, edited by Marshall Kaplan and Peggy L. Cuciti, 24–31. Durham: Duke University Press, 1986.

Schlossman, Steven, and Michael Sedlak. *The Chicago Area Project Revisited*. Santa Monica, CA: RAND, 1983.

Schneider, Eric C. *Vampires, Dragons, and Egyptian Kings: Youth Gangs in Postwar New York*. Princeton: Princeton University Press, 1999.

Schram, Sanford F. *Praxis for the Poor: Piven and Cloward and the Future of Social Science in Social Welfare*. Minneapolis: University of Minnesota Press, 2002.

——. *Welfare Discipline: Discourse, Governance, and Globalization*. Philadelphia: Temple University Press, 2006.

Seda, Eduardo. *Social Change and Personality in a Puerto Rican Agrarian Reform Community*. Evanston, IL: Northwestern University Press, 1973.

Seligman, Ben B., ed. *Poverty as a Public Issue*. New York: Free Press, 1965.

SenGupta, Gunja. *From Slavery to Poverty: The Racial Origins of Welfare in New York, 1840–1918*. New York: NYU Press, 2009.

Shaffer, Anatole. "The Cincinnati Social Unit Experiment, 1917–19." *Social Service Review* 45.2 (1971): 159–72.

Shaw, Clifford R. *The Jack-Roller: A Delinquent Boy's Own Story*. Chicago: University of Chicago Press, 1930.

Shaw, Clifford R., with Frederick M. Zorbaugh, Henry D. McKay, and Leonard S. Cottrell. *Delinquency Areas: Study of the Geographical Distribution of School Truants, Juvenile Delinquents, and Adult Offenders in Chicago*. Chicago: University of Chicago Press, 1929.

Shelby, Gertrude Matthews. "Extending Democracy: What the Cincinnati Social Unit Has Accomplished." *Harper's*, April 1920, 688–95.

Shepardson, Mary. "Navajo Tribe Factionalism and the Outside World." In *Apachean Culture History and Ethnology*, edited by Keith H. Basso and Morris E. Opler, 83–89. Tucson: University of Arizona Press, 1971.

——. *Navajo Ways in Government: A Study in Political Process*. Menasha, WI: American Anthropological Association, 1963.

Sherry, Michael S. *In the Shadow of War: The United States since the 1930s*. New Haven: Yale University Press, 1995.

Silko, Leslie Marmon. *Yellow Woman and a Beauty of the Spirit*. New York: Simon and Schuster, 1996.

Silva, Denise Ferreira da. *Toward a Global Idea of Race*. Minneapolis: University of Minnesota Press, 2007.

Simon, Jonathan. *Governing through Crime: How the War on Crime Transformed*

American Democracy and Created a Culture of Fear. New York: Oxford University Press, 2007.

Simon, William H. *The Community Economic Development Movement: Law, Business, and the New Social Policy.* Durham: Duke University Press, 2001.

Sinclair, Hamish. "Hazard, KY: Document of the Struggle." *Radical America* 2.1 (1968): 1–24.

Singh, Nikhil Pal. *Black Is a Country: Race and the Unfinished Struggle for Democracy.* Cambridge: Harvard University Press, 2004.

Sklar, Kathryn Kish. *Florence Kelley and the Nation's Work: The Rise of Women's Political Culture.* New Haven: Yale University Press, 1995.

Skurski, Julie, and Fernando Coronil. "States of Violence and the Violence of States." In *States of Violence,* edited by Fernando Coronil and Julie Skurski, 1–32. Ann Arbor: University of Michigan Press, 2006.

Smith, Anna Marie. *Welfare Reform and Sexual Regulation.* Cambridge: Cambridge University Press, 2007.

Smith, Barbara Ellen. "De-Gradations of Whiteness: Appalachia and the Complexities of Race." *Journal of Appalachian Studies* 10.1–2 (2004): 38–57.

Smith, Charles Sprague. "The Peoples' Institute of New York and Its Work for the Development of Citizenship along Democratic Lines." *Arena,* July 1907, 49–52.

——. *Working with the People.* New York: A. Wessells, 1904.

Smith, Dean Howard. *Modern Tribal Development: Paths to Self-Sufficiency and Cultural Integrity in Indian Country.* Walnut Creek, CA: AltaMira, 2000.

Smith, Jason Scott. *Building New Deal Liberalism: The Political Economy of Public Works, 1933–1956.* Cambridge: Cambridge University Press, 2006.

Smith, Jennifer B. *An International History of the Black Panther Party.* New York: Garland, 1999.

Smith, Sam. *Captive Capital: Colonial Life in Modern Washington.* Bloomington: Indiana University Press, 1974.

Sonnie, Amy, and James Tracy, "Uptown's JOIN Community Union from 1964–1966." *AREA Chicago,* December 2008, 26–28.

Southside Community Committee. *Bright Shadows in Bronzetown: The Story of the Southside Community Committee.* Chicago: Southside Community Committee, 1949.

Sparrow, Bartholomew H. *The Insular Cases and the Emergence of American Empire.* Lawrence: University Press of Kansas, 2006.

Spergel, Irving A. "Youth Gangs and Urban Riots." In *Riots and Rebellion: Civil Violence in the Urban Community,* edited by Louis H. Masotti and Don R. Bowen, 143–56. Beverly Hills, CA: Sage, 1968.

Spicer, Edward H. *Cycles of Conquest: The Impact of Spain, Mexico, and the United States on the Indians of the Southwest, 1533–1960.* Tucson: University of Arizona Press, 1962.

Spivak, Gayatri Chakravorty. "Can the Subaltern Speak?" In *Marxism and the Inter-*

pretation of Culture, edited by Lawrence Grossberg and Cary Nelson, 271–313. Urbana: University of Illinois Press, 1988.

——. *A Critique of Postcolonial Reason: Toward a History of the Vanishing Present.* Cambridge: Harvard University Press, 1999.

——. "In Response: Looking Back, Looking Forward." In *Can the Subaltern Speak? Reflections on the History of an Idea*, edited by Rosalind C. Morris, 227–36. New York: Columbia University Press, 2010.

Springer, Kimberly. *Living for the Revolution: Black Feminist Organizations, 1968–1980.* Durham: Duke University Press, 2005.

Statler, Kathryn, and Andrew Johns, eds. *The Eisenhower Administration, the Third World, and the Globalization of the Cold War.* Lanham, MD: Rowman and Littlefield, 2006.

Stead, William H. *Fomento: The Economic Development of Puerto Rico.* Washington, D.C.: National Planning Association, 1958.

Stears, Marc. *Demanding Democracy: American Radicals in Search of a New Politics.* Princeton: Princeton University Press, 2010.

Steinberg, Stephen. *The Ethnic Myth: Race, Ethnicity, and Class in America.* New York: Atheneum, 1981.

Steiner, Jesse F. "An Appraisal of the Community Movement." *Social Forces* 7.3 (1929): 333–42.

——. "Community Organization: A Study of Its Rise and Recent Tendencies." *Journal of Social Forces* 1.1 (1922): 11–18.

——. *Community Organization: A Study of Its Theory and Current Practice.* New York: Century, 1925.

Stoecker, Randy. "The CDC Model of Urban Redevelopment: A Critique and an Alternative." *Journal of Urban Affairs* 19:1 (1997): 1–22.

Stromquist, Shelton. *Reinventing 'The People': The Progressive Movement, the Class Problem, and the Origins of Modern Liberalism.* Urbana: University of Illinois Press, 2006.

Sullivan, George. *The Story of the Peace Corps.* New York: Fleet, 1964.

Sundquist, James L. *Politics and Policy: The Eisenhower, Kennedy, and Johnson Years.* Washington, D.C.: Brookings Institution, 1968.

"Symposium: Poor People's Movements." *Perspectives on Politics* 1.4 (2003): 707–35.

Tait, Vanessa. *Poor Workers' Unions: Rebuilding Labor from Below.* Cambridge, MA: South End Press, 2005.

Tanenhaus, David. *Juvenile Justice in the Making.* New York: Oxford University Press, 2004.

Textor, Robert B., ed. *Cultural Frontiers of the Peace Corps.* Cambridge: MIT Press, 1966.

Tharp, Everette. "The Appalachian Committee for Full Employment: Background and Purpose." *Appalachian South* 1 (Summer 1965): 44–46.

Thompson, Dorothy. "The Unit Plan of Health Administration." *National Municipal Review* 7.11 (1918): 596–99.

Thomsen, Moritz. *Living Poor: A Peace Corps Chronicle*. Seattle: University of Washington Press, 1969.

Tijerina, Reies López. *They Called Me "King Tiger": My Struggle for the Land and Our Rights*. Houston: Arte Público, 2000.

Torres, Andrés. *Between Melting Pot and Mosaic: African Americans and Puerto Ricans in the New York Political Economy*. Philadelphia: Temple University Press, 1995.

Tracy, James. "Rising Up: Poor, White, and Angry in the New Left." In *The Hidden 1970s: Histories of Radicalism*, edited by Dan Berger, 214–30. New Brunswick, NJ: Rutgers University Press, 2010.

Trolander, Judith Ann. *Professionalism and Social Change: From the Settlement House Movement to Neighborhood Centers*. New York: Columbia University Press, 1987.

Truman, David B. *The Governmental Process: Political Interests and Public Opinion*. New York: Knopf, 1951.

Truman, Harry S. "Inaugural Address, January 20, 1949." In *Public Papers of the Presidents of the United States: Harry S. Truman, 1949*, 112–16. Washington, D.C.: Government Printing Office, 1964.

Tullis, Tracy. "A Vietnam at Home: Policing the Ghettos in the Counterinsurgency Era." PhD diss., New York University, 1999.

Tyson, Timothy B. *Radio Free Dixie: Robert F. Williams and the Roots of Black Power*. Chapel Hill: University of North Carolina Press, 1999.

UK Colonial Office. *Community Development: A Handbook*. London: Her Majesty's Stationary Office, 1958.

UN Ad Hoc Group of Experts on Community Development. *Community Development and National Development*. New York: UN Department of Economic and Social Affairs, 1963.

UN Bureau of Social Affairs. *Social Progress through Community Development*. New York: United Nations, 1955.

UN Department of International Economic and Social Affairs. *Popular Participation as a Strategy for Promoting Community-Level Action and National Development*. New York: United Nations, 1981.

UN Office of Public Information. *The United Nations and Decolonization: Summary of the Work of the Special Committee of Twenty-Four*. New York: United Nations, 1965.

US Congress Joint Economic Committee. *Toward Economic Development for Native American Communities*. Washington, D.C.: Government Printing Office, 1969.

US Department of Labor. Office of Policy Planning and Research. *The Negro Family: The Case for National Action*. Washington, D.C.: Government Printing Office, 1965.

US Federal Security Agency, Social Security Administration, International Unit. *An Approach to Community Development*. Washington, D.C.: Government Printing Office, 1952.

US House Committee on Education and Labor. *Economic Opportunity Act Amend-*

ments of 1966: Report Together with Minority Views (to Accompany H.R. 15111). Washington, D.C.: Government Printing Office, 1966.

——. *Economic Opportunity Act Amendments of 1967: Hearings, 90th Congress, 1st, on H.R. 8311*. Washington, D.C.: Government Printing Office, 1967.

US International Cooperation Administration. "The Community Development Guidelines of the International Cooperation Administration." *Community Development Review* 3 (December 1956): 3–5.

——. *Report of the Interregional Conference on Community Development and Its Role in Nation Building, Seoul, Korea, May 6–12, 1961*. Washington, D.C.: US International Cooperation Administration, 1961.

US Senate. *Final Report of the Select Committee to Study Governmental Operations with Respect to Intelligence Activities*. Washington, D.C.: Government Printing Office, 1976.

US Senate Committee on Government Operations, Permanent Subcommittee on Investigations. *Conference on Problems Involved in the Poor People's March on Washington, D.C.* Washington, D.C.: Government Printing Office, 1968.

——. *Hearings: Riots, Civil and Criminal Disorders. 90th Congress, 1st Session*. Washington, D.C.: Government Printing Office, 1967.

——. *Hearings: Riots, Civil and Criminal Disorders. 91st Congress, 2nd Session*. Washington, D.C.: Government Printing Office, 1970.

US Senate Committee on Labor and Public Welfare, Select Subcommittee on Poverty. *The War on Poverty: The Economic Opportunity Act: A Compilation of Materials Relevant to S. 2642*. Washington, D.C.: Government Printing Office, 1964.

US Senate Committee on Labor and Public Welfare, Subcommittee on Employment, Manpower, and Poverty. *Hearings: Amendments to the Economic Opportunity Act of 1964*. Washington, D.C.: Government Printing Office, 1966.

US Senate Committee on the Judiciary. *Antiriot Bill—1967: Hearings on H.R. 421*. Washington, D.C.: Government Printing Office, 1967.

——. *Revolutionary Activities within the United States: The American Indian Movement : Hearing before the Subcommittee to Investigate the Administration of the Internal Security Act and Other Internal Security Laws*. Washington, D.C.: Government Printing Office, 1976.

US Senate Committee on the Judiciary, Subcommittee to Investigate the Administration of the Internal Security Act and Other Internal Security Laws. *The Puerto Rican Revolutionary Workers Organization: A Staff Study*. Washington, D.C.: Government Printing Office, 1976.

Vaughn, Roger. "The Real Great Society: Some Tough New York Slum Kids Team Up to Fight Poverty Instead of Themselves." *Life*, September 15, 1967, 76–91.

Vázquez-Calcerrada, P. B. "A Research Project on Rural Communities in Puerto Rico." *Rural Sociology* 18.3 (1953): 221–33.

Vigil, Ernesto B. *The Crusade for Justice: Chicano Militancy and the Government's War on Dissent*. Madison: University of Wisconsin Press, 1999.

Von Eschen, Penny. *Race against Empire: Black Americans and Anticolonialism, 1937–1957*. Ithaca: Cornell University Press, 1997.

Wale, Fred. "The Division of Community Education—An Overview." In "Community Change: An Action Program in Puerto Rico," edited by Charles F. Cannell, Fred G. Wale, and Stephen B. Withey, special issue, *Journal of Social Issues* 9.2 (1953): 11–22.

———. *Report of the Division of Community Education of the Department of Education: From July 1, 1949 to October 15, 1951*. San Juan, PR: Department of Education, 1952.

Wale, Fred, and Carmen Isales, *The Meaning of Community Development: A Report from the Division of Community Education*. San Juan, PR: Department of Education, 1967.

Walkowitz, Daniel J. *Working with Class: Social Workers and the Politics of Middle-Class Identity*. Chapel Hill: University of North Carolina Press, 1999.

Ward, Steven C. *Modernizing the Mind: Psychological Knowledge and the Remaking of Society*. Westport, CT: Praeger, 2002.

"We Have No Government." In *Black Protest: History, Documents, and Analyses*, edited by Joanne Grant, 501–5. Greenwich, CT: Fawcett, 1968.

Wei, William. *The Asian American Movement*. Philadelphia: Temple University Press, 1993.

Weisskoff, Richard. *Factories and Food Stamps: The Puerto Rican Model of Development*. Baltimore: Johns Hopkins University Press, 1985.

Weissman, Harold H., ed. *Community Development in the Mobilization for Youth Experience*. New York: Association Press, 1969.

———. "Overview of the Community Development Program." In *Community Development in the Mobilization for Youth Experience*, edited by Harold H. Weissman, 23–28. New York: Association Press, 1969.

Welborn, David M., and Jesse Burkehead, *Intergovernmental Relations in the American Administrative State: The Johnson Presidency*. Austin: University of Texas Press, 1989.

Weller, Jack E. *Yesterday's People: Life in Contemporary Appalachia*. Lexington: University of Kentucky Press, 1965.

Wells, Henry. *The Modernization of Puerto Rico: A Political Study of Changing Values and Institutions*. Cambridge: Harvard University Press, 1969.

West, Guida. *The National Welfare Rights Movement: The Social Protest of Poor Women*. New York: Praeger, 1981.

Westad, Odd Arne. *The Global Cold War: Third World Interventions and the Making of Our Times*. Cambridge: Cambridge University Press, 2005.

Whalen, Carmen Teresa. "Bridging Homeland and Barrio Politics: The Young Lords in Philadelphia." In *The Puerto Rican Movement: Voices from the Diaspora*, edited by Andrés Torres and José E. Velázquez, 107–23. Philadelphia: Temple University Press, 1998.

Whalen, Carmen Teresa, and Víctor Vázquez-Hernández, eds. *The Puerto Rican Diaspora: Historical Perspectives*. Philadelphia: Temple University Press, 2005.

Whisnant, David E. *Modernizing the Mountaineer: People, Power, and Planning in Appalachia*. Rev. ed. Knoxville: University of Tennessee Press, 1994.

Wight, Albert R., and Mary Anne Hammons. *Guidelines for Peace Corps Cross-Cultural Training*. 4 vols. Estes Park, CO: Center for Research and Education, 1970.

Wilkins, David E. *The Navajo Political Experience*. Rev. ed. Lanham, MD: Rowman and Littlefield, 2003.

Wilkins, David E., and K. Tsianina Lomawaima. *Uneven Ground: American Indian Sovereignty and Federal Law*. Norman: University of Oklahoma Press, 2001.

Will, Robert E., and Harold G. Vatter, *Poverty in Affluence: The Social, Political, and Economic Dimensions of Poverty in the United States*. New York: Harcourt, Brace and World, 1965.

Williams, Aubrey Willis, Jr. "The Function of the Chapter House System in Contemporary Navajo Political Structure." PhD diss., University of Arizona, 1965.

Williams, Robert A., Jr. *Like a Loaded Weapon: The Rehnquist Court, Indian Rights, and the Legal History of Racism in America*. Minneapolis: University of Minnesota Press, 2005.

Wilson, Gregory S. *Communities Left Behind: The Area Redevelopment Administration, 1945–1960*. Knoxville: University of Tennessee Press, 2009.

Withey, Stephen B., and Charles F. Cannell. Introduction. In "Community Change: An Action Program in Puerto Rico," edited by Charles F. Cannell, Fred G. Wale, and Stephen B. Withey, special issue, *Journal of Social Issues* 9.2 (1953): 2–3.

Wittman, Carl. "Students and Economic Action." In *The New Student Left: An Anthology*, edited by Mitchell Cohen and Dennis Hale, 170–80. Boston: Beacon, 1966.

Wittman, Carl, and Thomas Hayden. "An Interracial Movement of the Poor?" In *The New Student Left: An Anthology*, edited by Mitchell Cohen and Dennis Hale, 180–219. Boston: Beacon, 1966.

Wolcott, David, and Steven Schlossman. "In the Voices of Delinquents: Social Science, the Chicago Area Project, and a Boys' Culture of Casual Crime and Violence in the 1930s." In *When Science Encounters the Child*, edited by Barbara Beatty, Emily D. Cahan, and Julia Grant, 116–35. New York: Teachers College Press, 2006.

Woods, Robert A. "The Neighborhood in Social Reconstruction." *American Journal of Sociology* 19.5 (1914): 577–91.

Woodward, C. Vann. *Origins of the New South, 1877–1913*. Baton Rouge: Louisiana State University Press, 1951.

Young, Cynthia. *Soul Power: Culture, Radicalism, and the Making of a U.S. Third World Left*. Durham: Duke University Press, 2006.

Young, Robert W. "The Rise of the Navajo Tribe." In *Plural Society in the Southwest*, edited by Edward H. Spicer and Raymond H. Thompson, 167–238. Albuquerque: University of New Mexico Press, 1972.

Young Lords Party. "Position Paper on Women." *NACLA Newsletter* 14 (October 1970): 14–16.

Young Lords Party and Michael Abramson. *Palante: Young Lords Party*. New York: McGraw-Hill, 1971.

Yúdice, George. *The Expediency of Culture: Uses of Culture in the Global Era*. Durham: Duke University Press, 2003.

Zarefsky, David. *President Johnson's War on Poverty: Rhetoric and History*. Tuscaloosa: University of Alabama Press, 1986.

Zimmerman, Jonathan. "Beyond Double Consciousness: Black Peace Corps Volunteers in Africa, 1961–1971." *Journal of American History* 82.3 (1995): 999–1028.

Žižek, Slavoj. *Violence*. New York: Picador, 2008.

INDEX

community survival programs of, 214–18; global activities of, 233–43; Seniors Against a Fearful Environment (SAFE) program of, 217; UN initiatives of, 236–37, 242–43

Black Power Movement: emergence of, 111–12, 248; self-determination ideology and, 24

Black P. Stone Nation, 209–10

Blackstone Rangers, 142; antipoverty programs and, 209–13; coalition building by, 220–23; OEO and, 202–6, 311 n. 31

Boggs, James, 24

Bosque Redondo prison camp, 188, 306 n. 114

Bourne, Randolph, 38

Breathitt, Edward, 171

Bretton Woods Conference, 81

British Empire, Indian community development and, 59

British Guild Socialism, 46

"broad form" deeds, for mining rights, 162

Brock, Lawrence, 86

Brown Berets, 214, 219–20

Buckney, Edward L., 222

Burchell, Graham, 25

Bureau of Indian Affairs (BIA), 159, 185, 187–89, 194–96

Burgess, Ernest, 120

Bush, Rod, 183

Cabral, Amilcar, 238

Campos, Pedro Albizu, 200

Cannell, Charles F., 67–68

capitalism: community union project and, 164; conservative procapitalist reprisal and, 246–47; dependency and, 20–21, 263 n. 52; inequality and, 196–98; liberalism and, 148–53, 202–8, 245–47; neoclassical economics and, 16–17; poverty creation and, 13; racial formation of, 308 n. 3

Caribbean, colonialism and history of, 235

Carlton, Winslow, 123, 125

Carnegie Corporation, 89

Carter, Jimmy, 239–40

Catron, Thomas B., 93

Caudill, Henry, 169

census data, social unit plan and role of, 49–58

Charlo, Victor, 141

Cherokee Nation v. Georgia, 82–83

Chicago Area Project, 119–22, 149

Chicago Freedom Movement, 210

Chicago school approach: juvenile delinquency initiatives and, 119–22

Chicago Tribune, 210

Chicanos, nationalist framework for, 184

Children of Resurrection City (Afield and Gibson), 143

Children's Year Campaign, 53

Chow, Rey, 74–76

Cincinnati Academy of Medicine, 47, 54

Cincinnati Social Unit Organization, 8; accused of being socialist, 45–46, 54–57; block workers, in social unit plan experiments, 48–50; development of, 45–58, 270 n. 59; legacy of, 74–76; Visiting Nurses Association and, 54; West End Medical Society and, 54–55. See also Social Unit Organization

Cincinnati Tuberculosis League, 47

Citizens' Crusade Against Poverty, 128–29

citizenship: economic independence and, 14; political participation and, 27; for Puerto Ricans, 175; self-help/self-determination paradigms and, 19–25; social unit plan's concept of, 48–58

civic competence: political participation and, 151

Civic Culture, The (Almond and Verba), 151

Civil Rights Act (1964), 11
civil rights movement: Cold War
geopolitics and, 7–11; community
development policies and, 5, 8, 248–
51, 260 n. 22; poor whites and, 165
class conflict: Appalachian antipoverty
programs and, 171–72; Black Panther
Party's initiatives and, 215–20; poverty policies and, 14–15; Puerto Rican
community action and, 178–79;
social unit plan and issues of, 49–58,
270 n. 59
Cleaver, Eldridge, 201–2, 214–15
Cleveland, Harlan, 89
Cleveland Community People's Conference, 1
Cloward, Richard, 113–14, 118–19, 123,
126–29, 153, 290 n. 62, 296 n. 146
coal industry: community action and
resistance to, 161–72; mine workers'
community action and, 155–56; political power of, 162–72
COINTELPRO (FBI counterintelligence
program), 217–18
Cold War ideology: antipoverty programs, 3, 6–11; community action
programs and, 26, 58, 75–76; Native
American policies and, 84–88; Peace
Corps establishment and, 77–78; self-
determination and, 22–25; strategic
role of Puerto Rico in, 60–72; underdevelopment discourse and, 80–83
Coleman, Dovie, 2
Coles, Robert, 169
Collazo Ramos, Práxedes, 64
Collier, John, 37–45, 74, 84, 188–89
Colonial Development and Welfare
Acts (1940 and 1945) (United King-
dom), 59
colonialism: Appalachian poverty programs and, 172; global political community and legacy of, 234–43; impact
on Puerto Ricans of, 235; Indian community development and effects of,

59; Navajo National community programs and role of, 188–96; Peace
Corps training programs and influence of, 91–103; poverty policies and
decline of, 8–11; Puerto Rican community action and, 60–72, 183–84;
Puerto Rican nationalism and, 203–5;
self-determination ideology and, 22–
25, 203–5; slavery of African Americans and, 234–35; underdevelopment
discourse and, 77–109
"coloniality of power," 23, 264 n. 59
Columbia University: Division of
Urban Planning at, 207–8; juvenile
delinquency initiatives and, 123; social
outreach programs and, 90
Committee for Miners (CFM), 163,
166–72
"commonality of interest," poverty programs and, 196–98
commonwealth status, congressional
authorization of, for Puerto Rico, 62
communism, counterinsurgency and
ideology of, 220. See also New Communist Movement; socialism
Communist Manifesto, The, 220
Communist Party, Mobilization for
Youth and, 126
community action: gang involvement in,
205–9; mine workers' participation
in, 155–56; Mobilization for Youth
and, 122–25; poverty alleviation and
role of, 1–3, 8, 12
Community Action Program (CAP), 7–
8, 11–12; amendments to, 248–51;
civic competence ideology and, 151;
creation and control of, 27–28; delinquency theories and, 27; gang participation in, 211–13; juvenile delinquency policies and, 118–22; Native
American proposals for, 185; political
participation and role of, 114; urban
unrest and targeting of, 112–13,
131–36

"crisis strategy," Piven-Cloward concept of, 114, 126–29, 153, 290 n. 62, 296 n. 146

Croly, Herbert, 38, 46

Cruikshank, Barbara, 19

Crusade for Justice, 219–20

Cruse, Harold, 309 n. 9

Cuba, strategic role of Puerto Rico in relation to, 62–72

cultural paradigm: juvenile delinquency programs and, 120–22; Peace Corps training and, 89–90, 100–103, 107–8; poverty policies and, 26–27; Puerto Rican nationalism and, 66–72; underdevelopment discourse and, 80–83

Cultural Patterns and Technical Change (Mead), 91

"culture of poverty": 4–5, 67, 162, 277 n. 11; underdevelopment discourse and, 82–83

"culture shock" concept of, Peace Corps training and, 89–90, 97, 104, 109–10

Daily News newspaper, 125

Daily Optic newspaper, 102

Daley, Richard J., 1–2, 210, 212, 220–22

Dasgupta, Sugata, 272 n. 101

Davila, Orlando, 223–24

Davis, Rennie, 164

Dean, Mitchell, 4

Debs, Eugene V., 36

decentralization: democratic development and, 34; Navajo community development programs and, 187–88; OEO policy initiatives and, 134–35; policing strategies and, 150; poverty policies and, 3–4; social unit plans and, 57–58

Declaration on the Granting of Independence to Colonial Countries and Peoples, 236–37

Declaration on the Rights of Indigenous Peoples, 237

decolonization, 72, 218–19, 234–43: self-determination ideology and, 22–25; liberation vs., 241–42; UN and, 241–43

de facto discrimination, antipoverty policies and, 11–18

de jure discrimination, antipoverty policies and, 11–18

delinquency. *See* juvenile delinquency

Delinquency and Opportunity (Ohlin and Cloward), 123

Deloria, Vine, Jr., 23

democracy: community and, 266 n. 11; community action programs and ideology of, 35–36; maximum feasible participation ideology and, 116–18; social unit plan ideology and, 47–58; World War I rhetoric concerning, 37

Democracy Speaks Many Tongues (Poston), 97–98

democratic centralism, Young Lords Party's ideology of, 232–33

Democratic Party: African Americans and, 157; antipoverty programs as political strategy for, 12; New Deal programs of, 15–16; "no vote" campaigns and, 212–13

Denetdale, Jennifer, 306 n. 114

Denning, Michael, 57

Department of Agriculture and Commerce (Puerto Rico), Social Programs Administration of, 70

Department of Play Streets, 39

dependency theory, self-help and self-determination and, 20–21, 263 n. 52

development. *See* community development/community action programs; economic development; underdevelopment discourse

Devil's Disciples, 205

Devine, Edward T., 270 n. 61

Dewey, John, 38

Díaz, Manuel Jr., 174–75, 177, 181–82

differential opportunity structures, juvenile delinquency policies and, 118–22

Diné/Navajo groups, establishment of,
185–98, 193, 306 n. 114, 307 n. 125
Dinwiddie, Courtenay, 47–50
Disciples, 209–10
disruption, politics of, 122–31; Poor People's Campaign and, 151–53; Puerto
Rican Community Development
Project and, 177–84
División de Educación de la Comunidad
(DIVEDCO), 186, 58–72, 75–76; origins
in Puerto Rico of, 26, 63–64; popular
will and introspection in, 31–35
Doering, Edith, 130
domestic service work, exclusion from
old-age and unemployment insurance
for, 15–16
Downes v. Bidwell, 276 n. 142, 278 n. 20
Duany, Jorge, 71
Dulles, John Foster, 60
Dunbar-Ortiz, Roxanne, 238, 240–41
Duran, Rafael, 145
Durham, Douglas, 243
Durham, Jimmie, 238, 241, 243

East Harlem Prep School, 207–8
East Harlem Triangle Urban Renewal
Project, 208
East Harlem Urban Design and Planning Studio, 207–8
Eastland, James, 131–32, 243
Eastman, Roe, 50–51
East New York Action, 124
economic development: antipoverty
policies and preoccupation with, 16–
18; entrepreneurial poor and, 247–51;
foreign policy and ideology of, 59–72;
Galbraith's critique of, 258 n. 11;
nation-state and, 17, 81; neoliberalism
and, 251–54
Economic Development Administration
(Puerto Rico), 63
economic growth: entrepreneurial poor
and, 247–51; ideology of, 17–19, 258
n. 11

Economic Opportunity Act (EOA)
(1964), 7, 11–12, 18; community
action ideology of, 159; Green amendments to, 248–51; maximum feasible
participation ideology and, 115–18;
mine workers and, 156; Native Americans' exclusion from, 185; Poor People's campaign and, 142–48; "Special
Assistance to Rural Families" provision of, 157–58; Special Impact
Amendment to, 250; underdevelopment discourse and, 80–83; urban
unrest and, 111–12, 131–36
Economic Opportunity Amendments
hearings, 131
Economic Research and Action Project
(ERAP) (SDS), 1–3, 163–72, 209, 299
n. 26
educational programs, community
action initiatives for, 41–43
Education in the Peace Corps (Pagano),
100
Elliott, John Lovejoy, 46
Ely, Richard T., 35–36
Emancipation Proclamation, 14
Emerson, Haven, 42
"employable mother" rule, social welfare
policies and, 21
Enlightenment: self-determination ideology and, 22, 260 n. 24; underdevelopment discourse and, 81–83
Erazo, Joseph, 178–79
Escobar, Arturo, 11
ethnicity: foreignness and, 74–76; New
York Puerto Rican community action
and, 183–84; in OEO's policy assumptions, 160–61, 304 n. 86

Fager, Charles, 143
Fanon, Frantz, 215–16, 218
farm labor: antipoverty programs for,
157–58; exclusion from old-age and
unemployment insurance for, 15–16
FBI: American Indian Movement and,

hegemony (*cont.*)
nation-state, 219; of postwar United States, 9, 17; of Western culture, 22
Henry Street Settlement, 46, 122–23, 169
Hicks, Mary, 48, 50–51, 55
Highlander Center, 139
Hispano communities: community development programs and, 26; definition of, 265 n. 65; underdevelopment discourse and, 79–80; University of New Mexico Peace Corps training center and, 91–103
Holcomb, Robert, 170–71
Homestead Act (1862), 14
Honig, Bonnie, 74–76
Hoover, J. Edgar, 132, 217–18, 295 n. 130
Horton, Myles, 139
Hudson Guild settlement house, 46
human capital, theory of, 16–17
Humphrey, Hubert, 88, 191, 212
Hunter, John G., 187
Huntington, Samuel, 116
Hyde, Mary, 145–46

ideology, Jameson's theorization of, 5
Ignacio (film), 33–35, 70
immigrants, 38–39, 44, 48–49, 53, 56, 74–76; juvenile delinquency and, 119–22; New York Puerto Rican community action and conceptions of, 177–78, 182–84
imperialism: antipoverty programs and culture of, 200–201; Black Panther Party criticism of, 218–20; gang activity in face of, 202–5; global initiatives against, 233–43; liberal ideology and, 9–11; urban unrest and, 113
income distribution, poverty and inequalities in, 18
income maintenance, poverty alleviation through, 11
Independent Coal Operators Association, 170–71

India, community development in, 59
Indian Appropriation Act of 1871, 237–38
Indian Reorganization Act of 1934, 74–76, 187–89
Indian Tribal Relation Committee, 83
indigenous coalitions: international diplomacy efforts and, 237–43; political activism by, 203–5
individualism: antipoverty programs and ideology of, 18–25; Puerto Rican community activism and, 64–67. *See also* self-determination ideology
Industrial Areas Foundation, 210
industrialization, poverty creation and, 13
inequality, equivalencies in, 196–98
influenza epidemic of 1918, 53
informal economy, neoliberal social ethics and, 252–54
Inmates Liberation Front, 227
Innis, Roy, 24
Institute of Juvenile Research, 119
Institute of Rural Reconstruction (India), 59, 272 n. 101
Insular Cases, 82–83, 85, 276 n. 142, 278 n. 20
integrationist policies: African American resistance to, 111–12; Puerto Rican community action and, 178–79
intercommunalism, 219–20, 235–36, 241
Intercommunal Youth Institute, 217
interest group politics, community programs and, 196–98
Internal Security Act, investigation of activist groups and, 243
international development, poverty policies and doctrine of, 3, 11
International Indian Treaty Council, 28, 203; Declaration of Continuing Independence by, 237–38; international diplomacy initiatives of, 233, 237–43
International Labor Organization, 236–37

La Sociedad de Albizu Campos, 225

Latham, Michael, 90

Latin America: dependency theory in, 21; strategic role of Puerto Rico in, 60–72

"La Voluntad Que Ignacio No Tuvo" (booklet), 31–35

law-and-order ideology: antipoverty funding surveillance and, 213; international diplomacy efforts of activist groups and, 242–43; liberal enforcement of, 148–53

Law Enforcement Assistance Administration, 149

Lawrence, Ida Mae, 19–20

Lazarus, Sylvain, 232

League of Nations, 308 n. 6

Lester, Julius, 24

Lewis, Oscar, 67, 82

liberal antipoverty initiatives: criticism of, 199–200; political utility of, 12–18; radicals' negotiation of, 28; role of governance in, 3–6

liberal internationalism: indigenous coalitions and, 237–43; self-determination ideology and, 203–5, 308 n. 6

liberalism: antipoverty programs and constraints of, 202–5; future trends in, 245–47; gang activity and, 205–8; nation-state and, 219; state governance and, 148–53, 298 n. 15

liberal pluralism, poverty policies and, 159–61, 182–84, 197–98

liberation: decolonization vs., 241–43; liberty vs., 201–5

liberty, liberation vs., 201–5

Liberty Loan Committee, 44

Libros Para el Pueblo (Books for the People) series, 31–35

Life magazine, 9, 207

Lindeman, Eduard, 267 n. 11

Lindsay, John, 173

Lippmann, Walter, 38

local agencies: Cincinnati Social Unit Organization and, 47–57; federal antipoverty programs and, 12–18, 249–51; Navajo community development programs and, 185–96; police-community relations projects and, 150–53; Puerto Rican community action programs and, 70–72; Puerto Rican Community Development Project and involvement of, 179–80

Logan, Marian, 138

Long, Russell, 130, 291 n. 66

Lopez, Alfredo, 179

López Mateos, Adolfo, 95–97

Los Casos de Ignacio y Santiago (booklet), 32–35, 70

Lower East Side Neighborhood Association, 122–23, 169

Luce, Henry, 9

Lukachukai Navaho Demonstration School, 185

lumpenproletariat: Black Panther Party and, 214–20; gang involvement in antipoverty programs and, 209–13

Lytle, Clifford, 23

MacArthur, Douglas, 148

MacDonald, Dwight, 7

MacDonald, Peter, 194

macroeconomic theory, economic development and economic growth and, 251–54

Madigan, LaVerne, 85

mainstream journalism: images of striking mine workers in, 162–72; juvenile delinquency images in, 121–22; poverty images in, 4–5

Manhattan Trade School for Girls, 45

Mao Zedong, 218

March on Washington, 124

Markell, Patchen, 298 n. 15

Marshall, John, 82–83

Marshall Plan, 81–83

Martin, Franklin P., 53

National Institute of Mental Health, 123
nationalism: of African Americans, 24,
184; antipoverty programs and, 200–
205; Black Panther Party's programs
and, 218–20, 309 n. 9; immigrants
and, 74–76; of Native Americans, 23,
197–98; Puerto Rican community
action and ideology of, 60–72, 184,
224, 228–29; in Puerto Rico, 60–76
Nationalist Party of Puerto Rico, 230
National League of Women Workers, 45
National Liberation Front, 218–20
National Organization for Public
Health Nursing, 54
national security, poverty programs and,
16–17
National Welfare Rights Organization
(NWRO), 130–31, 138–48, 290 n. 62
nation-building ideology: decline in
community development and, 248–
51; Navajo community development
and, 195–96
nation-state, conceptions of, 4, 17, 22,
81, 219
Native Americans: concepts of poverty
among, 26–27; delegation to Puerto
Rico of, 85–88; development paradigm and policies toward, 83–88; dispossession of, 14; EOA programs and,
184–85; indigenous coalitions and,
202–5; international diplomacy
efforts of, 237–38; Peace Corps training programs and, 79–80, 103–6;
Poor People's Campaign and, 139–48;
Puerto Rican identification with,
229–30; self-determination ideology
and nationalism of, 23; termination
policy (House Concurrent Resolution 108) and, 26, 83–87, 140–41;
treaty obligations and, 159
Navajo Long Walk, 306 n. 114
Navajo Nation: chapter organizational
structure of, 186–87; community
action projects in, 27–28, 184–96;

Peace Corps training and, 89–90,
109–10; population statistics for, 185;
US military campaign against, 188;
War on Poverty and, 158–59
Navajo Tribal Council, 185–96
neighborhood: community organization
and, 267 n. 14; juvenile delinquency
initiatives and, 119–22; Puerto Rican
Community Development Project
and, 179–82
Neighborhood Youth Corps, 11, 185,
205–8, 297 n. 6; gang mediation in,
210–13
neoliberalism: community action programs and, 28; emergence of, 245–47;
social ethics of, 251–54
Neuberger, Richard, 88–90
Newark Community Union Project,
164–75
New Communist Movement, 219–20
New Deal legislation: antipoverty policies in, 15–16; race and gender
inequalities in, 15–16, 21, 260 n. 22
New Federalism programs, 248–49
New Left ideology: Appalachian com-
munity union movement and, 166,
197–98; community action and, 158
New Liberalism, 35–36
New Mexican newspaper, 101
New Mexico, colonialism and formation
of, 91–103
"new nationalism," Progressive Era and, 38
New Republic magazine, 46
Newton, Huey P., 202, 204, 216–20,
229, 237
New York Association for Improving
Conditions of the Poor, 45
New York Community Council
(NYCC), 57
New York Milk Committee, 45
New York Times, 37, 40, 46, 111, 147
Nieves, Josephine, 176–77
Night Comes to the Cumberlands
(Caudill), 169

Puerto Rico (*cont.*)
tion to, 85–88; self-determination
ideology and nationalism in, 23, 60–
72, 75–76
Puerto Rico Development Company, 63
Putnam, Robert, 253–54

Quadagno, Jill, 260 n. 22
Quentone, Allen, 87
Quijano, Anibal, 23, 264 n. 59

race and racism: antipoverty programs
and, 12, 157–61, 172; "coloniality of
power" and, 23, 264 n. 59; community union project and, 165–72; juvenile delinquency initiatives and, 120–
22; labor segmentation and, 14; law-
and-order ideology and, 149–53; in
New Deal policies, 15–16, 21, 260
n. 22; in OEO policy assumptions,
160–61; Puerto Rican community
action and, 182–84; social unit plan's
failure to address, 44–45, 48–49;
social welfare policy and, 21–25; in
War on Poverty programs, 157–61
race riots: in 1919, 44; counterinsurgency and, 131–36; policing strategies in wake of, 112
racial capitalism, 200–201, 218–20, 308
n. 3
racial uplift ideology, self-help and self-
determination and, 20
Radhakrishnan, Sarvepalli, 9
Rahnema, Majid, 81
Rainbow Coalition, 221–23
Raleigh County Community Action
Association, 169
Ramos, Manuel, 224
Ratliff, Thomas, 171
Ray, Jink, 171
Reagan, Ronald, 249–50
Real Great Society (RGS), 177, 202–9,
213, 224, 315 n. 81
recognition, 28, 65, 89, 156–57, 159–60,

188–89, 196, 202, 234, 236, 239–42;
theories of, 298 n. 15
recreation centers, development of,
41–42
Red Cross, 44
Red Guard Party, 219–20
Reedy, George, 155
Republican Party, 131; law-and-order
ideology and, 148
Resurrection City, 143–48, 150. *See also*
Poor People's Campaign
Reuss, Henry S., 88–90
revolutionary internationalism, Black
Panthers' ideology of, 218–20, 235–
36, 241
revolutionary nationalism, Young Lords'
ideology of, 229–30, 235–36
Reyes Ramos, Montserrat, 64
Rivera, Higinio, 69
Rivera Santiago, Concepción, 64
Robinson, Cedric, 200–201, 308 n. 3
Rodgers, Daniel, 13–14
Rodríguez, Zacarías, 68
Roldán, Julio, 226–27
Roosevelt, Franklin Delano, 15–16
Rosen, George, 53
Ross, Andrew, 18
Rothstein, Richard, 165
Rough Rock Demonstration School,
109–10, 185–86
roving picket movement, 156, 162–63,
166, 168
Roxborough, Ian, 61
Rubin, Lillian, 8
rural antipoverty initiatives, 157–61,
171–72
Rusk, Dean, 141, 146
Russell Square Community Committee,
119–20
Rustin, Bayard, 138

Saldaña-Portillo, María Josefina, 195–96,
263 n. 52
Sales, William, 183

unincorporation doctrine, 82–83
union organization, coal miners and, 162–71
United Auto Workers, 128–29
United Community Corporation, 131
United Front against Fascism, 221
United Mine Workers of America (UMWA), 161–72
United Nations: Black Panthers' diplomacy efforts at, 236–37; community action programs' petitions to, 28; community development policies of, 195, 303 n. 76; decline in community development support at, 247; growth-oriented development policies and, 251–54; indigenous coalitions and, 203–5; liberal internationalism and, 308 n. 6; Native American diplomacy efforts at, 237–43; Navajo community development projects and, 189–90; Puerto Rican commonwealth establishment and, 62; self-determination ideology and role of, 236–37; Social Commission of, 33–34
United Nations, Charter of 1945, 203, 236
United States, global indictments against, 234–43
United States Agency for International Development (USAID), 247
United States Conference of Mayors, 133–36
United States Forest Service, Hispano conflicts with, 94–97
United States Information Agency (USIA), 6–11
United States International Cooperation Administration, 66, 89
United States-Navajo Treaty of 1868, 188
United States State Department, Peace Corps and, 106–10

Universal Declaration of Human Rights, 236
universality, Peace Corps training and ideal of, 107–8
University of Chicago, 119–20; Campus Circle construction projects, 212
University of New Mexico, Peace Corps Training Center at, 91–103
University of the Streets project, 207–8, 213
Upper Kentucky River Area Development Council, 167
Upward Bound, 11
Urban Coalition Afro-Latin Unity Council, 208
urban migration, Appalachian poverty and unemployment and, 171–72
urban organizing: Black Panther Party and, 214–20; police-community relations and, 151–53; Puerto Ricans in New York City and, 173–84
Urban Progress Center, 1–2, 210
urban riots: counterinsurgency and, 131–36; gang activity and, 211–13; political participation and, 27, 122–31, 152–53
US-Mexican War, 82–83, 92

vagrancy law, work enforcement through, 14
Valentín, Gilberto Gerena, 139
Valle, Marte, 173
Verba, Sidney, 151
Veterans' Bonus March of 1932, 147–48
Vietnam War: counterinsurgency as response to, 203–5; domestic social policy and, 117–18; international community development decline and, 247; policing strategies and protest of, 112; Poor People's Campaign and, 137–48, 152–53
Vincent Astor Foundation, 206, 208
violence: Appalachian community action programs and, 170–72; liberal ideology and reliance on, 148–53;

violence (*cont.*)

political participation and, 27; political participation and role of, 114; Poor People's Campaign and, 136–48

vocational training, in Peace Corps program, 100–103

Volunteers in Service to America (VISTA), 11, 168–70

Voting Rights Act (1965), 11, 212

Wagner, Robert, 111, 125–26, 289 n. 54

Wald, Lillian, 46

Wale, Fred, 67–69

Walker, Tillie, 139

Wallace, George, 165

War on Poverty: Black Panthers' disaffection with, 214–20, 235–36; coal miners' strikes and, 163–72; Cold War geopolitics and, 7–11; Community Action Program and, 1–4, 12, 248–51; community-based political participation and, 156–98; disillusionment with, 200–201; gang initiatives and, 202–8, 213, 223; initiation of, 155; juvenile delinquency programs and, 118–22; liberal pluralism and, 197–98; maximum feasible participation ideology and programs of, 116–18; normative effects of, 18; Peace Corps parallels with, 108–10; political motivations behind, 160–61; Poor People's Campaign and, 129–31, 153; public welfare policies and, 128–31; Puerto Rican community action and, 173–84, 235–36; racial politics and, 157–61; self-help/self-determination paradigms in, 19–25; social unit plan compared with, 49–50; street gangs and policies of, 28; urban unrest and, 112–13, 117–18

Warrior, Clyde, 199–201

"We Are Nationalists and Internationalists" (Newton), 204–5

Weber, Max, 82

Welfare Recipients Demand Action (WRDA), 2–3

welfare rights movement, 113–14; civic competence ideology and, 151; emergence of, 128–31; Poor People's Campaign and, 137–48

Wells, Henry, 70

What Is to Be Done? (Lenin), 232–33

White, James O., 54

white poverty: Appalachian antipoverty programs and, 157–61, 171–72, 297 n. 8; civil rights movement and, 165; Rainbow Coalition and, 221–23

Wiley, George, 128, 138–39, 290 n. 62, 293 n. 91

Williams, Aubrey, 187

Wilson, Woodrow, 22, 37

Winant, Howard, 184

Wirtz, Willard, 141

Withey, Stephen B., 67–68

Wittman, Carl, 164–65

Woods, Robert, 267 n. 14

The Woodlawn Organization (TWO), 210–13

Woodward, C. Vann, 172

workingmen's clubs, development of, 41–42

World Bank: grass-roots development and, 247; NGO Working Group of, 254; poverty and participation rhetoric at, 251–54

World Court, 241

Wounded Knee (1973), confrontation at, 203, 237–38, 243

Wretched of the Earth, The (Fanon), 215–16

Wright, Nathan, 24

Yarmolinsky, Adam, 157–58, 297 n. 8

Yellow Brotherhood, 219–20

Young, Andrew, 141, 239–40

Young Lords Organization, 28, 183; antipoverty programs and, 209, 214; coalition building by, 221; community activities of, 224–33; formation of, 223–24; international activities of, 233–43; OEO and, 200, 202–5; political activities of, 223–33; Real Great Society and, 315 n. 81

Young Lords Party (YLP), 226–33; Ofensiva Rompe Cadenas (Break the Chains Offensive) of, 230–33

Young Patriots, 221

Youth Organizations United (YOU), 206–8, 213

Zayas, Francisco, 64–65

Žižek, Slavoj, 118

Alyosha Goldstein is associate professor of American Studies at the University of New Mexico.

Library of Congress Cataloging-in-Publication Data
Goldstein, Alyosha.
Poverty in common : the politics of community action during the American century / Alyosha Goldstein.
p. cm.
Includes bibliographical references and index.
ISBN 978-0-8223-5167-2 (cloth : alk. paper)
ISBN 978-0-8223-5181-8 (pbk. : alk. paper)
1. Community Action Program (U.S.)—History.
2. Economic assistance, Domestic—United States—History—20th century. 3. Community development—United States—History—20th century. 4. Social service—United States—History—20th century. 5. Public welfare—United States—History—20th century. 6. Poverty—Government policy—United States—History—20th century. 7. United States—Economic conditions—1945—I. Title.
HC110.P63G6593 2012
362.5'5250973—dc23   2011041901